D1271905

The Modernity of Others

Jewish Anti-Catholicism in Germany and France

Ari Joskowicz

STANFORD UNIVERSITY PRESS

STANFORD, CALIFORNIA

Stanford University Press
Stanford, California

© 2014 by the Board of Trustees of the Leland Stanford Junior University.
All rights reserved.

Published with assistance from the College of Arts and Science at Vanderbilt
University.

Library of Congress Cataloging-in-Publication Data

Joskowicz, Ari, author.
  The modernity of others: Jewish anti-Catholicism in Germany and France /
Ari Joskowicz.
     pages cm
  Includes bibliographical references and index.
  ISBN 978-0-8047-8702-4 (cloth : alk. paper)
    1. Anti-Catholicism—Germany—History—19th century. 2. Anti-Catholicism—
France—History—19th century. 3. Anti-clericalism—Germany—History—
19th century. 4. Anti-clericalism—France—History—19th century. 5. Jews—
Germany—Politics and government—19th century. 6. Jews—France—Politics
and government—19th century. 7. Secularism—Europe—History—19th century.
I. Title.
  BX1766.J67 2013
  305.892'404—dc23
        2013013482

Typeset by Thompson Type in 10½/14 Galliard

To my parents

Contents

Illustrations

Acknowledgments

It is a great pleasure to be able to thank the many people who helped me write this book. The final manuscript owes much to conversations I had as a fellow at the Herbert D. Katz Center for Advanced Judaic Studies in 2009. I am deeply grateful to all the members of the group working there on "Secularism and its Discontents." My fruitful discussions with Amnon Raz-Krakotzkin in particular helped me understand the political and theoretical urgency of rethinking the history of secularism. David Myers, Shmuel Feiner, and Rachel Manekin also pushed my work in new directions, while my forays into early modern history were aided by much-appreciated references from Maurice Kriegel and David Ruderman. Ethan Katz, with whom I have the pleasure of coediting a volume on secularism that features some of the work done at the Katz Center, has similarly remained an important interlocutor and offered helpful feedback on several chapters.

This work has also benefited from a wonderful group of people at the University of Chicago who helped me develop this project in its earliest stages. Michael Geyer, Paul Mendes-Flohr, Leora Auslander, and Bernard Wasserstein offered invaluable advice and encouraged me to consider the broader implications of my study. Special thanks are due to Michael Geyer, who always offered his engaged feedback, and to Leora Auslander, who was exceedingly generous with her support and offered insights that helped me rethink my project in crucial ways. I was also lucky to have many friends at the University of Chicago who thoroughly read and discussed individual chapters with me, including Rachel Brezis, Jerome Copulsky, Dan Koehler, Emily Marker, Avi Sharma, Andrew Sloin, and Ronen Steinberg.

Many others have also given me generous feedback over the years. I am grateful to Malachi Hacohen, Barbara Hahn, Jonathan Hess, Marc Lerner, Frances Malino, David Nirenberg, Jeffrey Sammons, Allison Schachter, Galili Shahar, Samira Sheikh, Helmut Walser Smith, and Todd Weir for reading parts of the book. I also received invaluable feedback from members of workshops sponsored by the University of Chicago, the Dubnow Institute in Leipzig, the Leo Baeck Institute in Jerusalem, the University of Mississippi, Vanderbilt University, Yale University, the Université de Montréal, Hebrew University, the University of North Carolina, and Duke University, as well as the Works-in-Progress workshop at the Association for Jewish Studies' annual conference. Others have served as important conversation partners. Stefan Nowotny has always encouraged me to explain my endeavors in broad conceptual terms. Manuel Borutta, Oliver Dinius, Michael Gross, Lisa Leff, Eva Lezzi, Till van Rahden, Michaela Wirtz, and Lisa Zwicker offered helpful advice at different stages of the project.

Various grants have made it possible for me to research and write this book. Two important research trips were funded by François Furet and Kunstadter travel grants from the University of Chicago and a Vanderbilt University Research Scholar's summer grant. Residential fellowships from the following institutions allowed me to work on this project: the Lady Davis Fellowship Trust, the Hebrew University's Franz Rosenzweig Minerva Research Center, the Simon Dubnow Institute in Leipzig (in cooperation with the German Academic Exchange Service), and the Herbert D. Katz Center for Advanced Judaic Studies. The *German Studies Review*, *Jewish Quarterly Review*, and *Jewish Social Studies* generously granted permission to include material I previously published in these journals. I am also grateful to Aron Rodrigue and Steven Zipperstein, the editors of the Stanford Studies in Jewish History and Culture series, for their support of my project and to my editors, Norris Pope and Stacy Wagner, for their encouragement and attentiveness throughout the publication process.

Finally, I wish to thank Julia Phillips Cohen, who has been among (so many) other things my most important reader, critic, and congenial intellectual companion.

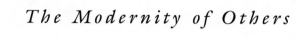

The Modernity of Others

Introduction

Throughout the early twenty-first century, debates over the relationship between Islam and the West have fundamentally influenced the way Europeans and Americans think about religion. The notion of a clash of civilizations figures in the writing of popular pundits as a category of analysis, while their detractors condemn the use of the phrase for creating the very conflict its proponents purport to describe. Whether affirmed or rejected, claims of religious and civilizational confrontation continue to shape the politics of secularism on a global scale. In Europe, a growing number of politicians and public intellectuals argue that secularism has become the very essence of what it means to be European. According to many of the same individuals, Islam is the antithesis of everything Europe represents because it never experienced its own process of secularization.

As a small minority, European Jews are marginal actors in this imagined clash of civilizations. Yet, in practice, they remain central to European debates over the place of religion in civil society: They both serve as constant points of reference and are among the most vocal commentators on the subject of secularism and Islam in Europe today. Often regarded as Europe's constitutive (if now domesticated) outsiders, European Jews are frequently asked to speak about how to "assimilate" Europe's more recent immigrant populations. Despite the invitations they receive to serve as expert voices in such situations, as a demographically small minority with a checkered past in Europe, Jews continue to face particular challenges as they participate in public debates over religion, secularism, and universalism in European society. Their responses reflect their peculiar position as partial outsiders in contemporary Europe. On the simplest level, European Jewish commentators oscillate between two positions: Many express their dedication to fighting Islamophobia—which they consider uncomfortably close to historical forms of antisemitism—while others find in European secularist fears of Islam the opportunity to build broader alliances with Christian and secular Europeans against Islamic fundamentalism. No matter where they stand, Jews' political identity in Europe is of necessity shaped by ideas about religion and politics that have emerged in response to debates about another religious minority.

This book explores the origins of these dilemmas and suggests that they are inherent to the challenges secularist debates have posed for minorities from their inception. Warnings of an impending clash of cultures also shaped religious politics in nineteenth-century Europe and gave birth to many of our current expectations about the proper place of religion in society. Employing stereotypes that may remind us of today's debates over Europe's relationship with Islam, European liberals of the long nineteenth century regularly portrayed the Catholic Church as the ultimate anti-modern power and Catholicism as a religion that turned its believers into docile and dependent followers of church leaders.[1] Like Jews, Catholics and the Catholic clergy often appeared in the accounts of their opponents as both effeminate and politically dangerous because of their transnational solidarities—as the antithesis of the patriotic educated male who symbolized the ideal political subject. As a result, the formative period of modern Jewish thought and politics overlapped with a period of growing battles between self-declared progressives, on the one hand, and the Catholic Church and its defenders, on the other.

Politically active Jews in the nineteenth century consequently faced challenges similar to those confronting European Jews in the new millennium. As in today's constructed conflict between the West and Islam, Jews were a highly visible third party in the nineteenth-century culture wars between liberals and Catholics; as today, they had a stake in the very notion of such a confrontation. They could either embrace or critique the idea of a liberal–Catholic conflict, but it was nearly impossible for them to remain neutral. Their position depended largely on their answers to a dilemma that resembles the one many Jews face today: Were anticlericalism and anti-Catholicism comparable to anti-Judaism and thus objectionable? Or did they offer Jews a means of finally defeating an institution that they believed to be a central enemy of Jewish equality, namely the Catholic Church?

Jews' responses to this dilemma were not predetermined. Many of the most influential Jewish authors and politicians of nineteenth-century Europe nonetheless clearly saw an opportunity in anticlerical politics and explained their place in the world in terms of their opposition to the Catholic Church or Catholicism. The rhetoric of anticlericalism (as it is commonly called in France) and anti-Catholicism (as it is commonly called in Germany) profoundly affected the way that Jews and non-Jews went about exhibiting their religiosity, organizing religion, representing it to the state, and explaining it theoretically. As today, Jews were affected by these debates even when they did not endorse the notion of a full-fledged clash of civilizations. Although anti-Catholicism represented neither an all-encompassing Jewish worldview nor a defining feature of the Jewishness of its proponents, it was a major part of the cultural milieu of modern Jewish intellectuals in both France and Germany. As such, criticism of the Catholic Church and its clergy significantly shaped the political environment that French and German Jews encountered during the first century of their transformation into citizens. Although it rarely appears in popular or scholarly portrayals of European Jewish history, anti-Catholic anticlericalism constituted a foundational element of modern Jewish politics—with enduring consequences.

This book traces how different Jewish individuals in modern Germany and France employed anti-Catholicism to articulate their own visions of modernity, national belonging, and proper forms of religion. It analyzes a range of moments in which anticlericalism allowed Jews to address major social, political, and intellectual issues of their day, moving from the Enlightenment and revolutionary politics of the late eighteenth century to the rise of mass political movements and parties in the late nineteenth and early twentieth century. At the same time, it is an entangled history of German and French Jewry, which highlights shared elements in their political rhetoric and approach to religion across the national boundaries that divided them.

Beyond the Marginal Jew

By analyzing the polemics that one politically marginalized group employed against another, the study of modern Jewish anti-Catholicism offers an opportunity to rethink the categories most often used to address marginality in Jewish history and in the study of minorities more generally. Indeed, while there exist traditions of studying Jews in relation to other immigrant, ethnic, national, or racial groups in the historiography of American Jewry as well as that of the Jews of the Habsburg, Ottoman, and Russian empires, historians of Jews in modern Western and Central Europe have tended instead to analyze Jews' social positions in terms of the dichotomous categories of majority and minority. This dichotomy appears in different forms—as Germans and Jews, the French and the Jews, Christians and Jews, or non-Jews and Jews—yet ultimately such pairings are formulated to understand how Jews related to an unmarked "center."[2] Recent discussions of Jewish integration, assimilation, and acculturation have offered ever more nuanced ways of understanding how Jews dealt with their exclusion from various centers, but they have rarely challenged the notion that the principal dilemma of nineteenth-century European Jews was their relationship with a "mainstream" or dominant society.

This model of Jewish integration as a story of center–margin relations makes sense in certain contexts, but for much of nineteenth-century Germany and France it explains little about Jews' experiences on the level of national politics. Jewish authors, activists, and politicians all confronted fragmented political arenas and societies. German Jews faced not simply an abstract, monolithic German nationalism but rather different sets of liberal, conservative Protestant, and Catholic nationalisms. French Jews, for their part, acted in a political sphere in which liberals and republicans disagreed with conservative Catholics over how to define the French nation. Jews might have been outsiders in a Christian state in both cases, but they could also behave like insiders in the more complicated constellations of nineteenth-century European religious and political conflicts. In Germany, for example, educated Jewish men could identify with the hegemonic views of middle-class Protestant men on questions of the place of religion in society, thereby distancing themselves from traits liberals condemned, such as effeminacy, irrationality, religiosity without decorum, and Catholic "fanaticism."[3] When positioned in relation to a multiplicity of other nonhegemonic groups, Jews appear as more than simple pariahs or parvenus.[4]

Jewish anti-Catholicism offers one example of this complex set of relations between different nonhegemonic groups. It thus challenges any simple narratives of Jewish marginalization by a clear and homogenous center. In this respect, Jewish critiques of the Catholic Church might be compared to the more widely studied phenomenon of Jewish orientalism, in which Jews acted as insiders to Western scholarship in their attempt to unlock the secrets of an unknowing yet precious East.[5] Even more than Western and Central European Jews' interest in things oriental, however, Jews' comments on Catholicism challenge our sense of center and periphery, inside and outside, power and powerlessness.[6] In the case of the Orient, the direction of the gaze from Europe and the asymmetry of access to powerful institutions are clear. Jews studying the Orient engaged with phenomena that had no political influence over them. This is not true for the Catholic Church, which, on the one hand, was liberalism's favorite proximate enemy yet remained, on the other hand, one of Europe's most powerful institutions. German political Catholics and the Catholic Church might have appeared as marginal in rhetorical terms, yet in a number of contexts they maintained significant social and political power. In France, the Catholic Church and political Catholicism laid claims to embodying French culture and nationhood. In both countries, Jewish polemics against the Catholic Church targeted an institution that was both systematically written out of the narrative of modernity by the Jews' liberal allies and an active force shaping these debates and the modern world. Like few other phenomena, Jewish anti-Catholicism and anticlericalism thus test our assumptions about dichotomous categories of power in modern Europe. The question of who is the political insider was itself part of the debate between Jewish and Catholic polemicists.

A more three-dimensional map of Jewish politics invites us to rethink a long-standing notion of Jewish history popular in a new guise in studies informed by the postcolonial turn: The idea that Jews inhabit a privileged position as outsiders, which allows them to recognize or resist the pathologies of modernity.[7] Although such scholarship focuses our attention on important traditions of Jewish dissent, it tells only part of the larger story of European Jewish modernity. Jews were not only the foil for the modern European nation but also—often uncritical—producers of nation-state discourses in which the nation's Others were not only Jews but also Catholics. Jewish writers such as Moses Mendelssohn (1729–1786) and Heinrich Heine (1797–1856), whom scholars within and beyond Jewish studies regularly invoke as models for resistance to the homogenizing forces of modernity, also reproduced liberal tropes about modernity's Others, albeit in a minoritarian key.

Making Jewish Anticlericalism Visible

Explaining Jewish experiences as the acts of precarious insiders operating within a fragmented political landscape draws attention to debates and challenges that other studies have noted but often relegated to the sidelines. Scholarship has tended to render Jewish criticism of the Catholic Church invisible in large part because scholars have considered the phenomenon an uncomfortable or politically fraught topic. This is largely due to the fact that Jewish anti-Catholicism first emerged as a subject of discussion among antisemites during the late nineteenth century. Although antisemites of all denominations made reference to the phenomenon, Catholic antisemites in particular used Jewish anti-Catholicism to legitimize their anti-Jewish *ressentiment* as merely a reaction to Jewish hatred. Understandably, few scholars have wanted to risk placing themselves within this tradition by accusing the victims of modern antisemitism of hating their persecutors first and thus having caused their own persecution.[8]

To absolve Jews from the accusation of hating Catholicism, nineteenth-century Jewish apologists as well as certain recent historians have depicted the comments of Jews who spoke against the Catholic Church as a mere reaction to Catholic antisemitism.[9] This position represents the mirror opposite of the arguments of nineteenth-century Catholic antisemites who claimed that their antisemitism was purely a reaction to Jewish anti-Catholicism. It also rests on the same fallacy: Just as Catholic discourses on Jews were not simply a result of Jewish hostility, Jewish comments on Catholicism were not simply a result of Catholic antisemitism.

Seeing in Jewish anti-Catholicism only defensiveness, moreover, denies political agency to Jewish actors and thus excludes them from all theoretical discussions about the nature of secularism and liberal citizenship. Studies of the anti-Catholicism of German Protestants, for example, point us to the paradoxical fact that nineteenth-century anti-Catholicism—which many today would identify as a prejudiced and illiberal position—was an inherent part of modern German liberalism.[10]

The suggestion that Jewish anticlerical polemicists were simply reacting to the provocations of the Catholic Church therefore presupposes that the foundational paradoxes of liberal modernity did not also apply to Jews. Instead, I argue, recognizing the paradoxes of minoritarian secularism elucidates some of the most important tensions that existed within different liberal projects in modern Europe.

Exploring the implications of Jewish anti-Catholicism as part of a broader study of the makeup and consequences of liberal political paradigms need not entail an endorsement of the antisemites' claim that Jews had a penchant for aggressive anti-Catholicism. Scholars have rightly insisted that categories like "prejudice" do not adequately describe the motivations of Jewish critics of Catholics and Catholicism. For the most part, modern Jewish anti-Catholic polemicists were not interested in stigmatizing, pathologizing, racializing, or excluding Catholics from society. Such aims would in any case have been misplaced among members of a small demographic minority still struggling to attain civil rights and social acceptance. It is, however, possible to agree with historians like Olaf Blaschke, who argue that—contrary to the accusations of Catholic antisemites—modern European Jews were rarely hateful or radical secularists, while simultaneously seeking to understand why, when, and how they found anticlericalism appealing.[11] For nineteenth-century antisemites, the question was only *whether* and *to what degree* Jews were anti-Catholic or anticlerical. We need not reproduce this question, which antisemites and their interlocutors have asked to prove or disprove Jewish complicity in their own persecution. Instead, I suggest, we should rather focus on *why* and *how* modern European Jews spoke against Catholicism and the Catholic Church.

By raising these questions and treating Jewish anticlericalism as a key to understanding the politics of modern secularism, my approach differs from those taken by previous studies that have dealt with the subject. While I largely concur with the empirical conclusions of the works of Jacob Toury, Uriel Tal, Lisa Leff, Zvi Jonathan Kaplan, and Jeffrey Haus, who have all discussed Jewish anti-Catholicism in either Germany or France, I depart from their basic understanding of the phenomenon.[12] Jews' anti-Catholicism was not simply an expression of their distaste for the Catholic Church, or merely the result of their pragmatic support for specific laws that limited clerical influence in society. Anticlericalism and anti-Catholicism were infused with a de-cidedly rhetorical quality: They consisted of popular images, terms, and narratives that invoked particular expectations of proper religiosity and formed part of political languages (to use J. G. A. Pocock's term) that shaped practices and experiences far beyond the confines of high poli-tics.[13] Jewish anticlericalism appears not only in overtly anti-Catholic statements but also in minor references and asides, such as when Jews denounced antisemites for being "medieval," a term that invoked a host of narratives about the Catholic Dark Ages and humanity's struggle to free itself from the stranglehold of the church. What is more, anti-Catholic polemics were, in many cases, not even aimed directly against Catholicism. Jewish reformers often found it expedient to use popular epithets drawn from anti-Catholic campaigns to attack their Orthodox Jewish opponents. Thus we find examples of self-declared Jewish pro-gressives denouncing their rivals as Jewish Jesuits or insulting Jewish Orthodox leaders as Jewish popes. In the German case, Jewish intel-lectuals criticized Protestant nationalists for pursuing "Catholicizing" forms of politics in their use of religious images and emotional appeals. Just as we can recognize the insult *Talmudism* (in the sense of using sophistry) as drawing on anti-Jewish traditions, we should similarly recognize terms like *Jesuitic* and *medieval* as forming part of an anti-Catholic repertoire, regardless of the identity of the individuals they targeted. Such references to Catholicism, the Catholic clergy, or Jesuits as a symbol or insult speaks to the way different European Jews articu-lated their ideas about emancipation, decency, autonomy, gender roles, and sensuality in a self-declared liberal culture war of progress versus reaction. Indeed, for many Jews, anti-Catholicism structured their sense of historical time, with a medieval, unemancipated "before" and a modern, increasingly emancipated "now." Jewish anti-Catholicism was not simply a reflection of Jewish–Catholic relations but a political lan-guage—revolving around ideas of privatized religion, good citizenship, and progress—that continues to define politics today.

Anticlericalism and the Polemics of Secularism

Focusing on the rhetorical quality of anticlericalism and its role as a political language also addresses a number of undertheorized aspects in the study of secularism. Many recent works in religious studies and anthropology—in contrast to scholarship on Jewish and European history—define secularism not as the opposite of religiosity but rather as a form of engagement with it, or—in the words of Gauri Viswanathan—as a "condition pertaining to the practice of religion."[14] Drawing inspiration from Viswanathan's approach as well as that of Talal Asad, I employ the term *secularism* to refer to a set of expectations about the practice of religion that affirm religion's role in the body politic and in society within strictly circumscribed boundaries.[15] This approach recognizes that different individuals articulate these expectations not only in legal terms but also through various forms of social pressure and in assumptions about proper and productive behavior. Contrary to its usage in many works of German, French, and Jewish history, I do not define secularism as a set of antireligious doctrines. Antireligious secularism was just one of many forms that secularist expectations took, and one that became prominent only in the last third of the nineteenth century.[16] My understanding of secularism encompasses instead what others have referred to primarily as middle-class religiosity. It is indebted largely to George L. Mosse's understanding of decency as a middle-class virtue that regulates, among other things, how individuals live their religion and organize their religious life.[17]

My work also departs from many studies of secularism in that I stress the importance of polemics—and anticlerical polemics in particular—over political principles. Anticlerical polemics are a useful guide to secularism because theoretical and philosophical approaches to secularism have varied widely, to the point of being clearly contradictory.[18] Geoffrey Brahm Levey, for example, has recently illuminated the tension between two different models of secularism: that of the neutral state and that of the nation-state.[19] The first approach consists of a set of models that scholars often trace back to early modern jurists and philosophers such as Samuel Pufendorf and John Locke. This version of secularism aimed to overcome conflicts within territories inhabited by Catholics and Protestants by removing the state from theological debates.[20] The increasing power of Europe's centralizing states since the seventeenth century thus went hand in hand with the rhetoric of self-constriction: According to this version of secularism, the state might assume authority in the earthly realm, yet its powers in religious realms had to remain limited. This form of secularism implied a particular type of separation of public and private spheres predicated on the state's self-limitation to public and worldly concerns.[21]

The second model of secularism emerged in the eighteenth century with new approaches to the state and the nation. The ideal of a strong centralizing state and of the nation-state in Europe presupposed certain cultural similarities between its members, which were to be fostered through education. Early nationalists and political economists in the service of the state began to differentiate between what they decided were the productive and unproductive elements of religion within a stable and prosperous social order. Jean-Jacques Rousseau's conviction that an obligatory form of civil religion was necessary to sustain the ideal state is only the most radical version of this approach.[22] More pragmatic renditions of the same idea are also recognizable in the efforts of eighteenth-century German representatives of police science.[23] In this new form, religion and religious texts became part of debates over the bonds that held society together.

While the first model of privatized religion required states to abdicate their influence over religious matters, the second nation-state model made religion a potential field of new interventionist state policies. Many Protestant conservatives in Germany and Catholic conservatives in France began to call for a religiously homogenous nation, while liberals and republicans put forward their own versions of state involvement in religious affairs. Retaining their rhetoric of opposition to intolerance and fanaticism, various republicans and liberals alike demanded that the state take over the education of the nation's youth to instill universal civic values. As they did so, they were influenced by their view that Christianity constituted a part of national culture as well as the bedrock of secular morality (*morale laïque*).[24]

Many nineteenth-century debates between liberals and their detractors revolved around these two seemingly irreconcilable models, both of which formed part of the larger phenomenon that scholars today call secularism. Both models have figured prominently in liberal political traditions despite the fact that they often contradicted one another, and both continue to appear in today's growing literature celebrating or critiquing modern secularism in turn. It is therefore futile to speak of one pure form of secularism based on distinctions between different theoretical approaches; in practice, there are only people who lay claim to certain models that have been called secularism at different junctures, and, more often than not, only in retrospect. It might be tempting to label as secularism only the neutral state model—with its emphasis on separation of church and state—as Geoffrey Brahm Levey and others writing within an Anglo-American tradition have done. Doing so would, however, mean that the myriad liberal and republican politicians who established state schools that taught secularized Christian ethics to combat the Catholic Church's influence on education would be excluded from our definition of secularism.[25] Indeed, according to the separationist interpretation of secularism, the vast majority of German and French politicians of the modern period do not appear as secularists. Such an omission becomes particularly problematic in the context of continental Europe. In the German-French sphere, separation demands were at times more typical of the Catholic side in conflicts with liberals and republicans.[26] Indeed, liberal and conservative Catholics alike called for religious freedom in an attempt to defend the Catholic Church's role in primary and secondary education.[27] Mainstream liberals, by contrast, often wanted the state to police religious groups rather than give more autonomy to the church within the state. The separationist definition of secularism thus implies that conservative Catholics were secularists, whereas state-centered liberals were antisecularists. Such a description would have been counterintuitive to nineteenth-century observers and is hardly intelligible in current scholarly debates.

How then to reconcile these differences? How can we make the term *secularism* productive for anything but the most localized investigation when its apparent meanings have so little in common? Does it even make sense to use the term *secularism* in the singular? In the pages that follow I propose that we move beyond a discussion of principles to start addressing these questions, while at the same time remaining cognizant of the import of political structures. Principles are crucial for political thought but are, by themselves, not helpful for understanding either everyday political divisions or the often unspoken assumptions behind political debates. The culture wars of nineteenth-century Europe that fueled the development of secularist understandings of religion were not an exercise in political philosophy. Rather, I argue, polemics determined modern Europeans' views on religion and politics at least as much as theoretical considerations. Liberals did not first believe that close-knit religious groups undermined the nation-state only to seren-dipitously discover Jesuits who they decided fit this description, for ex-ample. In practice, Enlightenment thinkers and liberals adopted both their anti-Jesuitism and their more abstract ideas about proper forms of religiosity at the same time.

Polemics, in other words, made secularism. The two theoretical models of secularism have this in common: They are both the result of the insults directed against those whom liberals came to describe as "fanatics"—a key term of eighteenth- and nineteenth-century debates on religion.[28] Once understood as polemical and rhetorical positions that shaped people's outlooks on the nature of religion and politics, anticlericalism and anti-Catholicism become constitutive elements of any history of secularism. Put another way, we can recognize distinct positions in the conflicts surrounding religion less through different speakers' abstract invocations of political theory than in the specific and even pedestrian polemics they employed against those they qualified as the enemies of "true" religion. Thus, when I use the term *secularism* in the pages that follow, I do so to refer to the set of expectations about proper religion that have always treated particular religious groups as a model while treating other religious groups as a foil.

The potential and the obstacles that *polemical secularism* has posed for minorities since its inception come into relief if we recall its two-pronged concern with minorities. Gruesome depictions of the persecu-tion of believers by fanatical priests and, later, by the defenders of the religion of reason—whom religious thinkers denounced as "fanatics of antifanaticism" beginning as early as the French Revolution—created interest in the fate of various marginalized religious groups.[29] Indeed, the stories that illustrated Enlightenment and liberal notions of prog-ress regularly involved religious minorities. When liberals condemned the Inquisition's persecution of witches, heretics, and converted Jews or decried the Catholic Church's mistreatment of Jews and Protestants during the medieval and early modern periods, they distanced them-selves from an institution they believed had no place in the modern age. In this sense, anti-Catholicism became dependent on references to those groups that had suffered under the church. Indeed, it is hardly a coincidence that Voltaire's most memorable polemics against the Cath-

olic Church were his horrifying rendering of the torture and brutal ex-
ecution of the Protestant Jean Calas.[30]

At the same time, religious minorities were also the targets of secularist critiques of fanaticism. The secularists' promise was that those
they regarded as fanatics, whether Catholics or Jews, would be neutral-
ized in a secularist political order, either because religion would remain
outside of political debates in a well-regulated society or because the
state would eventually reform its retrograde populations through its
educational and cultural policies.

As the principal non-Christian religious minority in Germany and
France, Jews confronted both those aspects of secularist discourse that
idealized minorities as victims of fanaticism and those that denounced
them as enemies of the nation and progress. Jews' own rhetoric similarly reflected both aspects of secularist polemics: Invoking middle-class
expectations about proper religiosity, they criticized secularist pressures when such pressures adversely affected their own status but also
endorsed polemics that affected other religious groups. Jewish anti-
Catholicism thus provides a unique perspective on the versatility and
trade-offs that modern secularism has offered to religious minorities.
It also illuminates the challenges and opportunities Jews faced as they
employed a political language in which they served merely as one foil
among many for debates on religion.

Rethinking Secularism and Nationalism in Germany and France

Recognizing Jewish criticism of Catholic antimodernism as examples
of polemical secularism also reveals crucial intersections between Germany and France thus bringing together the often disparate historiog-
raphies of these two countries in the modern period. While scholars
now suggest that the European path to secularization may have been
the exception rather than the rule, Germany, France, and a handful of
other European states remain a crucial part of current debates over
secularism because these countries continue to be the (sometimes unspoken) models for abstract discussions of secular paths to modernity.[31]
More precisely, France and Germany often stand in for two distinct

paradigms of secularism. In David Martin's seminal attempt at classifying secularism, France becomes the prototype of the "Latin" model: In his rendering, French secularists pursued an antireligious agenda and sought to remove religion from the public sphere through their fight against a unified and dominant Catholic Church.[32] For Martin, as for many nineteenth-century German theorists since the romantic period, Germany represented an opposite "Protestant" model of a more conciliatory path. According to this view, progressives in the North German states were willing to accord church-based religiosity a role in the making of a peaceful and well-regulated society. Liberal Germans in the long nineteenth century were, according to various portrayals, the children of the Religious Enlightenment recently described by David Sorkin, while the French appear more often as the inheritors of the atheist Radical Enlightenment posited by Jonathan Israel.[33] Yet, for nineteenth-century intellectuals, Germany was also the country of the *Kulturkampf*, the mostly legal and political struggle between the state and the liberals against the power of the Catholic Church. While reformers and conservatives across Europe could point to France as a model for the consequences of militant unbelief in politics, Germany— like Gladstone's England—became a classic example of secularism under conditions of denominational conflict.

The use of Germany and France as models is perhaps even more important for scholarship on nationalism. Since Hans Kohn's foundational work in the 1940s, political scientists have treated France and Germany as opposite paradigms for civic and ethnic forms of nationalism.[34] Such approaches suggest that the French created a state-centered, voluntaristic nation, whereas the Germans' focus on culture and origins exemplified an ethnocentric model, as Rogers Brubaker has famously described it.[35] Taken together, these models portray Germans as preoccupied with the creation of an ethnic nation in which religion, understood as a cultural phenomenon, became a legitimate element in nation building. In fact, nineteenth-century commentators and later scholars alike have continued to accuse German nationalists of adopting a confessional, and particularly Protestant, view of the nation. Others have assumed, by contrast, that French believers in a political nation were prone to opposing all religious establishments and thus embraced antireligious politics.

These distinctions between opposing forms of nationalism and secularism have also profoundly shaped the historiography on modern Jewry. Influenced by historical sociology, various modern Jewish historians have identified different Jewish "paths of emancipation," thereby mapping the fate of Jews onto national trajectories.[36] According to the classical narrative, French Jews were equal citizens throughout the nineteenth century in a nation imagined as voluntary, while German Jews had to struggle with exclusion from an ethnic nation during the same period. Although various scholars have started to question the idea that the integration of Jews in Germany and France should be understood in terms of fundamentally different paradigms, this approach nonetheless continues to leave its imprint on the field.[37]

There are, of course, good reasons to highlight these differences in light of the greatly divergent histories of Jewish emancipation in the two countries. In France, Jews gained full citizenship by 1791 and experienced restrictions on these rights only during two short periods—from 1808 to 1818, when Napoleon placed limitations on Jewish rights, and from 1940 to 1944, when Jews' basic civil rights were repealed under the Vichy regime's "Statute on the Jews." By the nineteenth century, French Jews could theoretically (if not always in practice) be elected or appointed to administrative and political positions. German Jews, by contrast, experienced emancipation as a protracted process completed only in 1871 with German unification. While German states had a variety of approaches to regulating religion, many shared a reluctance to give Jews full rights. Until the Napoleonic wars, Jews often lived as only temporarily tolerated individuals or families. Even after they obtained citizenship rights in the largest German states, such as in Prussia in 1812, Jews found their ability to practice a number of occupations limited, especially those associated with sovereign prerogatives.[38] Even in the most liberal parts of Germany, such as the commercially oriented city-state of Hamburg or the southwestern German kingdom of Baden, Jews did not gain basic civil rights until the 1840s.

This study offers an alternative to the dichotomous views of German and French secularism in general and to those concerning each country's Jewish experience of modernity in particular. By taking this approach, I do not mean to suggest that the differences between the two national contexts do not matter. It is undeniable that the ideal types outlined above would have seemed plausible, and at times quite compelling, to nineteenth-century German and French individuals preoccupied with gauging their own position by contrasting it with the situation that existed across the Rhine.[39] Indeed, in the writings of untold nineteenth-century observers, the antireligious Frenchman and the Protestant German liberal came to epitomize the two nation's distinct political cultures. Nor do I intend to claim that France and Germany should instead be considered similar in most respects. On the contrary, the present work builds on many of the distinctions already highlighted by scholars working in the field, while also adding some of its own. Ultimately, this book suggests that recognizing the similar manner in which modern Germany and France organized religion illuminates their entangled history and allows us to see crucial political developments in these two national contexts as part of a transnational story.

Building on the work of historians of the middle classes, gender, and religion, this study argues that Jewish anti-Catholic polemics were part of a larger consensus about the relevance of religion for nation building as well as social stability. Even though bureaucrats, liberals, and conservatives all pursued different agendas in the confessionalized German states and the nearly single-denominational French contexts, they shared ideas about progress and social peace that drew on and reinterpreted similar concepts of religious practice and dogma. Liberals in Germany and France alike fought the much-maligned "alliance of throne and altar" while continuing to pledge their support for a strong state and upholding their own positive notions about religion. Although this pattern is unmistakable in both countries, it is more commonly deemphasized in French history—with its focus on republicanism and the emergence of *laïcité*—than in German history. In fact, liberals' interest in religion continued in both countries, largely because it became shorthand for the ensemble of moral and transcendental commitments that held society together. As Gareth Stedman Jones has noted in the case of early socialists in Western Europe, transforming society implied a simultaneous vision for changing religion, even more than it implied a vision for changing the state.[40] Particularly in the first half of the nineteenth century, political and religious thought was therefore difficult to distinguish in both contexts.[41] In fact, it was precisely the shared politicized notion of religion that sustained the polemical concern with Catholicism and Judaism as foils across modern France and Germany.

In both countries, religion figured prominently in middle-class notions of decency, including those espoused by Jews. Being a good local and state citizen implied the capacity to regulate one's passions, cultivate the right emotions, and express them in the right place. In Germany and France, Jews' efforts to be seen primarily as a religious group, as well as their attempts to reform their religious practice, emerged from precisely this impetus to meet the expectations of respectability common to a wide range of milieus in both countries. Although French Jews had greater access to political rights and social opportunities beginning in the late eighteenth century, they nonetheless continued to face pressures to fit into middle-class models of proper religiosity that resembled those experienced by German Jews.[42] Such visions were an expression of a shared orientation shaped by broader European debates over the definition of fanaticism, the antiliberal tenets of the Catholic Church, and, to a lesser extent, the nefarious influence of Jews.[43]

Examining German and French history through the lens of these shared polemics offers new insights into nineteenth-century secularism and Jewish politics by showing that the champions of liberal secularism in both France and Germany were more willing to permit the public expression of religious identities than is often acknowledged. In this regard, the history presented here develops further various critiques of older narratives of Jewish assimilation. German and French Jewries regularly functioned as the textbook cases of minorities that tried to represent themselves as adherents of an exclusively privatized form of religion—as Frenchmen or Germans on the streets, and Jews only in the synagogue or at home. Indeed, it can hardly be argued that Jews in France and Germany attempted to articulate themselves politically as did Jews in Eastern Europe. In Habsburg Galicia and the Russian Pale of Settlement, Jews were more willing to make political claims as one nation among many in the context of the multinational empires in which they lived. Jews in France and Germany, by contrast, tended to emphasize their position as a confessional group with no political ambitions.[44]

In recent decades, scholars working on both countries have challenged the most radical version of this narrative of the confessionalization and privatization of Jewish religiosity. Among the most important interventions are a series of studies that show the ways and contexts in which nineteenth-century Jews spoke of themselves as linked by more than religion alone. Independently of each other, scholars of German and French Jewry have begun to explore the different means by which Jews employed self-descriptions that betrayed their adherence to essentialized cultural, and even ethnic or racial, definitions of Jewish identity.[45] This criticism has stopped short of completely revising the claims about Jews' tendency to efface their Jewish background in political contexts. Despite the divergent definitions German and French Jews employed to describe themselves during the long nineteenth century, they consistently demanded to be treated as a religion in official debates and in the realm of state legislation. Terms such as *tribe* [*Stamm*] or *race*, which Jews began to use in the nineteenth century, were meant to underline Jewish difference in a decidedly nonpolitical manner compatible with their complete devotion to their homeland.

A second challenge to the narrative of the privatization of religious identity in Germany and France goes further and is even more relevant to the present work: This challenge emphasizes the ways in which the notion of "religion" itself became politically potent beginning with the earliest debates on Jewish citizenship. Ronald Schechter has made this point persuasively in his analysis of representations of the Jews during the Napoleonic period: In 1806 and 1808, the French Emperor asked Jews to come together to declare their willingness to become citizens first and Jews second. Napoleon's attempt to turn Jews into Frenchmen and Frenchwomen of the Mosaic persuasion was a classic example of secularist expectations at work. Yet, although he promoted the idea that unmarked individuals rather than religious communities constituted the French nation, his policies nonetheless legitimized the expression of Jews' collective interest. Indeed, Napoleon's paradoxical request called on Jews to speak as a collective about their ability to become individuals. Although Schechter does not use secularism as the analytical frame for his discussion, his example shows that secularist rhetoric created a much more complicated situation than many theorists of secularism might have us think.[46] The pressure to become unmarked citizens of a secular state often led to the creation and strengthening of newly coherent subnational collectivities organized along religious lines.

This dynamic, which is central to the argument of this book, was at work in nineteenth-century Germany and France more broadly. In both contexts, Christian churches were driven toward state–episcopalian arrangements in which the state encouraged the formation of territorial churches. In the process, the state not only regulated, funded, and policed the churches under its jurisdiction; it also recognized their collective legitimacy.[47] In both countries this marked what French historian Jean Baubérot has called "the first threshold of secularization": By creating the status of recognized religions, the state stopped privileging the members and institutions of a particular denomination to further its own legitimacy.[48] Secularist expectations defined an ideal in which religious identities, instead of disappearing, were recognized and equitably regulated by a neutral state.

What does all of this mean for our understanding of secularism and polemics? I contend that in both Germany and France secularists used their polemics not so much to suppress religion or protect religious freedom as to legitimize the production and maintenance of boundaries. This meant, first of all, that when Jews invoked the values of secularism in their polemics against Catholics and other so-called fanatics, they were claiming their rights as a collective. The polemics of German and French secularism were more valuable in the hands of community builders than in the hands of those who sought to challenge communal projects. A particularly salient example is that of French Jewish liberals who used secularist polemics to reinforce Jewish communal boundaries against proselytizers in the 1840s, as described in Chapter Four. They did so by accusing priests of undermining the religious peace and overstepping the rules of decency by "seducing" Jewish women to convert to Catholicism. Such claims of Catholic disloyalty to the nation expressed patriotic and secularist expectations while also serving Jewish communal ends.

Contrary to the still powerful assumption that European secularism encouraged Jews to display Jewish belonging only in apolitical and private contexts, my analysis of various genres of nineteenth-century politics shows that secularist polemics encouraged Jews' public expressions of Jewishness in equal measure. The exploration of parliamentary speeches in Chapter Six demonstrates that, despite enduring assumptions about the modern European nation-state's attempts to create a universalist, neutral public sphere, Jewish deputies in both Germany and France found that they were free to speak as Jews on the nation's most public of stages. Not only did non-Jewish parliamentarians permit Jews to speak on behalf of their community, in some cases—most importantly, during debates over the role of the Catholic Church—non-Jewish parliamentarians invoked secularist expectations about religious speech to force Jewish members of parliament to emphasize their Jewish background.

Understanding secularism as a set of contradictory images and narratives about the modernity of Others highlights how malleable secularism was in two important modern European national contexts. In both Germany and France, secularism was at times a tool with which individuals demanded a complete leveling of differences and radical assimilation in society, while at other times it served to foster a view of society as an entity composed of multiple religious pillars. Despite the impression given in much of the literature on the subject, this was true even of "antireligious" French secularism. The following study of polemical secularism thus offers a *common* story of German and French politics from the late eighteenth to the early twentieth century. It also brings into question some of the certainties we have inherited about the nature of secularism as well as the effects it has had on society in general and religious minorities in particular.

Conceptualizing France and Germany: Beyond a Comparative Perspective

While identifying the shared elements of Jewish anti-Catholicism in the German and French contexts allows for a transnational history of polemical secularism in modern Europe, writing such a history is by no means a straightforward exercise. In order to write what is at once a comparative and an entangled history, I have found it necessary to employ certain terms and modes of analysis that will inevitably seem unconventional to historians of German and French politics and religion alike. An important example of the challenge of studying modern

Jewish anti-Catholic anticlericalism across national contexts is the fact that French and German historians have tended to use a different vocabulary to study related phenomena: As already noted, historians of France tend to speak of *anticlericalism*, whereas German historians have largely employed the term *anti-Catholicism*. Both labels emerged in the late nineteenth century in the midst of the very conflicts they were designed to describe. As a result, using one or the other term can obscure crucial aspects of the reality of nineteenth-century politics, in part because of the different valence each term has accrued since the nineteenth century. Whereas the label of *anticlerical* has at times been employed as a neutral or positive epithet by historical actors and is, furthermore, often used without reproach by historians of French re-publicanism to this day, the term *anti-Catholic* has primarily a negative connotation in the use of contemporaries and historians alike.[49] More-over, whereas there were numerous associations and journals that called themselves anticlerical in France—such as Léo Taxil's Ligue anticléricale and its organs *L'Anti-cléricale* (1879–1882) and *La République anticléricale* (1882–1885)—no groups or periodicals employed *antikatholisch* as a self-description in their name or title in Germany.[50]

As Manuel Borutta has argued in his comparison of anti-Catholicism in Germany and Italy, the use of the more neutral term *anticlericalism* invites scholars to deemphasize the uncomfortable fact that liberal po-lemics were often not aimed against all clerics but rather specifically against the Catholic clergy.[51] Indeed, much like their Italian fellow travelers, French liberals and republicans often supported Protestant pastors and Jewish rabbis in their attempts to limit the power of the Catholic Church.[52] In this sense, they were frequently as proclerical as they were anticlerical, in the narrow sense of the term.

There were certainly also anticlericals who were not anti-Catholic. Many self-identifying Catholics in Germany and France sought to renew and reform Catholicism at the same time that they called for an end to perceived abuses by Jesuits and the high clergy.[53] Still, by 1815, the dominant phenomenon was anti-Catholic anticlericalism, a posi-tion that was either denominationally indifferent or Protestant inspired. This form of anticlericalism was most intelligible across national bor-ders and was also the version accessible to Jews as a third party in con-flicts over the role of religion in society.[54] What French scholarship calls anticlericalism drew on images of conservative Catholicism as inherently antimodern, images that were similar to those embraced by anti-Catholics in Germany.

The term *anti-Catholicism*, used by historians of Germany, also has a complex and loaded history. Multiple studies have emphasized how denominational conflicts between Catholics and Protestants—both Lutheran and Reformed—intensified in nineteenth-century Germany.[55] Differences between the Christian denominations were important for daily interactions between Germans of all religious backgrounds, for the group identities conveyed through mass media, and in local and national political spheres, and also for the self-understanding of Jews.[56] That some form of confessionalization occurred in Germany is largely undisputed, yet the term *anti-Catholicism* potentially obscures the fact that many German conflicts about religion were intradenominational.[57] Indeed, the conflicts between religious groups, on the one hand, and those among liberals and orthodox factions within a single religious group, on the other, were often at cross-purposes. Members of one major anticlerical liberal association of Protestants in the German Empire, the Protestantenverein, were, for example, at times cautious in their relationships with another more overtly anti-Catholic Protestant association, the Evangelischer Bund, precisely because they wanted to keep up the fight against Protestant orthodoxy at the same time.[58]

While the terms *anticlericalism* and *anti-Catholicism* both capture important aspects of the polemical secularism that influenced political debates in France and Germany throughout the modern period, using one or the other term exclusively for a transnational history would inevitably privilege one historiographical tradition over the other. Anticlericalism and anti-Catholicism alike operated in both countries, and both terms, I suggest, can be useful as analytical categories as long as we remain mindful of their limitations. I have thus employed both *anticlericalism* and *anti-Catholicism* in this book. By doing so, I hope to help bridge the gap between disparate scholarship on religion and politics in each country.

Terminology is hardly the only challenge of a project with such a strong comparative component. One major difficulty of any history covering both the German and French contexts is caused by the divergent forms of state building each country experienced in the modern era.

France was a nation-state throughout the period covered by this book, whereas Germany remained a vaguely defined area consisting of various city-states, small principalities, middle-sized states, and the competing hegemons of Austria and Prussia throughout most of the nineteenth century. German historians—both those writing about pre- and postunification Germany—often resort to speaking about some territories more than others to advance tentative claims about the whole of Germany. Fully aware of the limitations of this approach, I have found no way around it. This study thus focuses mostly on the Protestant north and touches only peripherally on the German-speaking Habsburg territories, where conflicts over the role of religion in society played out differently. At the same time, I would venture that there are also compelling reasons to speak of Germany as a unit even before unification: The debates that I trace both transcended and aimed to transcend the context of individual German states. All of the German authors who appear in this book addressed their appeals to a wider German-language audience. My analysis is concerned precisely with the ways such individuals came to position themselves within this imagined community and space.

Finally, a short note on methodology is in order. While this is a comparative work, it is also an attempt to write an entangled history that traces connections among individuals as well as debates across national borders. Traditionally, comparative scholarship has tended to look for commonalities only as a framework to explain different outcomes. Scholars pursuing such approaches would find two countries that experienced some form of antisemitism, for example, and ask why antisemitism turned into an all-encompassing genocidal ideology only in one of them. The point of departure is thus similarity, while the conclusion explains the difference. Whenever possible, the approach I have pursued here is the opposite: I explore the different arrangements of religion and politics and of Jewish integration in Germany and France and then proceed to highlight what both contexts ultimately had in common. This approach is primarily a commitment to setting arguments in a particular order. As a consequence of this move, the roles of entanglements change. In a traditional comparative framework, connections are often either an obstacle or irrelevant to the argument. I am, by contrast, interested rather in the entanglements that illuminate shared patterns (even as they also hint at differences).[59]

The structure of this book reflects this commitment to an entangled approach. Rather than write separate chapters about each country and leave the comparative work for the introduction and conclusion—as most comparative studies do—I have structured each chapter around a discussion of common phenomena that appeared in Germany and France during a given period. It is perhaps too ambitious to call this approach a method. It is rather an aspiration to create a narrative structure that highlights the transnational nature of the pressures and trade-offs that one particular minority faced in a world in which secularism was always polemical and always also aimed at other religious groups.

My attempt to write both a history of Jewish anti-Catholicism and a cultural history of secularism in nineteenth-century Germany and France is structured both thematically and chronologically. Chapter One analyzes modern forms of antisemitism and anti-Catholicism through a comparative lens, from the early 1700s through the rise of political and racial antisemitism in the late nineteenth century. As I demonstrate in this chapter, Jews and Catholics were often subject to similar pressures to remake themselves to fit secularist ideas about proper religiosity. More importantly, discussions of Jews and Catholics regularly appeared in the works of the same author. Contrary to most studies of antisemitism or anti-Catholicism, which have tended to present diachronic studies of one or the other phenomenon over time, I show how polemics against different religious groups can be understood anew when discussed together. This first chapter also sets up the rest of the book, as it shows that antisemitism and anti-Catholicism were structurally connected and that Jews thus always engaged with their own social and political positions when they spoke about Catholics. This was as true for those Jews who were vocal anti-Catholics as it was for Jewish critics of anti-Catholic secularism.

The next four chapters focus on the transitional period from the mid-eighteenth to the mid-nineteenth century, which Reinhart Koselleck has identified as the period in which most of the concepts used to describe modern European society and politics were formed.[60] Indeed, most secularist expectations and tropes—including anticlerical images—emerged in this period. Chapters Two through Five examine different moments from the late Enlightenment—when German and French Jews engaged regularly with political debates in the public sphere for the first time—to the creation of the French Third Republic and a unified Germany in 1870–1871. In each of these chapters, I seek to show the entanglement of German and French stories while also charting new configurations of anticlerical polemics and their penetration into different levels of society.

Chapter Two explores the late eighteenth-century moment when Protestant and Catholic followers of the Enlightenment saw critiques of the church as evidence of a person's ability to free him- or herself from a state of ignorance. Enlighteners thus generally welcomed Jewish comments on the Catholic Church as proof of an individual Jew's intellectual refinement and viewed debates over the power of the Catholic Church as a political issue that anybody—even a Jew—invested in the fate of the state had the right to discuss. Accusations that Jews were intruding on an intra-Christian conflict with anticlerical statements emerged only during the Napoleonic era, with the rise of romanticism and new forms of religiously inspired nationalism, described in Chapters Three and Four. In these conflicts, anticlericalism emerged as an oppositional ideology, associated with the critique of the Restoration regimes and of anti-Enlightenment movements. Anti-Catholic polemics could even become a weapon in Jewish intellectuals' fight against Protestant antisemitism and ethnic nationalism, as I show in Chapter Three. It also served multiple other purposes, including community building and the articulation of a religious reform program within Judaism

The fifth chapter focuses on the most intensive period of anti-Catholic boundary making among Jews, which began around the time of Mortara affair of 1858. In the aftermath of this scandal, Jewish periodicals and Jewish intellectuals increasingly accepted the vision of a world divided into two camps: one progressive and liberal and the other Catholic and anti-modern. This language also penetrated intra-Jewish conflicts, as reform-oriented Jews increasingly denounced Orthodox Jews for "resembling" Jesuits or conservative Catholics. The few Jews who expressed sympathy with the papacy during this period were increasingly isolated and sometimes even ostracized, as Jewish newspapers issued reports of liberal–Catholic conflicts across the globe. Secularist understandings of religion and critiques of improper religiosity were now, more than ever, identified with opposition to Catholicism.

Chapter Six explores the varieties of secularism that emerged in the wake of the liberal–Catholic conflicts of the nineteenth century by focusing on parliamentary debates on Judaism or the Catholic Church from the 1840s to the rise of antisemitism in 1880s. In nineteenth-century French and German parliaments, as in today's Europe, Jews often found themselves in a position to participate in debates over the place of religion in society. An analysis of the rhetorical strategies of Jewish deputies as well as the responses their speeches elicited from other parliamentarians challenges the longstanding assumption that universalist secularism undermined Jews' ability to speak about their own particular interests in public. As it turns out, other parliamentarians criticized Jewish deputies not so much when they spoke about themselves as Jews but rather when they attempted to speak about other religious communities.

The last chapter describes the intensification and subsequent weakening of Jewish forms of anticlerical polemics through World War I. While the 1870s represented the zenith of Jewish anti-Catholicism in Germany, the rise of new suspicions against Jews made such polemics increasingly less attractive in Germany from the 1880s on. Jewish anticlericalism was similarly contested from the beginning of the French Third Republic (1870–1940). Only briefly, in the context of the heated conflicts between republicans and Catholics that culminated in the Dreyfus affair in the late 1890s, did representatives of French Jewry make opposition to the Catholic Church and "clericalism" central to their political rhetoric. This was also true in French colonial Algeria, where a few Jewish apologists drew on anticlerical images during this period. In this context, one Algerian Jew who took up this fight created the only Jewish periodical ever dedicated exclusively to the battle against "clericalism." By the turn of the century, in France and French Algeria, as in Germany, aggressive anticlerical polemics lost most of their political value, especially after the 1905 law for the separation of church and state was enacted in France. As they turned away from the anticlerical themes that had defined nineteenth-century secularism, early twentieth-century Jewish activists and writers once again followed the pattern of mainstream liberal and republican politics.

One   Antisemitism, Anti-Catholicism, and Anticlericalism

In 1902, the historian and Catholic political commentator Anatole Leroy-Beaulieu (1842–1912) published the first systematic comparison between antisemitism, anticlericalism, and anti-Protestantism.[1] Before this time, authors in Germany and France who had related antisemitism and anticlericalism to each other had done so largely through polemics: Catholic antisemites often claimed that their political positions were a reaction to Jewish anticlericalism, while Jewish critics of the Catholic Church frequently argued that they were merely defending themselves against Catholic opposition to Jewish emancipation. Although Leroy-Beaulieu's *Doctrines de haine* [Doctrines of Hatred] repeated these arguments, it also added what one scholar has called a structuralist explanation of these three forms of prejudice.[2] According to Leroy-Beaulieu, a number of common threads connected all three discourses: Proponents of each type of hatred similarly expressed their positions in terms of economic rivalry, religious antipathy, and racial prejudice as well as in the form of fantasies about the political intrigues of their imagined enemy.

Offering a critique of interventionist secularism and "tyrannical statism," Leroy-Beaulieu argued that all three doctrines of hatred resulted from the pressures of the modern nation-state.[3] In each case, representatives of a particular group demanded the unity of the nation, which, they claimed, was threatened by Jews, Protestants, or the Catholic clergy in turn. Yet, in Leroy-Beaulieu's estimation, it was not a particular group but rather the ideologies of antisemitism, anticlericalism, and anti-Protestantism that ultimately divided the nation. Leroy-Beaulieu's interpretation was unusual in his day but has since become a mainstay of the historiography on the European culture wars of the nineteenth century. Most scholars now favor the view that the nations of modern Europe were divided primarily by their most militant unifiers.

For most of the twentieth century, Leroy-Beaulieu's *Doctrines de haine* had little influence, despite the fact that its author is considered by many to be one of the greatest fin-de-siècle intellectuals and philosemites. Indeed, already before the Dreyfus affair, in 1893, Leroy-Beaulieu had opposed antisemites by writing a passionate and sophisticated apology of the Jews in a work entitled *Israël chez les nations* [Israel among the Nations].[4] A Catholic liberal from the upper middle class who taught at the prestigious École libre des sciences politiques, Leroy-Beaulieu was a rare voice of dissent in a period when many saw Catholicism, monarchism, and antisemitism as complementary political commitments. Given his unusual position, many centrist republicans welcomed Leroy-Beaulieu's intervention into the study of comparative marginalization as a noble endeavor yet soon forgot his work.[5] Jewish activists and journals of the day also enthusiastically supported him but did so selectively: They applauded his opposition to antisemitism but ignored his arguments about anticlericalism.[6] This disjointed reading of Leroy-Beaulieu's oeuvre continues to inform current scholarship, even though historians interested in anti-Protestantism and the genealogy of French *laïcité* have recently revived his notion of doctrines of hatred.[7] In general, the extensive scholarship on antisemitism has been less concerned with comparisons to the stigmatization and exclusion of other groups and more interested in establishing a singular narrative beginning with the history of Christian anti-Judaism. As a result, no study has picked up where Leroy-Beaulieu left off in 1902.

The dearth of comparative approaches is remarkable considering that Germany and France both gave rise to modern antisemitism and constituted focal points in the conflicts between liberals and Catholics. A vast literature on the history of antisemitism in both countries has explored how modern antisemites depicted Jews as members of an alien Oriental race whose attempts to gain wealth and social status weakened the position of their Christian neighbors. In tandem with this literature, a growing body of scholarship has pointed to the ways that liberals in the same countries portrayed Catholicism as backwards and similarly cast Jesuits as saboteurs who planned to subjugate the world and undermine the nation.[8] While these two literatures have not developed in isolation from each other, few works have tried to explore the parallels and entanglements between these different forms of othering.[9]

Given the striking similarities between anti-Catholicism and anti-semitism, it seems worthwhile to return to the comparative approach pioneered by Leroy-Beaulieu and to ask: Were different "doctrines of hatred" in fact connected during their formative phases? In which contexts did polemics against different groups reinforce each other, and in which contexts did they depart? This chapter pursues these questions by comparing antisemitic and anti-Catholic polemics in modern Germany and France, charting the emergence of polemical secularist politics through this double lens. By suggesting ways of rethinking the relationship between the claims different actors made against Jews and the Catholic Church in modern France and Germany, this chapter also offers a logical starting point for understanding the complex position Jews inhabited within the nineteenth-century European culture wars between liberal secularists and Catholics. Jews and Catholics alike had a fraught relationship with polemics that defined what secular citizenship and modern religiosity could mean. Focusing on the intersection of debates over the place of Judaism and Catholicism in different modern European contexts thus illuminates the stakes Jews had in depicting political conflicts in terms of a clash between a secular and a Catholic camp.

Although this chapter surveys the connection between antisemitism and anti-Catholicism in one long chronological sweep, my aim is to allow us to see new details of these discourses rather than flatten what we already know. I am therefore less interested in simply comparing these two phenomena and more concerned with exploring how they became entangled, reinforced each other, and together shaped different modern visions of political belonging and progress in two European countries. Although various modern thinkers and activists remained convinced that antisemitism and anti-Catholicism were diametrically opposed to each other, my analysis shows that secularism subjected Jews and Catholics alike to increased scrutiny, albeit with different consequences. Yet, I argue that it is not the hatred but rather the intense interest in Judaism and Catholicism as alien objects of inquiry that is most characteristic of European secularism in its various forms. In this interpretation, I take a cue from the sociologist Zygmunt Bauman, who has referred to the depiction of Jews as radical Others—whether in the form of antisemitism or philosemitism—as "allosemitism."[10] What follows is thus a story not merely of resentments, as Leroy-Beaulieu would have had it. It is instead an analysis of secularism as a regime of knowledge based on both allosemitic and allo-Catholic views of Jews and Catholics as foils as well as models for thinking about which forms of religion could be considered politically acceptable. These models, much like their attendant polemics, were frequently shared by influential figures in Germany and France.

The Challenge of a Comparative History of Different Doctrines of Hatred

Before engaging with the entangled history of antisemitism and anti-Catholicism it may be useful to contemplate some of the challenges involved in undertaking comparisons between such fundamentally different forms of Othering. A history of the coevolution of these two doctrines of hatred must, first of all, take into account the different emphasis of anti-Jewish and anti-Catholic rhetoric. Depending on the context, antisemitic authors and politicians inveighed either against Jews, Judaism, or Jewish institutions. The same distinction could be made among authors who criticized Catholics, Catholicism, or the Catholic Church. To a large degree, slippage between these different targets is characteristic of the heated polemics against religious and political enemies. A pamphlet that railed against the immorality of Eastern European Jews might quickly become a condemnation of the economic power of all Jews, for example, just as a history of Jesuits might rapidly turn into a critique of Catholic superstitions or the allegedly anti-modern nature of the Catholic religion. Because such polemics have such a wide range of imprecise targets, any selective grouping of texts can give the impression that Jews and Catholics were stereotyped in a similar way.

Looking at the larger corpus of texts makes clear that this was not the case. Most liberal critiques were aimed against Catholic institutions, the influence of Catholic clergy, the persistence or revival of superstitions that allowed clergy members to control their flocks, and Catholicism as a religious culture. The targeting of whole Catholic populations was nonetheless uncommon in both Germany and France, in spite of several glaring examples of enlighteners and, later, liberals who employed Orientalist imagery to depict Catholics as insufficiently modern.[11] Antisemites, by contrast, were primarily concerned with identifying the alien character of the Jewish population as a whole. Characterizing Jews as members of a different ethnic, racial, or national group, they argued against the political emancipation and social inclusion of Jews, an approach anti-Catholics seldom employed in their campaigns. Anti-Jewish and antisemitic activists and thinkers also rarely focused exclusively on rabbis, in contrast to anti-Catholicism's focus on the Catholic clergy.[12]

This different emphasis is most strikingly reflected in caricatures produced in Germany and France during the nineteenth century. While satirical magazines featured widely recognizable images of what they intended to be a Jewish type, they offered no equivalent of a recognizable typical Catholic. The accompanying two drawings from the Berlin satirical weekly *Kladderadatsch* illustrate this asymmetry. Both incidentally offer anticlerical messages. The first image was published during the debates on the Mortara affair of 1858, which erupted after Edgardo Mortara, a Jewish boy from Bologna—then part of the Papal States—was taken from his parents by the police following his baptism by a Catholic maid. According to the Roman authorities the boy, now a Christian, could no longer remain in the care of his Jewish family.[13] The affair became a cause célèbre for liberals across Europe. It also occasioned a great deal of anticlerical and satirical commentary.

In the wake of the Mortara affair, many contemporaries contemplated the potentially absurd consequences of a scenario in which a person's religion could be forever changed only because someone had sprinkled him or her with water. The first illustration offers a version of this type of humorous reflection: How could one protect oneself from baptismal water? Waterproofing, of course. The drawing shows a Jew putting on water-resistant clothing in preparation for his travels to Italy. While the illustration was intended as an anticlerical depiction, it employed standard allosemitic portrayals of Jews as essentially Other. Indeed, the only stereotypical figure in the drawing is the Jew, who is central to the satirical effect of the image. His figure—unlike the Catholic—was a stock

Figure 1.1. "Caution is the mother-in-law of wisdom. Zwickauer equips himself
for a long-planned trip to Italy." The headband and shirt say "waterproof."
Kladderadatsch, November 7, 1858, 208.

character that could be used not only to consciously denigrate Jews but
also to other ends, including anticlerical campaigns.

This contrasts with the second image, which depicts both the Catholic clergy and population in an unflattering way. To a large degree, the
humor of the drawing is produced through the caption, which need
not concern us here. On a visual level, the second illustration works

Figure 1.2. "*Ecclesia militans.* The war of the bishops against the government starts. They already sounded the call for collections and already they tear the collection boxes [or guns, *Büchse*] from the walls, to *gun down* everything that is *blocked* by the government." *Kladderadatsch*, June 29, 1873, 120.

through a conventional depiction of the costume and physiognomy of the Catholic clergy and draws on the familiar image of priests grown fat from overindulgence. The Catholics on the right of the drawing, by contrast, are stereotypical in their demeanor and perhaps in the prevalence of devout women, but they do not appear as caricatures of a single, easily identifiable type. Indeed, outside of the context provided with the illustration, they would not be recognizable as Catholics.

This contrast in visual representation hints at the fact that Jews and Catholics faced clusters of stereotypes with different emphases and implications about the possibility of their belonging to the nation. The trope of foreignness existed for both groups, but only the pair "Jews and Germans" or "Jews and Frenchmen" became an exclusive binary, whereas the opposition between Catholics and Germans or Frenchmen appears to have been unknown. Even ardent German Protestant liberals, who denounced Catholic beliefs and rituals as alien, rarely argued that Catholics could never be Germans. While claims of Jews' foreignness and irreconcilable racial difference became the central accusation of modern antisemites, the primary charge hurled against Catholics was rather that they remained stuck in the past and insufficiently rational. Not surprisingly, most nationalists and liberals in nineteenth-century France and Germany alike considered it much easier to abandon irrationalism than an alien origin or character. This difference in stereotypes was particularly pronounced in France, where most inhabitants were at least nominally Catholics. In French liberal and republican polemics, the term *Catholic* was largely defined by political commitments rather than religious heritage. To be Catholic in France was not, as in Germany, to belong to a distinct religious community that could be ethnicized. These reflections suggest that, while certain tropes in antisemitic and anti-Catholic discourse were similar, the emphasis on themes of foreignness and progress often remained different in each case, as did the particular targets of each of these doctrines of hatred. To continuously mark these differences, I therefore resist literary convention and address the connections between anti-Catholicism and antisemitism with asymmetrical terminology: In the pages that follow, I will refer less frequently to depictions of Jews and Catholics and more often to depictions of Jews and Catholicism or Jews and the Catholic clergy.[14]

Another issue that raises methodological concerns is that of the differing levels of vulnerability experienced by the targets of antisemitism and anticlericalism. Whereas Jews were a small minority that did not constitute more than 0.5 percent of the population in France or 2 percent of the population in the German states, Catholics formed the majority in France and many regions of Germany. Even when Jews and Catholics were both small minorities in predominantly Protestant cities such as Berlin—where Catholics and Jews constituted just over and just under 3 percent of the population, respectively, in the mid-nineteenth century—Catholics were part of a much larger religious group in Prussia and the German states as a whole.[15] This disparity is just as great if we compare the Catholic Church and the institutions of organized Jewry. French and German anticlericals targeted one of the single most influential institutions in their society, whereas antisemites largely imagined the collective power of the Jews in Europe.

Although this difference had an impact on the way Jews and Catholics lived and expressed their communal interests, it matters less if we want to understand how these two forms of Othering were connected discursively and historically. Protestant and Catholic liberals often discussed Jews and the Catholic clergy in related ways as they spoke about progress, proper religiosity, citizenship, and nationhood, despite the fact that the "real" targets of their invectives were fundamentally different.

Even if the realities of demography and power need not be central to rhetorical forms of exclusion, stereotyping often had an unequal impact on Jews and Catholics and, thus, meant something different to members of each group. Indeed one major difference separates Jewish and Catholic experiences in this regard: Jews did not retaliate against perceived injustices with riots in modern Germany or France, whereas German and French Catholics were both victims and perpetrators of mass violence at different moments during the long nineteenth century.[16] Does this mean, however, that hatred against Jews and Catholics cannot be discussed together for methodological and ethical reasons? Pierre Birnbaum makes this argument cogently when he argues against reviving Leroy-Beaulieu's idea of doctrines of hatred.[17] Because there was no Protestant or Jewish violence against Catholics in France, he contends that it makes little sense to use one overarching category for anti-Protestantism, antisemitism, and French anticlericals' critique of Catholics. Indeed, one might ask: Is the fact that both Jews and Jesuits were labeled as foreigners enough to justify treating them as equal victims, when it was only the small Jewish minority who suffered physical violence?

Without diminishing these methodological problems, a brief overview of the violence perpetrated against Jews, Catholics, and the Catholic clergy in nineteenth-century Western and Central Europe reveals that differences were not always as stark as one might assume with the history of the Holocaust in mind. Throughout the long nineteenth century, violence affected Jews, Catholics, and the Catholic clergy, even if unevenly and at different times. The most severe cases of violence against Jews occurred in 1819 in Northern and Western Germany and in Alsace during the revolutions of 1789, 1830, and 1848.[18] All of these major incidents transpired during the first half of the long nineteenth century, a pattern which offers evidence of the increasingly rare nature of anti-Jewish violence during the nineteenth century despite the rise of political antisemitism. Equally important, anti-Jewish violence in France and Germany became less and less lethal over the course of the nineteenth century. Even in the most notorious case of anti-Jewish violence, connected to blood libel accusations in Konitz in 1900, there was little bloodshed.[19] In metropolitan France, the last fatalities of anti-Jewish violence in the nineteenth century likely occurred in 1832.[20] Whatever the reason, the great wave of anti-Jewish protests of 1898 that exploded in the midst of the Dreyfus affair led to fatalities in Algeria but not in metropolitan France.[21] As in the case of Konitz, many late nineteenth-century riots were contained by the presence of the state's security forces.

Violence against the Catholic clergy was different but also common throughout the long nineteenth century in Western and Central Europe.[22] The French Revolution and the Commune of Paris in 1871 each brought about their own ideological persecution of priests in the name of the nation.[23] In various other instances there was also nonstate violence against the clergy and lay Catholics. This is especially true if we include riots against Catholic foreigners or Catholics who were also linguistic minorities. Even in Catholic France, religion was present as a symbol of difference in riots against Catholic immigrants. In 1893, for example, French workers killed between eight and fifty Italian immigrants in riots in the country's south—shouting "Death to the Cristos," and thus highlighting their victims' perceived religiosity and their own nonreligious identity.[24] While this does not necessarily suggest that riots were caused by religious motives or the victims' religious affiliation, the killing of individuals identified as "Cristos" cannot be disconnected from anticlerical rhetoric. Attacks against Catholic clergy and churches were also a form of political protest in France in the 1830s.[25] While this type of political violence was uncommon in Germany, some scholars have highlighted cases of riots that emerged from tensions between different denominational groups. The most famous—if also exceptional—case of such violence against a Catholic institution was the storming of Berlin's Moabit monastery in 1869 by a mob of 3,000 to 10,000 people.[26]

All of this should not obscure the fact that Jews—a smaller and more vulnerable minority in both countries—experienced violence in fundamentally different ways than did Catholics or Catholic clergy for most of the nineteenth century. Because both groups were threatened physically, however, it is worth asking whether similar patterns led from insult to violence. In both cases we might ask whether *longue durée* hatreds or local circumstances have more explanatory power.[27] While the following discussion focuses less on social realities and more on the depiction of Jews and Catholics in high- and middlebrow texts, this brief survey of the history of violence against these two communities in modern Germany and France indicates that—as long as we do not equate the two—there exist compelling reasons to pursue comparative and integrated analyses of modern antisemitism and anti-Catholicism in the social realm as well.

Jews and Catholics as Symbols during the Enlightenment

The Reformation marks a convenient starting point for any search for the prehistory of the entanglement between debates on Jews and Catholics in modern secularist discourse. While the Reformation did not necessarily make Jewish life in Europe any easier than it had been previously, it certainly made it more interesting as a subject of inquiry to Protestants in particular.[28] Representatives of all confessional parties—Lutherans, Calvinists, and adherents of the Tridentine Catholic Church—tried to bolster their own position through a reinterpretation of the Hebrew Bible and the history of the biblical Israelites. While the precedent from ancient Jewish history became central to intra-Christian conflicts over the role of the church in society, postbiblical Judaism also acquired new value as a living source of information about Israelite history. Some of the seminal works that reflect this new political interest in Jews bolstered arguments for the toleration of Jews while also advancing anti-Catholic positions.[29]

Texts most often discussed in the context of the history of Jewish–Christian relations are thus also part of the history of secularism and anti-Catholicism. We can see this clearly if we consider that the most important turning points in German and French opinions about Jews emerged in response to events in the history of Protestant–Catholic relations. One of these crucial moments was the 1685 revocation of the

Edict of Nantes, which sent large numbers of French Calvinists into exile. These exiles' attempts to come to terms with the theological and world historical meaning of expulsion and persecution influenced enlightened debates about Jews across Europe.[30] For members of the so-called moderate party among the Huguenots in the Dutch Republic, toleration was a weapon to be used against the types of religion that had turned them into refugees. We can see this motive in Bernard Picart and Jean Frederic Bernard's immensely popular *Cérémonies et coutumes religieuses de tous les peuples du monde* [Religious Ceremonies and Customs of all the People of the World] (1723), which included Jews as one among many faiths. Framed in part by Picart's deist commitments, rabbinical Judaism appeared in this encyclopedic overview of the world's religions as a tradition that needed to be understood—rather than judged—with the same methods that one would use to describe Lutheran and Calvinist Protestantism, Catholicism, Islam, and the so-called heathen religions.[31] Redefining religion as a universal anthropological phenomenon, this work depicted all religions as peculiar and capable of superstitious forms, making Judaism appear less exotic than it had in earlier European writings. At the same time, the book argued that some religions—most notably Catholicism—were more prone to fanaticism than others. The same approach that made Judaism appear familiar made Catholicism appear strangely unfamiliar.

The polemical undercurrent of Bernard and Picart's work could be ignored by readers who preferred to focus on the authors' other achievement, which was their popularization of a unified approach for the description of different religions. In other texts that developed out of the same Huguenot milieu, the polemical thrust was harder to ignore. Pierre Bayle's friend Jacques Basnage (1653–1723) more clearly used his discussion of Jews in an attempt to denounce other denominations. Basnage's search for the meaning of exile and the survival of communities of faith under persecution are major themes of his *Histoire des Juifs* (1706–1707), which has been hailed as the first comprehensive history of the Jews.[32] Although he depicted Jewish suffering as the result of the Jews' rejection of Jesus and, thus, of divine punishment, Basnage also showed much sympathy for their fate and demanded toleration for them. His position was not just an expression of empathy for another oppressed and exiled group, however. It also offered him an occasion to contrast Protestant practices with Catholic intolerance, which—according to Protestant polemicists—had prevented Jews from converting to Christianity.[33] The analogy between the development of a false rabbinic tradition out of true revelation and the similar corruption of God's word by the Catholic Church proved especially fertile ground for anti-Catholic commentaries.[34] Even though Basnage did not develop his anti-Catholicism "into a sustained allegorical argument," as the historian Adam Sutcliffe has noted, his anti-Catholic positions gave additional meaning to his description of Jewish beliefs and suffering.[35] Among the moderate party of the exiled French Protestants of late seventeenth- and early eighteenth-century Europe, as for many other European Protestants, sympathies toward Jews often had as much to do with their attempts to gain advantages in their confessional conflicts with Catholicism as with their efforts to promote new ideas of religious toleration. These early historical and ethnographic narratives of fanaticism and anti-fanaticism, both of which used Jews and Catholics as foils, created patterns of comparison that persisted in secularist debates through the present.[36]

The *Lettres juives*, published by the marquis d'Argens (1704–1771) between 1735 and 1737, offer another influential version of this entanglement of anti-Church criticism, secularism, and—in this case—nonreligious philosemitism. D'Argens was a nobleman from Provence who became a deist and prominent enemy of organized religion. Living and publishing first in the Dutch Republic, he eventually moved to Berlin in the 1840s, where he was close to Fredrick II as well as nonaristocratic enlighteners like Friedrich Nicolai (1733–1811).[37] Modeled on Montesquieu's *Persian Letters* (1726), the *Lettres juives* features the voice of a foreigner who writes an anticlerical ethnography of Europe's dark side.[38] Rather than allowing us to see France and other European countries through the eyes of Persian noblemen, however, the Oriental protagonist of d'Argens's work is a Jewish traveler from Constantinople named Aaron.

As in many other epistolary treatises of this type, the main character, introduced as an exotic outsider, appears less and less foreign the more he describes his alienating experiences in Europe. A tale of moral improvement, the book portrays its Oriental Jewish protagonist as successively more enlightened (and, by implication, more European) the more he observes, and distances himself from, Catholicism. Indeed, the true Orientals in d'Argens's novel are not the Jews but the Jesuits, whose origins and politics Aaron explains to his interlocutor Isaac with a reference to Muslims. "If you examine the conduct of the Jesuits carefully, you notice that they are very similar to the Muslims. They employ the same methods as the latter to expand their sects, and try like them to seduce men, flattering their passions and scaring them."[39] Thus the Jesuits appear intelligible to the Eastern traveler because of the "parallel between Turkish and Jesuitic politics."[40] Aaron, familiar with that other Oriental figure—the Muslim—recognizes in the Jesuit the true, fanatical, and superstitious Oriental. In d'Argens's novel, a Jewish character becomes the tool for the expression of anticlerical critique. Secularist ideas about proper religiosity thus emerged equally in the texts of Huguenot writers and deist Catholics as part of their shared rejection of what they qualified as Catholic superstitions and backwardness. Jews were crucial symbols in conflicts between Protestants and Catholics, as well as those between Enlightenment thinkers and conservative Catholics, because they helped anti-Catholic writers place their main foil—Catholicism—into greater relief.

D'Argens found successors not only in France but also in Germany, where such polemics were more often interpreted in the context of the competition between the Christian denominations. Here too we can detect the continuation of Basnage's attempt to simultaneously familiarize readers with Jewish history and defamiliarize Catholic Christianity. The most famous anti-Catholic work of the German Enlightenment, Friedrich Nicolai's *Beschreibung einer Reise durch Deutschland und die Schweiz, im Jahre 1781* [Description of a Voyage through Germany and Switzerland in the Year 1781], for example, frequently dwells sympathetically on the treatment of Jews in past and present.[41] Nicolai was an influential Berlin publisher, a friend of Moses Mendelssohn (1729–1786), and one of the most articulate proponents of a markedly Protestant vision of rational society in the late eighteenth century.[42] His travels through the southern parts of the German Empire were intended to introduce him and his northern German compatriots to regions of the fatherland he assumed were little known to his readers. Describing the Catholic South's traditions, economy, and its inhabitants' physical characteristics, Nicolai drew on the narratives of other Protestant travelers—particularly those from England—as well as d'Argens's fictive traveler who discovered much that was peculiar and exotic in the religious practices of Catholics.[43] Throughout the work, Nicolai's ridicule was reserved principally for the unbridled consumption patterns of the Catholic population and especially the clergy. Rarely did priests appear in Nicolai's narrative without large paunches nurtured by the excessive intake of food and alcohol.[44]

Unlike the geographic descriptions of most contemporaries, Nicolai's travelogue also addressed the persecution of Jews at various points along his itinerary, ranging from historical instances of anti-Judaism in Franconia to the humiliations Jews experienced in Nuremberg during his own day.[45] Although Nicolai did not claim that anti-Jewish persecutions were a genuinely or exclusively Catholic phenomenon (nor could he have plausibly done so), the emphasis he placed on Jewish suffering in his anti-Catholic description of Germany is nonetheless remarkable. For Nicolai, unlike most of the authors of his time, the construction of the Catholic St. Leopold Church on top of the destroyed synagogue in Vienna's old Jewish district was a poignant example worthy of inclusion in print.[46] This early anti-Catholic ethnography of German lands was thus also one of Germany's first national geographies of anti-Judaism.

The combination of ambivalent philosemitism and anti-Catholicism that was characteristic of the works of Basnage, d'Argens, and Nicolai was not the only model of anticlericalism available to European authors in the eighteenth century. Voltaire, the most famous Enlightenment thinker to write about both Jews and Catholics, offers perhaps the most dramatic counterexample to the anti-Catholic philosemitism of the previously mentioned authors. Scholarship on the place of Jews in Voltaire's work long took its cues mostly from Arthur Hertzberg, who argued that the emblematic Enlightenment thinker was a forerunner of modern antisemitism because his anti-Christian polemics against the Hebrew Bible went hand in hand with his depiction of Jews as an eternally alien race.[47] According to this reading, Voltaire's primary concern was to critique the Hebrew Bible as well as the Jews as the source of Catholic Christianity.

Various scholars have subsequently complicated this view, emphasizing instead the tensions inherent in Voltaire's work.[48] Indeed, in different contexts, Voltaire depicted Judaism both as the source of

Christianity and as something entirely distinct from it. Jews even served as a positive foil in some of his anticlerical arguments, just as they had for d'Argens. In his *Philosophical Dictionary*, for example, Voltaire noted that the Jews' "bottomless" intolerance was nonetheless limited by the fact that they were entirely unconcerned with those around them. In contrast, it was the Christians who became missionaries of fanaticism in Voltaire's view.[49] As he put it succinctly in his dictionary, "The Jews didn't want the statue of Jupiter in Jerusalem; but the Christians didn't want it in the Capitol."[50] Whereas the Jews were merely defending their own environment against encroachment from the Romans, in other words, the Christians tried to refashion the empire as a whole. In light of this dangerous Christian—and, in Voltaire's political context, Catholic—form of fanaticism, could one blame Jews for staying Jews?

Voltaire also praised the obstinacy of the Jews at times, portraying it, as Ronald Schechter has aptly noted, as a sign of their potential for fidelity.[51] In the *Henriade,* Voltaire's epic poem on civil war and religious fanaticism, he wrote of the auto-da-fés against Jews who were burnt "for not having left the faith of their ancestors."[52] Less dangerous than Christians and victimized by the Catholic Church for their unwillingness to abandon their convictions, Jews could sometimes appear as a (relatively) positive foil for the type of fanatical religion Voltaire intended to critique. Although he did not systematically depict Jews as victims of religious persecution, as some of his contemporaries did, Voltaire also participated in a tradition that connected discourses on Catholics and Jews in multiple and contradictory ways.[53]

Much like Basnage's *Histoire*, Voltaire's work offers no single pattern that connects philosemitism or antisemitism with anti-Catholicism, or a hatred of the Inquisition with a love for Jews. Like the other eighteenth-century examples noted here, reference to Voltaire's work can nonetheless illustrate how Judaism and Catholicism became closely imbricated in a variety of Enlightenment texts that exerted long-lasting influence on the narratives of later secularists. In many texts that offered a relatively sanguine view of the Jews, denominational and non-denominational polemics against Catholicism contributed to a shift in writers' understanding of Judaism as merely one religion among many. Although such depictions regularly depicted Judaism as a faith capable of fostering fanaticism, they also argued that Jews had also been unfairly persecuted for centuries, particularly by the Catholic Church. Anti-Catholicism—and with it allosemitism—was hardwired into the modern rhetoric of progress in both the French and German sphere.

Nationalism and the Turn to Religion as a Resource

Enlighteners like Nicolai, d'Argens, and Voltaire spoke about Judaism and Jews as part of their attempts to critique existing religious institutions and excise what they viewed as fanaticism from positions of power. During and after the Napoleonic wars, a very different intellectual tradition associated with romanticism gained strength on the left and the right. While the various romanticisms that emerged in this period had different political thrusts in Germany and France, they had one thing in common that explains their shared focus on both Judaism and Catholicism. In both countries, romantics turned to history and religion to explain the fate of nations and states. The romantics' critique of both Jews and the Catholic Church shaped this historically informed understanding of progress and national belonging.

The comparison of Judaism and Catholicism in romantic thought is, in many respects, unusual, especially to students of German history. In the German context, romanticism is most often associated not only with a celebration of Catholicism but also with a rejection of Jews as alien to the nation. Indeed, many scholars have suggested that the emergence of romanticism marks one of the points of origin of modern antisemitism.[54] Similar claims are rarely made about modern anti-Catholicism. As I will argue here, however, there are good reasons to analyze the relationship between romanticism and anti-Catholicism anew.

The romantic idealization of Catholicism, particularly in the German context, frequently implied a rejection of existing forms of Catholicism. Much like Judaism, Catholicism appeared to certain German romantics as something dead, which deserved to be brought back to life in a different form. Novalis's (1772–1801) famous idealization of medieval Catholicism as the model for any future politico-religious order in his essay "Christianity or Europe" was possible because he saw the existing form of Catholicism as irrelevant.[55] In other words, an idealized— and, in this case, cosmopolitan—version of Catholicism was in need of revival precisely because it had disappeared as a reality.[56] Indeed, for Novalis, Rome had been corrupted to the point that it stopped representing authentic Catholicism and had become instead another Jerusalem.[57] Powers of the Counter-Reformation like the (dissolved) Jesuits were similarly absent from Novalis's vision of Catholic renewal. He portrayed them only as an obstacle to the kind of Catholicism he believed would be reborn in a new reformation.

Although the romantics' rejection of contemporary Catholicism was different from their attacks on Jews, both Catholicism and Jews figured in their reflections on authenticity and political cohesion. Johann Gottfried Herder (1774–1803), one of the pioneers of this type of thought, offers a complicated case of such an entanglement. In his later years, Herder famously viewed Jews as a separate tribe that could serve as a model for the overlap of religion, language, culture, and nation he aspired to establish for the German people. According to Herder, the Jews and Irish were the prototypical national religious groups whose suffering had ennobled them. Precisely because he used them as a positive template for autonomous wholeness in a people, Herder also depicted Jews as eternally foreign to the German nation and to Europe as a whole.[58] Jews were foreigners, and their presence in Germany thus had to be regulated not by agreements concerning religious coexistence but rather according to the political exigencies of European states.[59]

Beyond suggesting that the Jewish people could serve as a model to the Germans, Herder argued that Jews and Germans also had important historical experiences in common. Like the Jews, Germans had to learn to mourn the loss of their original national religion, which was wiped out by Roman Catholicism, in order to recuperate a similar type of resilient national religious culture. Catholicism had replaced local vernaculars, which allowed for true national expressions of religion, with an abstract Latin pronounced by priests who distanced the people from God. Significantly, in his dialogues on national religion, Herder presented Jesus as a man of the people who barely understood the court language of Latin.[60] Herder's program of Germanic religion not only derided Latin culture but also suggested that German Catholics should abandon that legacy in order to become truly German. Herder similarly considered Hebrew and Latin prayers as incommensurable with German nationalism, which he believed should treat both religion and language as part of a larger national culture. Neither Jews nor Catholicism was truly German, in his view, but their role was fundamentally different in his analysis. Indeed, he suggested that Jews had nothing to offer to Germany despite the fact that Judaism could serve Germans as a model, whereas Catholics could be German as long as they abandoned Catholicism. Particularly in his later writings, Herder called for Germans to follow a Jewish model of nationhood in order to remedy Catholicism's corrupting influence on their own nation.

The implications of this type of thought for Jews and Catholics remained distinct. Whereas most German romantics hoped that their models would transcend the divisions between Protestants and Catholics, no such expectations existed about the distinctions between Jews and Christians. After their early liberal years in the late eighteenth century, many German romantics became enemies of full civil rights for Jews but not for Catholics or Protestants.

The writings of Herder and Novalis on the subject constitute only a fraction of the large corpus of German romantic texts from the period, yet both suggest an entangled history of romantic anti-Judaism and anti-Catholicism that has continued to go unnoticed in much of the scholarship.[61] Herder's romantic reimagining of Hebrew national religion, as well as Novalis's idea of an undivided medieval Catholicism, remained part of the repertoire of conservative and liberal nationalists alike throughout the nineteenth century. It was less their solutions than their way of posing the problem that influenced those who hoped that Germany—until 1871 an imagined country—would transcend its religious divisions. Herder was not alone among romantic thinkers in depicting Jews as the true outsiders to Germany and Europe. Paradoxically, this position allowed Herder as well as other romantics to portray Jews as less of an integral challenge to the formation of a unified German state than Catholicism, which many romantics described as central to the German predicament. For these Protestant romantics, a secularist vision of a nation transcending denominations relied on a vision of both Jews and Catholics as alien, with Jews serving as the foil for a primordial form of national unity and Catholicism as an obstacle to present and future spiritual unification.

In France, the romantic turn to religion and history had a very different impact on debates about Jews and Catholicism. In the French case little evidence of the overlap of anti-Catholicism and anti-Judaism can be found in the works of the most vocal opponents of Jewish legal equality, as was the case among influential German romantics. In the writings of Joseph de Maistre (1753–1821) and Louis de Bonald (1754–1840), the rejection of the revolutionary legacy of Jewish civic rights went hand in hand with these authors' advocacy of the return to a Christian, and specifically Catholic, state in France.[62] The growing influence of the French Counter-Enlightenment during the Napoleonic and Restoration eras, as well as the eventual emergence of the prominent anti-Jewish Catholic journalist Louis Veuillot (1813–1883) in the 1840s, made it easy for observers in the nineteenth century and today to identify Catholicism, monarchism, and anti-Judaism as key ingredients of early French romantic thought.[63]

These were not the only voices in the debate on religion and politics that appeared in France during the first half of the nineteenth century, however. French liberal thinkers and left-wing romantics were as concerned with the crisis of order and morality as were conservatives.[64] Much as in Germany, the renewed interest in the potential role of religion as a source of liberal or radical politics went hand in hand with a return to history as a source of legitimation and inspiration.[65] Political authors and historians such as François Guizot (1787–1874) in the 1820s, or Edgar Quinet (1803–1875) and Jules Michelet (1798–1874) in the 1830s and 1840s, all agreed that religion was crucial for the proper functioning of the state. As in Germany, it was no contradiction for individuals to be both anticlerical and to seek either the renewal of Catholicism or the rediscovery of an original form of Catholicism purified of its hierarchical, restricting, and superstitious accretions.[66] Such arguments were popular even among French socialists who continued the romantic's emphasis on religion as a basis for a social revolution, such as Louis Blanc and Etienne Cabet during the July Monarchy (1830–1848) and the Second Republic (1848–1852). Both political leaders extolled what they described as the true Christianity, a form of religion they distinguished from that upheld by the Catholic clergy.[67] Other French liberals promoted Protestantism or a reformed Christian religiosity as a solution, including Madame de Staël (1766–1817), Benjamin Constant, Guizot, and Quinet.[68] This turn to religion was substantially different from the outlook of Protestant and secular nationalists in Germany, however. Irrespective of the position they took, French liberals limited their debate to the way religion would come to structure society and state. They gave little thought to the question of how it would define the limits of the nation. In this debate, Catholicism was a much more important topic than Judaism.

On other occasions, calls to regenerate the nation by reforming religion shifted the focus back to Judaism as an atavistic religion incapable of reform. Although this type of argument never took center stage in France, as it did in Germany, it was not unknown among liberal French romantics. Madame de Staël adopted Herder's theories of national character in her early work, for example, and found relatively little to commend in the traditions of Jews, Catholics, or Muslims. In her *de la Littérature* (1800), she remarked on the incapacity of Jews and Muslims to experience the type of melancholy typical of the peoples of the North.[69] While Orientals regret only that they cannot live forever, she posited, northerners suffer from a deep melancholy of the mind that allows them to write great literature. Like Herder, Madame de Staël found positive traits within all literary traditions but saw Protestant culture as the most mature expression of the value of freedom. In her vision, inspired in part by German romantics like August Wilhelm Schlegel, the South included both the Near East and Rome. According to de Staël, neither region was capable of fostering a movement toward liberty. While her writings may have had some influence on early French romantics, however, her comments did not become constitutive of liberal romantic literature in France as a whole. More important still, the liberal romantic tradition in France did not produce a challenge to Jewish civic rights, as it had in Germany.

A different, more radical form of antisemitism and anti-Catholicism marked by a romantic turn to religion and history did emerge among supporters of the radical revolutionary legacy in France, however. Several French leftists embraced antisemitism as well as anti-Christian anti-Catholicism by building not only on the oeuvre of Voltaire but also on the racialized sense of national spirit that appeared in Madame de Staël's work. This pattern emerges clearly in the writings of Pierre Proudhon (1809–1865), who tried to save the monotheistic idea from association with Judaism. In Proudhon's words, monotheism was "so little a Jewish or Semitic idea that the race of Shem can be said to have been repudiated by it [. . .] Monotheism is a creation of the Indo-Germanic spirit and could not have arisen from any other source."[70] According to Proudhon, the racial origin of Judaism also explained the "wicked superstition called Catholicism."[71] One of the later representatives of this same school of thought was Gustave Tridon (1841–1871), a Blanquist and member of the Paris Commune. For Tridon, Judaism was a religion of human sacrifices that emerged from the cult of Moloch; it was the evil root at the core of all theism that could only be overcome through atheism.[72] Here antisemitism, anti-Catholicism, and anti-religiosity were married in a way that made it easy for believing Jews and Catholics to denounce all three discourses together as unacceptable forms of militant anti-religious secularism.

Despite their shared unease in the face of such arguments, Jews and Catholics experienced opportunities and limitations differently in Germany and France; in the two countries, these groups were regulated by different laws and had a different relationship to romantic politics. There were also similarities, however, that shaped Jews' and Catholics' perceptions of their position in society. The romantic concern with history and religion as political culture made Judaism, Catholicism, and Protestantism equally central political symbols of romantic discourse. As liberals as well as their detractors defined religion in cultural terms, religion increasingly became associated not only with ideas of a unified state but also with attempts to forge a homogeneous nation. Each religious community played a different part in this high-stakes game for the viability and world-historical role of different nations. Reference to different denominations and religions thus became relevant for secularist visions of good citizenship not as isolated symbols—as one might gather from literature focusing, for example, only on the rise of romantic antisemitism—but rather in permanent relation to other groups that stood in for progress and backwardness in turn.

Liberal Anti-Catholicism and Jewish Particularity

With the rise of liberal anticlericalism in the middle decades of the nineteenth century in both Germany and France, a new version of the entanglement of anti-Catholicism and anti-Judaism came into existence. Although the transition from romantic nationalism to liberal politics entailed strong continuities, for the purpose of this survey one discontinuity in particular is worth highlighting: Among nineteenth-century liberals, as well as democrats and republicans, the preoccupation with the Catholic Church became predominant, while interest in Jews diminished. In this age of liberal and middle-class ascendancy, the relations between church and state as well as expectations about decorum in religious practice took center stage. In the process, Catholicism emerged as the principal Other of the French and German liberal middle classes. Even though relatively few authors wrote directly about the place of Jews in society during this period, Jews emerged as important symbols in debates about Catholicism. We can thus see a tendency that began with the Huguenot authors of Amsterdam like Basnage before gaining traction in the mid-nineteenth century: Allosemitism, or the discussion of Jews as an essentialized Other, proved a common feature in debates about Catholicism.

The most successful anticlerical novel of the nineteenth century offers a clear illustration of this tendency. Eugène Sue's (1804–1857) *Le juif errant*, published in installments throughout 1844 and 1845, used the myth of the Wandering Jew as a frame narrative for a work aimed against the Jesuits.[73] The Wandering Jew, Ahasver, and to some extent the Wandering Jewess, Herodia, were the tragic heroes, but not the main figures, of Sue's novel. The principal protagonists are rather a persecuted Protestant family, the Renneports, and the Jesuits who seek to rob the Renneports of their wealth. Ahasver serves as the guardian angel of the novel's tragic victims but makes only a few appearances. The narrative receives its ultimate coherence through the machinations of the Jesuits, depicted as a combination of a global crime syndicate and a brutal cult.

In all these regards the novel can be understood as straightforward in its anticlericalism and philosemitic in its depiction of Jews. This impression changes if we focus not on the theme of evil but rather on that of sterility, which inscribes the story in the larger narrative of human progress and national development that Sue aimed to tell. Identifying the affinities between his cult and the Jesuits, the leader of an Indian religious sect of fanatical assassins who joins the Jesuits explains, "[The Goddess] Bowanee makes corpses which rot in the ground. The Society [of Jesus] makes corpses which walk about."[74] This is not just a reference to *"per-inde ac cadaver,"* the Jesuit principle of submitting oneself like a corpse, but rather to the manner in which the Jesuits stand for both evil and sterility or death in Sue's work.[75] For Sue, the Jesuits create continuity merely as a criminal organization, yet they bear no children and cannot offer anything to sustain the nation or move it into the future.

Curiously, the Jews of the novel, who are altogether positive figures, are equally sterile. The Wandering Jew, a shoemaker who denied Jesus a resting place before the crucifixion, represents the workers of the earth in Sue's depiction. When his time as protector of the Renneport family ends due to their demise, he too is allowed to die, as is the Wandering Jewess. His death, Sue informs us, means the redemption of the world's artisans who, like the Wandering Jew, forever toil and are driven from their rightful place. The two other Jews of the novel, Samuel, the keeper of the Renneport estate, and his wife Batsheba, are equally positive figures. Like the two mythical Jews of the novel, it becomes clear that they will die without offspring after their only son is killed in Russia. Symbols of great fidelity, the Jews of the novel have no progeny and disappear once their role is fulfilled. Their disappearance, however, announces a new productive age, symbolized by the family of a Napoleonic soldier who turns to agriculture. In this anti-Catholic *roman feuilleton* both Jews and Jesuits have a role in the future of the nation and humanity only in the sense that their demise marks the beginning of a new age. In a manner typical of liberal French authors of the period, Sue not only used the philosemitic image of the Wandering Jew—and by extension all Jews—as the symbol for suffering humanity; he also employed the anti-Jewish trope of Christian supersession in secularized form to push his anticlerical agenda.

The close relationship between anticlericalism and allosemitism is even more tangible in the case of German liberals active between 1840 and 1880. For reasons that are disputed among scholars, German liberals switched to a more welcoming attitude toward Jews at some point around 1844–1845.[76] In the process, they also started to vote for Jewish civic rights in certain state parliaments. While anti-Jewish statements did not disappear, the majority of liberals across the German states represented in the Frankfurt Parliament of 1848 abandoned demands that civic equality would either presuppose or result in Jews and non-Jews being indistinguishable.[77] By this time, when liberals could vote on national legislation, their decisions regarding Jews as well as a religiously neutral state approximated the opinions expressed in the French parliament of spring and summer 1848.

Precisely as issues of Jewish emancipation became less contentious in German circles, liberals' conflicts with the Catholic Church and its supporters became most pronounced. After the *Trierer Wallfahrt* of 1844, when approximately 500,000 pilgrims went to Trier to see the exhibition of the Holy Coat, stereotypes of the gullible, superstitious Catholicism and a manipulative Catholic Church entered political debates in an unprecedented manner.[78] The most intense period of conflict between 1858 and the end of the *Kulturkampf* in the late 1870s was also the period when Jews seemed most welcome as political allies of Protestant liberals in Germany.

Liberal anti-Judaism continued in spite of this lull in debates, but its relationship to philosemitism and anti-Catholicism became more complicated as German liberalism became increasingly inviting to Jews. Evidence of these simultaneous shifts in opinions toward Jews and Catholicism is unmistakable in the *Staats-Lexikon*, a multivolume dictionary published by two Southwest German authors in several editions meant to form the definitive collection of liberal thought in Germany.[79] Much like Diderot and d'Alembert's *Encyclopédie* of the eighteenth century, Rotteck and Welcker's encyclopedia depended on the contribution of different like-minded scholars and was thus not of one piece. Rather than represent a single liberal opinion, its entries created a conversation on the most important political and legal issues of the day.

In the first edition of the *Staats-Lexikon* published between 1834 and 1843, Jews and Jewish themes did not feature prominently. Before the Jewish reformer Sigismund Stern contributed to the third edition in 1863, only two entries referred to Jews at any length. The first of these dealt exclusively with the Hebrews of the Biblical period and was written by H. E. G. Paulus, a liberal Protestant theologian and opponent of Jewish equality.[80] The second, offering the only discussion of a modern Jewish topic, was an entry by the linguist Franz Bopp (1791–1867) on "Judenschutz und Judenabgabe," two expressions used for the special taxes and concomitant protective relationship with the sovereign that defined Jewish life in German lands well into the nineteenth century.[81]

As many historians had done since Basnage, Bopp documented the exclusion and persecution of Jews in meticulous detail. Yet, whereas Basnage drew mainly theological lessons from his account of Jewish suffering, for Bopp the same history held a different message, which was that nations should never become dependent on other nations for protection. Given this perspective, no guarantees were sufficient "to protect the descendents of an Oriental tribe [*Volksstamm*] from oppression and persecution."[82] Bopp certainly advocated an end to the persecution of Jews, but his historical description left open the question of whether the Jews remained Orientals or whether their separate existence had come to an end through assimilation in the modern era. Whatever Bopp's final judgment on Jews' foreign character might have been, his main aim was to highlight his opposition to fanatical religion and to champion national strength. For this purpose, the persecution of the Jews could serve as a morality tale.

If the *Staats-Lexicon* articulated a sympathetic if ambiguous vision of Jews, its overall position on the Catholic Church was self-consciously critical. Although the multitome work was written predominantly by Protestant liberals, the editors left the entry on Catholicism to a representative of conservative Catholicism, Johann Baptist Hirscher (1788–1865).[83] Compared to the entries on Jewish themes, this article is remarkable in its defensive tone. Hirscher, a professor of theology at Tübingen, opened by justifying the inclusion of an entry on Catholicism in an encyclopedia of political science. The welfare of the state depended on the respect different groups showed one another, Hirscher wrote: "This is therefore the place to vindicate the honor of the millions who confess adherence to Catholicism by showing the essence of this denomination, even if it will not be possible to ensure the approval of those who disagree with us."[84] Hirscher went on to argue for the usefulness of Catholicism to the state before pleading with his readers to show patience as Catholicism took the necessary steps to become a modern religion. Rather than attempting to simply describe Catholicism, Hirscher offered an apology aimed at retaining the honor of his denomination, just as many Jews did in this period.

The entry on the constitution of the Catholic Church offered a counterposition to Hirscher.[85] The author distinguished between ultramontane and episcopalian strands within the Catholic Church, claiming that episcopalian Catholicism was its only authentic interpretation. This, in turn, meant that the dissident German Catholics, who organized communities outside the Catholic Church after 1844, were the true representatives of Catholicism. Thus redefined, Catholicism had to reject the principles of a pope-oriented and historically false church "that every Protestant or true historical mind [*Geschichtsforscher*] would also deny."[86] Catholicism, in other words, had to transform its very core to embody the type of Christianity that liberals viewed as compatible with the state.

The anti-Catholic character of this vision comes into focus in the entries on those institutions that Catholics were expected to abandon in order to participate in the liberal state. The lexicon's essay on "Monasteries," for example, was dedicated to proving that the activities of monasteries were contrary to religion as well as "a rationally organized state."[87] In an effort to challenge the very existence of such institutions, the author put much effort into proving that it was a historical error to believe that monasteries had been useful as centers of culture even in the Middle Ages.

No article on Judaism or Catholicism could match the paranoid language of S. Jordan's long entry on "Jesuits," however.[88] Much as Jules Michelet and Edgar Quinet would do in their French lectures at the Collège de France a few years later, Jordan spoke not only of Jesuits but also of a corrupt system based on intrigue and skillful manipulation, which he referred to as Jesuitism. As he explained it in his entry, the ultimate aim of the Jesuits and Jesuitism were "the resurrection of Rome's rule in its full glory on the ruins of the destroyed Reformation, to build on the ruins of civilization the empire of darkness and superstition, and thus bring back a time of barbarism, inquisition, and auto-da-fés."[89]

Unlike Voltaire's double interest in Jews as both victims and examples of intolerance, the vision of Jewish suffering at the hands of Catholic persecutors remained dominant in this German compendium of liberal thought. Even before the southwest German liberals who stood behind this anthology started to support Jewish rights in local parliaments, their interest turned more decisively toward Jews as victims of medieval fanatacism and the Inquisition, which, they alleged, the Jesuits were trying to reinstate.[90]

A similar dynamic is characteristic of the works of Gustav Freytag (1816–1895), who is remembered today principally as the author of the most successful antisemitic novel in German literary history, entitled *Soll und Haben* [Credit and Debit] (1855). There is, indeed, little in this notorious novel that would merit a reevaluation of such an assessment. Written in a didactic style, each of its characters is an overdetermined representation of a societal trend or type. The main Jewish characters are all physically inadequate, including the central Jewish villain Itzig, the corrupt Schmeike Tinkeles, and the valiant but unworldly Bernard. Each of these Jewish characters embodies the opposite of the healthy, nationalist, masculine Protestant main character, Anton. While readers follows Anton's slow but honorable coming of age before witnessing his transformation into a great man, they see the Jews' precipitous rise and fall through personal disgrace or their death due to physical weakness. There are no Catholic figures that are equivalent to these Jewish characters. Indeed, Catholicism hardly figures in the novel. Although it is possible that the Polish insurrectionists that appear in the text are Catholics, Freytag never makes this explicit to his readers. Because the novel allows only for one personification of each type, the Polish characters appear above all as foreigners to the German nation. Freytag avoids complicating this distinction further by exploring the differences between German Protestants and Catholics. The other principle group that he depicts as antithetical to the ideal new caste of ethical trader-citizens are aristocrats. Their vanity and inflexibility ultimately corrupts them. Ruined by excessive pride but unwilling to engage with the world of trade, in Freytag's novel they mirror the Jews—who are similarly greedy, if even more viscerally driven to profit at all cost and more cunning in their endeavors.

The entanglement of discourses on Judaism and Catholicism did not disappear among liberal nationalists like Freytag, however. The connection between debates on Jews and Catholics comes into focus once again if we look at Freytag's anticlerical works, such as his *Bilder aus der deutschen Vergangenheit* [Pictures from the German Past].[91] Freytag wrote this tremendously popular attempt at cultural history between 1859 and 1867, around the time when he began to declare himself an enemy of anti-Jewish agitation (even if his own apologetics in favor of Jews and against Richard Wagner reproduce many anti-Jewish stereotypes).[92] According to Freytag's later work, both Jews and the Catholic Church were too proud of their past to accept a universal message of love.[93] Both groups take the place that was occupied by the aristocracy in *Soll und Haben*: They are self-absorbed and, at least in principle, unable to modernize.

Unlike in *Soll und Haben*, however, in *Bilder aus der deutschen Vergangenheit* it is not the Jews but rather the Jesuits that became Freytag's dominant foil for his depiction of a citizenry grounded in Christian and commercial ethics. Comparing the progress of Jews and Jesuits in the modern period, he wrote:

> This new *Bildung* also raised the Jews, their fanaticism had disappeared since Christian zeal stopped persecuting them. The grandchildren of this Asiatic wandering tribe are our compatriots and brotherly comrades. The clerical Society of Jesus on the other hand, [. . .] is until today—just like on the first day they immigrated to Germany—alien to German life.[94]

It should be noted that even in this vision Jews remained a recently naturalized group that was understood to have descended from an Asiatic wandering tribe. The fact that the Jesuits were higher on the list of Germany's dangerous enemies than Jews in this depiction did not erase the suspicion that Jews were not Germans; on the contrary, Freytag's rhetorical games conserved that difference. His juxtaposition of Jesuits and Jews was meant to work because of his suggestion that both groups, in their unredeemed state, were examples of a foreign form of fanatic religiosity. Freytag's position was, in this regard, typical of debates on national belonging that centered on the question of the comparative Germanness of various groups. Even if they were more German than Jesuits, the Jews continued to elicit concern about their alien character.

The evidence from German and French debates from the 1840s to the 1860s shows that discussions about Catholicism partially eclipsed the interest in Jews. Liberals now viewed Catholicism as the main antagonist in their quest for a peaceful and fertile society of decent, authentic, and rational citizens. Paradoxically, this new preoccupation also kept alive the peculiar secularist concern with Jews as a foil. Until the rise of political antisemitism in the late 1870s, both negative and positive images of Jews surfaced in the heated liberal polemics about Catholicism. Although Catholicism became the principal target of the ascendant liberal middle classes of the mid-nineteenth century, even when they hoped to join anti-Catholic campaigns, Jews could not easily disentangle their own position from that of Catholics. They remained symbols of sterility and of a people superseded that stood at the core of liberal ideas of progress, even if liberals did not commonly treat Jews as the main obstacles to the new era they envisioned.

The Kulturkampf, the Guerre des deux France, and the Antisemitic Movement

While few writers theorized the relation between antisemitism and anti-Catholicism before 1870, after this point a large number of individuals began to venture explanations about how one phenomenon had caused the other. In 1870s Germany, the notion was popular that Jewish involvement in liberal campaigns against the Catholic Church influenced the way different groups perceived Jews. This idea has regularly been repeated since. Starting in the late nineteenth century, commentators have noted that the antisemitic movement began as the *Kulturkampf* ended. In the early 1870s, writers for Catholic periodicals such as *Germania* denounced Jews as part of a liberal–Protestant alliance that was—in their eyes—determined to undermine both the Catholic Church and religion.[95] This trope was soon picked up by Protestant antisemites, who accused Jews of undermining the nation by sowing dissent among Germans of different Christian denominations.[96]

Jews and Catholics were inextricably linked in these renewed debates on secularism, though in new configurations. In many such discussions, Catholics came to stand for resistance to modernity and secularism while Jews came to represent a destructive form of modernity and a radicalized, materialistic secularism. At other times, both groups continued to figure as enemies of the nation. Even the narrow group of dedicated antisemites in Germany was split between those who condemned the *Kulturkampf* in their writings and those who saw it as a model. Otto Glagau (1834–1892) supported the former position. He believed that the Germans had been fighting the wrong *Kulturkampf*—that is, that their fight against Catholics had been misplaced and that they should have been fighting instead against Jews. A Protestant who received support from antisemitic Catholics, Glagau claimed that Jews had inflamed the tensions between the Christian denominations to cover up their intention to defraud non-Jewish Germans.[97] Eugen Dühring (1833–1921), another prominent antisemite of the era, was perhaps more typical when he articulated a preference for the exclusion of Jews from society without fully condemning campaigns against Catholicism. For Dühring, the anti-Catholic *Kulturkampf* served mainly as inspiration for future anti-Jewish legislation: Citing the 1872 law that expelled all Jesuits from Germany, including those in possession of German citizenship, Dühring suggested that similar measures could be taken against Jews.[98] At the same time, Dühring inverted the strategy Freytag had used in *Bilder aus der deutschen Vergangenheit*: He made the Jesuits the foil that explained the inherent malevolence of Jews without fully exculpating the Jesuits. While for Dühring Jesuits merely followed a corporate law that could be overcome by individual members of the order, the Jews could never abandon their Jewishness [*Judenhaftigkeit*], which was an inherent feature of their very being.[99] According to Dühring, Judaism, like Islam, could only be intolerant or dead; there was no humane form of Judaism.[100]

These disagreements about the relationship between antisemitism and anti-Catholicism in Germany occurred in the face of the antisemitic movement's difficulties in attracting anti-Jewish Catholics. The denominational tensions between Protestants and Catholics that had peaked in the *Kulturkampf* limited antisemites' ability to create a sustained political movement. The identification of the antisemitic movement with Protestantism made Catholics in the German Empire—unlike in Habsburg Austria, for example—less likely to support antisemitic parties.[101] The *Kulturkampf* in Germany was thus not so much a cause of political antisemitism as a factor that limited its success.[102] Anti-Catholicism offered both a model for political antisemitism and an obstacle to its development, in other words.

Although certain racial antisemites employed racist discourse in a conscious attempt to overcome denominational divisions between

Protestants and Catholics, confessionalization nonetheless tended to remain an impediment to their projects. In his 1912 political treatise *Wenn ich Kaiser wär* [If I were Emperor], for example, the Pan-German leader Heinrich Class (1868–1953) depicted Catholics as respectful of authority and conservative in outlook. Explicitly arguing against a new *Kulturkampf*, he asked Protestants to be patient and to exert less pressure on Catholics as they attempted to integrate into German society.[103] Jews, on the other hand, constituted a racial enemy who did not deserve political or even basic civil rights. Yet there remained a tension in the statements of such Protestant nationalists between their open calls for denominational reconciliation and their embrace of anti-Catholic Protestant positions in other contexts. This tension is well exemplified in Class's own life and writing: Although his 1912 treatise called on Protestants to support Catholic attempts to integrate into German society, he also presided over the *Alldeutscher Verband*, an organization that had as its motto, "Without Judah, without Rome, we will build the all-German [*Alldeutschen*] dome."[104]

In this context, an outright overlap of enmity toward Jews and Catholicism appeared only in the works of anti-Christian antisemites such as Richard Wagner (1813–1883) and Houston Stewart Chamberlain (1855–1927) in Germany or Georg von Schönerer (1842–1921) in Austria. Especially for Chamberlain and Schönerer, the battle ahead would be waged against both "Judah and Rome."[105] Chamberlain's *Foundations of the Nineteenth Century* (1899) was perhaps the most prominent expression of this idea. In this foundational text of racial antisemitism, Chamberlain transposed the hope for a renewed Germanic, post-Church Christianity into the language of biological, *völkisch* racism. Germanic religion was destined to overcome the type of Christianity that had emerged from Judaism and that found its more recent incarnation in ultramontane Catholicism. Predictably, anti-Catholic organizations such as the *Evangelischer Bund* welcomed Chamberlain's work, while Catholic Germans looked on with dismay.[106] Even though the influence that anti-Catholic racist antisemites had in the larger Protestant milieu in late nineteenth-century Germany is debatable, they were certainly vocal enough to shape the opinions of a small group of dedicated antisemites in their day. In these circles, we can also find several theories about a secret Jewish–Jesuit alliance that remained marginal in the nineteenth century but would later gain prominence among various Nazi propagandists.[107]

The perspective from France was quite different. Shulamit Volkov's suggestion that antisemitism could serve as a cultural code that marked a speaker as a member of a particular anti-emancipatory position applies to nineteenth-century France even more than it does to the German case.[108] In Germany, where civil society was fragmented into sociore-ligious milieus, this code was intelligible primarily among Protestants who identified each other as belonging to competing liberal and con-servative milieus.[109] When applied to France, however, the concept becomes even more powerful. There antisemitism operated as a code that invited contemporaries to view society as split between two large heterogeneous camps, one secular, or *laïque,* and one Catholic.[110] In late nineteenth-century France, antisemitism became identified with a Catholic camp defined by its opposition to republican laicism, which many Catholic writers denounced as the result of Jewish and Masonic plots.

The boundaries between antisemitic and anticlerical camps were thus much clearer in late nineteenth-century France, as was the idea that each doctrine of hatred had caused the other. French political antisemitism of the late nineteenth century was more compact in its unifying de-nominational character and better integrated into mainstream Catholic structures than German antisemitism.[111] This is not to say that antisem-itism was more widespread in France. The case of Algeria demonstrates that the intensity of the antisemitic movement was not related to the creation of clear boundaries between a republican and a Catholic camp. The three French departments of Algeria are considered the French provinces where antisemitism was strongest. Unlike in the Hexagon, Algerian antisemitism emerged out of an alliance of a radical republican tradition and right-wing and clerical forms of French nationalism. In Algeria during the late 1890s, the anticlericalism and antisemitism of European settlers thus became entangled as nowhere else on the conti-nent, with masonic lodges and socialists at the vanguard of the antise-mitic movement.[112]

In metropolitan France, anticlericalism and antisemitism were much more antithetical. The camp opposing Catholic antisemitism in France, although neither homogenous nor hermetic, identified not only with the principal of emancipation—as Volkov's original model for Germany suggested—but with anticlericalism as well. Bound together by a common enemy, French liberals, opportunists, leftist republicans, and some socialists were willing to ignore their differences during certain periods to unite in their opposition to Catholics.[113] Conspicuous distancing from either Catholics or Jews thus clearly signaled to individuals from different backgrounds adherence to opposing exclusive political causes. It was in France more than in Germany during the late nineteenth century that suspicions against the Jews and the Catholic clergy became mutually sustaining.

Conclusion

During the eighteenth and nineteenth centuries in both Germany and France, anti-Catholicism shaped perceptions of Jews as much as anti-Jewish polemics shaped perceptions of Catholics. Opposition to one group often served as a foil for the relative integration of the other. At other times, the interest in one group kept interest in the other alive. The Jew and the Jesuit, or Judaism and Catholicism, both became the polemical targets of reformers who sought to define notions of proper religiosity and modern citizenship in France and Germany alike. The histories of antisemitism, anticlericalism, and anti-Catholicism cannot be understood in isolation; nor can we grasp the larger history of modern secularism without recognizing their entanglement. The interrelationship between these different forms of Othering appeared not at the margins but rather at the core of Western and Central Europe's modern political traditions.

Whenever German and French Jews spoke about Catholics in the modern period they inevitably engaged with their own position in society. This was the case because modern secularist expectations about religion invariably linked them to discussions on Catholicism. When Jews attacked what they characterized as the anti-modern, hierarchical character of the Catholic Church, they did so in the context of debates in which their friends and detractors depicted Jews and Catholics in relational terms. At the same time, they engaged with their own status as a religious community because the very idea of a religion—defined by their contemporaries as a proper religion deserving of legal guarantees—incorporated both Catholics and Jews as a foil. Antisemitism and anticlericalism were ultimately also attempts to keep the notion of religion pure, against those Jews and Catholics who allegedly hid their political and base motives behind the façade of religion.

Finally, it should be noted that the entanglement of anti-Jewish and anti-Catholic rhetoric is something that emerged only rarely as explicit statements in Jewish or Catholic texts. The opinions that Jews and Catholics expressed about one another were seldom consciously shaped by the particular historical narrative presented here. As far as most contemporary Jews were concerned, Jews and Catholics had little in common.[114] Indeed, when Jews reflected on anti-Catholicism and when Catholics thought about antisemitism, they frequently did so without recognizing their intimate imbrication in such debates.

The same is true for other nineteenth and twentieth-century observers. The connection between different constructed enemies was obscured by the fact that they ultimately appeared to motivate different sets of thinkers. Nineteenth-century contemporaries often summarized the political map of Europe in the following manner: Liberals attacked Catholicism, whereas conservatives attacked Jews. Commentators who identified the intersection of anti-Jewish and anti-Catholic positions among anti-religious leftists primarily viewed the phenomenon as a mere curiosity. The fact that Leroy-Beaulieu was nevertheless able to bring the two enmities together was the result of his principled criticism of nationalism and statism as major containers of modern secularism. He rejected the logic of integral Catholic nationalists and of republicans, seeing both anti-Catholicism and antisemitism as expressions of secular nationalism and its demands for homogeneity in society. We can understand the limited reception of Leroy-Beaulieu's interpretation if we consider that the French republican state achieved one of its great symbolic triumphs just as his *Doctrines of Hatred* appeared. After their victories in parliamentary elections starting in 1898, republicans strengthened the powers of state while passing new laws to weaken the churches. In 1905, the French parliament decreed the separation of church and state, which was widely understood as retaliation against the role conservative nationalists had played in inciting the country during the Dreyfus affair. In the polarized atmosphere of the early twentieth century and with optimism about the potential for a reinforced secularist order at its height, few observers were willing to follow Leroy-Beaulieu when he claimed that Jews and Catholics faced similar challenges. Today, as liberals' faith in progress and the modern state comes under increasing scrutiny and as the conflicts between liberals and Catholics have been all but put to rest, it is time to rethink this connection once again.

Two Jewish Anticlericalism and the
Making of Modern Citizenship in
the Late Enlightenment

When Leroy-Beaulieu explained the pressures the nation state exerted on different religious groups, he argued against a set of expectations about proper religion that began to solidify in France and Germany during the eighteenth century. Only during the Enlightenment did boundary making against the purported evils of fanaticism and superstition—terms associated with the anticlerical discourses of the eighteenth and nineteenth century—become constitutive of ideas of citizenship and proper sociability. Starting in the 1780s, the first generation of Jewish thinkers to gain prominence as enlighteners intervened into these debates and expressed their own expectations in anticlerical terms. As they did so, they joined much broader debates. At the same time, they took a position that was fundamentally different from that of Catholic or Protestant enlighteners.

The case of Moses Mendelssohn's seminal work of political philosophy, *Jerusalem* (1783), illustrates this peculiar social and intellectual position. The first Jew to become a public figure in German intellectual life was often painted as a "reluctant apologist" who primarily sought to "extricate himself from [. . .] controversy," when it came to engaging in religious debates.[1] Yet Mendelssohn opened *Jerusalem* with statements about the Catholic Church that are hardly apologetic. In the book's very first pages, he contrasted the enlightened form of sociability he admired with "despotism," which he described as a suppression of freedom of conscience. Elaborating on the phenomenon, he explained: "[Despotism] has a definite answer to every question. You need not trouble yourself any more about limits; for he who has everything no longer asks: 'How much?' The same holds true for ecclesiastical government, according to Roman Catholic principles."[2] In Mendelssohn's portrayal, the Catholic Church appeared as the epitome of an institution that assured a "horrible peace" by regulating all aspects of life at the expense of its believers' freedom of thought. Turning to the issue again a few lines later, Mendelssohn noted, now in a more sarcastic tone: "He who considers tranquility in doctrine and life to be felicity will find it nowhere better secured to him than under a Roman Catholic despot; or rather, since even in this case power is still too much divided, under the despotic rule of the church itself."[3] For Mendelssohn, only the Reformation had struck a blow against the monolithic and all-encompassing system of oppression typified by the Catholic Church to bring about freedom of religion and thought.[4]

Such polemics against the Catholic Church raise a set of issues distinct from those raised by the various other forms of criticism Mendelssohn issued in *Jerusalem*. Speaking out against Catholic despotism offered him a particular tool with which to articulate his larger philosophical agenda. Certainly, Mendelssohn also expressed his criticism of the coercive power of the rabbinate and was equally willing to denounce the actions of the Anglican clergy when their example served his arguments. Yet, different varieties of anticlericalism—opposition to the power of Catholic priests, Protestant ministers, or rabbis—implied fundamentally different types of self-positioning. Anti-rabbinic anticlericalism expressed Jews' willingness to engage with what both Jews and non-Jews alike understood to be a problem specific to Jews. When Jews spoke about the rabbinate, they spoke about their own communal future, invoked Jewish traditions, and frequently wrote in Hebrew, even as they adopted themes drawn from the wider European Enlightenment. However, when Mendelssohn and others started to address what they considered problematic aspects of Christian churches in their country's vernacular, they claimed a position as members of an enlightened republic of letters independent of their religious affiliation. Mendelssohn's first paragraphs in *Jerusalem* mark his commitment to writing more than simple apologetics. Opening with a targeted attack on Catholic despotism rather than rabbinic fanaticism, he attempted to mark himself as an Enlightenment philosopher and as a member of a universalist conversation.

Mendelssohn's volleys against the Catholic Church in *Jerusalem* also had wholly different implications than the accusations he made against

Protestant clergy in the same work and elsewhere in his oeuvre. Describing the Catholic Church of his day as a remnant from an unreformed past, Mendelssohn adopted a view of history that he shared not only with Protestants but also with many Catholic deists. In the context of debates on the abuses of the Catholic clergy (especially the higher clergy and the Jesuits), Catholicism stood for stagnation, even for those who did not see Protestantism as an acceptable alternative. Unlike critiques of Anglican clergy or Lutheran pastors, Mendelssohn's commentary on Catholic despotism was entangled with his (and various other enlighteners') very notion of progress. His criticism of Catholic despotism was thus one of the first attempts by a Jew to claim his own modernity as well as that of Judaism through the rejection of one of Christianity's internal symbols of the nonmodern.

Mendelssohn and his contemporaries allow us to explore modern Jewish anti-Catholicism during its earliest moments. Understanding the role anticlericalism played in Jewish attempts at integration and—by extension—the political integration of subjects and citizens more broadly also expands on recent scholarly debates on the religious character of major strands of the Enlightenment in two principal respects.[5] First, doing so adds an analytical layer to the recent scholarship on the relationships between Jewish and non-Jewish attempts to rethink rather than overcome religion in the eighteenth century, such as David Sorkin's work on Moses Mendelssohn and the Religious Enlightenment.[6] In contrast to Sorkin's approach, my analysis focuses not on the transfer of epistemological and theological models across denominational and linguistic boundaries but on the translation of polemics from one context to another. Religious enlighteners—within a Catholic, Protestant, or Jewish framework—shared not just ideas on the nature of religion but also examples of religious pathologies across borders and religious cultures. The alleged abuses of the Catholic Church were high on that list of perceived superstitions and fanaticisms.

Second, paying attention to the emergence of Jewish anticlericalism reinforces the role that anticlericalism and denominational divisions played in the Enlightenment more broadly. Although scholarship to date has not challenged the notion that anticlericalism was a central feature of various European strands of the Enlightenment, recent studies of eighteenth-century history—especially the works on religious forms of

Enlightenment—have nonetheless deemphasized its importance.[7] Our understanding of the history of anticlericalism and anti-Catholicism in different Enlightenment contexts still awaits comprehensive treatment. By exploring how Jews such as Mendelssohn learned to use anticlerical tropes as they became modern political subjects, I suggest one means of reinserting anticlericalism into the broader study of the politics of enlightened secularity and religiosity across Europe's linguistic borders.

The modern aspects of Enlightenment anticlericalism are highlighted when we examine the way marginal Jewish individuals desirous of gaining acceptance from non-Jewish allies understood anticlerical polemics as part of their political repertoire. Anticlerical Jews were not representative of the Enlightenment at large or of most of German and French Jewry during the late eighteenth century, but they were nonetheless visible individuals who helped to shape broader public debates about Enlightenment, citizenship, and progress.[8] The fact that individuals with a relatively precarious position could employ anticlerical tropes underlines the importance of these polemics against the Catholic Church for the emergence of new forms of civic and social belonging in a period in which Jews and others became, or dreamed of becoming, citizens for the first time.

Confessionalism and Sociability in a Protestant Context

We can similarly grasp the novelty of modern anticlericalism and its decisive engagement with new modes of citizenship by analyzing the period before the rise of the Berlin Enlightenment in the eighteenth century. Although Jews had taken positions on the Reformation in conversations with other Jews throughout the early modern period, they had done so mostly in Hebrew and for internal consumption.[9] Even before Jews in France or German lands started writing pamphlets or publishing in non-Jewish periodicals, however, isolated Jewish statements about Catholicism found their way into larger debates. One such case reaches us through a court investigation against a Jew in Breslau that lasted from 1696 to 1697. In that city, then controlled by the Catholic Habsburgs, the unnamed son of Jacob Victor, a Jew from the Polish town of Krotosyn (later Prussian Krotoschin), reportedly circulated a coin at the market that was interpreted as an egregious insult against the Catholic Church. According to a witness, the boy had attempted to entertain his non-Jewish peers with the coin. When none of his onlookers showed any interest, he explained that this particular piece of currency showed the pope on one side and a nun on the other. The exact nature of the insult was never explained in the court records, but we can assume that the two sides together evoked some type of sexual innuendo. Indeed, the other boys seemed to have understood the joke well enough to threaten to denounce their Jewish companion. According to a witness, the boy's father soon appeared and claimed that this type of humor would amuse everybody and would thus prevent his son's punishment. The authorities, who soon learned of the provocation, were keen to prove the opposite.[10] While Jews had written critically in Hebrew about the Catholic Church earlier, an image like the one on the Jewish boy's coin could travel across social boundaries without the help of theological experts. In the process, it exposed Jews' critiques of Catholicism to new scrutiny.

The Victors' crime was interpreted not only as a religious affront but also as a political act. In the year the Jewish merchant was interrogated, Silesia was governed for the Habsburgs by Franz Ludwig von Pfalz-Neuburg (1664–1732), who also acted—among many other clerical and nonclerical titles—as lord bishop of Breslau. According to the agreements of the Peace of Westphalia (1648), Breslau was one of a select number of cities where Lutheran, Reformed, and Catholic Christians were all allowed to practice their religion freely. Yet Neuburg was at the forefront of the Habsburgs' attempt to roll back the Reformation in their territories. His task was particularly difficult in a city like Breslau, which was predominantly Protestant. Given the government's effort to re-Catholicize the province, the mockery attributed to this local Jew and his son was not simply an insult to Christianity but a challenge to the sovereign.

While Jews like Jacob Victor engaged in political speech, however unintentional, by mocking the Catholic Church, their ability to gain a broader audience as they did so was highly limited. Neither Jacob Victor's concrete countervision nor his ideas about religion and the political order appeared in the court documents. His voice remains muted on this matter. This changed in the 1780s, as members of Mendelssohn's

generation who employed anticlericalism as part of their public engagement with the political concepts and governmental practices of the Enlightenment. Mendelssohn's *Jerusalem* is among the first examples of
such engagement and also marks a shift in the Jewish Enlightenment's
concerns from intracommunal educational reform to more overtly political goals.[11] It is similarly the product of a moment when individual
Jews in the German states began to engage with the politicized issue of
confessional difference as they created new alliances.

These alliances built on the linkage between philosemitism and anticlericalism among the non-Jewish writers described in the previous
chapter. Mendelssohn was close to some of the most prominent anticlericals who had become advocates of Jewish civil rights in eighteenth-
century Berlin, such as Friedrich Nicolai and the Marquis d'Argens.[12]
Indeed, according to Nicolai, d'Argens had even helped Mendelssohn
acquire his personal privilege to stay in Berlin.[13] Mendelssohn was
also familiar with other works with strong denominational overtones
against Catholics, such as Jacque Basnage's *Histoire des Juifs*.[14] While
there is no indication that Mendelssohn thought systematically about
the way these figures combined their rejection of the clergy with support of Jewish equality, he could not but notice that many of the
greatest champions of Jewish rights were also enemies of the Catholic
Church.

Mendelssohn was—as Wolfgang Altgeld notes—also influenced by
renewed debates about the prospect of unifying the Christian churches
in German lands.[15] Reacting to the rise of deism among Berlin writers,
orthodox thinkers like Benedikt Stattler (1728–1797) and Johann Caspar
Lavater (1741–1801) demanded the return to a positive form of Christianity that would be both based on revelation and circumscribed within
the bounds of traditional faith and a unified church. Although several
of these opponents of the Enlightenment were Catholic, others, such
as Lavater and the French émigré J. A. Starck, were Protestants. Anticlericalism became pivotal in these debates because Berlin enlighteners
such as Mendelssohn's friend and publisher Friedrich Nicolai created
the bogeyman of a Catholic Counter-Enlightenment and Counter-
Reformation to denounce representatives of orthodoxy, independent of
their denominational affiliation.[16] For the anticlerical polemicists who
operated with images of denominational divisions, even Protestants

could be fellow travelers of the Catholic Counter-Enlightenment: Such individuals earned the convenient label "crypto-Catholics."[17] Although the conflict was not necessarily a reflection of a Protestant–Catholic divide, late eighteenth-century enlighteners often made it seem as if this were the case.

Mendelssohn's comments thus signaled to his readers that he sought to affiliate himself with the Protestant enlighteners around him. Even passing remarks identified his antagonism toward the Catholic Church and its persecution of alleged heretics and unbelievers. His language was a sign of his participation in an intellectual milieu in which it was not unusual to use the term *Jesuitry* as a synonym for *hypocrisy*, as Mendelssohn himself did at one point in *Jerusalem*.[18] It was a turn of phrase he also used in a letter sent to his younger friend Herz Homberg (1749–1841), in which Mendelssohn referred to evils such as "hypocrisy and priestly conniving" [*Heucheley und Pfaffenlist*], "Jesuitic stratagems," [*jesuitische Kunstgriffe*] and the "*Clerisei*," a pejorative term for the clergy.[19]

Mendelssohn's remarks could also be understood as emerging from a particularly Jewish experience. Regarding ritual murder accusations against Jews, for example, Mendelssohn reported in the preface to his translation of Menassah ben Israel's *Vindiciae Judaeorum*: "I conversed with many intelligent, and, in other respects, not illiberal Christians, from Poland and other Catholic countries, who could not entirely divest themselves of those prejudices against my brethren."[20] He certainly did not need to read the works of Christian enlighteners to condemn his contemporaries for such beliefs. The fact that he limited his accusations to inhabitants of Catholic countries as well as his decision to express this observation in a treatise addressed to a non-Jewish audience nonetheless suggests that he was drawing on a widely comprehensible language of denominational anticlericalism as he did so. In this respect, Mendelssohn's comments were once again a reflection of his ability to speak to members of an intellectual circle that was more likely to suspect Catholics than Protestants of being unenlightened.

Taking sides and making these allies also exposed Mendelssohn to critique. By 1782, he was much more willing to engage with religious issues than he had been in the 1760s, when he famously explained to Lavater that he was unable to enter into open debate on religion due to his insecure status as a member of a minority.[21] The change in his approach in the early 1780s set Mendelssohn up for the charge that he was attacking Christianity. Among the critics of *Jerusalem*, Mendelssohn's anti-Christian polemics became a primary concern, forming part of the long history of fears about Jews maligning Christianity and Jesus, which had been growing since the Reformation.[22]

Jerusalem sparked some of the most heated debates in its arguments against the clergy's use of oaths, which, Mendelssohn posited, could never be given in a truthful way. In one instance, the book mentioned the example of Anglican bishops in the House of Lords who had sworn to accept the Thirty-Nine Articles of Anglican faith even though they did not believe in them.[23] Johann David Michaelis (1717–1791), a Hebraist who had opposed Jewish civil rights since the 1750s, seized on this passage in his review of *Jerusalem*.[24] Michaelis declared that he did not just disagree with Mendelssohn but also rejected the idea that a Jew could ever have the right to issue critical statements about Christian clergy. In response, Mendelssohn attempted to modify his own position by claiming that he had intended not to accuse the bishops of perjury but only of "abuse and contempt of a solemn declaration."[25] Mendelssohn's defensive reaction to Michaelis attempt "to play a trick on" him—as he called it in a letter to Nicolai—illustrates how even a short passage that critiqued the clergy could make him susceptible to anti-Jewish polemics.[26]

The type of debates that developed around Mendelssohn's criticism of Anglican practices, however, did not emerge as a result of his statements on Catholic religious despotism. This should not come as a surprise in the case of Michaelis, who was himself a Protestant anticlerical. Even Benedikt Stattler, an avowed Catholic writer who opposed Mendelssohn's work in his *Wahres Jerusalem* [True Jerusalem] (1787), did not take issue with the book's opening remarks, however.[27] Mendelssohn's comments on Catholicism were apparently read as the political arguments that their author meant them to be and thus did not scandalize either his friends, the authorities, or even his enemies.

Less denominationally determined forms of anticlericalism also appeared in the writings of other Jews from Prussia, such as the poet Ephraim Moses Kuh (1731–1790).[28] His case once again illustrates the special position Jews occupied in eighteenth-century anticlerical politics, even as they participated in wider debates alongside their non-Jewish contemporaries. Born in Breslau into a wealthy family and educated in religious and secular subjects, including Latin and modern languages, Kuh moved to Berlin in 1763 to work for his uncle Veitel Ephraim, one of the most important medalists and jewelers of the city. During this time he cultivated his interest in poetry and met with Mendelssohn. After Kuh lost his money in unknown circumstances and was forced to leave his employment in the midst of a scandal, he used his remaining funds to travel. Returning to Breslau in 1771 as a poor and broken man, he seems to have experienced a complete psychological breakdown and lived off charity from his family for some time. After several years, he eventually reappeared in the public arena as a poet. In 1784–1785, Kuh composed a series of epigrams for Christian Wilhelm Dohm's journal, *Deutsches Museum*. Some of these gave poetic expression to the particular challenges of Jewish integration into Christian societies, while others were reflections on Christian religious debates.[29]

Among Kuh's favorite religious topics was false piety, which he described as a problem emerging primarily within a Christian context. In an epigrammatic piece entitled: "To Klimene, who cleansed herself when she wanted to go to Church," he wrote: "Are you going to God's house, Klimene? / Why all that trumpery? / God would rather see a tear, / Than a diamond."[30] In another poem parodying artificial piety, written in 1784, Kuh gave his moralizing criticism a more sexual spin. Entitled "The Penitent," it read:

Miss Lais was a pious woman.
Even if courting was her pastime,
She nevertheless never did it—if we believe the myth
On the holy Easter Day,
When she went to the Lord's Supper
Receiving Christ's flesh and blood.

No paramour had then the pleasure,
None even received a kiss,
Until she, for two ducats
Was cleansed of all her misdeeds.
O, take her, time and posterity,
As a model for true piety.[31]

Kuh depicted the ancient Greek (and pagan) hetaera Lais as a devout Christian woman who used ceremonies of penitence without ever changing her sinful ways. Calling the courtesan who superficially washed off her sins the ideal of piety, Kuh played ironically with the popular image of Mary Magdalene as a redeemed prostitute and symbol of penitence. Perhaps more identifiably Protestant in character was his criticism of salvation through works—and monetary contributions—in the poem. Cleansing herself for "two ducats," Lais might appear to Protestant readers as a typical exponent of the absolutions of the Catholic Church. In a way that resonated with Protestant critiques of pious works but also critiques emerging from within the Catholic Enlightenment, Kuh's poem implicitly denounced such practices as pagan.

Kuh's use of the themes of deception and false piety were by no means unique. They are nevertheless remarkable because he included these poems in a series meant to impress readers by showing that even a Jew could write in proper style. Like Isaschar Falkensohn Behr (1746–1817), the first Jewish author to publish poetry in German, Kuh was always described as a Jew and advertised as a curiosity. Kuh's poems were introduced with the words "by a Jewish scholar" [*von einem jüdischen Gelehrten*] and Behr's as "by a Polish Jew."[32] Yet the main attraction of their work was not that a Jew could write something stylistically original. Beyond some notes on the dreadful situation of Jews in Poland and Prussia, these two Jewish poets seem to have been expected above all else to show their ability to adopt accepted poetic forms.[33] In Kuh's case, this was partly achieved through the intervention of Karl Wilhelm Ramler (1725–1798), who edited his texts so that they would conform to the tastes of the readership of the *Deutsches Museum*.[34]

The fact that Ramler, who made all editorial choices, included the poems that dealt with false religion and clerical deceit in his selections for the *Deutsches Museum* shows that he considered these themes to be a particular sign of integration and enlightenment. Attacks against the church and certain forms of religion by Jewish authors, in other words, were not simply accepted in certain circles; they could even be appreciated as an art form and evidence of refinement, as long as they conformed to certain models.[35]

Another, younger German Jewish thinker of the late eighteenth century assumed even greater liberties in his expression of religious criticism with a confessional edge: Moses Hirschel (1754–?), a polymath from Breslau.[36] The son of a weapons purveyor, Hirschel received a Jewish education that was meant to prepare him for career as a rabbi. He abandoned this path early on, turning to business, then travel, and eventually probably lived mostly from the wages he earned as a chess instructor. In the 1780s, Hirschel started a campaign aimed at the forces of "orthodoxy" and the legal powers of rabbis, which drew on universalistic, anticlerical language. In 1788, he published a book entitled *Kampf der jüdischen Hierarchie mit der Vernunft* [The Struggle of the Jewish Hierarchy against Reason], which described a thousand-year-old rabbinic conspiracy to keep Jewry in shackles.[37] These arguments did not just sound like borrowings from Voltaire's writings; they were clearly inspired by the French writer. For Hirschel, Voltaire was the "most important mainspring of the tolerance now prevalent in Europe."[38] The anti-Jewish elements in Voltaire's writing were not an obstacle to Hirschel's veneration of the French philosopher. On the contrary, Hirschel fused tropes from Voltaire's anticlerical and anti-Jewish writings to arrive at his own brand of critique of clerical power within Judaism.

In 1793, Hirschel published *Apologie der Menschenrechte* [Apology of Human Rights], in which he toned down his criticism of the rabbinic establishment.[39] Explaining his new approach, he argued that he had learned that his aggressive attacks were not a useful educational tool and had only earned him the contempt of his peers.[40] He nevertheless described the infringement of human rights as the work of fanatical rulers and priests, with the latter being the main target of his polemics. In one such passage, Hirschel once again referred to Voltaire, citing a stanza on priests who slay innocents from the French thinker's narrative poem on the Wars of Religion, *La Henriade* (1728): "Those furious monsters, hungry for carnage, / excited by the voice of bloodthirsty priests [*blutgierige Priester*/*prêtres sanguinaires*], / invoked the Lord while slitting their brothers' throats, / and their arms, all drenched in innocent blood, dared to offer God this execrable incense."[41] The memory of the violence of the Wars of Religion had been central to the critique of clerical power as well as the imagination of both a strong state and the nation in eighteenth-century France and Germany.[42] Mediated through Voltaire and used here as a general indictment against the clergy, this story without Jewish victims now became part of a Jewish argument for tolerance.[43]

Hirschel's criticism made him part of the radicalized *Haskalah* (Jewish Enlightenment), a role he is regularly assigned in depictions of the movement.[44] He was much more than a reformer of Jewish life, however: He also developed a critique of Catholicism that was unique among his Jewish contemporaries. The opportunities for Hirschel's particular engagement with the Catholic Church grew out of his connection with the Catholic physician Johann Joseph Kausch (1751–1825). The Jewish writer first contributed to one of Kausch's publications in 1789 when the latter launched the short-lived periodical *Wahrheit und Freimüthigkeit in schwesterlicher Umarmung* [Truth and Honesty in Sisterly Embrace]. The two also coedited the only existing collection of Kuh's poems. When Kausch wrote a short treatise on Silesia in the tradition of German political economy (or cameralism), he offered his friend Hirschel an opportunity to respond in one of his publications.

Kausch's work described how one might improve the province, touching on issues such as taxation but also on the way the Catholic and Jewish populations of Silesia could be made more productive and enlightened. Hirschel wrote four letters correcting Kausch on various points.[45] Two of these—the second and third letter—discussed the Catholic Church and Silesian Catholics in a way that was unprecedented for Jews. In the second letter, Hirschel went far beyond the demands other Jews had dared to make publicly when he proposed that the Catholic Church should be expropriated in Silesia. According to Hirschel, the law protected only legal property and thus did not apply to the church, which he claimed could not have acquired its property in a legitimate manner. Policies such as those decreed by the Habsburg Emperor Joseph II (1741–1790) in the 1780s to seize church lands for the state were thus justified in Hirschel's view.[46]

Hirschel pushed the issue further in his next letter, in which he proposed that Catholics be made more productive in society, a suggestion not without its irony because it was one that non-Jews frequently employed when speaking about Jews.[47] Whereas other Jewish (and non-Jewish) enlighteners spoke about the negative influence of the rabbinate, as Hirschel himself had done in the past, he now applied the same language, albeit with a slightly more moderate tone, to the Catholic clergy and its flock. According to Hirschel, the Roman curia was by definition backward, and because of its influence the Silesian clergy was backward as well. Together, papal and local influence encouraged the Silesian Catholics to adopt a mindless religion of practice that left them in eternal darkness.

Hirschel's explanations of the relationship between knowledge, sovereignty, and confession are as significant as his arguments about Catholics. In the beginning of the first letter, Hirschel announced that he was presenting the "criticism of pure and unprejudiced reason," claiming an objective position for himself.[48] In his fourth letter, however, he introduced himself as a Jew, explaining that he had no intention of commenting on Kausch's description of his coreligionists. According to Hirschel, issuing a comment about his fellow Jews might make him appear to have illegitimate interests; he could, however, speak about Catholicism because he had no stakes in the conflicts between Protestants and Catholics. Hirschel thus moved from his self-description as an objective commentator to what he considered a neutral position on Catholicism, based on his status as an outsider to intra-Christian debates. His comments on the government similarly underlined the importance of confessional divisions in debates over the place of the clergy and religious politics. Because the Prussian king was a Protestant, he could not initiate the type of top-down reform programs of the clergy that Catholic rulers could, Hirschel ventured. Although the Catholic clergy would always cry out against neology when attacked, in the case of a Protestant monarch, they would also denounce intolerance—"and this must be avoided as much as possible (especially under the current circumstances)," Hirschel added.[49]

There is no evidence that contemporaries challenged Hirschel's attacks on the clergy. On the contrary, a reviewer in the *Neue allgemeine deutsche Bibliothek* enthusiastically applauded Hirschel's comments on the Catholic population of Silesia and beyond.[50] In fact, the review treated him just the way Hirschel would have wanted to be treated, as a neutral, enlightened thinker who desired only to uplift an oppressed community that—in his view—had allowed itself to be left behind by progress. As in Mendelssohn's and Kuh's cases, Hirschel's comments on religion, Catholics, and the Catholic Church were apparently accept-able to his contemporaries, and even encouraged by other Enlighten-ment thinkers.[51]

The philosopher Mendelssohn, the poet Kuh, and the polemicist Hirschel all used criticism of Catholic institutions, rituals, and clergy to express their visions for an improved society populated by enlightened individuals. Images of Catholic clerics were certainly not the only foils at their disposal: In some cases these individuals were much more in-terested in speaking about the clergy of all religions as well as false piety more generally than about the Catholic Church (especially in Kuh's case). The denominational context of these debates made them mean-ingful to contemporaries without limiting Jewish self-expression. Most of their interlocutors accepted Jewish anticlericals' position as a reason-able, universalist stance rather than suggesting that Jews were entering conflicts on one side of an old feud between Protestants and Catholics. In France, where the denominational character of anticlerical polemics was much less of an issue, some politically active Jews adopted anticleri-cal themes in a remarkably similar manner.

Jewish Confessional Polemics in France before the Revolution

In the late eighteenth century, no Jewish author in France produced a systematic work on religion and politics comparable to Mendelssohn's *Jerusalem*. Nor was there a movement comparable to the mature Berlin *Haskalah* of the late 1770s and 1780s. Nonetheless, French Jewry did experience transformations of traditional authority structures and the emergence of small centers with an enlightened stratum.[52] Among the few French Jews who entered larger debates about religion, state, and the civic status of Jews during this time was Zalkind Hourwitz (1738–1812). A native of Poland, Hourwitz had moved to France with no financial and few linguistic resources.[53] Within a couple of years, he learned French and embarked on a path of self-education that, accord-ing to his own account, consisted mostly of reading the literature of the Enlightenment. Despite being a man of few means and his status as a foreigner, he managed within fifteen years of his immigration to become one of the best-known apologists for Jewish civil rights in

France. Hourwitz was also peculiar because he lived and wrote in Paris at a time when few Jews were permanently settled in the French capital and when even fewer entered the circles of enlightened bureaucrats and *philosophes*.

His first known article was a response to a letter from Warsaw published in the London-based *Courier de l'Europe* in 1783.[54] The anonymous author of the letter had inveighed against equality for Jews, describing them as robbers and usurers who were in their essence Arabs and consequently could never become truly French, German, or Polish. The letter's author rejected the idea that Jews were to be treated like religious dissidents because, he claimed, they were unlike other sects that professed to honor the name of Poles and valued the common fatherland. In his view, Jews were inherently hateful and slanderous and thus could be excluded from society without contradicting the Gospels' call to be patient with one's neighbor.

Hourwitz's response was printed in the same journal shortly afterward. It marked the beginning of his career as a highly polemical writer who was not shy to draw on tropes from anticlerical and sometimes antireligious strands within the Enlightenment. Hourwitz opened his piece with the following charge:

> It appears that the author of this letter is a defrocked Austrian monk, who in his ambition to damage the Jews also hopes to censure indirectly the sage and humane conduct of his Majesty the Emperor [Joseph II] who gave so many privileges to the Jews, as he did to all the heterodox sects, while suppressing the convents and appropriating for the demands of the state the wealth of those who took an oath of poverty. My suspicion is confirmed by the fact that he accuses the Calvinists of being less tolerant.[55]

Surmising, based on his analysis of the text, that the author of the piece was an embittered monk who hoped to get back at Joseph II by attacking the Jews, Hourwitz mobilized anticlerical tropes to counter the anti-Jewish rhetoric of his adversary. He inverted the image of commercial greed that the anonymous author had employed as part of an anti-Jewish stereotype by noting that the priests who vowed poverty nonetheless hypocritically amassed great wealth. According to Hourwitz, it was therefore not he (the self-declared "Polish Jew") who acted out of mere personal interest but rather his interlocutor, the foe of Jewish equality, who was motivated as much by private feelings of revenge as by political calculations. In the words of the historian Frances Malino, Hourwitz understood that "hatred toward the Jews would be used as a weapon in the struggle against secularization and reform."[56] It might be added that he also understood that hatred toward the clergy could be used as a weapon in the struggle for Jewish political equality.

Hourwitz continued to draw on similar imagery after he became more widely known as one of the three writers awarded the prize of a competition by the Academy of Arts and Science of Metz in 1788. Several years after the debates in Germany surrounding Dohm and Mendelssohn and Joseph II's Edicts of Toleration of the early 1780s, the Metz academy solicited contributions on the question: "Are there means to render the Jews more useful and happy in France?" Hourwitz published a revised version of his winning entry in 1789, which also included a new supplement. In this version he responded to the academy's criticism that his work had not sufficiently taken into account the procedural difficulties and popular resistance involved in giving equality to the Jews. Rather than addressing the concerns of the Academy, he attacked its very question, asking: "What would the French say if the Academy of Stockholm had proposed the following question twelve years ago: Are there methods to make the Catholics more useful and happy in Sweden?"[57] Certainly the French would not have been amused, Hourwitz suggested. Yet "the same Frenchmen, who would be surprised by that question in relation to the Catholics, are equally surprised that it is not made regarding the Jews!"[58]

Hourwitz did not remain content with challenging the question through a counterexample. He continued with a more radical elaboration of the dubious qualities of Catholic loyalty that resembles Hirschel's later statements on Silesian Catholics:

> As for me, I would think the opposite. I find the Swedes just and humane regarding the Jews but too generous toward the Catholics. The intolerance that the latter have toward the Lutherans, their dependence in spiritual matters on the court of Rome (which often influences the temporal), the annates and the other contributions that they pay, which are lost to the country that they leave, the ambition of that court to always make proselytes and to realize one day the profits that they give

in partibus infidelium, the treason of many Catholic lords toward the late king of Prussia when he was at war with a power of their religion — all that and many other considerations would dispose me against the admission of Catholics in a Lutheran state. At the same time, it has absolutely nothing to fear from the Jews, who have no princes of their confession, who do not form a corporate group and whose religion makes them incapable of civil and military employment, and who thus cannot become a nuisance for the state.[59]

Hourwitz went beyond the criticism of the Catholic Church found in Mendelssohn's work and radicalized the anticlerical rhetoric of his first article. Turning the charge that Jews lacked loyalty on its head, Hourwitz described Catholics as potential traitors. He even used the mercantilist argument that Jews might damage the economy by exporting valuable assets to other lands against Catholics, as he described Catholic Church donations in similar terms. The tenor of these polemics is particularly noteworthy if we consider that Hourwitz stressed his status as a foreigner and non-Christian by regularly giving himself the epithet "*juif polonois*." Rather than apologizing for his precarious position as a foreign Jew, he entered into polemics that were at once an attempt to undermine all questions about the usefulness of religious groups through irony and more straightforward attacks against the Catholic Church and Catholics.

There were few public reactions to Hourwitz's pamphlet, but one official response suggests how Hourwitz's statements were read in his day. The document was written by Hourwitz's censor, Gaston-Armand Camus, who was a Jansenist and acted as the lawyer for the clergy when he evaluated the *Apologie*, including the preface and supplement not submitted originally to the academy. Although Camus made some corrections to small parts of the preface, which he deemed improper, he nonetheless accepted the previously quoted passage.[60] Concerning Hourwitz's statements about Catholicism, Camus wrote: "One should not be surprised to hear a Jew express himself with little precision on some points concerning the Catholic religion: all one can demand from him is moderation and I find that his work is in fact written in a moderate style. There are some thoughtful reflections here and a broader and more cultivated erudition than one might have believed [. . .] to exist among the Jews."[61]

As one of the more outspoken Jansenists within the Order of Barristers of Paris and later a key player in the convention where he championed the civil oath of the clergy, Camus certainly had a reformist agenda concerning the Catholic Church and the state.[62] It is nevertheless remarkable that even while he was employed by the clergy Camus did not find Hourwitz's anticlerical statements particularly objectionable; nor was he offended that a Jew had made them. As in the Prussian case, we are thus left with a significant indication that Hourwitz's polemics and his satirical anticlericalism did not scandalize his enlightened readership as improper or out of place.

As a strategy of inclusion, these polemics mark Hourwitz as a self-declared adherent of the aggressively anticlerical Enlightenment associated with Voltaire of the 1750s. Unlike Mendelssohn, whose comments signaled his participation in a loose alliance of enlighteners with the monarchy, Hourwitz's anti-Catholicism can be viewed as a criticism of the crown. In both Mendelssohn's and Hourwitz's cases, the function of boundary making vis-à-vis the Catholic Church and Catholics was to position Judaism polemically within ongoing debates on legal equality. These Jewish efforts continued in a new key as debates on the clergy radicalized with the coming of the French Revolution.

The French Revolution and Jewish Anticlericalism

The position that politically active Jews took toward the church in the French revolutionary debates was conditioned not so much by the opinions of individual clergymen but rather by the development of state–church relations during the Revolution. Starting with the secularization of church property, the abolition of clerical privileges in 1789, and the passing of the Civil Constitution of the Clergy in July 1790, the early Revolution redefined itself in opposition to the church, which revolutionaries had come to regard as one of the key institutions (and therefore culprits) of the ancien régime. The Civil Constitution regulated the election of clergy by the local citizenry, curbed the influence of the pope on clerical appointments, and subjected the church to the state and to popular influence.[63] Shortly thereafter, on November 27, 1790, the National Assembly decreed that all clerics had to swear an oath to the nation and the king. With all of these changes in place, the break between the new revolutionary state and Catholic Church seemed unavoidable. Even before the pope's condemnation of these moves in the spring of 1791, political clubs and newspapers employed an increasingly fierce and militant rhetoric against the pope and the alleged threat emanating from so-called refractory or nonjuring priests who rejected the oath. Just around the time when Sephardi and Ashkenazi Jews in France gained citizenship—in 1790 and 1791 respectively—the Revolution and the Catholic Church became fully antagonistic.[64] The conflicts over the large number of refractory priests reinforced the association of revolutionary patriotism with anticlericalism and made the specter of an aristocratic and clerical Catholic conspiracy more tangible.[65]

The few Jews who entered the public sphere during the Revolution adopted the language of patriotic and progressive anticlericalism. One of the most militant among them was once again Hourwitz, who—for the only time in his life—found regular employment as secretary and interpreter at the Bibliothèque Royale between 1789 and 1792. During this period, in 1791, Hourwitz published several articles for papers associated with the Girondin faction, at a time when popular debates about the oath taking of priests were at their height. More than before, his articles for the *Chronique de Paris* now used the genre of sexually charged irony to denounce the enemies of the state and the people.[66] In February of that year, Hourwitz demanded information about "certain physical and moral phenomena" that had been associated with the clergy because, as he explained, tongue in cheek, he was unfamiliar with the "natural history of the clergy" in France.[67] As in his earlier articles, Hourwitz continuously identified himself as a foreigner only to play the game of anticlerical politics as if he were a post-Catholic Frenchman. He asked in Voltairian fashion: "How is it that during the ancien régime the majority of your prelates and beneficed clergy had such beautiful nieces? How is it that the number of these nieces has diminished considerably since the Revolution?"[68]

In another article, Hourwitz attacked "wicked priests" [*mauvais prêtres*] in a manner that was mindful of his earlier critique of priestly greed. In his opinion, the wicked priests alone were trying to defend Church property, as they had always profited from the church's usurpation of power. After citing the Deuteronomic statement that Levites were not to have property, Hourwitz challenged the wealth of the clergy and ended his article with the following admonition: "But let these Messieurs [the Abbé Maury and the Company of Jesus] be reassured, it is not we who will be damned for having taken back our property, but those who wish to hold on to it with all force in contempt of God's commandment: *Thou shall not steal.*"[69]

In her biography of Hourwitz, Frances Malino points out his striking use of the personal pronoun "we" in this context. She notes: "Hourwitz's attitudes were predictable, popular, and familiar. But they are no less significant, for they reveal the extent to which he had appropriated the Revolution's future, and thus ironically France's past, as his own."[70] Indeed, Hourwitz expressed his membership in the French nation to a large extent by making the church the lightning rod of his writings. His willingness to adopt the rhetoric of patriotic belonging was underscored by the fact that his attacks on the clergy and aristocracy followed prevalent discourses and were not substantially different from the articles submitted by other contributors to the same journals. Neither the target nor the means distinguished Hourwitz from his environment. Perhaps for the first time in modern history, a Jew declared his belonging to the French nation by fully appropriating a radical anticlerical discourse.

In the months and years after Hourwitz's articles appeared, revolutionaries became increasingly obsessed with defining and ferreting out the nation's enemies. Accusations of clerical conspiracies had become so commonplace by early 1793 that anti-Jewish Jacobins in Alsace started to draw on anticlerical themes in their campaigns against local Jews. In March of that year, rumors appeared about the Jews supporting the pope. On March 23, 1793, a *Courrier de Strasbourg* correspondent reported from Rome that "the Jews brought a considerable quantity of silverware from their synagogue to the public treasury. His Holyness [the pope] had it returned to them, however, and thanked them for their efforts."[71] The story immediately found its way into the German-language *Wochenblatt*, where the neutral one-liner became much more aggressive. This Jacobin paper from Colmar noted that the money was meant to pay for the war against France, adding ironically: "They [the Jews] were not so magnanimous in our department, as the Jewry of Rappotzweiler claimed that the silverware of their synagogue was pawned."[72] The *Wochenblatt* thus used reports about Jewish support for the pope to bolster the charge that Jews were only feigning insufficient funds when they did not support the revolutionary cause. The article also reminded readers of rumors that French troops had been defeated and slaughtered at Frankfurt am Main because the Jews betrayed them. (Allegedly, Jews had opened the city gates to the Prussians and Austrians and thus made the carnage possible).

These accusations also found their way into a petition of March 27, 1793, which was composed by the directors of the district of Colmar to the National Convention's commissar for military conscription in the name of several small towns in the vicinity of Colmar. The Jews' alleged support of the pope and their purported collective treason was one of the reasons the authors listed to buttress their appeal to exclude the Jews from the revolutionary armies.[73] Two weeks later, the Jacobin directors of the district of Colmar demanded from their department the expulsion of all Jews. According to the directory's letter, events in Frankfurt and Rome, among others, had proven that the Jews were the most dangerous enemies the nation had in its midst.[74] Whereas some antirevolutionaries denounced Jews as enemies of Catholicism, important Jacobins in Alsace claimed that Jews were collaborating with the pope to destroy the new order.

In light of these accusations, anticlericalism became even more symbolically charged for Jews. Six months after Jacobin administrators in Alsace sought to expel Jews with such arguments, polemics against the clergy appeared in the patriotism of Jewish communal elites in Lorraine. On October 21, 1793, the Jews of the city of Metz joined the rest of the town's population to publicly celebrate the victory of republican troops against an army consisting mostly of Austrians and French émigrés at Thionville. The two texts that emerged from this event—which have been analyzed by Ronald Schechter to different ends—engaged in a new type of official anticlericalism.[75]

The first text was a canticle in Hebrew entitled "Fallen, Fallen is the Wicked Kingdom," [*Nafelah nafelah malkhut ha-resha'*], which the Jewish community allegedly sang to the tune of the Marseillaise for the occasion.[76] The text of the piece was written by the Jewish enlightener and mathematician Moses Ensheim (1750–1839), who had been associated with the Berlin *Haskalah* journal *Ha-measef*. Ensheim had also worked as a tutor in Mendelssohn's home in Berlin and had returned to Metz in 1785, where he became an integral part of the city's wealthy Jewish community.[77] His canticle depicted the abolition of the French monarchy and the victories of the early revolutionary wars in biblical language: He wrote of the fall of the ancien régime in terms of Isaiah's prophecy that Babylon would be overthrown.

The second text emerging from the celebrations was a translation of Ensheim's Hebrew song into French by Isaac Berr Bing (1759–1805). Bing, the director of local salt works in Metz, was a Jewish enlightener who acted as a translator and popularizer of many writings, both Jewish and non-Jewish, that emanated from the Berlin Enlightenment.[78] Part of the small group of prosperous Ashkenazi Jews of Metz, Bing was also fairly well connected in non-Jewish circles, as his position at the salt works, his appointment to the Metz municipal council, and his eventual membership in the editorial committee of the prestigious *Décade philosophique* all indicate.[79] Although he was hardly a Jacobin or a militant, Bing clearly knew how to speak the language of the Revolution.

In his perceptive analysis of the Hebrew and French versions of the celebratory canticle, Schechter focuses on the multitude of expectations concerning citizenship that were encoded as biblical allusions in the Hebrew text and more explicitly stated in the French version. Apart from targeting the monarchy, which becomes associated with luxury and idolatry in the canticle, he suggests that the opposition between aristocracy and citizenry was constitutive of both texts.[80] The only enemy that Schechter does not mention, however, is the clergy, despite its prevalence in both versions.[81] Indeed, enmity toward the clergy emerges much more prominently than anti-aristocratic images in either text. In Ensheim's Hebrew, the following stanza—reproduced here in English—can be understood as offering an implicit criticism of the priesthood:

> The people with hairy mantles
> with a flattering mouth make ruin
> they abandon [their] good name with [false] oaths
> and your sins will not be blotted out.[82]

The key term here is *hairy mantles*, or *aderet se'ar* in Hebrew, which literally means a coat or mantle of hair. The phrase appears only once in the Hebrew Bible, in Zachariah 13:4, where it refers to the clothing worn by false prophets.[83] According to Schechter, Ensheim employed this phrase to denounce members of the aristocracy by alluding to their fur coats, thereby reproducing classic revolutionary anti-aristocratic rhetoric to express his patriotism.[84] There are several problems with this interpretation, however, the first being that the aristocracy was not usually identified through its use of fur in clothing.[85] Furthermore, if we want to grasp this image mainly in visual terms, it is far more likely that the reference is in fact to another mantle of hair: wigs. Debates about wigs had been common during the ancien régime and the Revolution. They often dealt with questions of convenience and naturalness, which also became central themes of social critique—including claims of the corruption of the Gallican Church.[86] Wearing wigs, however, was not necessarily associated with monarchist leanings or aristocratic lifestyles. Even after the Revolution there were republicans who wore wigs. The distinguishing feature of the wigs people chose was their length, with republicans preferring a distinctively shorter style.[87] If Ensheim indeed meant to use particular visual clues, they were ambiguous.

Bing's French interpretation of this stanza is also less anti-aristocratic than critical of the abuse of religion. The stanza in Bing's loose translation reads as follows:

> And you as well, who take religion as a pretext for
> your pointless fury! Your hope has evaporated; for your
> destructive projects you will obtain nothing but indignation from
> the true and sensible hearts.[88]

The allusions to "religion as a pretext"—like the original context of Zachariah's false prophets—seem to point more to the clergy than to the aristocracy. This interpretation also makes more sense given the particular political context of Ensheim's text: Ensheim did not write his canticle from scratch but rather drew extensively on another poem he had published two years earlier in *Ha-measef*.[89] Of the nineteen stanzas of the original poem, he reused fifteen and added sixteen new ones for the celebration at Metz in October 1792.[90] Major additions to the text were the references to oath taking, which can be explained as part of the standard script for patriotic festivals such as the one that formed the background for the poem's performance. By introducing elements of oath taking, the Jews of Metz who sang Ensheim's canticle symbolically swore their allegiance to the state and nation through their song—affirming the civic oath that they had to swear publicly between December 14, 1791 and January 10, 1792.[91] Yet Ensheim may have intended the new reference to oaths to have an additional meaning. Unlike the situation when he had written his first version in 1789, by 1792, the main targets of public polemics were the priests who refused the civic oath, and suspicions of clerical conspiracies were running high. The second to fourth lines of the stanza about the people with hairy mantles can thus also be read as a reference to the prevailing skepticism of false oaths: "With a flattering mouth make ruin / they abandon [their] good name with [false] oaths / and your sins will not be blotted out." The men with the fur coats are here those who swear false oaths like dissimulating monarchist priests.

Because Ensheim's text was meant mostly for internal Jewish consumption, we might also wonder what type of enemy Jews identified as a threat to the Republic and themselves. From this perspective, the clergy was a more proximate enemy than the aristocrats. In the summer of 1789, priests had contributed to the anti-Jewish violence that had swept the Alsatian countryside as part of the riots and mass hysteria of the Great Fear.[92] Given the many allusions to the clergy in both versions of the canticle as well as the broader historical context in which they were composed, it is ultimately more plausible to read Ensheim's poem as an exercise in revolutionary anticlericalism than as an anti-aristocratic piece.

If Ensheim's depiction of the Republic's enemies remained somehow ambiguous because of its complicated biblical coding, Bing's language in the French version leaves no doubt about his use of revolutionary anticlerical language. Indeed, the French version of the poem never mentions the aristocracy directly and makes only several possible allusions to them: for example, when it mentions "dark schemes" of some of the "perverted children" of the country and denounces oppressors who "live under gilded panels."[93] The only group explicitly identified in Bing's version, in contrast, is the clergy:

The time is no more when fanaticism fed by some
bloodthirsty priests sowed hatred and divisions between
the children of a single father! The benevolent philosophy
brought together all in their brotherly bonds. [94]

Bing thus appropriated the Voltairean trope of "bloodthirsty priests"
that we have already encountered in the writing of Hirschel and gave
it a Jewish twist by alluding to the confluence of republican and Jewish interests.[95] Written in October 1793, one month after the *levée en
masse* was decreed, the stanza can thus be read both as a warning about
"bloodthirsty priests" who were conspiring to lure France into war and
as a Jewish commentary on the anti-Jewish agitation of priests throughout the country. Other stanzas leave the same possibility for a double
reading. The Jews who were swearing their oath in Metz—unlike the
refractory priests—hoped to display and announce the identity of their
interest as Frenchmen and as Jews. The citizenship they imagined and
forged as they swore this oath was shaped by evoking a common anti-
Jewish and anti-republican clerical enemy.[96]

We can see from the unpublished writings of some Jewish revolutionaries that these opinions were not just public rhetoric but also privately held beliefs. This becomes clear, for example, in the writings of
Abraham Furtado, who was part of the wealthy Jewish elite of Bordeaux and, as a representative of the Sephardi community of that city,
had actively lobbied for the inclusion of Sephardi Jews into the 1787
decrees benefiting (Christian) non-Catholics.[97] A Girondin during the
Revolution, he was one of the founding members of Bordeaux's Société
des Amis de la Constitution, together with several other Jews.[98]

Furtado embraced a radical anticlericalism in his unpublished work
"Folie de Jeunesse," which he most likely composed in 1791.[99] Like many
other revolutionaries of his day, Furtado followed the paradigm of anti-
religious anticlericalism, championing a universal humanistic form of
morality. Within this worldview, progress demanded the end of religion
as well as of the priests who abused religion to establish a form of despotic rule to their own benefit. Defining the Revolution's achievements
at the beginning of his text, Furtado made his case thus: "The French
Revolution struck a terrible blow to the power of the clergy; and since

the power of religion was dependent on that of its ministers, we could see one weaken with the other. Both were simultaneously discredited wherever the progress of the enlighteners pushed them both away."[100]

Furtado was only marginally concerned with Judaism—and even Christianity—and was mainly interested in revealed religion in abstract terms. Yet, in his philosophical reflections, he argued that the attacks against the Catholic Church and the clergy, the most powerful purveyors of religious sentiment and superstition, had to continue. Abstract philosophy and concrete policy recommendations were thus closely entangled. It was superstition and despotism, Furtado wrote, "that entirely hinder the reestablishment of order. The issues that are most important, if we think of the principle causes of the Revolution, are the discrediting of priests and the weakening of the influence of religious opinions."[101] To counter the continuing influence of the clergy, who, Furtado claimed, were cunningly masking their insidious interests, his main recommendation was the establishment of a universal, national educational system.

Furtado's treatise was universalistic in two senses. First, it avoided emphatic French patriotism. Second, and equally important, Furtado did not identify himself as a Jew within the text. Rather than stress the French character of the developments he described, he spoke of universal progress and the fate of religion in Europe more broadly. In other words, he wished to convey the message that the Revolution and measures against the church concerned him as a human being (or a "universalistic" European) and not as a Jew. This position clearly contrasted with his public persona before the Revolution, when—as a representative of the *nation* of the Sephardi Jews of Bordeaux in Paris—he had been marked as a Jew in political debate.[102] Furtado's remaking into a French citizen concerned with the revolutionary order as well as a European advocate for humanity was mediated through the politics of anticlericalism. Opposing the church and religion in the name of progress was part of the process that helped transform the Bordelais Jew Furtado into the humanistic citizen Furtado who aimed to contribute to civil society.

The anticlericalism of many politically involved French Jews during the early years of the Revolution attests to the attraction not just of anticlericalism but also of a political and national project that put anticlericalism at its center. Hourwitz, Ensheim, Bing, and Furtado all wrote in different contexts, highlighting their Judaism in different ways, and yet, read together, they illustrate the emergence of a form of anticlerical citizenship that allowed Jews to participate in universalistic political discourse through their attempts at boundary making against the Catholic Church and clerics. Although not all of them followed an anti-religious line of argumentation, they all agreed that the power of the church and its priests presented a major political problem. Through their criticism, they made themselves part of a revolutionary struggle that defined itself in opposition to Catholic institutions.

During the years of so-called de-Christianization (1793–1794), however, which overlapped with the Terror, revolutionary Jews like Furtado did their best to keep a low profile. For Furtado this also meant a personal break with that part of the Enlightenment legacy, which he associated with the Terror and anti-religious thought.[103] The absence of anticlerical texts from the period of the Terror, even from the pen of a militant critic of the church and clergy such as Hourwitz, attests less to the fact that anticlericalism and citizenship had become dissociated in France in the period than to the precarious nature of open political positioning in general at this moment. Hourwitz, for example, returned to his pet theme—the history of church persecutions as well as clerical plots—during the period of the Directory (1795–1799). In an article he penned in 1797, Hourwitz replied to an anonymous author who demanded that the state introduce special taxes for Jews. As he had done in the period before the Terror, Hourwitz defended the rights of Jews by implying that enemies of Jewish emancipation were also enemies of the republic. The church, which had oppressed Jews through the ages, he asserted, had also been responsible for burning heretics and thus threatened to target the proponents of the current revolt against the church in his day as well.[104]

The story of another foreigner, a German Jewish émigré to France, offers similar indication for the possibility of anticlerical integration after 1794. Abraham Lembert (1766–1832), an accountant from Mannheim, became a Jacobin in the early years of the Revolution, eventually moving to Strasbourg in 1793.[105] After surviving the purges and internal conflicts among the German émigrés in Alsace during the Terror, he became part of a group of German Jacobins who were active in the new French Departments established east of the Rhine. Here he contributed to and likely also edited the *Republikanische Wächter*, a Jacobin semiweekly from Haguenau. The paper's main obsession was the identification of the nation's enemies, with a special focus on the nonjuring priests, the *"ungeschworene Pfaffen."* The *Wächter*'s preoccupation with priests was particularly strong in this linguistic border region, where they competed with the church for the favor of German-speaking "republican-minded Catholics."[106]

In 1797, Lembert published *Der Wahlmann*, which aimed to mobilize voters in the department of Mont-Tonnerre (located in today's German province of *Rheinland-Pfalz*) for the elections to the *corps législative*. The period leading up to the elections overlapped with Napoleon's successful campaigns in Italy, in which he defeated the troops of the Papal States and forced the pope to accept a peace treaty. Yet conflicts between republicans and the refractory priests continued. All these developments were reflected in Lembert's journal, which frequently featured stories about the nefarious influence of the *"eidscheue Priester"* [priests dreading oaths].[107] Reacting to the claim that all republicans were atheists, which he clearly perceived as a political threat, Lambert explained that only anti-republican emigrants and traitors were trying to claim that God and the priests were the same thing.[108] This did not stop him from printing a number of contributions by Jacobins that denounced all religious practices as unnecessary.[109]

Apparently, in certain contexts, militant anticlericalism could still be understood as a sign of loyalty after the Terror, even if the author of such polemics was clearly marked as a Jew. For the editor of the prorevolutionary *Rheinische Kronik*, for example, Lembert, "a citizen of Israelite religion" proved his "true republicanism" with his patriotic writings in the *Wahlmann*.[110] Such approval came not just from other publicists but also from the state. Lembert's activities launched him on a career that was remarkable for an unconverted Jew in the late eighteenth century. In 1798, he became the director of the central police office of the department of Mont-Tonnerre in Mainz.[111] Probably converting to Protestantism at a later date, Lembert eventually worked as *notaire impérial* under Napoleon between 1803 and 1813.[112] By the early 1800s,

Lembert—like most other revolutionary Jews—dropped his anticlerical stance. His suggestions for a reorganization of the departmental school system published in 1801–1802, hinted at the lacking teaching competence of the clergy but avoided all polemics in this regard.[113]

Anticlerical Citizenship, Horizontal Alliances, and Confessionalism

Jewish polemics against the Catholic Church and clergy signal a departure from the common practice of early modern Jewry of forming vertical alliances with the state and the monarch—a phenomenon referred to as the "royal alliance" first by Salo Baron and much elaborated on by Yosef Hayim Yerushalmi.[114] The emergence of Jews' horizontal alliances with other social, religious, and political groups went hand in hand with new polemics, new media, and new audiences.[115] Starting in the late eighteenth century, anticlericalism forms one among several efforts by Jews to build new coalitions and find novel ways of belonging in the modern period—be it to a particular milieu, body politic, nation, or the European Enlightenment writ large. Jews such as Hirschel, Hourwitz, Ensheim, Bing, and Lembert appropriated anticlerical polemics when they joined efforts at nation building. They were constructing alliances within civil society and toward the state at the same time. Even in the German case, Mendelssohn's comments on Roman Catholic despotism—which were not meant as a form of nation building—can be understood in similar terms. Although Mendelssohn's remarks were not part of a performative self-inclusion into a larger citizenry, they expressed his participation in enlightened Protestant circles in Berlin and were part of the language for theorizing state sovereignty and cultured sociability available to him. Ultimately, none of the comments on the church already discussed were merely reactive. They were neither simple complaints about Christian, Catholic, or clerical Jew-hatred nor a form of religious polemic. Rather, they were meant and understood as political commentaries.

In fact, such Jewish polemics against "Catholic despotism" and "bloodthirsty priests" made sense only in the context of debates within civil society and of the slow nationalization of politics. In this sense,

they marked a departure from the classic Jewish alliance politics oriented toward princes that still dominated the political realities of most
Jews in the German states, France, and the rest of Europe during this
period. Put more succinctly: The adoption of a new form of political
anticlericalism, which singled out the Catholic Church as its main target, marked the entry of German and French Jewish elites into the field
of modern European politics. Even more broadly, it signaled the invention of secularist politics of legal equality.

In those cases in which Jews were able to integrate into new social
and political spheres through anticlericalism—such as in parts of the
Berlin and Breslau Enlightenment and the French Revolution before
the Terror—their strategies were successful in that they were not attacked for overstepping the boundaries of proper religious discourse.
In the contexts of the late French monarchy or Prussian enlightened
absolutism, neither Mendelssohn, nor Kuh, nor Hirschel met with any
criticism for their statements against clerics or the church, despite their
precarious legal status and their clear identification as Jews. Nor were
Furtado, Ensheim, Bing, or Hourwitz attacked by their republican allies for joining in the chorus of anticlerical voices during the French
Revolution. Being enlightened and thus a legitimate participant in politics implied not simply that people could overcome the limitations of
their origins. It was also based on the privilege of attacking the enemies
of the Enlightenment with anticlerical polemics.

Despite these similarities, important differences also existed between
the ways this story unfolded in France and in Prussia during the second half of the eighteenth century. The examples from the Berlin Enlightenment show the importance of confessional differences for Jewish
attempts to integrate into circles whose principal members defined
themselves in Protestant and universalistic terms at the same time. In
France, by contrast, the Revolution opened the door to a more confes-
sionally neutral and explicitly political form of anticlericalism.[116] Irrespective of the confessional or nonconfessional nature of the alliances
they forged, however, the polemics late eighteenth-century Jewish anticlericals employed were similar in the broader shift they marked in
the practice of citizenship. Even if the anticlerical descriptions of religion that we find in Mendelssohn and Kuh were associated in Prussia with particular progressive Protestant circles, they were also part of

a general Enlightenment lexicon that could be understood in France. Perhaps even more important, they served similar political purposes in both countries.

The anticlerical character of these texts also exists independently from each author's particular position on the issue of God. In this respect, these thinkers were not on the same page: Whereas Mendelssohn publicly endorsed the view that religion was based on revelation, many of the other Jewish thinkers of the late eighteenth century mentioned here spoke in deistic or atheistic terms.[117] These differences make clear that the question of the religious character of the Enlightenment cannot be equated with that of its anticlericalism. Anticlerical polemicists certainly concerned themselves with religion and religious institutions, but the authors discussed here—as well as most of their interlocutors—nevertheless understood their interventions to be primarily political in nature. Indeed, it was precisely their political character that allowed Jews to enter into a debate that might otherwise appear as a dispute among Christians. Like few other texts can do, Mendelssohn's comments on "Catholic despotism" in *Jerusalem* encapsulate this convergence of religious and political concerns, illustrating how modern forms of alliance politics found their expression in the idiom of anticlericalism.

Three Romanticism, Catholicism,
and Oppositional Anticlericalism

In late-Enlightenment Berlin and during the French Revolution, anti-clericalism had formed part of Jewish enlighteners' efforts to create new horizontal alliances without alienating their monarch or government. When Jews like Moses Mendelssohn and Ephraim Kuh in Prussia, or Zalkind Hourwitz, Abraham Furtado, Moses Ensheim, Isaac Beer Bing, and Abraham Lembert in revolutionary France, publicly em-braced anticlerical ideologies in an attempt to signal their participation in enlightened circles, they remained loyal to the sovereign. During the period of Napoleon's ascendancy in the early nineteenth century, however, anticlericalism became a more radical and thus riskier strategy. For the next half century, taking anticlerical positions put Jews at odds with the state in France or German lands, as it marked their opposi-tion to sovereign attempts to rebuild the state, the nation, and society with the help of traditional religious institutions. This pattern was most noticeable in France, where the Napoleonic regime (1798–1814), the Restoration Monarchy (1814–1830), and, eventually, the July Monarchy (1830–1848) all sought accommodation, if not outright alliances, with the Catholic Church.

In France during the Restoration period, especially during the 1820s, liberals used anticlericalism to challenge the Bourbon monarchs, claim-ing in newspaper campaigns, for example, that the kingdom was con-trolled by a Jesuit cabal.[1] To chime in with these oppositional voices involved positioning oneself against the state. Even during the July Monarchy, founded in the summer of 1830 following an anticlerical revolution, the government showed little patience with those who tried to continue to support the politics that had brought the new regime to power. Preoccupied with consolidating his rule, the "Citizen King"

94

Louis Philippe sought to ease societal tensions rather than enflame them. The continuing outbreaks of anticlerical violence in the countryside, as well as anticlerical campaigns in the capital, were an obstacle to his program of appeasement.[2] Early in the regime, in 1831, France's Jewish consistories won a victory in their quest for equality when they gained access to state funding for rabbis en par with that already afforded to Catholic and Protestant clergy. Under these circumstances, Jewish representatives had little to gain from anticlerical polemics that were too revolutionary for a regime in need of consolidation.

Why then did certain French Jews engage in anticlerical polemics during precisely this period? Those who did so had the clear understanding that they were working outside the constraints of communal or consistorial politics and that their anticlericalism was now a subversive position. The new brand of anti-Catholic anticlericalism that emerged in the post-1815 Restoration period accompanied the rise of a markedly liberal and radical form of politics among small groups of Jews. Their anticlericalism developed in conjunction with the anti-Jewish rhetoric of Catholic romantics and reactionaries active during the first decades of the nineteenth century. While the Catholic Church lost a great deal of its power following the revolutionary period, dedicated Catholic monarchists remained vocal and posed a serious threat to Jews from the right.[3] Jewish community leaders had little reason to enter into polemics with such groups. In contrast, Jewish intellectuals and activists interested in speaking in political terms believed that engaging in debates about Catholicism offered them a crucial platform on which to express their new vision of social arrangements.

While anticlericalism was risky if appealing for radical Jewish authors in France, the situation in Germany was even more complicated. Although romantics in Germany had divergent political aims, most had one position in common: No matter whether they were radical opposition figures persecuted by censorship or the advisors to Restoration rulers, nearly all German romantics rejected the legal equality of Jews in a state that they envisioned as an organic whole based on Christianity.[4] Romantic models of a Christian state were at the core of long debates triggered by the publication of Christian Ludwig Paalzow's anti-Jewish tract *Über das Bürgerrecht der Juden* [On the Civic Rights of the Jews] in 1803. According to one estimate, the extended debates created by romantic nationalism inspired the publication of approximately 2,500 works on the topic of Jewish emancipation between 1815 and 1850.[5] Especially in the case of the small circles of middle-class Jews and Jewish students in German cities, it is also important to remember that the romantics' call for the exclusion of Jews from citizenship rights and civil society went beyond mere demands. Exclusionary measures also separated Jews from Christians in a number of different locales. The Berlin salons that had given rise to early romanticism were partly replaced by organizations like the Deutsche Tischgesellschaft, which excluded Jews and others whom its members did not consider to be respectable [*wohlanständig*].[6]

Despite the fact that romanticism challenged Jews' civil rights in Germany, there is nevertheless something puzzling about German Jewish anti-Catholicism. Why would Jews oppose the anti-Jewish tendencies of German romanticism with anti-Catholic polemics? In spite of a small number of prominent German converts to Catholicism among literary and artistic romantics—such as Friedrich Schlegel (1772–1829) and Johann Friedrich Overbeck (1789–1869)—the vast majority of romantics in North Germany were Protestant. There was also nothing particularly Catholic about the growing nationalist movement. What is more, Protestant manifestations of German romantic nationalism often fueled anti-Jewish activities. Indeed, the celebration of the 300th anniversary of Luther's Reformation at the Wartburg in 1817 turned into a foundational moment of nationalist and anti-Jewish agitation. The Hep Hep riots that shattered German Jews' sense of security in 1819 were similarly never identified as particularly Catholic; on the contrary, they began in predominantly Protestant cities like Hamburg.

The more important connection between Catholicism and romanticism was intellectual. Many contemporaries viewed the romantics who gave birth to an anti-Jewish brand of integral German nationalism as avid enthusiasts for Catholicism. Few works were more seminal in propagating that image than Heinrich Heine's *Die Romantische Schule* [The Romantic School] of 1835, which depicted romanticism as a reactionary movement most deeply influenced by Catholicism. The connection Heine drew was not self-evident, however. Indeed, one can argue—as I have in Chapter One—that some of the Protestant romantic's renewed interest in Catholicism was highly ambivalent toward the lived Catholicism of their day.

Much as in France, German Jewish anti-Catholicism was thus more than a mere reaction of members of a minority to their detractors. Using anti-Catholic rhetoric during the romantic era offered individual Jewish authors and activists opportunities to critique particular forms of nationalist exclusion that emerged during the Napoleonic War, to join oppositional circles of the Restoration period, and to experiment with new aesthetic and literary art forms. My aim in this chapter is to understand both the range of Jewish reactions to the nexus of romanticism and Catholicism and how certain Jews employed anticlericalism to change the political status quo. My guides in this endeavor will be four posttraditional Jews, who drew on anticlerical and anti-Catholic tropes in their writings: Joseph Salvador (1796–1873) and Léon Halévy (1802–1883) in France, Saul Ascher (1767–1822) in Germany, and Heinrich Heine in both contexts. Some of these writers do not fit into easy political or denominational categories. My use of terms such as "posttraditional Jew" or even "Jew" should not obscure this fact. These liberal authors adopted anticlerical positions that grew out of universalistic political programs, even as they also attempted to overcome their own personal predicaments of partial exclusion as Jews. Their combined efforts illuminate the central role Catholicism played as a productive foil for liberal secularist thought in the age of romantic nationalism. They also show how entangled denominational polemics were in two national contexts that are usually seen as having divergent romantic traditions and a distinct denominational and political character. At the same time, the juxtaposition of these two countries illustrates both the different opportunities anti-Catholic polemics offered Jewish intellectuals and how their texts were read and misread across linguistic borders.

Catholic and Liberal Romanticism in Restoration France

In postrevolutionary France, Napoleon's policies created a pluralism of recognized religions that offered protection not only to Catholics but also Reformed Protestants, Lutherans, and Jews. Individual agreements, starting with the 1801 Concordat and ending with the creation of official Jewish community bodies known as consistories in 1808, created a state-sanctioned structure that remained in place in France until 1905 (with the exception of the regions of Alsace and Lorraine, where it is still in force today). While it promised social peace, the Napoleonic settlement did not resolve the conflicts between different groups in France. According to Jean Baubérot, Napoleon's pluralism of recognized religions was based on an imagined consensus to be brought about through a compromise wherein Catholics would stop trying to be a hegemonic group while the Enlightenment's heirs would stop being anti-religious.[7] In a period in which neither the term *secularism* nor *laïcité* was used, this consensus—as Baubérot suggests—constituted the French path of secularism. Such expectations, however, were almost immediately broken on all sides. Rather than offer a lasting solution, the purported consensus of the Napoleonic order created a situation of heightened sensitivity to breaches by Catholics and anti-clericals alike. Catholic polemicists continued to describe liberals as anti-religious schemers while liberals warned of a Catholic conspiracy to reestablish the ancien régime.

Paradoxically, even Napoleon nurtured a resistance to this settlement through his religious politics. Hoping to divide the monarchist opposition with symbolic gestures of reconciliation toward the Catholic Church—particularly with Napoleon's coronation as emperor in December 1804—the state moved closer to the model of a Catholic monarchy.[8] Catholic monarchists, who opposed the French emperor, were emboldened by such attempts to seek new forms of accommodation with the Catholic Church.[9] After the first wave of amnesties was issued to émigrés who had fled during the revolutionary period, French anti-revolutionaries found new opportunities to promote their ideas. Expressing their outrage at the *philosophes'* alleged atheism, various right-wing romantics, such as Louis de Bonald and Joseph de Maistre, theorized about the need to ground the body politic and society in traditional religion.

Pierre Birnbaum has underlined how much the increasingly Catholic and Christian self-definition of the French Consulate (1799–1804) and First Empire (1804–1814, 1815) negatively affected the standing of Jews of early nineteenth-century France.[10] The position of the 1801 Concordat with the Catholic Church that Catholicism was "the religion of the great majority of French citizens" is indicative of the dilemma French Jews faced during this period. Such a statement might be understood as a rejection of the notion that France was simply a Catholic country, yet it also seemed to suggest that the state would not be averse to favoring Catholicism.[11] In this constellation, anti-Jewish voices also found new venues. On February 8, 1806, Louis de Bonald published an article in the *Mercure de France*, entitled "Sur les Juifs," that demanded the abolition of Jewish legal equality. The piece may have inspired Napoleon when he reevaluated the state's policies toward the Jews that same year. Soon after Bonald issued his plea to "unemancipate" the Jews, Napoleon limited the economic freedom of Alsatian Jewry (May 30, 1806) and eventually passed the *décret infame*, which infringed on Alsatian Jews' civil rights (March 17, 1808).[12] These decrees remained in place for a decade, until Louis XVIII failed to renew them. From that point on, the political equality of French Jews remained in place (through 1940). Yet political Catholics' continuing challenges of the legal and social equality of Jews, particularly during the period of the Bourbon Restoration, should not be underestimated. As Julie Kalman has argued, it was only by the late 1820s that Jews could feel secure that the theocentric political theories of counterrevolutionaries like Bonald, François-René de Chateaubriand, and de Maistre—whose ideas of a Christian state left no space for Jews—would not bring about a reversal of the state's policies toward the Jews of the realm.[13]

These worries became acute when anticlerical rumors reached vulnerable communities. A confidential report of 1829 on popular sentiment in southwestern France, for example, notes an atmosphere of fear among Jews regarding the possibility of such a reversal of state policies. In a letter to the Ministry of the Interior, the prefect of Landes warned of widespread popular anxieties concerning a ministerial rearrangement of the same year, which had given conservative Ultras more influence. The prefect noted the outbreak of great panics—"*une terreur pannique*"—among liberals in the region. In this case, the panic spread to the Sephardi Jewish community of Saint-Esprit-les-Bayonnes. Alerted by the news that the Papal States had enacted harsher laws against the Jews, local Sephardi Jews apparently spread rumors that such laws were also imminent in France.[14] In their disquiet surrounding talk of the revival of prerevolutionary policies, Jews shared their concerns with Catholic peasants, who expressed their fear of a return to the ancien régime and thus of their subjugation to seigniorial power.[15]

Even though anticlerical rumors affected Jewish communities, Jewish representatives were wary of entering the high stakes game of anticlerical politics. The first official Jewish responses to the anti-Jewish rhetoric of Catholic romantics followed traditional apologetic strategies and affirmed the status quo and with it, the Christian character of the empire. Berr Isaac Berr's proposal on the regeneration of the Jews, written shortly after Bonald's "Sur les Juifs" of 1806, is a case in point.[16] Berr's text complained of the persistence of Christian hatred against the Jews in France, suggesting that such hatred was "contrary to the spirit of the Gospels."[17] Berr thus recognized the Catholic symbolism that had accompanied the establishment of the empire. There was therefore little space for anticlerical statements in such an appeal to the Catholic emperor, even if Berr's opponents were self-declared Catholic critics of the regime.

Berr's reluctance to appear as a transgressor of this consensus by sympathizing with anti-government anticlericalism also characterized the approach of the smaller Jewish communities. This is illustrated by the reaction of the Jewish notables of the Alsatian town of Lauterbourg to anticlerical campaigns from the left. On May 14, 1831, the liberal Paris newspaper *Courrier français* published a short letter accusing the Catholic Church of organizing illegal Corpus Christi processions in the town.[18] Article 45 of the Organic Articles passed in 1801 prohibited religious ceremonies in public squares when other religions had houses of worship in the same city. Because Lauterbourg had a Jewish majority and a Jewish synagogue, according to the note, the public celebrations of Corpus Christi on May 8 and 9 of that year were a violation of Jewish rights and French law. While processions had long been a contested issue between anticlericals and the Catholic Church, the emphasis on offenses against Jewish feelings was less common.[19] The 1831 letter issued by the *Courrier français* offers an example of the liberal discovery of Jews as victims of organized Catholicism, a discovery that served anticlerical efforts to break the dominance of the Catholic Church in society.[20] A similar logic continued to appear in anticlerical polemics throughout the nineteenth century, reaching its zenith in the Dreyfus affair, when Dreyfusards united behind a Jewish officer accused of treachery in large part to oppose his enemies, at whose helm—they alleged—was a clerical cabal working insidiously to undo the French secular order.[21]

The Lauterbourg episode of 1831 departs from the received narrative of nineteenth-century liberal politics, however, because in this case the affected Jews reacted vocally to anticlericals' attempts to speak on their behalf and to "protect" their religious rights as Jews. What made sense for French liberals in the capital did not, it turns out, necessarily appear as helpful or even desirable to Jews in this Alsatian town. Worried that observers might believe that local Jews had denounced the church, the Jewish notables in Lauterbourg immediately tried to counteract this impression in collaboration with the town's mayor. In separate letters, the Jews and the mayor sought to convince the subprefect that these reports were neither in the interest of local Jews nor their doing.[22] As any observer familiar with the region would know, the mayor explained, Lauterbourg did not have a Jewish majority as the newspaper in faraway Paris had claimed. A small town of 2,649 inhabitants, the mayor estimated that only 211 Jews lived in Lauterbourg, or less than 10 percent of the population. The Jews had neither a consistory nor a permanent rabbi. Both letters skillfully withheld the only legally relevant detail: that there was a small synagogue in town.[23]

The letter by Lauterbourg's mayor also offered some explanations concerning the Jews reluctance to identify with the piece in the *Courrier français*. News of the article had spread quickly in the town and surrounding communities, he reported, putting economic pressure on local Jews who were commercially dependent on their Christian customers. If rumors that Jews had caused the end of the processions grew, their livelihood would soon be seriously endangered.[24] The letter of the Jewish community of Lauterbourg to the subprefect is equally revealing in its analysis of the effects of Paris-style anticlerical secularism on Jewish–Catholic relations in the countryside. The Jewish notables who authored this official response denied any local Jewish involvement in the attempts to hinder Catholic celebrations. In fact, they assured the authorities, the Jewish community wished nothing more than to see the Catholic processions continue. Rather than express a desire to remove all religion from public spaces, the Jewish community's leaders invoked an ideal of "reciprocal tolerance," which had allowed both Catholics and Jews to perform their rituals publicly. This ideal was diametrically opposed to the perspective offered by the Parisian newspaper article. Lauterbourg's Jewish notables explained their position as follows: "We prefer, Mr. Subprefect, to understand and practice religious liberty as we have understood and practiced it until this day; for interpreted in this way it seems more rational and real to us than if we were to adopt the restrictive system of the law."[25]

Explaining to an official that they preferred a pragmatic solution even if it contravened the law might not appear, at first glance, like the most prudent of strategies, but in this case it was exactly what government representatives wanted to hear. The prefect not only instructed the subprefect to allow further Catholic processions in the town on account of the Jewish community's support for such a move; he also recommended the publication of the letter of Lauterbourg's Jewish notables.[26] The prefect's decision in turn earned the support of the minister of the interior, who praised the Jews of Lauterbourg for their demarche, which—he suggested—proved they possessed an admirable "spirit of religious tolerance."[27] The Jews' example, in the minister's view, could even serve as a model for those anticlerical Catholics who were intolerant toward their own religion.

Both the French authorities and the Jews of Lauterbourg were typical in their reaction. Neither the state nor local Jewish elites—nor more influential Jewish leaders such as Berr—wished to inflame religious passions or deal with the violent consequences of political polarization. Such considerations were, however, not convincing to those intellectuals who desired change. Among oppositional authors of the center and left, a new type of religious politics developed, creating the template for a novel style of polemical secularism. Liberals like Benjamin Constant, Madame de Staël, and the constitutional monarchists around Pierre Paul Royer-Collard were as interested in religion and history as Catholic romantics but diverged from them in that they did not see the reconstruction of a powerful Catholic Church as their aim. Influenced by these thinkers but also radicalizing their positions, a sizeable group of young men and women educated in the Napoleonic lycées began using a religious language to challenge both Catholicism and the Restoration regime by the 1820s.[28] Diverse in their ideological commitments, many were influenced by the renewed status history had gained as a source for philosophical and political inquiry during the romantic era. Catholicism and Protestantism alike became much more attractive as political symbols than they had been during the Enlightenment.

A new polemics of secularism—or, in other words, of the politicized expectations toward religion—emerged out of this romantic attention to religions as symbols for historical processes. Several Jews from the so-called generation of 1820 who—unlike the Jews of Lauterbourg—were not directly dependent on the goodwill of priests or believers discovered this rhetoric for themselves. In the process, they not only created their own version of a religiously inspired counterproject to conservative Catholics, as Lisa Leff has shown; they also developed a new type of oppositional anti-Catholic rhetoric.[29] The lives and work of Joseph Salvador and Léon Halévy, two prominent members of this group of French Jewish anticlericals active during this period, illustrate this new pattern of Jewish engagement with early nineteenth-century French politics.

Egypt and Rome in the Writings of Joseph Salvador

Joseph Salvador was arguably the first Jewish thinker in France to create an anticlerical work aimed at legitimizing Judaism within a romantic framework.[30] Born in Montpellier in 1796, Salvador grew up in a family that was distinctly multiconfessional. His father was a Sephardic Jew who had gained entrance into non-Jewish circles around the time of the French Revolution, while his mother was a Roman Catholic and his brother Benjamin married a Huguenot.[31] Salvador first studied medicine in his hometown and then moved to Paris, where his academic interests expanded to include the history of religions. According to his own testimony, in 1819 the anti-Jewish Hep-Hep riots in Germany persuaded him to dedicate his life to the defense of Jewish dignity and the study of Jewish antiquities.[32] Because he had not been introduced to Jewish learning during his early years, Salvador's training in Jewish sources was mostly autodidactic, save a short period of instruction with the chief rabbi of Paris.[33]

Salvador's first work, published in 1822 as *Loi de Moïse* and then in 1828 as *Histoire des institutions de Moïse et du peuple hébreu* in a substantially expanded version, was a form of oppositional historiography. Among the work's most controversial aspects was its attempt to describe Jesus and early Christianity as part of Jewish history as well as Salvador's claim that Jesus' trial had been conducted fairly. Indeed, according to Salvador, Jesus was a blasphemer whose conviction and punishment were the result of due process and a legitimate interpretation of the law.[34] The central claim of Salvador's work was less controversial, however: He argued that the ancient Hebrew commonwealth—and Mosaic Law in particular—represented the first truly republican order. Although republicanism was usually understood as the opposite of monarchism in France and Germany, Salvador portrayed constitutional monarchy as the ideal republic. Salvador's Hebrew republic was, in other words, not a Jacobin republic. It was closer to the kind of state imagined by liberal defenders of the constitutional charter of 1814, in which the Restoration King Louis XVIII had been forced to guarantee freedom of religion and basic civil rights. Contradicting those romantics who referred to Christian history to legitimize conservative political theories, Salvador insisted that the Jewish religious past he described offered an alternative genealogy for a liberal religious order inspired by the revolution of 1789. In Salvador's view, Mosaic Law expressed the popular will and was thus founded on ideas diametrically opposed to those defended by Catholic conservatives. In his words, "The [Mosaic] Law was not just rule, as Bonald defined it, but a rule invested with the assent of all."[35]

In Salvador's description, Mosaic Law was also the source of modern rational philosophy. In fact, according to his historical analysis, modern thought had emerged from Mosaic republicanism but had been suppressed by Catholicism. To support his view, Salvador argued that "Roman Catholicism hampered thought in multiple ways: it removed all examination and discussion from matters of faith, it relegated activities of the spirit to a concern about another world, [and] it placed passive obedience above free choice."[36] In its opposition to the stagnation of Catholicism, in Salvador's view, the Reformation had initiated a renaissance of Mosaism [*mosaïsme*] by opening new paths for modern philosophy.[37] Yet, for Salvador, Protestantism did not complete this history. It reinvigorated Christianity and humanity through its renewed focus on the ancient Hebrew system of laws but was "only a preparatory and incomplete return to Mosaism restored in its purity."[38]

Although such candid commentaries on Catholicism were the exception in Salvador's writing, we can nonetheless find several other, if subtler, remarks about the church throughout his work. In a discussion of the innovations of ancient Judaism, Salvador described the situation in Egypt before the birth of Moses as characterized by the rule of privileged, priestly castes that constituted a "theocratic monarchy." In this system, the Egyptian elites used religion principally to gain earthly pleasure. Salvador suggested in his analysis that a closer look at the way ancient Egypt's ruling classes fostered superstition and excluded lower orders would "finally show such striking points of resemblance between those times and those closer to our own that I find myself forced to cry out again: There is nothing new under the sun!"[39]

Published during the period of intense anticlerical campaigns by the liberal opposition to Charles X (r. 1824–1830), Salvador's allusion to the alliance of throne and altar would have been obvious even though he did not mention Catholicism explicitly. His Egyptian clergy served as an allegorical stand-in for the Catholic clergy of his day. Elsewhere in his work, Salvador offered the key to his use of allusions in his history. In the alphabetical index to his book, he included the following entry with reference to the preceding quote: "Catholicism. Plunging itself into the Egyptian system."[40] Other anticlerical statements can also be found in his index. The entry for "clergy" reads: "Catholic clergy following in the steps of the Egyptian priesthood." On the corresponding page to this entry, there are no explicit references to Catholicism. Instead he contrasted the Jewish Levites with the Egyptian priests and the modern clergy at large.[41] For Salvador, Judaism emerged as a reaction to the practices of the Egyptian priesthood.[42] He described Mosaic republicanism as the result of a Hebrew rejection of the abuses of Egyptian clergymen, while implying in other instances that Catholicism was inherently as undemocratic as the religion of the Egyptian priesthood. In the words of historian Eugène Fleischmann, Salvador's concept of the Catholic Church "can be summarized in a single phrase: intellectual oppression."[43]

Like François Guizot, Augustin Thierry, and François Mignet, Salvador can be seen as a liberal romantic who put religion at the center of a leftist historical narrative with an anticlerical bent.[44] Within this group, Salvador was among the earliest oppositional historians. Indeed, his work of 1822 predates the breakthrough of liberal romanticism in France by several years.[45] Salvador's sympathetic description of the Reformation in the late 1820s should also be understood in the context of French intellectuals' increasing turn to Protestantism as a symbol for an alternative model of state–church relations in France. In this regard, Salvador was similar to prominent liberals such as Guizot and Benjamin Constant, both of whom combined political anticlericalism with a particular fondness for Protestantism in their writings from the era.[46]

Although Salvador's politics in the French context were remarkable because he allowed Judaism to take the place of Protestantism in this type of anti-Catholic polemics, from the perspective of transnational Jewish history, they stand out for their universalism. Unlike other contemporary Jewish thinkers, Salvador made use of Jewish history to put forward broader arguments about liberal politics. The young students and scholars of Judaism who participated in the Verein für die Cultur und Wissenschaft der Juden (1819–1824) in Germany aspired to show what was essential in Judaism as part of their fight to prove Jews' readiness to become citizens.[47] In the course of their work, they focused their anticlerical arguments on rabbis rather than priests because it was the clerical leaders of their own community who were most relevant to their concern for the regeneration of Judaism. In the rare cases when the Verein's members nevertheless drew on the Protestant anti-Catholicism of their Berlin environment, they did so as part of their agenda within Judaism rather than aiming to change German or European politics.[48] Salvador's ability to engage with current non-Jewish politics, to draw on the renewed interest in the Bible as a cultural text during the 1820s, and to use anticlerical language to communicate his arguments all contributed to the lasting impression his works made on a variety of French and European thinkers, including John Stuart Mill.[49]

The French reception of Salvador's early publications was also a function of the politics of his readership. Catholic newspapers across the board rejected the work of the liberal Jew who attacked Christianity. They also warned of the detrimental effects Salvador's book might

have on religious thinking more generally. In contrast, liberal reviewers from newspapers such as the newly founded *Globe* typically gave
Salvador's attempts a positive reading, even when they did not find his
anachronistic arguments compelling.[50] The liberal *Constitutionnel* was
similarly sympathetic, siding with Salvador's interpretation of the Bible
as a liberal document against the readings of Bonald and Lamennais.[51]
Salvador's work also continued to be used as an occasion for anticlerical
comments in the heated debates of the second half of the nineteenth
century. One reviewer of the 1862 edition of his book claimed that Salvador showed compellingly the ways in which Catholicism had dis-
torted the Bible in its quest to dominate the world.[52]

Léon Halévy: From Saint-Simon to Luther

As one of the earliest Jewish thinkers to use religion as a tool in the fight
against new exclusionary movements in the postrevolutionary state,
Salvador also inspired other French Jews who tried to shape their own
political language in the style of the (Christian) religious revolutionary
tone of the early decades of the nineteenth century.[53] During the 1820s,
Salvador's immediate influence can be detected in the writings of Léon
Halévy, the son of the maskil Elie Halévy (1760–1826) and brother of
the composer Jacques Fromental Halévy (1799–1862). After graduating
from the Lycée Charlemagne in Paris, Léon Halévy worked as Henri
de Saint-Simon's (1760–1825) private secretary in the writer's last years.
Halévy had been among the earliest members of Saint-Simon's circle,
after the two met in 1823. He was also one of the few people present at
Saint-Simon's funeral at the cemetery of Père-Lachaise in 1825.[54] Shortly
thereafter, Halévy cofounded a newspaper with other Saint-Simonians
called *Le Producteur* (October 1825 through October 1826), yet soon
found himself alienated from its other editors, particularly Pére Enfantin, as the group it represented increasingly transformed into a religious
sect.[55] Abandoning the Saint-Simonians just as various other upper-
class French Jews came to find the movement attractive, Halévy became
a more mainstream liberal, contributing to periodicals such as *Le Globe*.
In 1832, he married the daughter of the Catholic architect Hippolyte Le
Bas (1782–1867), who designed the church of Notre-Dame-de-Lorette.

His son, Ludovic, was baptized a Catholic in 1834, two years after his birth.[56] From 1837 to 1853, Léon Halévy was employed at the ministry of education, while he continued a successful career as a playwright. It seems that many of Halévy's lifelong personal connections emerged from his relations to his Catholic in-laws rather than through his earlier engagement with the circle around Saint-Simon.[57]

Halévy's career as an anticlerical writer began with the same genre as Salvador's works: He published two books on the history of the Jewish people, one on antiquity (1825) and one on modern times (1827–1828).[58] Unlike Salvador's books, which presented themselves as innovative scholarship, however, Halévy's writings had little scholarly ambition. Instead, they carried a strong political message. In fact, Halévy's political position was made clear even by his choice of publication venue in Lecointe's series of short historical summaries or *Résumés abrégés*.[59] The most successful book in this series had been Félix Bodin's *Résumé de l'histoire de France jusqu'à nos jours* [A Short History of France to the Present] (1821), which went through multiple editions for the decade that followed.[60] A deputy at the time, Bodin wrote a work of liberal historiography, emphasizing the importance of the Revolution of 1789 against the Jacobin period that began in 1792. Bodin had also added a theoretical postscript to his work, which explained the need for the separation of powers, a statement that positioned him as an opponent of the Ultras dominating the Bourbon monarchy in the 1820s. Reacting to critiques of the series, and of Bodin's work in particular, the editors' published apology for their project further elucidates the context of Halévy's historical study. Explaining their willingness to depict the dark episodes of French and human history, the editors defended themselves against the accusations of the Catholic press that the attacks on priestly misconduct issued by various works in the series were antireligious. Restating the anticlerical line of their series, the editors asked rhetorically why the clergy did not embrace the Gospels and the law of the land instead of defending aberrant priests mired in the ways of the past.[61] Insisting on their right to depict the Reformation in positive terms, the series' editors further positioned themselves against right-wing legitimists through the symbolic politics of philo-Protestantism.[62] At the same time, they also emphasized how much the very form of the works they published went against the grain of most scholarly publications. In fact, their short histories were prohibited at the university because students were expected to master material in a profound way without taking the shortcut of such highly synthetic summaries. The *résumés* were, in other words, politically subversive CliffsNotes, marketed officially to a general, nonscholarly public.[63]

The editor's decision to hire Halévy made sense in this context. Many of the series' authors were nonspecialists with strong political opinions, whose main task was the reproduction of common knowledge in accessible form. For this purpose, Lecointe and Durey secured the collaboration of prominent men of letters like Bodin but also of younger still less-known liberal writers like Philarète Chasles and Léon Halévy. In Halévy's case, it is fair to say that he faced more than the usual set of challenges in undertaking such a project: Most important, he did not know Hebrew, in spite of the fact that his father was a prominent Hebrew poet.[64] In Halévy's first volume, covering Jewish history until the destruction of the Second Temple, he drew on French biblical studies and on the translated biblical text, whereas for his work on modern history—covering everything since the destruction of the Second Temple to his day—Halévy was much more dependent on a limited number of works, including Basnage's *Histoire des Juifs*. In spite of these handicaps, Halévy's first volume at least appears to have been successful. The 1,500 copies Lecointe printed of the 1825 *Résumé* sold out quickly enough to merit the reprint of another 1,500 copies within a few months, as well as another edition in 1827.[65]

As was true of Salvador, Halévy's politics became legible through his religious polemics. Considering the abbreviated nature of his history, Halévy dedicated a great deal of space to a discussion of the ancient Egyptian priesthood, which he described as a paradigmatically corrupt clergy in terms already familiar from Salvador. As an anticlerical who claimed that the history of the Hebrews had something to offer to nineteenth-century liberals, Halévy found one passage in the Hebrew Bible particularly troubling. He struggled with Genesis 47:20–22, which reported that Joseph had bought all of the land in Egypt except that of the priests as a result of his role as the pharaoh's plenipotentiary. If the Bible was an account of good governance, how could Joseph reduce all to servitude but empower the priests? Rather than critique Joseph, Halévy decided to abandon his anticlericalism in this instance to draw on the theories of enlightened priesthood that would become prominent in the Saint-Simonian movement during its phase as a religious sect. Here, Halévy argued that the priests were more enlightened than other Egyptians while also venturing that centralization always led to civilizational progress.[66] As a caveat, however, Halévy added that Joseph's decision nonetheless had the ironic effect of leading to the future persecution of the Hebrews by the all-powerful Egyptian priests many generations later.

Halévy's politics emerged less from his approach to Christianity in general, a topic that has received some attention in scholarship to date, but rather to Protestantism and Catholicism in particular, both of which—as noted—served as potent political symbols during this period. Halévy, a Jew who married into an influential Catholic family, did not follow Saint-Simon's general rejection of Protestantism in his last works.[67] While Saint-Simon had reserved some of his most pungent criticism for the Catholic Church, his treatment of Protestantism was, in a sense, even more dismissive.[68] Catholicism was both the greater threat and the more interesting model, which Saint-Simon adopted when he envisioned a new clergy and a new pope. Even the Christian Middle Ages, while hardly a period to be emulated, appeared to Saint-Simon as an important stage in human history when an enlightened clergy moved humanity forward toward progress.[69] In his focus on collective freedom, Saint-Simon was fundamentally opposed to a Protestant path. He saw Luther as a necessary destructive force in historical developments but never as the key to the future organization of society.[70] Thus, although modern Catholicism was the central target of Saint-Simonians, the individualism of the Protestant Reformation was less appealing to them than it was to most other liberals of the time. Halévy was aware of Saint-Simon's position on Catholicism and Protestantism alike when he wrote his short histories of the Jews. Indeed, he had collaborated in putting them into print in the form of Saint-Simon's last work, the *Opinions littéraires, philosophiques et industrielles* of 1825.[71]

Yet even in his first *Résume*, written while he was still involved with the Saint-Simonians, Halévy signaled his departure from other followers of Saint-Simon by expressing his interest in Protestantism. In that work, Halévy noted that Luther had salvaged the religious core of the ancient Mosaic tradition much as Jesus had before him.[72] This approach became more pronounced in his second volume, written after Halévy broke with the Saint-Simonian movement sometime around early 1826.[73] Disenchanted with the group's increasing transformation from a loose association of intellectuals seeking to implement a new science of society into a hierarchical churchlike sect, Halévy also rejected the simultaneous anti- and philo-Catholic politics of the group. In his second volume, he argued that the Reformation had struck a blow against the Catholic monks who persecuted Jews, hinting at continuities to the Egyptian priests who had persecuted Jews long before.[74] In Halévy's view, Protestantism was closer to the "primitive Christianity that has been disfigured in such a peculiar manner by the Pharisees of Catholicism."[75] It was thus Protestantism that gave moderns access to an unadulterated Jewish tradition worthy of redemption.

Taking a position that was typical of liberals laboring during the 1820s and 1830s, Halévy suggested that religion, if understood properly, was destined to allow for secular politics. His political faith in Protestantism seems to have increased in line with his alienation from the Saint-Simonian movement he had helped to found. In a poem published in 1831, Halévy mocked the papist principle underlying the church organization of the group's new leader, Prosper Enfantin.[76] Losing his faith in the group's ability to create an anti-reactionary form of political religion, Halévy turned again to Protestantism as the religion that stood most clearly for opposition to the despotic aspirations he associated with Catholicism.[77] In 1834—the same year he baptized his son as a Catholic—Halévy translated Friedrich Ludwig Zacharias Werner's (1768–1823) drama *Luther* from German to French, referring to Luther in his introduction as "that great Christian philosopher, that bold champion of political and religious liberty."[78] At the same time, Halévy condemned Werner for eventually converting and becoming an "intolerant and exalted Catholic," remarking that "it is urgent that all the friends of progress and reason reunite to propel [proper] religious sentiment into the future—a religious sentiment which seeks to reemerge and which certain political passions want to exploit in a purely retrograde way."[79] According to Halévy, dire consequences would ensue if liberals were to surrender all religious sentiment to reactionary Catholicism—which, in his mind, was scheming to "rebuild its empire."[80]

Yet Halévy's Protestantism was neither a denomination nor even a church. It served, rather, as a symbol for rationalism in the face of a religiously charged form of political reaction. Halévy, like other Jews after him, turned to Protestantism in the face of a potent political anti-Protestantism from the right.[81] Theirs was a defiant philo-Protestantism that had little to do with their everyday denominational commitments. Halévy's work—like Salvador's before him—attests to the strategic function that boundary making toward the Catholic Church had for those modern European Jews who tried to combine a positive reevaluation of Jewish history, an appreciation for Protestantism, and liberal politics. At the same time, their political anti-Catholicism—and, in Halévy's case, philo-Protestantism—shaped the way they described their expectations toward religion. These authors' statements on the topic of Christian denominations made little sense outside of the politics of secularism; they were always more about citizenship and social cohesion than about transcendence or belief.

Reading Salvador in Germany

The writings of these French Jewish thinkers were not equally appealing to their German coreligionists. Whereas Halévy had little impact in the German states, Salvador's work captured the attention of German Jews.[82] The most important Jewish periodical of the time, the *Allgemeine Zeitung des Judenthums*, published several articles about Salvador in the late 1830s, just as his work on the history of Jesus appeared in French.[83] One article by the German-French poet Alexandre Weill called Salvador "the First Jew of France to be accepted as such," claiming (not without reason) that he was France's most prominent Jewish intellectual.[84] Eduard Gans (1797–1839) mentioned Salvador's early work in the written version of his lectures on Hegel's *Philosophy of Law*, which introduced a whole generation of students to Hegel's thought.[85] At the same time, various German Jewish reviewers suggested that Salvador was more well meaning than profound. For Gans, Salvador's project seemed forced and did not meet the standards of German scholarship. He also pointed out the irony of the fact that Salvador could manage to express his progressive views only in dialogue with right-wing Catholics, such as Bonald or Lamennais.[86]

Yet interest in Salvador's writings continued in German lands. In 1835, eight years after the French original appeared, his *Institutions de Moïse* was issued in a German edition. The work omitted several of the critical remarks concerning Catholicism featured in the index of the French volume but added an introduction by Gabriel Riesser (1806–1863), the most prominent champion of Jewish emancipation in Germany during that period. In many respects, Riesser was an unlikely choice for this role because he had been reluctant to mix his advocacy of Jewish rights with theological positions. Rather, as a lawyer, he had focused on the material he knew best: legal principle and positive law. Riesser's introduction to Salvador's work nonetheless indicated that he had an acute understanding of the context in which the book had been produced and that he embraced its religious and political program without reservation.

Riesser described the work as a simultaneous attack against Voltaire-ans who tried to undermine Judaism as part of their religious criticism and French ultramontanes, whom he equated with German "obscurantists."[87] Riesser explained the French constellation to German readers as a fight against a school "which called the altar to the aid of the absolute throne and which wanted to destroy freedom with the help of misinterpreted religion."[88] According to Riesser's reading, Jews who had been given their civic rights by those who employed the French rhetoric of freedom now had to invoke this freedom as a divine right, as Salvador had done with his historical-theological treatise.[89] For Riesser, this religious project was not so much an apology for emancipation as a product of the French culture of freedom, which he hoped would also lend dignity to Jewish readers in Germany in the near future. Through his introduction we can see that Riesser had much sympathy for Salvador's project in the French context but considered his conflict with ultramontanes as relevant to German Jews principally as a parable about liberty and self-esteem.

Riesser's explanations and Gans's skepticism about Salvador's reliance on the foil of Catholic conservative enemies offer a first hint of the different situation in France and Germany. Salvador's anti-Catholic polemics were not easily translated into the German context, where Catholics had not been the main proponents of an exclusive nationalism or anti-Jewish campaigns. Even as German Jews were curious about French anticlerical polemics during this period, in other words, they also faced challenges of translating them into their distinct German context. Turning to two intellectuals with a Jewish background who developed their own unique style of anti-Catholic polemics in Germany, the next sections will illuminate the political constellations that made such polemics meaningful for German Jews in ways that speak to the parallels, differences, and entanglements of anticlerical politics in Germany and France.

Saul Ascher: Anti-Romanticism in an Enlightened Key

The work of Saul Ascher offers a particularly rich example of the complex symbolic politics that linked Catholicism and Judaism in Germany during the early nineteenth century. Ascher was one of the earliest writers to develop an elaborate anti-Catholic criticism of German romanticism. He was born into a Jewish family that had been in Berlin for generations.[90] Because his father had been a bank agent, his family had the protected status of *Schutzjuden*. Although Ascher composed several apologetic texts defending Judaism against its detractors, he showed little interest in Jewish communal politics and earned his living as a bookseller and publisher.[91]

A marginal figure in earlier historical accounts, Ascher has been rediscovered in recent decades as one of the pivotal authors of modern Jewish political thought. Indeed, scholars now describe him as one of the earliest champions of an alternative Jewish modernity and his first major work, *Leviathan* (1792), as the beginning of Jewish political theology.[92] In the history of German nationalism and confessional conflicts, Ascher has similarly earned a special place. According to Wolfgang Altgeld, he was one of the few authors of his time who did not imagine Germany as a nation that needed to be religiously unified, ultimately "recognizing precisely in the Catholic Church and in Catholic Germany a bastion against the 'German theocracy.'"[93] The following analysis challenges this interpretation, although Ascher's criticism of the romantic movement made him a vocal proponent of religious pluralism, he was no champion of Catholicism. Instead he used the notion of a stagnant Catholicism against anti-Jewish romantics, making his work an early example of a type of anti-Catholic criticism of Protestantism that would reappear in many German Jewish intellectuals' writings over the next century.

Ascher's critique of romanticism and the Catholic Church can be found already in his early publications, which developed an anticlerical narrative of German history. In his *Ideen zur natürlichen Geschichte der politischen Revolutionen* [Ideas for a Natural History of Political Revolutions], which was forbidden by the Prussian censor 1799 and published only in 1802, Ascher constructed a stage theory of human history based on the hypothesis that revolutions reestablished the original equilibrium of presocietal humanity.[94] Revolutions, in other words, created a natural state and were thus the result of a natural drive, "the spirit of revolution." Three paradigmatic revolutions occurred in world history, according to Ascher's rendering: The first was economic, the second religious, and the third moral. Rather implausibly—even to his only known contemporary reviewer—Ascher asserted that the first economic revolution already had taken place in the eleventh century with the rise of the Third Estate, leading to the destruction of vassal systems.[95] This development led, in turn, to a religious revolution, the Reformation, which allowed reason to regain its power over the sensualism of the Catholic Church. Constituting the last stage experienced at the time of Ascher's writing, the French Revolution created a system of political rule, which allowed the popular will to be better represented politically.

Like other German enlighteners and liberals, Ascher integrated the Reformation seamlessly into his narrative of progress by reinterpreting religion as another articulation of politics. Christianity was consequently merely the expression of a political will and, according to Ascher, came into its own only after it had developed a hierarchy.[96] This hierarchy constituted a global governmental body that eventually became a problem when it abused its status. Once this occurred, Christianity became another form of despotism until the "revolutionary spirit" that existed in all of humanity took its course. In Ascher's view, nature was thus on the side of Martin Luther and against the church hierarchy.[97] Ascher's account idealized the Reformation as a necessary link in humankind's progression toward an ideal government, much as Mendelssohn had done before him (and also much as Hegel would do later). Omitting Judaism completely from the picture, the *Ideen* constituted an attempt to explain the victory of secularized and secularizing Protestantism. Anticlericalism was one feature of progress in this secularist vision.

Ascher's second outline for a stage theory of world-historical progress was written under the influence of the debates on Jewish emancipation triggered by Paalzow and other romantics. Under the impression of a nationalist movement that made claim to popular support and authenticity while rejecting Jewish civil rights, Ascher sought political reforms now mainly from a strong outside ruler. In his *Napoleon oder: Über den Fortschritt der Regierung* [Napoleon or: On the Progress of Government] (1807), he depicted the French emperor as the end point of a long evolution toward proper forms of government.[98] Once again, religious politics was pivotal in his world-historical schema. In Germany, Napoleon's greatness lay in his overcoming of nationalism and religious intolerance. According to Ascher, this intolerance had been driven by confessional conflict.[99] The religious schism between Catholicism and Protestantism had clouded the vision of the Christian faithful, making them believe that certain rights were restricted to certain denominations. As the Christian confessions increasingly guarded themselves against each other's possible encroachments, the Jews—as the third party with no territory to claim—remained without protection.[100] Only the introduction of French idealism, which went beyond nationalism, could lead to the enforcement of religious tolerance, according to Ascher's analysis.[101] Distinct from both the French Jewish romantics like Salvador and Halévy as well as German romantics who sought solutions to political problems in history, Ascher demanded a rational reordering of society that could interrupt the organic flow of history.[102]

As German romantic nationalism grew more militant in its opposition to Jewish civil rights, Ascher focused increasingly on the critique of exclusions that, in his view, emerged from Christian denominational divisions and the politics of exclusion. In reaction, he developed a language of political anti-Catholicism as a weapon against anti-Jewish Protestant romantics. His most vocal criticism of the exclusive nationalism of his day appeared in his two best-known political pamphlets, *Die*

Germanomanie [Germanomania] (1815) and *Die Wartburgs-Feier* [The Wartburg Celebration] (1818). The immediate occasion for the former text was Friedrich Rühs's publication of his "Ueber die Ansprüche der Juden an das deutsche Bürgerrecht" [The Claims of the Jews for Civil Rights in Germany] (1815).[103] Rühs, who had made his name as a translator and scholar of Scandinavian literature, had called for the isolation of the Jews through legal discrimination.[104] Because Jews constituted a foreign national element in Rühs's eyes, their presence in Germany was irreconcilable with the Christian-German character of the state he imagined. In response to his diatribes, Ascher responded to both Rühs's claims and the rise of anti-Jewish sentiment among romantic nationalists more broadly. These nationalist hotheads, in his view, deserved to be characterized as "Germanomaniacs" on account of their extreme and naïve devotion to ideas of a Christian and Germanic nation-state.[105]

Once again, Ascher explained the exclusion of Jews in terms of intra-Christian denominational conflicts. He was convinced that the main obstacle to the romantics' vision of a unified nation had been the insuperable antagonism between Protestants and Catholics in Germany.[106] To overcome this division, Protestant nationalists drew on a sentimental religious language that allowed them to make their Protestant Christianity look more like Catholicism. As Ascher put it, unity was to be created "through a Protestantism that was exaggerated to the point that it became Catholic."[107] Accordingly, Protestant nationalist romantics tried to unite the Christian confessions by Catholicizing Protestantism. In the process, they also came to conceive of anything that did not fit into their notion of an exaggerated or enhanced Christianity [*gesteigertes Christentum*] as an enemy of the true Germans they represented. This "Protestant Papism," as Ascher called it in the *Warburg-Feier*, rejected all liberal movements within Christianity while simultaneously denouncing Judaism.[108]

It was ironically in the Protestant north that this Catholic-style "sanctimonious religiosity" [*frömmelnde Religiosität*] found most of its adherents, according to Ascher. The "idealized Catholicism" that these Protestants constructed for political reasons was much more intensive than "real Catholicism" as it was practiced in the majority Catholic areas of Germany in his view.[109] The reason Ascher offered for the greater spread of this fanaticism among Protestant thinkers was not particularly flattering to Catholics. Catholics had been less receptive to these latest developments because they were already used to "symbolic and ceremonious representation of religious truths."[110] In other words, they lacked the depth of spirit that made a person susceptible to such fanatical ideas as those being developed by the "Catholicizing" Protestant nationalists. Moreover, he explained that these romantic nationalists received no support from the princes who gathered at the Congress of Vienna because—and here we find Ascher's positive countervision—society had reached a stage in which it functioned primarily on the basis of the principle of law.

Many of Ascher's interlocutors—his enemies included—shared his basic suspicion of Catholicism. In this sense, Ascher had chosen his language well: It allowed him to tap into the common German romantic distrust of both ceremonial Judaism and Catholicism and play one against the other. Indeed, Ascher attempted to take the sting out of romantic antisemitism by appealing to the anti-Catholicism of certain radical nationalists as well as their conservative detractors.[111]

We can see this approach at work in Ascher's relations to August von Kotzebue, a successful conservative playwright who was assassinated by a German nationalist student in 1819. Kotzebue might have been considered a friend to the Jews when compared to the German nationalists of his day but not to later liberals: Although he defended the idea of Jewish citizenship in principle, he also rejected full equal rights as long as Jews did not convert.[112] Kotzebue was also an anti-Catholic. Like Basnage and other Protestant thinkers since the Reformation, he combined his reservations about Catholicism and Judaism by claiming that the influence of Papism on Christianity prevented the conversion of the Jews.[113] Rather than appeal to Kotzebue's fragile support of Jewish rights, Ascher relied on their common critique of the pomp and ceremony of nationalist politics that both authors associated with Catholicism. When Ascher sent his pamphlet against the nationalist students' celebration at the Wartburg in 1817 to Kotzebue, he recounted the events there by satirizing them as a carnivalesque and overly pompous procession in an attached letter.[114] Kotzebue seemed to agree with Ascher's understanding of their common enmity, as he soon defended Ascher against the anti-Jewish slander of his nationalist detractors, sympathetically citing Ascher's accusations against "Protestant Papism" in his newspaper.[115]

Ascher's letter to Kotzebue also signaled his late turn to conservatism. Unlike Salvador, Halévy, and, later, Heine, who all treated anti-Catholicism as a tool with which they opposed the Restoration regimes, Ascher adopted anti-Catholicism as a defensive position meant to mitigate against radical nationalism. Because romantic nationalism had proven that emotive elements could be mustered against tolerance and rationality, Ascher was willing to move increasingly closer to conservative pragmatism to sustain his countervision. After the *Burschenschaften* and romantic nationalists started clashing with reactionary regimes around 1815, Ascher—who had started out with Jacobin sympathies—came to express his affinity with the governments that were suppressing the nationalist political student organizations. Shortly before new censorship laws were enacted in the Carlsbad Decrees (1819) in reaction to Kotzebue's assassination, Ascher addressed a short piece to the Federal Assembly, which laid out his plan for a "limited freedom of the press" for Germany. He urged the censorship of any text that expressed insolence toward religion or good morals. Anticipating that such wide-reaching restrictions on the freedom of speech might be abused by governments hoping to deflect legitimate criticism, Ascher proposed that censorship should apply only to the form, but not the contents, of publications: All authors should limit themselves to speaking like "a man of truth, simple, unadorned, modest, and in earnest."[116]

Caught at the end of his life between the repressive system of Metternich and nationalist reactions to his style of politics, Ascher became increasingly anti-romantic to the point of proposing the prohibition of the satirical style he himself had practiced in much of his earlier writing. Ascher's anti-Catholicism formed part of this anti-romanticism, and both were part of his rationalist, pluralistic, and cosmopolitan vision of society. His confessional politics adopted a particular Protestant language of anti-Catholicism to plead for a denominationally neutral form of secularism. In this sense, Ascher argued less against Catholicism than against something he described as the Catholicizing tendencies of Protestant nationalist romantics. The use of the term *Catholicizing* served as a code for the potential of any religion to stir the uncontrolled emotions of the population in support of an integral nationalism. Here the otherwise exceptional Ascher was typical of many self-declared progressive Jews in nineteenth-century Germany: Catholicism remained less an interlocutor or even an immediate enemy than a convenient argument in the direction of his true opponents, Protestant nationalists.

Heinrich Heine: Anti-Catholicism with a Transparent Mask

The shifting symbolic valence of anti-Catholicism becomes particularly visible in the works of Heinrich Heine, who lived and published in both France and Germany, where his denominational politics were differently received and took on different meanings. To put the difficulties of his border crossings—between Germany and France as well as Judaism and Protestantism—into stronger relief, I will focus on the decade after Heine's conversion to Protestantism, when he first relocated to the French capital. In his attempts to use denominational differences while also destabilizing them, Heine's works illuminate how debates on Catholicism and secularism could reflect a particularly Jewish predicament. His writings expose the entanglement of the poetics of emancipation with debates on Catholics, European secularism's other Others. What is more, unlike Salvador, Halévy, and Ascher, Heine became a true celebrity and gained a wide audience in both France and Germany among Jews and non-Jews alike. By exposing the many divergent readings and misreadings his work encountered across national boundaries, Heine's work allows us to further explore the similarities and differences of anti-Catholicism on both sides of the Rhine. Whereas the German reception of Salvador and Halévy's works illuminates the challanges of crossing these boundaries from west to east, Heine's case demonstrates the difficulties of translating these polemics when texts and individuals moved in the opposite direction.

Heine, who famously mocked Ascher as a dry preacher of Enlightenment reason—with "abstract legs and wearing a suit of transcendental grey color"—nevertheless shared with the object of his derision a mistrust of the political message of romanticism.[117] While the two drew fundamentally different conclusions about the aesthetic appeal of Catholic forms, both took a critical distance toward Catholicism for political reasons.[118] In contrast to Salvador, Halévy, or Ascher, however, Heine employed anti-Catholic polemics against the background of his attempts to perpetually rewrite his biography. These attempts at personal reinvention were based on his conversion to Protestantism in 1825, a step he struggled with from the start and that he took mainly to gain employment as a civil servant. Although his baptism crucially shaped his later anti-Catholic polemics, the true turning point in his approach to denominational politics occurred only in the wake of a number of conflicts in which he became embroiled later in the same decade.

One such conflict revolved around a sympathetic review Heine had written of *Die deutsche Literatur* [German Literature] by Wolfgang Menzel.[119] Heine had applauded Menzel's Protestant nationalism, which Metzel had expressed by denouncing Catholicism as servile and eternally bound to the past. In reaction to this review, which intervened into the denominational conflicts between Catholics and Protestants, Heine became the target of an influential leader of conservative Catholicism in Munich, Ignaz Döllinger, a priest, theologian, and publisher of the Catholic journal *Eos*. Döllinger's main tool of criticism against the well-known Jewish convert was anti-Jewish prejudice. He sought to discredit Heine's anti-aristocratic and egalitarian philosophy in a series of pungent comments on the monetary orientation that Heine "must have acquired with his mother's milk," making reference to Heine's inalienable Jewishness.[120] Another review in *Eos* from the same period, possibly penned by Döllinger as well, challenged Heine's identity as a Christian. The Catholic paper depicted Heine as a man who had "neither religion nor fatherland"; Heine was a man who lost his religion because "he became stuck in the chasm between abandoning an old belief and accepting a new one."[121] A central issue that Döllinger and his colleagues addressed with their anti-Jewish diatribes was the right of a non-Christian to enter into the debates between Catholics and Protestants. Depicting Heine alternately as a Jew and a person who had no authentic identity, they implied that the former Jew was not authorized to be anticlerical or anti-Catholic in public.

Shortly after facing Döllinger's comments, Heine engaged in a new controversy with August von Platen, a poet whom Döllinger praised enthusiastically in his publications.[122] Like Döllinger, Platen attacked

Heine as a Jew, humiliating him with anti-Jewish insults in his play, *Romantic Oedipus*. Given Döllinger's sympathy for Platen, Heine identified him incorrectly with the clerical anti-Jewish campaign in the Munich *Eos*.[123]

Heine's sense of a Catholic cabal working against him inspired a change in his approach to religion. Identifying Catholicism as the force driving his political and personal enemies, Heine discovered a new strategy during an extended trip to Italy. Whereas his conversion to Protestantism in 1825 was a pragmatic move, he now started to reinterpret his choice as a potential basis for another step: the appropriation of a Protestant version of anti-Catholicism for political purposes. We can see early indications of this change in his letters from this period, which report on his negative impressions during his travels in Italy and his intention to cultivate these resentments. Writing from the Baths of Lucca, which later became a central location for volume three of his *Reisebilder* [Travel Pictures], Heine wrote to his friend Moses Moser: "My love for human equality, my hatred against the clergy was never stronger than now, I have nearly become one-sided because of it. But to act people must be one-sided."[124]

Although Heine had previously been unable to find a voice in the conflicts between Catholics and Protestants, he now discovered a new means of "taking sides." Heine's most pronounced anti-Catholic polemics before he moved to France appear in "Die Stadt Lucca," which he began around 1829 during his travels in Italy and completed in 1830, while in Germany.[125] In this story, published in the fourth volume of his *Reisebilder*, Heine's confessional polemics, or, rather, his trained one-sidedness, became an integral part of his program of political, aesthetic, and personal emancipation.

The main target of Heine's sarcasm in "Die Stadt Lucca" was state-supported religion, which, he suggested, ultimately worked to undermine the state, damage religion, destroy freedom, and hinder the revolutionary unification of Germany.[126] Heine portrayed denominational conflict as the result of the politicization of religion, blaming these conflicts in turn for the weakness of his imagined fatherland. Curiously, his text nevertheless engages in precisely the type of religious politics that he rejected. While condemning religious division, Heine was anything but a neutral or even-handed critic of all religious fanaticism. Although Heine claimed at one point in the text that his observations might apply to "the whole diplomatic corps of God"—including rabbis and muftis—his main criticism was directed against the Catholic Church, whether in Germany or Italy.[127] Heine never wrote anti-rabbinic polemics that used the type of language found in his descriptions of the grotesque physiognomies of Italian priests (even if physical features appear in his satirical characterizations of Jews as well).[128]

At the same time, Catholicism was not a single entity for Heine. In some passages, Italian Catholicism is the butt of his criticism, while in others it served as the positive counterexample to German Catholicism. When Heine commented extensively on the disfigured faces of the Italian Catholic priests he claimed to have seen in a procession, for example, he depicted the Italian clergy as representatives of all Catholicism. In another passage, he argued that the Catholic clergy was less hypocritical in Italy than in Germany. Whereas German clergy tried to pretend they were as pious and unblemished in their private life as their public position made them seem, Italian priests knew their flock had no problem with hearing their sermon even after having found them drunk "in the muck of the street" the previous night.[129]

Heine described this peculiar form of a double life with particularly vivid imagery. According to Heine, Italian priests had a better sense of irony; they didn't mind what he called the "transparency of the mask" [*Durchsichtigkeit der Maske*].[130] The Italian clergy pretended to be dignified representatives of God, even as they pursued illicit pleasures in plain view. These priests were openly dissimulating in their official function and thus not dissimulating at all; their transparent masks hid nothing but rather symbolized a shared ironic understanding of human nature.

The idea of a transparent mask, which appeared only once in the text, also serves as a useful metaphor to describe the way Heine depicted himself as a Protestant and how this literary pose affected his criticism of Catholicism. Unlike the discussions of mimicry and masks offered in postcolonial writings from Frantz Fanon to Homi Bhaba, Heine's transparent mask defines a strategy of those who have the capacity to centrally shape hegemonic languages even if they do so from partially marginalized positions. The concept of the transparent mask is thus less applicable to the challenge of being autonomous in the face of colonization than it is about finding a stronger voice, in this case, by abandoning the uncomfortable role of Jewish poet in favor of a more complicated, and ambiguous, persona.

Nowhere does Heine's peculiar form of transparent masks appear as clearly as in the romantic scenes of his "Die Stadt Lucca." A key moment combining his religious criticism, his anti-Catholicism, and his idiosyncratic identity games unfolds as the narrator discovers his beloved Franscheska praying in a church. Franscheska is depicted as an attractive, sensual yet pious Catholic woman, who—as the readers of the earlier parts of the travel stories knew—was in love with the priest Cecco. The narrator eventually accompanies Franscheska, moved to tears by her prayers, through the empty streets of Lucca. Franscheska barely looks at him and remains in a kind of religious trance, her gait "gloomily Catholic."[131] Slowly, Heine entwines the description of religious acts with sexual innuendo. As Franscheska passes holy images she finds herself "crossing her head and breast; she refused my offer to help."[132] Suddenly, as they pass a marble Madonna statue, Franscheska kisses the narrator, whispering "Cecco, Cecco, caro Cecco!"—the name of the priest she loves.[133]

Heine's narrative voice explains: "I accepted these kisses quietly, although I well knew that they were intended for a Bolognese *abbé*, a servant of the Roman Catholic Church. As a Protestant, I had no qualms in appropriating the goods of the Catholic clergy, and on the spot I secularized Franscheska's pious kisses. I am aware that the priests will be furious about this; they will certainly clamor about theft of church property, and will wish to visit the French law of sacrilege upon me."[134] To the narrator's disappointment, Franscheska slams the door in his face once she arrives at home and proceeds to offer repentant prayers well into the night. Standing in front of the door, the narrator Heine's alter ego, combining Catholic with erotic imagery, makes the ultimate offer to his beloved:

> For this single night, if you will grant it to me, will I become a Catholic—but for this night only! O beautiful, blessed Catholic night! I would lie in your arms, believing like a pious Catholic in the heaven of your love; with our lips we will kiss and gain the lovely confession that the word will become flesh, faith will become tangible in form and substance; what a religion! You priests [*Pfaffen*] celebrate your Kyrie Elei-

son, [. . .] that is the body!—I believe, I am blessed, I fall asleep—but as soon as I wake the following morning I rub sleep and Catholicism out of my eyes, and once more see clearly into the sun and into the Bible. I am once again reasonable and sober like a Protestant.[135]

Thus in "Die Stadt Lucca," Heine—the Jew who was troubled by his conversion to Protestantism—had his narrator assume the role of Protestant who contemplated a temporary conversion to Catholicism so that he might gain the favors of a sensual Catholic woman. Heine's carnivalesque approach to religious affiliation has a clearly symbolic value in these passages. By satirically undoing Catholicism, he distanced himself from the politics identified with it while at the same time hinting at his fascination with Catholicism's aesthetic and sensual elements.[136] The "secularization of Franscheska's pious kisses" can be understood as a metaphor for his attempt to appropriate the emotive immediacy of religious forms for a churchless politics.[137]

At the same time, Heine's satire stylized Catholicism as the exotic Other, which allowed him to appear to his audience as a Protestant rather than a Jew through the person of his Protestant narrator. His discussion thus implicitly shifted from the opposition between Jews and Christians to one between Protestants and Catholics, as he wrote himself into the position of the insider. Paradoxically, Protestantism, which he identified primarily with rationalism, became his ticket to experiment with sensual pleasure in the narrative. The emancipatory hope of the story (expressed from an exclusive, masculine perspective) is encapsulated in the promise that the Jew-turned-Protestant might be able to fulfill his carnal desires.

Heine was well aware that he could not convince a German audience to forget his Jewish origin, which several reviewers at the time had noted in their critiques of his writings.[138] Not only did Heine have no illusions about his readers' perceptions of his past, but their lingering suspicion that he was still somehow Jewish was in fact essential to the satirical thrust of the text. Like the Italian clergy in his description, Heine wore a transparent mask. His claim that as a Protestant he had a right to Franscheska's kisses was in fact a simultaneous gloss on Protestant self-confidence, the Catholic clergy's collaboration with restorative powers (in the 1825 French law of sacrilege that he cites), and, most important, his own attempts to escape his critics' tendency to reduce him to his religion of birth. Heine claimed to be Protestant for comic effect and satirized the very act of donning masks. Drawing on the tensions between Catholics and Protestants prevalent during the period in which he wrote, Heine exposed the entanglement of citizenship, social position, and public religious identity that precipitated his conversion.

Heine's satire was made both rich and enticing because of the omnipresent possibility of being recognized under the mask. Like the ironic Italian priests of his story, whom he admired for their sexual adventurousness, Heine did not mind the transparency of masks. "Die Stadt Lucca" works with the assumption that his readers would grasp the fact that Heine inhabited a strange position as not quite Protestant, not quite Jewish, and clearly not Catholic.

This strategy made sense in the context of the tensions between promoters of the emphatically Protestant and Catholic visions of politics that had been on the rise in Germany since the romantic period. In Heine's hands, these debates between proponents identifying in some way with one or the other Christian denominations became an opportunity to challenge his marginal status. Put otherwise: Heine's anti-Catholicism was not just a way of critiquing Protestant nationalism, as it had been for Ascher, but was instead closely entangled with his perception of his fundamental predicament as a former Jew.[139] Using anti-Catholic tropes as the basis for an emancipatory attempt to re-imagine himself as a desirable seducer and rational man, Heine did so from a position that was both obviously unsustainable and purposefully undermined by his own prose. In this way, Heine both reinforced anti-Catholic stereotypes and used them to unhinge the very system of confessional differentiation that allowed for this stereotyping to operate in the first place.

The French Reception of Heine as Protestant Author

The evolving literary and political valence of Heine's anti-Catholicism as well as the different role denominational polemics played in Germany and France come into clearer focus if we compare the very different reception of his work in these two countries, as well as his own reactions to the different interpretations of his oeuvre and religious identity in each context. In Germany, Heine had to face various reviewers who regularly reminded his readers of his Jewish origin and denounced his attempts to appear Protestant as purely instrumental. This was not the case in France, where the press was initially more willing to accept Heine's self-presentation as a Protestant. Although a few important French commentators, including the historian Edgar Quinet, noted Heine's Jewish origins, others described him simply as a Protestant.[140] In 1835, the critic Philarète Chasles—Halévy's fellow author in the Lecointe book series—wrote a portrait of Heine in the *Revue de Paris* in which he condemned the German author's destructive "Protestant spirit," for example.[141] Whereas Chasles may have intended his insult as a metaphorical one—much as Ascher used the label of Catholicizer—another reviewer in the same journal was more clearly misguided in his interpretation of Heine's background. This reviewer attempted to explain Heine's anti-mythical and—implicitly—his anti-Catholic inclinations as the result of his supposedly Protestant upbringing.[142] Another anonymous reviewer for *La Quotidienne* even attacked Heine for daring to make anticlerical comments as a Protestant.[143] Such misunderstandings should hardly surprise us, however. First, Heine was seen less as a Jew and more as a German in France—where Germany was associated with Protestantism. Just as importantly, Heine himself did everything he could to keep his religious affiliation ambiguous in his new home.

In fact, Heine was unwilling to accept either a straightforward ascription as Jewish or as Protestant. In reaction to a comment issued in the *Journal des débats* that identified Ludwig Börne (1786–1837) and Heine as Jewish liberal leaders, Heine responded in a letter to the editors of the French periodical that "he did not belong to the Jewish religion" and "never set a foot in a synagogue."[144] The journal continued, "Member of the Community of the Confession of Augsburg, he [Heine] never renounced the title he attached to this respectable church, which does not simply profer spiritual bliss but also temporal rights in many German states."[145] In spite of these hints that Lutheranism offered certain pragmatic advantages in Germany, Heine's contemporaries could only understand this to mean that Heine had always been Protestant.[146]

Despite all of his efforts to be recognized as a Protestant in France, in a twist typical of Heine, the elusive author also rejected being identified as a believing Protestant in other instances. In 1833, the newly founded journal *L'Europe littéraire*, which defined itself as strictly apolitical, published Heine's essays on German romantic literature on the cover page of its first issue. Perhaps reacting to the article's political undertone, the paper added a disclaimer to Heine's second article. Beyond clarifying that signed pieces did not represent the ideas of the journal, its editors also explained their choice of author: "Thus Germany finds herself judged by a Protestant writer, because, in our opinion, intellectual Germany needs to be presented to Catholic France from a Protestant perspective."[147] Heine chose in this case to resist a simple identification as a Protestant in France. He responded with an explanation of the nature of his confessional commitments in a foreword to the first German edition of *Zur Geschichte der Religion*. According to Heine, he had told the publishers of *L'Europe littéraire* that France was not Catholic while he was only nominally Protestant. This position, he continued, merely expressed "the fact that I have the pleasure of parading in the Lutheran Church book as a Protestant Christian, which allows me to voice any opinion in my scholarly books, even those that contradict Protestant dogma. The [journal's] comment that I was writing from a Protestant perspective, on the other hand, puts me in dogmatic shackles."[148] French readers could find a similar passage in the essays Heine wrote for the *Revue de deux mondes*.[149] There he remarked:

> Protestantism was for me not just a religion but a mission. For fourteen years I have been fighting for its interests and against the machinations of our German Jesuits. Later, of course, my enthusiasm for the dogma faded and some years ago I declared openly in my writings that my Protestantism consists only of being entered into the church register of the Lutheran community as a Protestant Christian.[150]

These statements are interesting for multiple reasons. Heine explained to his French readers once again his understanding of Protestantism as a political stance defined by its opposition to reactionary Catholicism, in this case epitomized by the "German Jesuits." Consequently, Heine dated his involvement in this mission to the beginning of his career as a writer and not to his formal conversion.[151] The German version, on the other hand, makes explicit some of the literary strategies underlying Heine's confessional polemics, which were not to be understood as denominational in the narrow sense. The last thing Heine wanted to be associated with was a Christian church. The French journal had misunderstood his self-presentation as Protestant to indicate his involvement in Protestantism as a confessional milieu or an expression of religious sentiment. In contrast, German commentators had either ignored Heine's claim to be Protestant, when they were positively disposed toward him, or criticized his attempts at masking his identity when they were not. Only certain French journalists, apparently unable to wrap their heads around Heine's provisional, politically instrumental Protestantism, took him seriously as a Protestant. Having accepted Heine's claims at face value, the editors of *Europe littéraire,* along with many French reviewers, reframed Heine's satire, turning slippery political humor, which aimed for literary effects above all, into a German expatriate's rather straightforward exercise in confessional polemics. Only in the face of these French interpretations did Heine feel compelled to make explicit that his nominal Protestantism was a strategically chosen identity that allowed him to take an oppositional stance in religious, political, and aesthetic matters.

The complicated shifts in Heine's public identity also speak to the ways that he adapted his literary and political strategies in response to different pressures—particularly as they pertained to his multiple religious identities. For a German audience, Heine could joke that he was drawing on his (newly acquired) rights as a Protestant in his description of his efforts to "secularize" the kisses of the Catholic woman he desired, trusting that the irony of the scene he portrayed would not be lost on his readers. Given the record of Heine's reception in France, however, the humor of episodes such as the Franscheska scene from "Die Stadt Lucca" must have remained largely impenetrable to a French audience with little sense of Heine's religious background. Believing him to be either Jewish or Protestant, or in other cases not thinking in terms of denominational divisions at all, many French readers were not privy to the complex religious past of a writer who remained strategically ambivalent in his denominational self-presentation. If Heine had been a believing, Church-oriented Protestant, both his flirtation with the violence of Protestant anti-Catholicism and his erotic stories might have seemed purely violent. The reviewer who complained in *La Quotidienne* about Heine's audacity to write such comments as a Protestant would have been right to be uneasy with the German author's choices.

Yet, in fact, Heine never wrote as a Protestant in an unproblematic way: His transparent mask had become opaque in the French context. The political intentions of his stories thus remained lost on an audience that could not see through his purposeful posturing.

Heine's frequent glosses on his texts also reflect the different character of denominational polemics in Germany and France. His attempt to discredit romanticism as a Catholic invention had a sharper tone in Germany, where his work reinforced the association between a rising liberal camp and Protestant milieus—all the while mocking the false universalism of Protestant secularism. In France, debates on the division between Protestantism and Catholicism were mostly fought between Catholic secularist liberals and political Catholics, whereas Protestantism served primarily a symbolic function in public debates. Nonetheless, certain French readers appear to have interpreted Heine's literary expressions as a form of denominational politics penned by a believing Protestant. Heine thus played a double game in the French context. On the one hand, he tried to continue his German polemics, which were based on concrete divisions between Christian denominations. On the other hand, he also hoped to rid himself of the identification as a denominational Protestant and tried, rather, to join those French authors who—like Halévy—announced their attachment to Protestantism as a symbol of progress.

Conclusion: Anticlericalism and Romanticism

Although Heine was, without a doubt, the writer who most tangibly crossed boundaries—between denominations and between countries—all of the Jewish anticlericals discussed here shared some element of creative self-redefinition and border crossing. What is more, they all enjoyed a privilege that the Jewish notables of Lauterbourg did not have. Romantic and anti-romantic anticlericalism was for the most part an affair of individuals who were hard to pin down, even though none of their anticlerical positions would have made sense without their will to oppose anti-Jewish agitation. Each of the individuals portrayed in this chapter was invested in an understanding of universalism that they tried to ground in Judaism while also moving beyond it. Ascher thus expressed Enlightenment positions, while Salvador and Halévy defended the liberal values of 1789 with an eye to doing more than simply making a point about Jews. Like Heine, they tried, above all, to create an enticing global interpretation of society that would change the way Judaism was perceived once religion and history were accepted as central resources of political debate.

The romantic reevaluation of religion and history also left certain legacies that differed from those of Salvador, Halévy, Ascher, and Heine. Indeed, there existed a small number of Jewish thinkers who—for different reasons—did not adopt liberal anti-Catholic ideas but instead championed Catholicism as a symbol or an intellectual tradition. Three such individuals can serve to illustrate the wide variety of opinions that were at odds with the thinkers discussed thus far: The most prominent figure of Jewish origin to invest political hopes into Catholicism was Ludwig Börne, another German in Paris. Like other liberals, he idealized the legacy of early Christianity and saw the Catholic Church as an heir to its promise. Börne became a supporter of the Catholic radical Félix de Lammenais, after the former ultramontane priest turned toward religious liberalism and socialism. He eventually translated Lammenais's programmatic exposition *Paroles d'un croyant* [Words of a Believer] into German in the hope of spreading the revolutionary gospel to German artisans in Paris.[152] Lamennais had spoken of an original Christianity based on equality that had been purposefully corrupted by a conspiracy of evil kings. A return to original Christian principles would go hand in hand with an end of the corruption of wage labor, he reasoned. In his polemics against his fellow expatriate and opponent Heine, Börne explained that Catholicism was not destroyed by enlightened critique but rather cleansed and thus restored as a political force for progress.[153] Although he remained uninterested in church organization, Börne adopted the arguments of Lammenais, which drew on a particular idealization of Catholic tradition.

Isaac Pereire (1806–1880), a prominent French financier who, together with his brother, ran the Crédit Mobilier bank and invested in various industrial projects around France, represents another version of this position. One of the Jewish followers of Saint-Simonianism, Pereire originally strove, together with fellow members of the emergent religio-political group, to create a movement that could viably compete with Catholicism. Even after the group dissolved, Pereire preserved the Saint-Simonian's interest in the Catholic Church as a corrupted institution that nonetheless had the potential, once it was returned to its purest form, to play a role in a rational reordering of society in the future. Like Börne and the romantic French left, Pereire had many good things to say about Jesus as a revolutionary but, unlike them, he was also willing to engage with the existing church hierarchy.[154] As late as 1878, Pereire tried to convince the pope to transform Catholicism into a religion of industry according to the Saint-Simonian model.[155]

Another Jewish thinker went beyond these other writers' romantic interest in a renewed Catholic Church and even had positive things to say about the Catholicism of his day. The young Aaron Bernstein (1812–1884)—later one of the most important journalists and newspaper editors in the German language—argued in the 1830s that Catholicism was close to Judaism because its councils allowed for a revision of dogmas. Protestantism, not Catholicism, was the stagnant religion because of its reliance on an unchanging text. Judaism and Catholicism, by contrast, were the truly rational religions because they could adapt to the demands of each era.[156]

This short review of the alternative positions Jews or former Jews adopted toward Catholicism makes clear that there is more than one story of the boundary-making efforts modern European Jews employed by making reference—and giving preference—to one or the other Christian denomination within their symbolic political universes. Indeed, even among the anti-Catholic Jewish writers of this generation, the positions individual authors took, as well as their reasons for doing so, were diverse.

The polemics of Salvador, Halévy, Ascher, and Heine demonstrate this diversity well, even as they also show us some of the limited options Jewish liberals faced when dealing with national belonging and secularism. In Germany, many anti-Jewish romantics, like Herder and Fichte, were also anti-Catholic. Ascher and Heine drew on the negative depictions of Catholicism that one could find among these romantic writers in order to mobilize their contemporaries against Protestant nationalism. According to Ascher, the Germanomaniacs were Catholicizers, while Heine eventually denounced romanticism at large as an outgrowth of Catholic irrationalism in *Die romantische Schule*. Although

Heine, as a self-styled Jewish-Protestant jester, was much more ironic in his anti-Catholicism than Aschwer was, the effect of their polemics were similar: Both authors attempted to use anti-Catholicism to combine a greater liberal vision with a means of ensuring their personal emancipation as members of a still vulnerable—and only partially emancipated—minority. Both writers used Catholicism as the stand-in for the irrational element in politics that had to be squashed (Ascher) or creatively managed (Heine). In this regard, they could expect positive responses from anti-Catholic German readers and interlocutors, even if their critique of romantic nationalism received a less favorable reception.

In France, anti-Catholic romantics were more likely to be friendly to Jews. The question surrounding the role Catholicism would play in state affairs became the pivotal challenge for the left and the right, with both Judaism and Protestantism serving as symbols for potential toleration and diversity or—in the case of Protestantism—for individualism. Salvador and Halévy were much more in tune with their environment than their German coreligionists were. Their anti-Catholicism was not aimed at undermining a particular exclusive version of nationalism but at inscribing Judaism into the project of a leftist romantic alternative to both enlightenment individualism and Catholic collective thought.

In both Germany and France anti-Catholicism formed part of oppositional politics but never in exactly the same way. Writers in each context were often aware of the polemics occurring across the border and identified with their broadly similar aims while also remaining conscious of their different implications. Often texts crossed linguistic barriers, most visibly in the case of translations, such as Halévy's translation of Werner into French, the German translation of Salvador's early French works, or with many of Heine's essays and stories, which were translated from German to French and, later, sometimes from French to German. Tracing how such works were read in contexts with different denominational configurations and different aesthetic and political fault lines shows us how the use of individual religions—Judaism, Protestantism, Catholicism—as political symbols created mutually intelligible new options and challenges for Jews in Germany and France.

Four Reforming Judaism, Defending the Family
Jews in Catholic–Liberal Conflicts at Midcentury

The 1840s witnessed conflicts between liberals and Catholics that shaped the political landscape of Western and Central Europe for the remainder of the nineteenth century. These conflicts radicalized the opinions liberals held on the topic of religion and created new expectations about the proper place and form of religious practices. Unlike secularist polemicists of the late eighteenth century, early nineteenth-century secularists were influenced by romanticism's idealization of religion and thus rarely promoted anti-religious programs. By the 1840s, liberals in both Germany and France declared their quest for a pure form of religion in tune with progressive cultural and moral sensibilities. Such a religion—they claimed—stood in contrast to the politically problematic religious beliefs and practices they still observed in their day. Although liberals sometimes pointed to Pietism and Lutheran Orthodoxy as examples of inadequate or inappropriate religions, Catholicism was highest on their blacklist.

In Germany, the renewed politicization of religion was initially the result of clashes between the Catholic Church and the conservative Prussian government. Prussia had been predominantly Lutheran until 1815, when it acquired the Rhineland, an area with a large Catholic and substantial Reformed population. Like various other states that became more denominationally diverse after the post-Napoleonic settlements, Prussia soon enforced a variety of policies intended to integrate its territory.[1] Among these was state legislation meant to facilitate marriages between Protestants and Catholics, which in the eyes of many Catholics in the Rhineland constituted a direct attack on their position in the new provinces. In fact, they alleged, because large numbers of Protestant men had relocated to the newly incorporated Rhineland as adminis-

134

trators, Prussian policies encouraged local Catholic women to marry the Protestant civil servants sent to the area by the Berlin authorities. The next generation would then follow the denomination of their fathers, leading to a slow dwindling of the Catholic population. When the archbishop of Cologne spearheaded a campaign to enforce a papal ban on all intermarriages except those in which both partners promised to raise their children as Catholics, the Prussian state retaliated. After the authorities arrested the archbishop in 1837, Catholic resistance — in particular from the local nobility — became increasingly politicized.[2] Although liberals were originally not party to the conflict, many found their own reasons to support the policies of the Prussian state against the Catholic resistors in this instance.[3] Although many liberals opposed the regime during this period, they were more wary of what they considered a church that manipulated its flock into a religion of subservience than of a state that made religious institutions subservient.[4] Later conflicts across Europe — especially those in the states with large mixed-denominational populations such as Switzerland, Baden, and Württemberg — followed this pattern. Conservative government policies suddenly dovetailed with the principled secularism of liberal nation builders.

Within a few years, the conflicts surrounding the 1844 pilgrimage to the Holy Coat in Trier sparked new outrage from liberals, who expressed their middle-class expectations about proper forms of religiosity by voicing their surprise and indignation when nearly half a million German Catholics flocked to venerate the holy relic. Seeing in this new popular piety a form of superstition rather than the moralizing religion they endorsed, many liberals were adamant that the modern pilgrimage appealed mainly to the uneducated lower classes. Equally important, they attributed the growth of such popular piety to the manipulations of the clergy.[5] With the new scrutiny of both the government and liberals toward Catholic practices and the policies of the Catholic Church, religion became one of the central political issues in Germany.[6]

In France, conflicts between liberals and Catholics also intensified with similar results. Anticlericalism became the defining question of a new group of thinkers on the left and in the center of the political spectrum in the 1840s.[7] The focal point of this latest French anticlerical wave was a debate on the university's ability to regulate the curriculum of secondary schools. Discussions about the so-called monopoly of the university raged in the press, in parliament, and in the lecture halls of the Collège de France. The historians Jules Michelet and Edgar Quinet revealed to packed audiences in 1843 how the Jesuits schemed against kings, society, and the institution of the nuclear family. The works they published, including the reprint of their lectures, *Des jésuites* (1844), became canonical in the European culture wars.

As in Germany, the debates that raged in France were not just about the formal relations between church and state but about the role of religion in society; as in Germany, conflicts surrounding ultramontane Catholicism shaped ideas about the proper place, and thus the proper meaning, of religion and religiosity. While women had also figured in liberal polemics against the Trier pilgrimage in Germany, in France the role of women and gender relations became central issues of anticlerical campaigns.[8] This interest in questions of gender and religion was both kindled and expressed by one work more than any other: Michelet's widely read *Du prêtre, de la femme et de la famille* [Of the Priest, the Woman, and the Family], published in 1845 (and later republished as *Le prêtre, la femme et la famille*).[9] The pamphlet, which went through nine editions in its first year, warned of the clergy's systematic use of women in its bid for state power.[10] Drawing on long-standing ideas about the clergy's disruption of a family-based sexual order, Michelet denounced celibate priests as men living in an unnatural state. In his view, priests were both perpetrators—because they sowed discord in normal families—and victims—because their celibacy made them vulnerable.[11] Lacking their own families, they became pawns in the hands of an ancient system of domination that Michelet called "Jesuitism."[12] According to Michelet's definition, Jesuitism controlled the church, using priests who were not actually Jesuits to accomplish its ends.[13] Faced with what he believed to be a systematic grab for power starting at the level of society's smallest unit, Michelet called for a battle to be waged over the soul of French families. That battle, he asserted, could be won only if the priests lost their sway over women. Only then would marriage once again be the stable institution that he imagined it had been before the encroachments of the Catholic Church. Only then could it be restored as the foundation of society.[14] To justify his warnings, Michelet offered an exemplary story of the decomposition of familial life through clerical intervention but also of the redemption that was possible through love. Love, in the form of marriage, education, and patriotism, was to become the glue of society and to deflect the constant attacks of Jesuitism.[15] Michelet also believed love to be a crucial element in a rationally organized world: Sentimental attachment at home made rational actions possible in public. Such gendered visions of public and private, and of sentiment and rationality, became mainstays of anticlerical liberals across Western and Central Europe.

The discovery of politicized and sentimentalized religion as a central tenet of liberalism in Germany and France occurred at a moment when Judaism was also experiencing massive transformations. In at least two respects the 1840s were a turning point in German and French Jewish history. First, the rise of a large number of Jewish periodicals throughout the 1840s substantially reshaped and expanded Jewish public spheres in Europe and beyond. The Jewish press changed the way that Jews in both national contexts came to relate to each other and articulate their common interests.[16] Second, the 1840s saw the rise of a broad movement among German Jewry to reform religious life. Although reforms of synagogue services had begun already in the 1810s, it was only with the increase in reform-oriented associations and the Rabbinic Conferences in Germany in the mid-1840s that the movement found a wider popular base.[17]

Both phenomena were part of a longer history of Jewish embourgeoisement. During the hundred years that passed between the late eighteenth and the late nineteenth century, increasing numbers of Jews in Germany and France alike moved from a state of general impoverishment into the middle classes.[18] Their periodicals and voluntary organizations—including new synagogue communities—offered forums that nurtured a new, often aspirational, middle-class habitus.[19] These new organizations and media restructured the ties that Jews had both within and beyond the nation. The various weekly and monthly periodicals that appeared in Paris and in the mostly Protestant German cities of Magdeburg, Berlin, Leipzig, and Hamburg all created new spaces for discussions of religious and political topics and involved more participants with a stronger sense of connectedness than had been the case in the previous decades.

This chapter explores how politically engaged Jews in Germany and France both reacted to broader debates about the role of Catholicism in society and began to embody and espouse middle-class religiosity in new ways throughout the 1840s. It suggests that we cannot understand such major transformations as the Jewish reform movement, the preoccupation of Jewish leaders with women's religiosity, and minoritarian understandings of secularism without taking the religious conflicts that preoccupied the non-Jewish world into consideration. Although Jews did not adopt the new discourses of anti-Catholicism and anti-Jesuitism in full, many nonetheless found aspects of such anticlerical language helpful as they attempted to reenvision and reshape their role in society.

The attempts of Central and Western European Jews to imagine themselves as practitioners of a middle-class form of religion are part of a broader story of the Catholic–secular conflicts of 1840s Europe. Yet, these conflicts took different forms in different national contexts. In Germany, the principal religious transformations Jews experienced emerged as a result of the growth of Reform Judaism. While no such movement took root in France, Parisian Jewish journalists and public intellectuals remained equally interested in finding new politicized ways of speaking about religion throughout the decade. They did so by focusing their energies on what they considered to be a communal battle for the "souls" of Jewish women and, eventually, through a more overtly polemical engagement with conservative Catholicism as well. Examining the similarities between German and French developments during this period sheds new light on how the first wave of *Kulturkämpfe* shaped a common language that would soon inspire Jews' perceptions of a global conflict between liberalism and Catholicism.

Deutschkatholiken, Jewish Reforms, and Secular Religiosity

The decade of the 1840s was a period of religious dynamism across different denominations in Germany. Just as Jewish laypeople and rabbis began to speak of liturgical reforms and organized new synagogue associations, new religious groups emerged within both Catholicism and Protestantism. On the Protestant side, the Lichtfreunde combined the congregationalism familiar from Anglo-American evangelical religion with an emphatic rationalism. In places like Mannheim, these groups invited unbaptized Jews to join their ranks, although Christian members generally hoped for the conversion of their Jewish members at some point in the future.[20] The group that appeared among Catholics eventually had an even greater influence on German Jews, many of whom found the idea conveyed in the name of the new group— the Deutschkatholiken, or German-Catholics—particularly attractive. The Deutschkatholiken originated in the protests of the (suspended) Catholic priest Johannes Ronge (1813–1887) against the exhibition of the Holy Coat of Trier. In his open letter to Bishop Arnoldi of Trier, Ronge attacked the mass pilgrimage to the relic as a form of idolatry, describing Arnoldi as the Johann Tetzel of the nineteenth century.[21] In the aftermath, independent church groups coalesced around Ronge with the intention of creating what they envisioned as a modern and rationalist alternative for Catholics.[22] The small church communities they founded were interdenominational in orientation and emphasized individual freedoms. Among the areas that developed the strongest presence of these dissident communities were Silesia and Saxony, even though large meetings and individual conversions were also recorded in other German areas. The group's independent church communities quickly became the base and medium of social protest in these regions, while its avowed rationalism also attracted the interest of non-Catholic liberals.[23]

Although the Deutschkatholiken did not create significant enduring organizational structures, they became a topic of political debate that changed the way that German liberals came to imagine and articulate their political and religious positions during this period.[24] In the face of this pluralization of religion through the emergence of new progressive religious groupings, many liberals began to offer their support to independent church organizations. The early Jewish reformers were influenced both by this general environment of religious debate and in particular by the Deutschkatholiken. The group was Christian in its rituals, but the fact that it had parted from the Catholic Church with an anticlerical, liberal message gave it an air of universality that appealed to Jews searching for an accessible religious experience. In this regard, the attraction of this new Catholic movement for many German Jews was similar to the interest certain middle and upper-class French Jews had shown in Saint-Simonianism a decade and a half earlier.

Among the movement's earliest admirers was the Jewish writer Berthold Auerbach (1812–1882), who encountered the group shortly after his *Schwarzwälder Dorfgeschichten* [Village Stories from the Black Forest], published in 1843, earned him fame across German-speaking lands.[25] His stories depicted a basically harmonious rural society, where different religious groups were integrated into a civic life built on tradition and neighborliness. Like many of his contemporaries, Auerbach was fascinated by the promise of inclusiveness offered by Ronge's program, which seemed to represent a model of a democratic religion in tune with the world Auerbach created in his fictional stories. After hearing Ronge preach to a large crowd in Weimar in December 1845, Berthold Auerbach wrote enthusiastically about the movement to his old friend Jacob Auerbach that the Deutschkatholiken "can become the true deliverance of humanity and also of the Jew."[26] Auerbach was certainly captivated by Ronge's charismatic leadership and the movement's emotive appeal. Like many other German liberals, he was also fascinated by the political implications of the new group's attempts to combine romantic, sentimental religiosity with rationalism.[27]

Similar concerns also found expression in the correspondence of Abraham Geiger (1810–1847), a scholar of Jewish intellectual history and one of the most influential Jewish religious reformers of nineteenth-century Europe. In a letter written to his friend David Honigmann in 1845, he commented that

> The *neukatholische* movement refreshes the spirit and makes it receptive to a new untarnished understanding of religion, even if I see it more as a demonstration of general liberalism against the interference of a power-hungry hierarchy into individual freedoms than as a religious-progressive movement [. . .]. It also inspires in other denominations ideas and decisions that are fertile [for the development] of a noble humanity and the purification of religious forms.[28]

Geiger understood the new Christian group as an expression of secular politics that resulted in a religious phenomenon. Like Auerbach, he believed that the Deutschkatholiken (whom he called "New Catholics") could serve as an inspiration for contemporary reformers of Judaism, who were beginning to organize new platforms with the aim of establishing binding norms for their nascent movement. In the same letter, Geiger also spelled out a concrete organizational plan for a Jewish reform movement. He put his trust in the efforts of his friend Sigismund Stern (1812–1867) as well as Berthold Auerbach, hoping that these two young Jews who had gained a certain renown would publicly declare their reformist agendas and thus serve as a catalyst for a productive schism within Judaism. Building implicitly on liberal fantasies of a mass defection from Catholicism, Geiger believed that the new Jewish group would eventually leave Jewish reactionaries isolated.[29] Even if Auerbach and Geiger did not intend to join the Catholic dissident movement, it nevertheless inspired their own articulations of an ideal version of reformed religiosity and liberalism.

During the same period, groups of Jewish laypeople began to come together in Frankfurt am Main and Berlin to create new reformed congregations. Sigismund Stern, whom Geiger had envisioned as a potential community builder, ultimately became one of the fathers of the association in Berlin, founded in March 1845 as the Genossenschaft für Reform im Judenthum [Society for Reform in Judaism], which transformed into the Berlin Reformgemeinde [Berlin Reform Congregation] in 1850.[30] Contemporary Jewish commentators continuously measured Stern's association in relation to the Deutschkatholiken and—indirectly—to the Catholic Church. As in the case of the Catholic dissident group, Berlin's Jewish reformers saw themselves as a free community of believers who opposed conservative religious institutions.[31]

Although there were good reasons for many observers to view Stern and his followers as somehow related to the anti-papal Christian dissenters, the exact nature of the parallels between the Jewish and Christian movements remained contentious.[32] The Berlin correspondent for one of the new reform-oriented papers, the *Israelit des 19. Jahrhunderts*, for example, explained that Johannes Ronge had created an immense tension and expectation among Jews until Stern had supplied the "tinder that would enflame this combustible material."[33] One month later, in the face of a series of anti-reform polemics in the Jewish press, the same author claimed that comparisons between Ronge and Stern were baseless. The main parallel, he argued now, was rather between Stern's detractors and the Catholic Church, which had also opposed the

Deutschkatholiken. Michael Sachs, a Berlin rabbi and a critic of Stern, had acted like the Roman Catholic hierarchy, the reform-oriented correspondent continued, "abusing the pulpit in order to make ridiculous and inappropriate insinuations."[34] After attempting to distance himself from the comparison he had once drawn between Stern and Ronge—a comparison that might have damaged Stern's credibility among certain Jewish readers—the correspondent for the *Israelit des 19. Jahrhunderts* now declared that the rejection of despotic institutions like the Catholic Church was the common denominator between reformers of different faiths.

Another Jewish paper, *Der Orient*, offered more ambivalent coverage of Stern's endeavors but was equally consistent in framing Jewish reform movements as an outgrowth of a religio-political moment that began with the liberals' anticlerical and anti-Catholic campaigns. The orientalist Julius Fürst (1805–1873), the journal's editor, published a whole series with documents produced by reformers in early 1845, optimistically entitling it, "The First Stirrings of a German-Jewish Church," modeled after the name of the German-Catholic Church.[35] Fürst even explicitly cited Ronge's innovations as the main inspiration for Jewish reformers.[36] The paper's correspondent from Breslau took the opposite route, criticizing Stern and other reformers, a fact that offers evidence of the wide range of opinions that could be voiced within a given periodical during this period. Yet the Breslau correspondent clearly agreed with Fürst that the Jewish and Catholic reformers were cut from the same cloth: He called the members of the Rabbinical Conference, which took place in his town, a meeting of "our Rongeanists."[37] He also mockingly spoke of "*Juden-Rongeanisten*" and "*Deutsch-Juden*," who, he suggested, were merely witnessing the "last fatal convulsions of the reform illness."[38] In another article, the same Breslau author argued that although certain Jewish reformers pretended to fight against powerful religious institutions within their own community, the end result was a mere parody of the "New Catholics."[39] He even went so far as to suggest facetiously that such individuals might soon refer to themselves as "Catholic Jews" [*katholische Israeliten*].[40]

These insults were an expression of public Jewish figures' commitment to enforcing new boundaries of communal belonging in the face of disorienting shifts in Jewish religious and political affiliations. Other reformers, such as Ludwig Philippson, who also acted as the first guest preacher of the Reformgenossenschaft's synagogue in Berlin in 1845, insisted on the difference between Christian dissenters and Jewish reformers.[41] Philippson had encountered the competition of the Protestant reformist Lichtfreunde in his hometown of Magdeburg, where he acted as rabbi. In articles and public lectures, Philippson argued that true reformers did not abandon revelation. The Lichtfreunde as well as the Deutschkatholiken, by contrast, had become caught up in their idealizations of the individual and were therefore simply new pagans.[42] Despite Philippson's attempts to deny any similarities between the Christian and Jewish reform movements of his day, his comments on the subject make clear that the claim that the different groups had influenced each other was common enough to merit an elaborate refutation.

A central aspect of the Jews' relationship to intra-Christian dissent was their dedication to German nationalism. One work that illustrates this concern in its most radicalized form is *Eine deutsch-jüdische Kirche die nächste Aufgabe unserer Zeit* [A German-Jewish Church, the Next Task of Our Time], published by an anonymous Candidate of Jewish Theology in 1845.[43] The pamphlet called for Jews to follow the Deutschkatholiken in their quest for a dynamic form of religiosity that was free of clerical oppression. The author developed this theme in comparisons between what he alleged were the crimes of "rabbinism" and those of the Catholic Church. Had the rabbis not opposed intermarriage just as much as the Catholic bishops had?[44] According to the author, the Deutschkatholiken freed the people of papist influence and thus raised the flag of true patriotism.[45] Similarly, Jews would only discover their true Germanness once they followed the example of the Deutschkatholiken and purged the despotic elements within Judaism, once and for all.[46] Like other writers of his day—both Jewish and non-Jewish—the author saw women as the victims of unreformed rabbinic law. The traditionalist rabbis' harsh rules and lack of true religious sentiment crushed women's "feelings of femininity," in his view.[47] Toward the end of his text, the young author issued a plea in which all the different themes of reform and oppression reappeared:

> Assemble, O you German men of Israel! Be true and express your inner conviction in a solemn declaration! Proclaim that you abjure rabbinism

and orientalism, that you are German and German in the fullest sense of the word! Your church is oriental and rabbinic no longer, but rather a *German-Jewish* one![48]

Even those critics who were uncomfortable with the anonymous theology student's insinuation that many reforming Jews were merely copying Catholic dissidents nonetheless agreed with his nationalist message. One commentator for the *Israelit des 19. Jahrhunderts* argued that the term *Kirche* was unfortunate in its implications but that he could subscribe to the idea that German Judaism was fundamentally different from other forms of Judaism, particularly its Polish incarnation.[49] Various Jewish reformers in Germany similarly expressed their investment in making their coreligionists at once more modern and more German during this period.[50] Their nationalism was another reason the model of the German-Catholics had such a broad appeal among Jewish reformers.

Even though some Jewish reformers refrained from making explicit references to intra-Christian debates, by the 1840s their project borrowed from a common language of religiously inspired liberalism that was originally formulated against new forms of Catholic piety. Jews who embarked on a collective enterprise to transform Judaism according to their standards of modernity thus necessarily defined themselves and their own actions according to the principal reformist religious movements of their time. In this sense, they did not adopt the rhetoric of the *Deutschkatholiken* so much as draw on a common liberal language that addressed religious practices and organization and politics in equal measure. As a result, engaging with Catholicism and its dissidents offered German Jews a means through which to articulate their vision of Judaism as a middle-class religion perfectly suited to the modern age.

Jews, Catholics, and Church–State Relations in Germany

While Jewish activists found the example of the new Christian anti-clerical groups inspirational, they remained, on the whole, reluctant to compare their political situation with that of Catholics. The few explicit comparisons Jewish authors offered to this effect tended, instead, to contrast the situation of Jews and Catholics, a trend that became more pronounced throughout the 1840s.[51] There were, without a doubt, reasons to see the political struggles of the two groups as separate. While Article 16 of the German Federal Constitution of 1815 guaranteed Catholics and Protestants equal rights before the law, in most German states Jews did not gain full legal equality until the last third of the nineteenth century. Whereas the Catholic Church existed under public law everywhere in Germany, Jewish religious institutions were officially treated as private organizations until 1847 in large parts of Prussia. In this context, many observers believed the aims of Jewish and Catholic activists to be diametrically opposed: The Catholic Church sought to regain some of the autonomous rights it had lost since the eighteenth century, while Jewish advocates argued that they had no particularistic political aspirations (such as the hope for a messianic restoration of a Jewish state) in order to prove worthy of full citizenship. The fact that Germans—Jews and non-Jews alike—adapted the term *emancipation* from British debates on Catholic rights in the 1820s to the Jewish struggle for legal equality remained an exception.[52] It was likely more palatable to Jewish reformers because it was not a domestic example. Within Germany, little connected Jewish and Catholic struggles over their relationship with the state.

These differences between Catholic and Jewish political aims became more meaningful the more Jewish intellectuals became invested in a Protestant narrative of world history. This was the case with individuals such as Sigismund Stern—the founder of the abovementioned Berlin reform community—whose example illuminates the role anti-Catholic polemics played for Jews who were socialized into Protestant liberal intellectual traditions. It also shows how far liberal anticlericals could take their ideas about the relation of religion and politics.

Born in a small town in Posen, one of Prussia's poorest provinces and one with a large Jewish population, Stern received a traditional Jewish upbringing before he was sent to a German *Gymnasium* and eventually enrolled at the University of Berlin as a student of philology and philosophy.[53] In 1835, he became the principal of Berlin's Jewish boys' school, after the historian of Jewry Isaak Markus Jost vacated the position. By the early 1840s, Stern had become one of the most prominent among a group of laymen who pushed reforms further than most rabbis had previously been willing to do.[54] The basic demands of most of the new reformers, such as those united in the Frankfurt Reformfreunde, were that Jews adapt traditional rituals to their understandings of modern, middle-class propriety, that they clarify that Jews no longer hoped for the messiah to return them to Palestine, and that they declare the Talmud invalid in legal matters.[55] Although Stern was sympathetic to such positions, he created a program that was even more far-reaching in its interpretation of state–church relations.

Stern's career as a reformer took shape in 1843, when he published an article demanding the acceptance of Judaism as a state religion in Prussia.[56] Although he did not make the comparison explicit in this text, Stern imagined an arrangement that replicated the French consistorial system.[57] According to Stern, Judaism was finally moving out of its medieval isolation into the stream of world history. As Jews became modern, two rival models were possible, according to him. They could become a religious group with its center of gravity outside of the state, thus remaining in permanent conflict with their country. This was the model of Catholicism in his view. Alternatively, Stern believed Jews could turn into a state organ and follow the pattern of Protestantism.[58] Judaism naturally followed the latter path, Stern argued. By taking this position, he joined an expanding number of Jewish reformers who had outlined what they believed to be the merits of Protestantism starting in the 1810s.[59]

In 1845, Stern elaborated his plans for the reform of Judaism in a series of highly popular lectures he gave in Berlin.[60] While other reformers had attacked the idea of a Christian state, Stern endorsed it and even pushed it further.[61] Repeating his earlier arguments to a wider audience, he claimed that Prussia was not so much a Christian as a Protestant state.[62] Even if there were other states that had a large Protestant majority, Prussia had the mission to become the pillar of Protestantism in the Christian world.[63] Trained in philosophy at the University of Berlin, Stern employed a Right Hegelian framework as he unfolded his Protestant view of religious world history to his audience. Christianity was a necessary offspring of Judaism, in his view, because the latter had been unable to overcome paganism in surrounding communities. Yet, over time, medieval Christianity increasingly acquired many pagan qualities, such as the distinction between priest and laity.[64] According to Stern, Protestantism had risen against these pagan elements and challenged the popes' desire for unlimited temporal power. Protestantism, he argued, reached the zenith of human and conceptual development with the Prussian state and the idea of statehood itself. When Protestantism restored Christianity to its purest form, Stern continued, it also released Judaism from its isolation, thus allowing the Jews to comprehend their universal mission once again. As he made these claims, Stern elaborated a Jewish version of a Protestant-Hegelian narrative in which Protestant Christianity prepared the final stage of Judaism's mission. Jewish philosophers—including Ludwig Philippson, Hermann Cohen, and Franz Rosenzweig—revisisted such a revised Hegelian account on their own terms over the next century.

Because Judaism was as capable of engendering loyal and rational citizens as Protestantism was, Stern suggested that Protestant Prussia should deal with Judaism as it had with Lutheranism: by creating a Jewish State Church. If Jews were to declare themselves a church in an autonomous act from below they would merely form a sect, he warned his listeners.[65] A Jewish church needed to be created by the will of the nation, as expressed by the state. Jewish communities thus had to be made subservient to the state to achieve legitimacy. Only then would the Jewish "church" enter "into the higher organism" of the state.[66] In all these respects, Stern noted, Judaism was different from Catholicism, which was unable to accept freedom of conscience and was always grounded in loyalties beyond the country's borders.[67]

Stern's plan relied on the fact that the Prussian government had begun to tolerate religious reform among its Jewish subjects, in contrast to its restrictive policies of the 1810s and 1820s. His proposals were, however, based on what was most likely his purposeful misinterpretation of the premise of these new opportunities. Reform in Prussia became possible in part because the central authorities were beginning to accept some of the claims of reformers and—more importantly—because the state showed itself increasingly indifferent to the religious activities of Jewish communities.[68] Indeed, as Michael Meyer has noted, there is evidence that the king's evangelical views and idealization of a corporate Christian state made him more welcoming to the internal fragmentation of the Jewish community.[69] In his correspondence with his ministers, Friedrich Wilhelm IV was primarily focused on having Jews govern themselves as part of his plan to reorganize Prussia along corporate lines. Having repeatedly expressed his desire to leave Jewish religious issues in Jews' hands, he eased the prohibitions against the creation of new, separate prayer houses, which had blocked Jewish reformers' efforts in earlier periods.[70] The Christian state proved less interested in the religious practices of its Jewish subjects, whereas liberal politicians and administrators who rejected the corporate state sought reforms that would allow the government to increase its supervision of rabbinical training and Jewish education.[71]

Stern was working with an unusual strategy in this situation because he did not turn to liberal discourses of natural equality but instead appealed to the romantic ideals that underpinned the king's plan for a Christian state. What he proposed was not a religiously indifferent state but that Prussia should become a Judeo-Christian, or, rather, a Judeo-Protestant state. Such a plan held little chance of success, of course, as Stern's contemporaries understood. In fact, when Stern's fellow reformers came together to realize his plan by forming the liberal Genossenschaft für Reform im Judenthum in 1845, his proposal to found a church proved unpopular, and the group limited its aims to the creation of a private association.[72] Although parts of Stern's vision were clearly unrealistic, his statism and his understanding of secularism were not so different from the positions taken by his peers. Like many others in his day—including his French Jewish contemporaries—Stern hoped for a secular order that would recognize Judaism as a proper agent of state building. In Stern's view, secularism did not mean separation. It was rather the reinvention of religion as a political and potentially national institution. While most Jews did not join Protestant intellectuals in their more aggressive anti-Catholic campaigns during this period, for many Jewish intellectuals in Germany such as Stern, anticlerical narratives nonetheless played a significant role in shaping their view of religion, good citizenship, and a tolerant secular order.

The Damascus Affair

Ideas about middle-class religiosity developed under different circumstances in France. Although France also witnessed the rise of lay piety and the growing popularity of religious language among political groups from the center to the left, no influential dissenting reform movements emerged either within Christian or Jewish circles.[73] As a consequence, the opportunities Jews in France had to imagine themselves as part of a liberal anticlerical milieu were distinct from those German Jews encountered during the same period. In France, both Jewish officials and independent intellectuals felt the impact of the new conflicts between anticlerical liberals and committed Catholics more keenly.

Several scandals and debates marked the path of French Jews into the midst of these conflicts. The turning point most frequently analyzed in the existing literature is the Damascus affair, the infamous blood libel case that took place in 1840 in the Ottoman city, at the time under the military control of Muhammad Ali of Egypt. The affair indeed became an important *lieu de mémoire* for French Jews, symbolizing a change in the history of Jewish relations to liberal and republican anticlericalism. From the start, the affair revolved around Catholic clergy: After a Capuchin friar and his servant were reported missing shortly before the Jewish festival of Passover in February of that year, the Jews of the city were accused of having killed the cleric for ritual purposes. Instrumental in the escalation of the incident was the local French consul, Count de Ratti Menton, who gave his support to the accusations. The governor of the city, Sherif Pasha, had members of the Jewish communal elite arrested and tortured with the aim of forcing their confessions. Two of the imprisoned men died in the process, and many others were maimed.[74]

Although the affair led to an outcry also among German Jews, only in France did it profoundly change domestic relations between Jews and members of different Christian denominations. As Lisa Leff has argued, it was during the affair that French Jews began to argue that France was not (or should not be) the protector of Christians abroad but rather of "civilization" writ large. From this moment on, Jewish politicians like Adolphe Crémieux (1796–1880), Jewish journalists like Samuel Cahen, and members of the Jewish consistories invoked the French civilizing mission as they competed with conservative Catholics over issues of foreign policy. To the extent that liberal and republican universalism was by definition in competition with Catholic universalism, Jews can be said to have joined an anticlerical camp in greater numbers beginning in 1840.[75]

While the Damascus affair accelerated Jews' alliance building with anticlericals, it did not, however, lead directly to a rise in Jewish anticlerical polemics. In spite of Jews' renewed alliances with anticlericals, and also despite the fact that ultramontane Catholics like Louis Veuillot began agitating against Jews during this period, few Jews issued public comments about the actions of the Catholic Church during the affair. Indeed, most Jewish activists of the era pointed to the Christian origins of the blood libel and the effects of exporting flawed Western traditions abroad rather than criticizing Catholicism and the Catholic Church in particular.[76]

Only two French Jewish authors framed the affair in terms of Jewish conflicts with the Catholic Church, the conservative Rabbi Lion Mayer Lambert (1787–1862), and the textile merchant Auguste Fabius (1804–1885). Although the responses of each of these writers to the Damascus affair were unusual for Jews of this period, their statements on the topic nonetheless illuminate new possibilities for Jewish polemics against Christianity and the Catholic Church. Of the two, only Lambert could claim to speak for wider segments of the French Jewish population. Known, among other things, for serving as the first principal of France's rabbinic seminary in Metz (1829–1838), Lambert also authored a Jewish catechism that rejected liturgical reform.[77] Following the precedent set by Salvador and Halévy, Lambert published his polemics in a short history of the Jews from antiquity to the present, albeit in one aimed at a principally Jewish readership.[78] A political liberal, Lambert celebrated the civic achievement of the French Revolution while condemning its excesses.[79] Although he understood his own era as an age of toleration, he believed the agents of this new age were limited to the government and the upper classes, which nonetheless had to share their streets with the fanatical members of the lower classes who still belonged to another age.[80] Lambert consequently considered it his mission to educate those with less refined sensibilities and to enlist religion for that purpose. A powerful rabbinate was a crucial part of this vision. Even in the widest sense of the word, therefore, Lambert was hardly an anticlerical: He believed that only rabbis and other members of the clergy were willing to defend revelation and spread true spiritual civilization through tolerance.[81]

The Damascus affair appeared to confirm certain tenets of Lambert's worldview while contradicting others. While it convinced him that much work had to be done to complete the task of civilizing the world, the torture of innocent Jews also exposed a moral weakness in the ranks of both the European upper classes and their official representatives. Like others who saw their faith in progress and the state challenged during this moment, Lambert explained the calamity by pointing to dark forces scheming behind the scenes. While Lambert portrayed Capuchins and other monks as the main culprits in the transmission of anti-Jewish blood libel accusations, he nonetheless alleged that the true schemers continued to remain hidden. With generous doses of hyperbole Lambert wrote that the year 1840 had revealed "the most criminal and savage project since the creation of the world" and one that entailed "nothing less than the extermination of all Hebrews from the surface of the globe."[82] His only explanation for the recent developments was a conspiracy, which he expressed in terms that could only be understood as an accusation against the Jesuits. According to Lambert, Father Thomas, the monk who had gone missing in Damascus, was quite possibly still alive in a convent somewhere. Alternately, Lambert proposed, if Father Thomas was indeed dead, the very same people who had constructed the story might have in fact killed him. He explained, "One knows the maxim of the Jesuits that the aim sanctifies the means."[83] Reviewing various possible scenarios, he concluded that "one no longer needs to convince the sensible reader that this is a conspiracy devised by a secret society *which has its seat in Europe.*"[84]

As he issued such statements, Lambert was one of the few French Jews of his day to embrace a paranoid style of religious politics.[85] His anti-Jesuitical polemics shared much with the discussions of liberals who contrasted Jesuit practices with their vision of a positive secularist religion. Even though he was a conservative in religious matters, through his polemics, Lambert nonetheless embraced a central tenet of secularist religion. This was the idea that any true religion had to be a power for progress. His insinuations that the Jesuits were scheming to expunge the Jews from the face of the earth was his attempt to make sense of the failure of the educated and powerful classes he had once trusted to protect the Jews. A voice from the center of the rabbinic establishment, Lambert shows the possibility of French Jewish forms of anti-Catholicism that were far from anticlerical in the broader sense. Indeed, Lambert was, in his own way, a proclerical anti-Catholic.

While his theories did not attract much attention from the general public, the statements of the much less prominent Fabius did, to the chagrin of the French Jewish elites who worried about the public image of their religion. Fabius, who, as a young merchant in Lyon, was something of an upstart and marginal to the Jewish establishment, gave two sermons in his local synagogue in 1842, the second of which critics perceived as being deeply offensive to Christianity and Catholicism.[86] The first person to draw attention to the printed version of Fabius's sermons seems to have been the editor of the *Archives israélites*, who denounced the publication to the "paternal authority" of the Jewish Central Consistory in January 1843, immediately after its appearance.[87] The Consistory made several inquiries about the sermons and their author but managed to keep the affair out of the newspapers.[88] This all changed once the anti-Jewish journalist Louis Veuillot began to attack Fabius's pamphlet in the pages of his periodical *Univers religieux*, claiming that Fabius should be considered antipatriotic and an enemy of the French people and state for daring to insult the religion of the vast majority of French citizens.[89]

As was true of many other liberals of the period, Fabius had indeed ridiculed representatives of the French state—the Damascus consul Ratti Menton and (by then former) Prime Minister Adolphe Thiers—but he had not in fact polemicized primarily against Catholicism. The thrust of his argument was instead primarily anti-Christian, as the minister of justice soon discovered after inspecting the pamphlet.[90] Employing a language that no doubt struck many in the audience as rather out of place for a Rosh Hashanah sermon, Fabius mocked Christianity for being a mere continuation of paganism. Fabius heaped onto Christianity a wide range of insults drawn from the quiver of nineteenth-century liberal religious thought, claiming that it was a materialistic, amoral, violent, irrational, deadening, and mystical cult that passed as proper religion. While his sermons were thoroughly anti-Christian in tone, certain passages could also be considered as a provocation toward the Catholic Church. Fabius, for example, repeated Lambert's claim that the Jesuits had been pulling the strings during the events of the

Damascus affair. In his words, former Prime Minister Thiers "wanted to have us forget that the whole horrible drama of the disappearance of a monk could only have been the infernal invention of the school of Loyola in order to assassinate [. . .] Jewish men with greater ease and under the cloak of [just] vengeance."[91]

The affair surrounding Fabius's sermons did not last long. Within a short time, the Jewish communal institutions publicly renounced Fabius's positions and explained that he had assumed an authority he did not in fact possess when he gave a sermon in a consistorial synagogue. His statements nevertheless came to haunt European Jews for the rest of the nineteenth century, as various Catholic antisemites—including the influential Prague theologist August Rohling—continued to refer to his work to prove the anti-Christian and anti-Catholic attitudes of Jews.[92] Fabius's statements also became the subject of two prominent libel trials in Austria and even forced the Central Consistory in France to clarify its position that Fabius lacked all authority in the Jewish community as late as 1884.[93]

Although Lambert and Fabius were both exceptional in their day, their approaches to anti-Christian and anti-Catholic polemics became increasingly influential for politically active Jews in France during the second half of the nineteenth century. Lambert may have been the first conservative Jewish voice to openly embrace an anti-Catholic position in nineteenth-century France, but he would hardly be the last. In the following decades, several other conservative Jewish journalists forged a similar path between religious traditionalism, liberal politics, and an avid opposition to the alleged anti-modern schemes of the Catholic Church. Fabius, for his part, remained less typical in his opinions, yet the long and checkered fate of his statements serves as a window onto the pressures Western and Central European Jews experienced from the mid-nineteenth century on. The Jewish communal elite's problem with Fabius stemmed less from the contents of his polemics than from the place he had chosen to announce them. Religiously infused political polemics were unacceptable within the synagogue. When Fabius attacked the religion of the majority within a Jewish place of worship, the Central Consistory showed that it was willing to use its authority to police the synagogue and to protect it against any attempts to use it as a platform for anticlerical or anti-Christian campaigns.

Crucially, both cases also illustrate how little the Damascus affair changed the character of Jewish polemics in mid-nineteenth-century France. Lambert was largely ignored, while Fabius was unanimously rejected by all official and semiofficial spokespersons of the Jews. The shift to a more aggressive style of anti-Church polemics came not when Jews felt most vulnerable and disappointed by their liberal allies but rather when they gained new confidence and discovered new anticlerical friends.

Anticlericalism and Conversion Fears in France

While the Damascus affair served as both a trigger and legitimation for Jewish anticlericalism in the long run, the more immediate incentive to use anticlerical language was the mix of romantic religion and anticlerical secularism that became fashionable among certain members of the French middle classes in the 1840s. The group most inclined to embrace an anti-governmental anticlerical vision wholeheartedly was originally rather small. It consisted mostly of ambitious individuals from a younger generation of French Jews, whom the historian Michael Graetz has put at the center of his account of the peripheral Jews (as he calls them) who helped to found the single most important institution of nineteenth-century Jewry, the international philanthropic organization Alliance israélite universelle.[94] Among these individuals were Eugène Manuel (1823–1901) and Isidore Cahen (1826–1902), the son of the editor of the *Archives israélites*, who studied with the doyens of academic anticlericalism such as Michelet, Quinet, and Adam Mickiewicz (1798–1855).

The wave of anticlericalism that hit France in the 1840s ultimately made ripples well beyond the circles of Jewish students. Due to a scandal that alarmed many Jews involved in communal affairs in 1845, a wide group of French Jewish authors and activists ended up embracing explicitly anticlerical and anti-Catholic polemics to guard against what they perceived as outside threats to their community. Various scholars have discussed this case—the so-called Terquem affair—to explain the anxieties French Jews expressed in the face of Catholic attempts to convert their coreligionists or as an example of the challenges of modern identity formation once religious boundaries became more porous.[95] Yet the case also offers a window into the way that French anticlerical secularism of the mid-nineteenth century shaped new concepts of religiosity and domesticity among Jews in France.[96]

The scandal started with the death of Dr. Lazard Terquem, a physician from Metz, who died in Paris in February 1845. Terquem had been an active member of the Metz Jewish community, teaching physics, chemistry, and natural history in the rabbinic seminary of the city throughout the early 1830s and offering his medical services to the institution's students free of charge.[97] He had also published a book about circumcision from a medical perspective in 1843 and taught on the subject at Metz's rabbinic seminary.[98] Yet Lazard Terquem's lifestyle was, as one author in the *Archives israélites* put it, "half-secular." Terquem had, in other words, both involved himself deeply in Jewish communal affairs and kept a skeptical distance from religious practice.[99] To the Jewish public, he was also known as the brother of Olry Terquem (1782–1862), a mathematician who had promoted far-reaching religious reforms—including the abrogation of circumcision and the celebration of Sabbath services on Sundays—in controversial open letters he had written under the pseudonym Tsarfati since 1821.[100]

In 1816, Lazard Terquem had married Rose Daniel, the daughter of an observant Jewish family from Verdun.[101] After twenty years of marriage, which resulted in four children, his wife converted to Catholicism together with their oldest daughter.[102] The couple moved to Paris, where their remaining two daughters were baptized. By 1845, only Lazard and his son remained Jews. In early 1845, Lazard fell seriously ill, and it quickly became clear that he was near death. According to both Jewish and Catholic sources, Lazard was baptized in this weakened state on February 15, 1845, by Abbé Théodore Ratisbonne (1802–1884), the most famous Jewish convert to Catholicism in France at the time. Lazard died two days later. In spite of protests from Jewish members of his family as well as the chief rabbi of Paris, Lazard was interred as a Catholic at Montparnasse cemetery. Questions over his burial marked the beginning of a well-publicized conflict about the role of priests in Jewish and non-Jewish family life.

Shortly after his brother's death, Olry Terquem sent an official complaint to the Jewish Consistory of the Seine, explaining his brother's domestic situation and asking for official support in halting the Catholic burial. Like many of the other texts produced in the debate that ensued, this document became known to the public through the Jewish and non-Jewish press, as well as through an independent reprint.[103] Olry wrote of his brother's tribulations, how he had abhorred Catholicism and had left Metz because he could not bear the shame of living in his hometown as part of a Catholic–Jewish couple. In Olry's interpretation, his brother's wife had been "of an extremely overbearing character," whereas his "poor brother had no force of character and was bent completely under the burden of his tyrannical companion."[104] According to Olry, Lazard was forced to make a deal with his wife: She could convert the daughters, but their son would remain a Jew.[105]

Olry was unambiguous about his brother's attitude toward Judaism and Catholicism. Just a month before Lazard's death, Olry wrote, the brothers had pronounced the Jewish prayer over the dead, the Kaddish, for their father in synagogue. He added that well through early February Lazard had "rejected in horror the mysteries and practices of Catholicism."[106] Olry claimed that his brother had prohibited all signs of Catholicism in his house because he considered them a form of idolatry.[107] But then sickness struck. Lazard's mental state had deteriorated quickly, Olry continued, and by February 15 he had been unable to recognize him. It was at this point, according to Olry, that Abbé Ratisbonne secretly baptized Lazard while Olry was distracted in the kitchen of his brother's house. Ratisbonne's only witnesses were eight Catholic women, which Olry considered inadequate. In his first open letter he explained, "Always the women! There was not one impartial witness."[108] In a letter to the *Courrier français*, Olry explained that Lazard had believed in divine unity, not trinity. This allowed Olry to assert with "mathematical conviction" that his brother was on his deathbed "still anti-Catholic to the highest degree."[109]

For all involved, female religiosity and family values were at the core of the issue. For Olry Terquem, female spirituality itself was not a problem. On the contrary, he explained that "the sole consolation for all members of our family [. . .] is to think that the best and weakest of husbands is henceforth protected by the angelic piety of his wife."[110] It was only "treacherous apostasy" that was unacceptable, he argued.[111] Terquem's main worry was Lazard's son, who was still Jewish and under the tutelage of his Catholic mother. He expressed his expectation that he—unlike the women in the family—would resist the influence of Ratisbonne's "coterie" because "there is Terquem blood in his veins, and I will not lose hope in his loyalty."[112]

These themes resonated with wider concerns of French political debate. In fact, around the very time of the scandal over Lazard Terquem's baptism, Quinet and Michelet held their lectures at the *Collège de France* condemning ultramontanism and Jesuit activity as threats to both the state and the family. The language of *Le prêtre, la femme et la famille*, which Michelet had published just before the scandal surrounding Terquem broke, immediately appeared in the Jewish press. Contributors to the *Univers israélite* and the *Archives israélites* had indeed noted the rise of Jesuit activity in France with concern before the Terquem affair and warned against what they labeled an ultramontane reaction.[113] Although they never spoke of a Jesuit conspiracy as had Lambert and Fabius, increasing numbers of Jewish contributors to Jewish periodicals began to refer to the threat of "Jesuitism," as Michelet had mostly famously done during the same period. This was the case despite the fact that the Jesuit order had nothing to do with the Terquem affair.[114] In the aftermath of Lazard Terquem's death, contributors to the *Archive israélites* and the *Univers israélite* became even more responsive to the anticlerical message emanating from the university.[115] In the *Archives israélites*, the Jewish bookseller and educator Gerson-Lévy (1784–1864), who had known Lazard Terquem personally in Metz, added long quotes from Michelet's text in his first report on the affair.[116]

Michelet's general warnings had pertained to the Christian family.[117] Gerson-Lévy appropriated his text, giving it a new meaning and urgency for Jews. While Michelet had painted scenarios of family discord in which young Christian women were lured to leave rationalism behind in exchange for a numbing obedience masked by the mysticism of the church, in Gerson-Lévy's scenarios the threatened women would also necessarily be abandoning the religion of their forefathers. French Judaism, like French society as a whole, in other words, would be unmade by women. In this type of discourse, women were portrayed as simultaneously too weak to resist the lure of priests and too strong or overbearing for their husbands, as in the case of Lazard's wife.

Crucial in this context was the notion of Catholic seduction, an idea that preceded the debates about the potential abduction and baptism of Jews often attributed to the Mortara affair of 1858.[118] Already in 1845, Gerson-Lévy issued a public appeal for the improvement of Jewish education, invoking the following scenario in light of the Terquem affair: "Fathers of families! This example has at least one positive result for us. It exhorts us to give our daughters a religious instruction that can shelter them from the sweet seductions of the first seminarian who comes their way."[119] As can be seen in this last quote, and unlike the debates concerning the threat proselytizers posed to the old and poor, discussions of women's vulnerability to conversion also allowed Jewish male activists to invoke sexualized images to bolster their arguments. The seduction they imagined was based precisely on those qualities they believed made Jewish women important for Judaism. In their rendering, Catholic priests had the ability to corrupt the potential for love that fueled women's religiosity and made them the ideal keepers of the Jewish family and home.

These ideas about female and male characteristics and the strategies that the Jewish community had to adopt to secure the integrity of the Jewish family found expression in multiple articles published during this period. One anonymous correspondent to the *Archives israélites*, for example, was critical of the fact that the affair had apparently given the French Jewish community free license to denounce feminine religiosity.[120] In his response, the paper's editor, Samuel Cahen, explained that he and Judaism as a whole had a deep respect for women but that he was nonetheless convinced that their "fertile imaginations" had to be dealt with in a realistic manner.[121] Ultimately, there appeared to be little space to challenge this depiction of women as naturally inclined toward religion (for better or for worse) within the French Jewish public of the mid-nineteenth century.

We might read all these comments on gender and the household as part of Jewish reactions to the real threat posed by conversions. If women were targeted by proselytizers, was it not natural that the Jewish community should react? Proselytism and conversions offer only a partial explanation of the impassioned pleas French Jews provided on the subject in a powerful contemporary idiom. As Todd Endelman has argued with regard to denunciations of female conversion in various European countries, these accusations tell us much about the commentator and little about conversion trends or the motivations of proselytes.[122] In fact, conversion records from the diocese of Paris do not show a significant predominance of female conversions during this period.[123] If we look only at the small sample for the period before the affair for which we have solid data from archival records (during the years 1837 to 1843), we find that only ten (48 percent) out of twenty-one converts from Judaism were women.[124] Of the fifteen converts who were adults, eight (53 percent) were women and seven (47 percent) men.[125] Celebrity cases make a big difference in public persecutions, of course, even if quantitative data does not confirm them. This may explain the tone of debates in the 1830s, when the conversion of men from the highest ranks of French Jewish society—such as David (Paul) Drach, Simon Deutz, and Theodor Ratisbonne—moved to the center of public attention and inspired a concern with treason and (male) responsibility.[126] The Terquem case of the following decade was, however, based neither on significant changes in conversion patterns nor on the case of a prominent woman's conversion. This absence is confirmed by a second conversion that followed quickly on the heels of the Terquem affair. A few months after Lazard Terquem's death, the Jewish community was shocked by the news that the wife and children of the Central Consistory's president, Adolphe Crémieux, had been baptized.[127] Even though Crémieux stepped down from his position in the Consistory as a result, the conversions of the women in his family did not elicit any debate on the level of the Terquem affair. Indeed, in response to this later development, the Jewish press issued only a few brief exchanges questioning the viability of Jewish communal officials whose close relatives converted to Christianity.[128]

The Terquem affair and the outpouring of anticlerical gender discourses it sparked, particularly in the pages of the *Archives israélites*, can be better understood in terms of the values that Jews found they could express in response to the questions the affair had raised. The Terquem affair did not simply articulate Jews' perennial fears that the Jewish community would dissolve once social boundaries between different religions started to weaken, in other words. Such fears were certainly present, yet—much like the ideas about Jewish political solidarity that emerged with the Damascus affair and crystallized with the founding

of Zionism later in the century—they were reinvented and reinvigorated when Jews discovered a political language that allowed them to
communicate their positions in terms that made sense to broader communities.[129] Jewish opposition to proselytism expressed in anticlerical
terms was part and parcel of mid-nineteenth-century French Jews' self-
understanding as defenders of Judaism as a middle-class religion—the
same notions that reformers in Germany endorsed as well.

This also explains why anticlericalism started to appear in the pages
of Jewish journals with a different—and less gendered—focus. In the
Univers israélite, Simon Bloch (1810–1879), for example, initially reported on the Terquem case in a tone similar to the one adopted by the
Archives israélites. Bloch, a self-declared religious conservative who attempted to instill in his readers a sense of pride in their Jewish heritage,
saw in the Terquem case an ideal opportunity to fulfill that mission.[130]
According to Bloch, Lazard Terquem was "a martyr of Israel whom the
French synagogue will keep in its holy and eternal memory."[131] Rather
than belabor the point about the demise of the family in the face of
female apostasy, Bloch quickly turned to a more traditional anti-Jesuit
line in his paper, a position to which he would return on many occasions over the following decades.

Several months after the affair first broke, Bloch published a three-
part article that exemplified his approach. It was entitled "The Jesuits,
the University, and the Synagogue."[132] In this essay, Bloch responded
to the statements of Pierre Louis Parisis, the archbishop of Langres, on
new state ordinances for the Jewish community in May 1844. According to Parisis, the Jewish community's silence in the face of regulations
that gave a secular character to their communal organization—by sub-
jugating Jewish institutions to civil oversight and allowing laymen to
dominate their consistories—proved that Judaism was no longer a living religion.[133] In his reply, Bloch compared the different relationships
of Judaism and Catholicism to the state: "In effect," he wrote, "if we
examine the organization of the Catholic Church closely, we necessarily
arrive at the conclusion that Catholicism is a separate and distinct institution from all other intuitions of the state. It has, as a consequence,
different interests than does [the rest of] society."[134] As a result, Bloch
argued, the church should be treated like a foreign state.[135] Even more
problematic, in Bloch's analysis, was the fact that the church not only

insisted on protecting its embassy, as any other state might, but that it also demanded immunity for all of its institutions, including its schools. Adopting an anti-Jewish theory from the eighteenth century that Jews were *in civitate* (in society) but not *de civitate* (of society), he concluded, "An exotic institution, the Catholic Church cannot take roots in the middle of another country; it may exist *alongside* of the state but is not *in* the state."[136] The loyalty of clerics rested abroad, Bloch claimed, adding that their members had no children to consecrate to the future of the nation.[137]

Jews, by contrast, made themselves entirely at home in their state because Judaism "must assure the welfare of all of humanity and penetrates into the blood of any society's life."[138] In short, while Bloch argued that those dedicated to the Catholic Church were to be held under suspicion for lacking loyalty, he ventured that Judaism was by nature patriotic.[139] In the aftermath of the Terquem affair, the *Univers israélite* presented Catholicism as a pernicious form of religious internationalism to underscore the loyalty that Judaism engendered. Bloch thus deflected many of the accusations of particularism direct at Jews by Catholic Frenchmen by attributing the same characteristics to the Catholic Church. Like Stern in Germany, Bloch viewed the Catholic Church's resistance to being subsumed under the umbrella of the nation-state as a necessarily unpatriotic position. Unlike his Prussian coreligionists, however, he used this accusation more directly in polemics against a Catholic opponent.

By the second half of 1845, only a few months after Lazard Terquem's baptism and death, the message the Jewish French press issued was clear: There were forces within the Catholic Church that worked transnationally to undermine the state, seduce the weakest members of society, and destroy the bonds of harmonious love that joined together the family, the Jewish community, and the state.[140] At the same time, the anticlericalism of these different Jewish papers was not anti-religious. Borrowing from the spiritualist anticlericalism of Michelet, contributors to the Jewish press attempted to design their own kind of religious anticlericalism, one that underlined their commitment to sustaining a Jewish identity in accordance with all they believed to be French. Inverting claims about Jews' status as disloyal outsiders within the nation, gendered discussions of Jesuitism as an international enemy conveyed

French Jewish men's sense of masculinity and allowed them to stake their claims as insiders to the nation.

Conclusion

Scholars often refer to the new forms of religiosity that developed in Western and Central Europe beginning in the early 1800s and accelerated in the 1840s as a middle-class form of religion. It is precisely within this context that they tend to speak of Jews' confessionalization. Reform Jews and many Orthodox Jews made great efforts to prove that Judaism was merely one denomination among others within the larger multidenominational context of their secular nation or state. This interpretation went hand in hand with a shift in the center of Jewish religious life from the male-dominated study hall to the home, family, and communal centers, a trend often referred to as the feminization of religion. This process offered new—if still highly circumscribed—roles for Jewish women.[141]

Many of these developments overlapped in the 1840s, as middle-class Jews in Germany sought to reform their religion while middle-class Jews in France began to adopt the anticlerical language of social romantics. The beginnings of the *Kulturkämpfe* changed the way participants in new Jewish public spheres, consisting of newspapers and lay associations, came to speak about Jews' interest in morality, nationalism, and modernity. This increasingly widespread approach to speaking about religion represented a particular form of secularism, which did not focus on freedom of religious expression.

Unlike earlier generations of reformers in Prussia who had suffered from the intrusions of an interventionist state, by the 1840s Jewish liberals of various stripes linked their arguments to liberal secularism to argue that their religion was capable of moralizing society in the service of the secular nation and state. Rather than suggesting that Jews had a right to forms of piety that were independent of the state's demands—a position reminiscent of the line of liberal Catholics during the period—Jewish authors and activists tended to argue that Judaism was compatible with a romantic-secularist project. Catholicism was less an interlocutor than a foil for imagining this romantic vision of a simultaneously secular and religious society.

In France, Jews expressed their attachment to this form of secularism in their polemics against proselytizers, whom they accused of undermining the very foundations of society. Anticlerical tropes allowed Jewish men to express their outrage at attempts to convert Jews in a language that resonated with the concerns of French secularists. This gendered, anticlerical language made the conversion of Lazard Terquem and his family a particularly appealing topic of debate. According to Jewish activists, proselytism required regulation because it threatened the general peace and the nation. As the lawyer Isaïe Bédarride, writing under the impression of the Mortara affair, put it several decades later: Among "well-policed nations" there was no reason to allow these attempts to manipulate the weak, such as women, children, or slaves.[142] The secular state, imagined as the arbiter between competing (private) religious claims, was also meant to protect certain individuals from the lure of boundary crossing. Liberal French Jewish activists imagined women both as a weak link that allowed for these boundaries to break down and as the element that allowed religion to survive within the family and thus among Jews and the French nation at large. Polemical secularism was, in this sense, aimed less at promoting individual freedoms than at securing the survival of Judaism as a useful religion in the context of the modern nation-state.

German Jews shared aspects of this approach to secularism. Throughout the mid-nineteenth century, Jews in the German states continued to fight against their continued exclusion from civic rights. While certain liberals still accused Jews of lacking the will and ability to assimilate, conservatives who rejected full Jewish citizenship as incompatible with their concept of the Christian state became Jews' more important (and in some respects, more convenient) opponents. Jewish journalists, rabbis, and active laypeople in Germany responded to accusations from both sides of the political spectrum with the claim that their form of Judaism—properly understood—allowed them to contribute to the moralizing of the general public and thus be part of the well-ordered society that both liberals and conservatives promised to establish. German Jewish publicists thus shared a basic assumption about the nature of secular citizenship with their French counterparts. The main difference at this point was that German Jewish reformers did not invoke anticlericalism to argue for state intervention as French Jews did.

Although Jewish intellectuals and activists in both Germany and France adopted anticlerical polemics during this period, they expressed little sympathy for the struggles of their coreligionists across the border. In spite of the many parallels in their campaigns, and Jewish periodicals' permanent adoption of texts drawn from both national contexts, most Jewish authors of the period do not appear to have perceived their activism as forming part of a common project. German-Jewish reformers' association with anticlerical dissidents did not resonate with their French coreligionists. Although French Jews undertook various initiatives to improve the decorum of synagogue services and to pursue a program of consensual liturgical modernization, most French "progressive traditionalists," perceived German developments as unnecessarily divisive—and thus ultimately opposed to their vision of Judaism's unified mission within the French nation and abroad.[143]

For their part, German Jews largely ignored the debates that raged among French Jews about how to protect the integrity of their communities and their families against proselytizing priests and Jesuitical plots. Indeed, although German-Jewish periodicals reported on some of the French conversion scandals, the topic led neither to wider debates about the issue nor to clear articulations of a political program in the German context.[144] This was the case despite the fact that individual correspondents wrote about similar incidents of proselytizing occurring in Germany.[145] For German Jews, the more important targets of criticism and the primary source of their anxieties were Protestant missionaries, yet there existed no equivalent to the anticlerical language prevalent in France that would have allowed them to denounce Protestants as retrograde enemies of a stable religious order.[146] The lack of a common target for these polemics against proselytism may have contributed to the fact that there was no common front and little sustained conversation about these issues across the Rhine. This distinguishes the Terquem scandal from the 1858 Mortara affair, in which Jews in the German state, France, and other countries invoked shared visions of paternal authority, familial integrity, and the hostile politics of the Catholic Church. Not only did Jews in both countries have a shared target during the Mortara affair, they also developed a broader sense of a common conflict by this later date. While the examples from the early *Kulturkämpfe* described here underscore the relevance of anticlerical politics for Jewish self-understanding in the 1840s, they also signal an important shift that led German and French Jews to think of themselves as part of a global clash between the forces of liberalism and the Catholic Church in the following decades. Although the period after the Damascus affair saw the beginning of cooperation and interest in helping disenfranchised Jews outside the "civilized" world, it was only in the period of intensified *Kulturkämpfe* of the 1850s and 1860s that Jews developed the patterns of perceptions that made sense of these debates as part of a large transnational conflict.

Five Jews in the Transnational Culture Wars
Secularism and Anti-Papal Rhetoric

At some point in late December 1870, Simon Bloch sat down in Paris to write a review of the past year for his paper, the *Univers israélite*. His retrospective included a long list of events that merited mention. France had entered into a poorly planned war against Prussia and its allies, which led to the quick demise of the imperial regime after Napoleon III was captured in battle on September 2. Soon afterwards, the Third Republic had been formally declared, but the new government was unable to reverse the fortunes of war. By September 19, Paris was under siege. Reflecting on his situation, Bloch began his essay by lamenting the grave state of affairs in the capital. Food and coal had become scarce, and Bloch's work was made more difficult by the fact that little news had reached the city in the past months.[1]

Looking back at this year full of dramatic developments, Bloch identified the single event that he believed to matter most to his readers:

> The main Jewish event that we can report for the year 1870 was the deliverance of our coreligionists from papal oppression; an oppression all the more odious as it took religion as a pretext and God as an accomplice. Through the fall of the pope's temporal power, God and religion are in turn liberated from the monstrous complicity that the self-declared vicars and representatives of God on earth imposed on them.
>
> Pius IX said to the [Jewish converts, the] Abbés Lémann: "What then can I do for your [Jewish] nation? If I weren't so preoccupied at the moment, I would have many things to say on the subject. At the moment I cannot do anything but pray; and I pray much for [your Jewish nation]." These prayers of the pope were granted: our *nation* was delivered . . . from him.[2]

According to Bloch, while France's fate was still uncertain, the history of the Jews had already taken a positive turn. The fall of Rome had been the direct consequence of the retreat of French military support for the pope because of the country's decision to concentrate its efforts toward the struggle against the German states. As a French citizen and a republican patriot, Bloch condemned the Prussians' attacks on France. Yet as both a political liberal and a self-declared religious conservative who emphasized the unity of the Jewish people, he welcomed the consequences of the war. While his homeland was occupied, his coreligionists had been liberated and progress had defeated fanaticism.

Curiously, the Jewish paper in Germany closest to Bloch's journal issued very similar comments in the wake of the war. Rather than succumb to the general enthusiasm surrounding France's defeat, the *Israelitische Wochen-Schrift* repeatedly pointed out the cost of war. A week after the Prussian king accepted the imperial crown of the unified German Empire, the paper complained about the bloodshed caused by the hostilities. Its editor, Rabbi Abraham Treuenfels (1818–1879), wrote,

> It is to be hoped that it is more than patriotic wishful thinking that the misery of war will be a blessing for Germany. Already the overthrowing of Cesarism and the temporal rule of the papacy are events that compensate for the great sacrifice and the awful suffering. In other words: God guides all events so they will have a good outcome; but it is certain that the fact that "God decided to let it end well" does not change anything about "You meant to do evil."[3]

The general wariness of war found in the pages of the *Univers israélite* and the *Wochen-Schrift* was typical of Jewish organs in both countries during the conflict. None of the editors of the Jewish periodicals in either country were enthusiastic about the conflagration.[4] Historian Christine Krüger has argued that the emphasis on the dangers of war and nationalism was a distinctive feature of the German-Jewish public when compared to non-Jewish, liberal papers in Germany.[5] The same might be said of the opinions expressed in French-Jewish periodicals. Contributors to the Jewish press in both Germany and France reiterated the willingness of Jews to fight for their homeland but expressed sadness about the prospect of mass death and armed conflict between two European states. Isidore Cahen, the editor of the *Archives israélites*, was even bold enough to argue against a circular by the French chief rabbi asking Jews to join a patriotic subscription during the war. In his view, clerics of any religion had no place getting involved in the war effort: Their role was rather to pray for the wounded and humanity as a whole.[6]

The one outcome of the war that Jewish journalists on both sides of the Rhine celebrated was the fall of Rome. Although in both Germany and France they published articles bemoaning the devastation, they nonetheless suggested that liberalism had emerged victorious after French troops abandoned their positions in the remaining papal territories.[7] From Paris, an article issued by the *Archives israélites* referred to the entry of Italian troops into Rome as "one of the most important events of our century,"[8] while from Magdeburg Ludwig Philippson claimed in his *Allgemeine Zeitung des Judenthums* that "the civilized world is now being liberated from the existence of a church-state."[9]

What had prompted these prominent Jewish intellectuals to interpret the war of 1870–1871—which had remade the map of continental Western Europe—in terms of its consequences for the papal regime? Why had the oppression of the several hundred Jews who lived in Rome assumed such importance that their liberation appeared to lend meaning to the death of thousands as well as the occupation of France? What inspired various Jewish activists to proclaim divine intervention and delivery from evil when they spoke of Italy's newfound sovereignty over the city of Rome?

In answering these questions, this chapter explores the creation of a shared German and French Jewish preoccupation with the papacy and the Catholic Church between the ascendancy of Pius IX as pope in 1846 and the Italian annexation of Rome in 1870. During this period of just over two decades, the opposition between liberalism and Catholicism became a powerful paradigm that helped Jews in Germany and France interpret national as well as international politics. In the pages that follow, I seek to understand how self-identified Jewish writers inscribed themselves into these conflicts and reshaped their religious outlooks to such an extent that the fall of papal Rome appeared to them as an event of supreme importance.

The explosion of anti-Catholic and Rome-centered discussions in the Jewish public sphere after 1858 overlapped with the rapid urbanization and integration of Jews into the middle classes in both France and Germany.[10] In France, this period also brought about the movement *en masse* of Jews from rural Alsace to Paris, which became the new center of Jewish life in the country. Concomitant with these geographic and social movements, increasing numbers of Jews came to regard their Judaism as an expression of their German and French patriotism and their liberal political identities writ large. The Italian conquest of the Papal States—a process that inspired religious, national, and political fantasies about a new age—offered Jewish journalists and intellectuals an opportunity to articulate these new commitments. Both the competition between French and German Jews as members of two distinct national communities and their growing willingness to work together toward common Jewish causes were intimately connected with their position toward Catholicism, as the debates of the decades before 1870 demonstrate. Polemics against the papacy stood at the center of German and French Jews' nationalization, internationalization, and even the religious and theological narratives that supported their different visions of a tolerant and secular political order from the mid-nineteenth century on. The image of Roman fanaticism became part of a debate about Judaism's role in a secularist order that was now fully intelligible across different national contexts.

The Jewish Press and the Early Years of Pius IX (1846–1858)

Although Jewish intellectuals and activists had publicly expressed their political criticism of the Catholic Church since the Enlightenment, their preoccupation with the living conditions of Rome's Jews was a relatively recent phenomenon. Jewish periodicals came to cover Roman life and politics in regular installments beginning in the 1840s, during the early years of the confessional press's expansion. Various writers for these papers provided editorials rather than simple reports: Many highlighted what they considered to be the profound contradiction between the spiritual claims of the papacy and the reality of its severe restrictions on the Jews under its protection. Despite the new attention Jewish authors and audiences began to give to the topic of Rome and the Jews beginning in the midcentury, however, they did not immediately situate the struggles of the papal Jews within the frame of a civilizational or global conflict between liberalism and the papacy.[11]

Indeed, precisely as liberals across Germany began to champion equal citizenship for Jews in the mid-1840s, changes in Rome gave grounds for optimism about an imminent shift toward more inclusive policies in the Papal States as well. In this context, the German and French Jewish press enthusiastically welcomed the ascendancy of Pius IX in 1846.[12] Journalists in both countries reported on the celebratory texts Jews in Italy wrote in honor of the new pope: Like many Italian Jews, they expected him to put an end to the humiliation of Rome's Jewish community.[13] Shortly after Pius's election, the *Archives israélites* even published a Hebrew poem that described Pius as savior [*moshiach*] and pious man [*Pius ha-Hasid*].[14] Different Jewish serials similarly reported about the changes the new pope was implementing, ostensibly with the aim of dismantling the ghetto.[15]

The idea of a liberal pope also inspired Jews who were neither professional publicists nor communal officials during this period. The Jewish community of the village of Nackel in Posen, for example, sent an address to Rome that was signed by fifty-five of its members.[16] The villagers conceded that they risked ridicule for presuming that anybody would care about expressions of solidarity issued by the members of their small community with the Jews of Rome. Given the momentous nature of the change they witnessed, however, they had wanted to communicate their gratitude to Pius IX directly, also adding that they had no doubt that his benevolence toward Jews would advance Christianity to new heights.

Positive reports on the new pope continued to appear in the Jewish press until Pius was forced to flee Rome on the declaration of the Roman Republic in February 1849.[17] After his return to the city in 1850, Pius IX grew much more conservative. His subsequent decision to reestablish the ghetto ended the short-lived romance between the Jewish press and the new pope. Pius IX soon emerged as the most prominent symbol of Catholic anti-modernism in the nineteenth century, among both Jewish and non-Jewish liberals.[18] It was also at this time that Jewish interest in the Jews of Rome became one of the focal points of the tensions between Jews and conservative Catholics.[19]

The change in papal policy alienated authors who had supported Pius IX even during the time of the Roman Republic, which had declared Jews equal citizens.[20] From Paris, Simon Bloch argued in late 1849 that the flight of the pope had damaged religious authority everywhere.[21] Once reports arrived from Rome about what the pope planned for the country's Jews after his return to power in 1850, however, Bloch reversed his position and returned to an anticlerical and anti-Catholic line he first rehearsed during the Terquem affair. It was one that he would cultivate throughout the rest of his tenure as editor of the *Univers israélite*.[22]

In France, the turn from optimism to estrangement was also reinforced by domestic developments. At the beginning of the 1848 revolution, the Catholic Church and liberal revolutionaries appeared to have come to a tentative understanding.[23] By the summer of 1848, however, lower-class unrest began to force a shift in alliances. When a strengthened conservative camp closed down the state-run national ateliers, a workers' uprising shook Paris. After the ensuing clashes and massacres by state forces of late June 1848, the newly formed conservative Party of Order came to dominate parliament with the promise to keep the left out of power. The church now became the conservatives' ally in their quest to appease the lower classes and return to the status quo ante.[24]

This alliance was solidified with the election of Louis Bonaparte as president in December 1848.[25] Among the new measures that symbolized this political realignment were France's military intervention against the Roman republic, the reinstatement of the pope in May 1849, and the passing of the *Loi Falloux* on March 15, 1850.[26] The latter law, which permitted clerics to teach in primary and secondary schools with a letter of support from the church, led to the growth of a large Catholic school system in France.[27] At the same time, the ultramontanes, who favored a centralized pope-oriented church, prevailed over liberal Catholics and Gallicans, who had supported more autonomous French church structures.[28] To contemporary observers, ultramontanism and Louis Bonaparte, with his absolutist desires, were colluding. Such perceptions inspired a new wave of anticlericalism from the left.[29]

Jews felt the consequences of the revival of conservative Catholicism and the return of a new alliance of throne and altar immediately. The issue was brought home in an unexpectedly personal way to the Jewish press when the campaigns of ultramontane journalists and clergy led to the unmaking of the career plans of Isidore Cahen, the son of the editor of the *Archives israélites*. In October 1848, the young Cahen was appointed to teach at a secondary school in the Vendée, which was considered a deeply Catholic province.[30] Within a matter of days, two ultramontane papers in Paris, *La Voix de la Vérité* and *l'Univers*, called for his replacement.[31] Soon the bishop of Luçon joined the campaign and wrote a pastoral letter condemning the appointment of a Jewish teacher in his region. Hoping to avoid further commotion, the responsible Ministry of Education transferred Cahen to a new position, in another region. Refusing to budge, Cahen resigned.

The resulting scandal received extensive coverage in the Jewish and non-Jewish press. Anticlerical papers such as *Liberté de Penser* discussed the affair not long after it broke.[32] Responding to Cahen's misadventures, the *Archives israélites* also took a newly strident tone as it criticized the intolerance Jews experienced at the hands of conservative Catholics and—by extension—under papal authority in Rome.[33] The affair surrounding Cahen's appointment in the Vendée even became a topic of debate in the Chamber of Deputies on January 14, 1850, and was likely one of several reasons why the Central Consistory offered its collective resignation in the same year.[34] From Germany, Philippson's *Allgemeine Zeitung des Judenthums* also made the Cahen affair known to readers, describing it as part of the clergy's plan to gain control of the educational system again.[35] Although Simon Bloch of the *Univers israélite* rarely mentioned Isidore Cahen by name—likely as a result of his ongoing journalistic competition with Isidore's father—he nonetheless discussed the larger issue of clerical threats to Jewish equality during this period.[36]

By the early 1850s, the editors of France's two major Jewish periodicals had become anticlerical in their personal outlook and publically critical of the government's benevolent policies toward the Catholic Church and Rome. If their newspapers did not become platforms for aggressive anticlerical views, this was at least in part the result of the political repression that followed Louis Bonaparte's coup d'état of December 2, 1851, and his ascendancy to the throne as Napoleon III shortly thereafter. Even as enemies of the alliance of throne and altar,

Jewish intellectuals were increasingly wary of criticizing the emperor openly.[37] Both periodicals also vacillated between expressing their sympathies for liberal projects and their loyalty to a monarchy that relied on the church's support. As a result, the Jewish press came to feature fewer articles on the church in the years after the founding of the Second Empire (1852–1870), as compared to its outspoken opposition to the pope toward the end of the Second Republic (1848–1852).

Although the German Jewish press rejected Catholic support for the restoration regimes, even more than in France, its representatives expressed little interest in vocally anticlerical platforms between the 1848 revolution and the Mortara affair one decade later. Philippson's *Allgemeine Zeitung des Judenthums* offers a clear example of this moderate approach to anti-Catholicism at the midcentury. Articles about ultramontanism virtually disappeared from the Jewish press during the years of reaction in the early 1850s in Germany and France. The reasons for this shift were different in each context, however: Whereas anticlericalism became increasingly risky in France because it conflicted with loyalty to the Catholic emperor, German Jewish periodicals now offered fewer discussions of the Catholic Church because it ceased to be their principal concern. During a period of reaction under the ministry of Otto von Manteuffel (1850–1858) in Prussia, it was not Catholics but rather a group of Protestant conservatives, led by Ernst Ludwig von Gerlach and Julius Stahl, that spearheaded a movement aimed at disenfranchising Jews.[38] Based on Stahl's theories of a Christian state, conservatives such as Herrmann Wagener fought for the removal of article 12 of the constitution of 1850, which guaranteed freedom of religion to Prussia's subjects. Engaged in rhetorical battles with Protestant groups, the *Allgemeine Zeitung des Judenthums* gave less attention to Catholicism throughout much of the 1850s.[39]

Mortara and the Specter of Religious Fanaticism

The Mortara affair of 1858 marked a slow transformation rather than a single watershed, changing the way Jews related to the Catholic Church for many years to come. Because of its designation as an "affair," like the events surrounding the Damascus blood libel some two decades earlier,

"Mortara" has garnered a great deal of attention in modern Jewish historical studies.[40] It consists of a well-documented series of events, all meticulously reconstructed by David Kertzer in his book on the subject.[41] In Bologna, the former nanny of a young Jewish boy, Edgardo Mortara, confessed to her priest in 1858 that she had secretly baptized the child several years earlier when he had been sick and remained in danger of dying. The priest passed the information on to his bishop. With the argument that the boy was now a Christian and could not live any longer with his Jewish family, the papal police then seized the child from his parents. Desperate to get their son back, the family turned to the Jewish communal bodies in the Papal States, hoping in vain that the traditional lobbying channels could help them retain custody over their child.

In August 1858, the Jewish communities of neighboring Piedmont sent an urgent letter to the representative bodies of French and British Jewry asking for their support in the matter. The missive prompted a series of interventions by Jewish and non-Jewish statesmen as well as the general outcry of European liberals. All of these efforts failed, however, and Edgardo Mortara was raised in papal institutions even after Italian unification in 1860–1861 and the conquest of Rome in 1870. He was soon ordained and remained a priest until the end of his long life.

Although they represented a material failure, scholars have described the profound effect that the activities surrounding the affair had on the way Jews in Europe came to conduct politics. The affair has often been credited with refocusing Jewish activism from *shtadlanut*, or private lobbying through intercessors, to public campaigning and the creation of new institutions for the expression of Jewish solidarity. There is little doubt that the affair changed the rhetoric of European Jewish politics and simultaneously created new opportunities for Jewish intellectuals to deploy anticlerical polemics in the long run. Yet, much like the Damascus affair, the Mortara affair was even more powerful as a *lieu de mémoire* than as a trigger of immediate changes in Jewish political strategy. It did not lead to an immediate spike in anti-Catholic polemics.

In the earliest responses of Jewish public figures to the Mortara affair, the politics of intercession and lobbying remained important, as did rhetorical strategies that were incompatible with secularist polemics. As various Jewish periodicals attempted to direct rescue efforts, they often employed a conciliatory language that stood at odds with the more aggressive tone of the outright anticlerical polemics they embraced at other times. Philippson's *Allgemeine Zeitung des Judenthums* offers the best example of these strategic constraints. The liberal editor and rabbi found the field for activism wide open because there were no centralized Jewish organizations in Germany able to lead a Jewish campaign for Edgardo Mortara. When the French Central Consistory sent an address to the French emperor on the subject, Philippson decided to draft his own petition intended for the pope. Like all petitions it was formulated in a respectful language that Philippson was careful not to contradict in his opinion pieces on the affair. It is thus hardly surprising that Philippson toned down his one-time polemics against the church after circulating a petition containing lines such as this one: "The humble undersigned Rabbis of the German and Prussian Jewish communities come before the throne of your Honorable Holiness, in front of the distinguished seat of the leader of the great Catholic Church, the sublime sovereign of the Papal States, trusting to find a receptive ear, because they come in the name of justice and love for humankind."[42] Philippson, like most of his journalistic peers in the early months of the affair, focused his energy on persuading the pope that his government should stop a practice that "was unworthy of any church."[43] Arguing at the same time that Mortara's delivery into the hands of the church was a typical case of Catholic religious fanaticism would hardly have served his cause.

Even once Jewish journalists realized the futility of their lobbying efforts, they refrained from drawing on the full repertoire of anticlerical insults available to them. In fact, in spite of the ever-intensifying anti-Jewish campaigns undertaken by the French ultramontane press led by Louis Veuillot and his *Univers religieux* during the affair, Jewish activists continued to avoid aggressive rhetoric.[44] Even in France, where Jews were increasingly drawn into the gravitational field of republicanism, it made little sense to react to the affair with anticlerical invectives. One reason for this was that members of the most anticlerical contingent of French Jewish elites—the journalists emerging from the conflicts of the 1840s with clear ideas about the nefarious influence of Catholic conservatives—had now become institution builders. Isidore Cahen was one such individual. After losing his career as a teacher due to an ultramontane campaign, Cahen became the principal contributor to the *Archives israélites*. By November 1858, after the strategy of gathering petitions proved ineffective, Cahen came up with the idea of a Comité de défense israélite that was soon renamed the Alliance israélite universelle.[45] Over the next years and decades the project grew into the largest Jewish philanthropic organization of the nineteenth century with a vast school system throughout North Africa and the Middle East.[46] While anticlericalism constituted an important part of the organization's congenital make-up—as Michael Graetz and Lisa Leff have argued in their descriptions of the origins of the organization—the Realpolitik necessitated by the Alliance's mission from its inception also made journalistic polemics inopportune.[47]

Although Jewish activists and journalists now avoided explicit insults to the church, a more subtle yet sustained change in their tone was undeniable. One way to gauge this rhetorical shift is to see how various Jewish individuals began to portray Catholicism as a special case of fanaticism, distinct from other religious traditions. Jewish journalists were able to make sense of the pope's policies by comparing the Mortara affair to religious violence in other contexts. In the process, they defined their understanding of proper and improper religion in relational terms.

By the time that the Jewish press in Germany and France first offered reports about Edgardo Mortara's fate in late August and early September 1858, the topic of "religious fanaticism" featured regularly within their pages. The label was, however, generally reserved for non-Europeans and exotic places. In its initial exposé of the Mortara case, the *Archives israélites* mentioned the petition of the Piedmontese communities on behalf of the Mortaras in the context of an article concerned mainly with the alleged fanaticism of Muslims abroad. Cahen's main focus in this first report on Edgardo Mortara's fate was the killing of the French and British consuls in the Ottoman port city of Jeddah, which he depicted as a paradigmatic case of religiously motivated "barbarism."[48]

As the Mortara affair developed, the killings in Jeddah as well as claims of Muslim fanaticism more generally remained a point of comparison. Olry Terquem, the radical reformer and brother of Lazard Terquem, for example, argued that the "dry" (state-based, nonviolent) crime perpetrated against the Mortara family was worse than the bloody one in Jeddah because the simple people could not comprehend its cruelty.[49] The official address of the Jewish Central Consistory to Napoleon III also warned that such intolerance in the heart of Christianity played into the hands of anti-Western Muslim fanatics.[50] In a world globalized by colonial rule, French Jewish champions for Mortara portrayed the breakdown of secular expectations in one part of the world as a dangerous precedent for the non-European "fanatics" in the French colonies. At the same time, such statements hinted at the exoticism of the Vatican in the heart of Europe.

Discussions of religious fanaticism could, however, cut both ways. News of the police intervention in the case of Edgardo Mortara reached the European press just as reports appeared of a young Jewish man who had stabbed and seriously wounded a missionary priest in an Amsterdam church on August 1, 1858. In an editorial he published on the topic in the *Archives israélites*, which was later translated and reprinted in the *Allgemeine Zeitung des Judenthums* in Germany, Cahen claimed that such an act of overt religious violence was an aberration among Jews.[51] He also attempted to suggest that the young Jewish assailant had been provoked. The Scottish missionaries had brazenly built their church in the middle of a Jewish quarter, after all. According to Cahen, although the overly sensitive young perpetrator had clearly gone too far, he was not the only one who had been appalled by the missionaries' shameless attempts to convert the Jews in their own neighborhood. Brawls between Jews and the missionaries had already been recorded. In Cahen's view, Jewish fanaticism in Amsterdam was merely a response to the fanaticism of the missionaries in their midst—a logic he did not apply to the killings in Jeddah, which he continued to insist were the product of the innate, unprovoked fanaticism of Muslims.[52] From Strasburg another Jewish journalist, the lawyer S. Honel who edited a local Jewish paper entitled *Le Lien d'Israël*, similarly argued that the fanatical activity of the Protestant missionaries in Amsterdam should be considered an extenuating circumstance.[53]

While Jewish journalists did their best to lay the blame on the missionaries, the crime remained an embarrassment and undermined their attempts to depict Judaism as an ideal civic religion. Cahen and Philippson soon took a new position that helped them solve this problem. Attributing the stabbing to the individual pathology of the young Jewish perpetrator, they argued that there was nothing particularly Jewish about the violence that had taken place in the Amsterdam church that summer. According to the reports the *Archives israélites* and the *Allgemeine Zeitung des Judenthums* issued in the wake of this latest affair, the young Jewish aggressor likely suffered from *monomania religiosa*, a particular religious form of the psychological affliction that rendered the diseased incapable of making proper judgments.[54] To distinguish this incident from the events surrounding the Mortara family, Philippson and Cahen also emphasized that the case involved a single perpetrator and—like the killing of the consuls in Jeddah—was the result of a crime of passion rather than a preconceived policy. Unlike the papal authorities' abduction of Edgardo Mortara, the stabbing in Amsterdam was thus not a political issue. In the depiction of the Jewish press, Muslims and Jews exhibited a form of fanaticism characteristic only of agitated masses or the mad rather than the carefully orchestrated fanatical policies of the Catholic Church. Because journalists like Cahen and Philippson also argued that there was nothing inherently Jewish about an isolated act of a deranged Jewish individual, they suggested that it need not be understood as a disruption to the narrative of progress that framed their interpretation of the Catholic Church's backwardness.

Yet another, third, incident appeared in comparisons between different types of fanaticism and challenged Jewish commentators' hopes for progress in religious politics. During the summer of 1858, reports told of six Swedish women who had been deprived of their property and sentenced to live in exile for converting from Lutheranism to Catholicism. The German Jewish press remained silent on the subject. In France, Olry Terquem was one of the few Jews who publically reacted to the affair. He called for a subscription in favor of the persecuted Swedish women through the pages of the *Univers israélite* and suggested that the Jewish Central Consistory could direct the initiative.[55] His call remained unanswered. Although Jewish journalists offered regular reports of Protestant "fanaticism"—whether among orthodox Lutheran or German Pietistic Christians—their coverage did not inspire similar outrage or motivate collective action as did cases involving the Catholic Church in particular. French and German Jews appear to have lacked a narrative that would have made such responses appealing. In France in particular, Jews often regarded Protestants as members of a fellow minority and Protestant anti-Judaism as merely a deviation from the norm. The Mortara affair only strengthened their sense of Jewish–Protestant solidarity, both within France and internationally: The Evangelical Alliance working out of London became the principal non-Jewish organization to cooperate with French Jewish lobbyists for the return of Edgardo Mortara, while the Alliance israélite universelle later showed its gratitude by intervening for persecuted Protestants in Spain in 1863.[56]

German and French Jews' reactions to the Mortara affair, like their response to religious violence and persecution in Jeddah, Amsterdam, and Sweden, were shaped by narratives about the role of particular religions in society and politics. In this sense, the events that unfolded in the home of the Mortara family in Bologna were not simply the catalyst for later Jewish critiques of the Catholic Church but also a symptom of Jews' historical understanding of religious fanaticism as a political problem. Moreover, Jews' responses to this moment were influenced not only by grand narratives of Protestant progressiveness and Catholic and Islamic backwardness but also by the sense that Europe was returning to a path of progress after the temporary reaction to the failed revolutions of 1848. In Prussia, the future Prussian king and German emperor Wilhelm I became the prince regent in January 1858, inaugurating a period of liberal reforms and liberal electoral successes.[57] The suggestion that Jews would finally gain equal civil rights excited the passions of many Prussian Jews during this period. German and French Jews also looked beyond the Channel to find signs of better times. In 1858, the very year that the young Mortara was taken from his family, Lionel de Rothschild was the first Jew to take his seat in the British House of Commons.[58] Just as the Papal States engaged in actions liberals associated with obscurantism and religious fanaticism, the rest of Europe appeared to be making new strides toward religious equality. These shifts reinforced the contrast liberals drew between the so-called civilized European states and papal rule in Italy. While the Jews who mobilized in the name of the Mortaras in different countries across Europe and beyond were often motivated by local concerns, this perception of a broader political realignment helps explain the timing of the incident as a transnational event.[59]

In the wake of the affair, the contributors to the Jewish press consistently expressed their understanding of religion and politics by making reference to Catholicism as the ultimate example of fanatical religion. Throughout the decades that followed, various Jewish newspapers across France and Germany found opportunities to discover new Mortara cases.[60] Bloch even turned the events of the affair into an adjective, speaking of the "apostolic, Roman, and Mortarian Church."[61] Cahen, for his part, began to refer to clerical circles as the "place where one commits and approves of *Mortarism* [*mortarisme*]."[62] Other scandals such as the 1864 conversion of the Roman Jewish boy Giuseppe Coen against his parents' will added to the repertoire of stories Jews told each other about the persecutions their coreligionists underwent at the hands of the papal regime.[63] The continued references to the events of 1858 reinforced the idea, now increasingly popular among French and German Jews alike, that Judaism existed in a fundamental opposition to a particular brand of Roman Catholicism. In the language of Jewish reformers and activists, "Roman fanaticism" became the benchmark for other—Pietistic, Jewish, or Islamic—forms of fanaticism. Even though Jewish journalists repeatedly claimed that they were not engaged in "a battle between Judaism and Catholicism," the Mortara affair made clear that increasing numbers of politically engaged Jews considered opposition to the temporal rule of the papacy an obvious position. [64]

Can a Jew Support the Pope?

The degree to which opposition to Rome became a fixture of public Jewish life after 1858 became apparent in a scandal that surrounded the French journalist and lawyer Joseph Cohen (1817–1899).[65] Cohen was an advocate in Marseille when he started to write for the *Archives israélites* in the 1840s. In 1842, he and the president of the Jewish Consistory of Marseille, Jacques-Isaac Altaras, were charged with writing a report on the state of Algerian Jewry and to make recommendations for their civic improvement.[66] Among their suggestions was the creation in the newly acquired French territories of a consistory, which would oversee Algerian Jews' transformation in the image of modern European Jewry. The state followed their proposals, and Cohen became the first president of the newly formed Consistory of Algiers in 1845, after he had moved to Algeria to become a state-appointed defense lawyer.[67] In 1850, he returned to the Hexagon and became a journalist for various dailies and a member of the Jewish Consistory of Paris and later of the Central Committee of the Alliance israélite universelle.[68] Adding to his fame was a well-received apologetic work, entitled *Les Deïcides*, which showed why it was incorrect to accuse Jews of having committed deicide in Jesus' trial.[69] Cohen's main intellectual outlet was, however, his own Jewish weekly, *La Vérité israélite* (1860–1862). The paper appears to have met with some success, judging by the irritation it caused his competitors. Bloch, who had made the *Univers israélite* his life's work, was clearly disconcerted by this upstart in the Jewish publication business. To the veteran publisher's distaste, Cohen brought new marketing techniques to the trade, when he advertised his *Les Deïcides* (which had been a series in the *La Vérité israélite* first) in synagogues with large posters.[70]

In 1862, the respect Cohen had gained among Jewish communal elites quickly evaporated when he picked two inopportune fights. First he offended members of the rabbinate when he accused them of being responsible for the decline of Judaism.[71] After receiving angry letters from two important rabbis, Cohen promptly apologized for his critique. A second article damaged his reputation even more seriously among liberal Jews and led to the scandal that hastened the demise of his newspaper. In September of that year, Cohen argued in the conservative daily *France* that the temporal rule of the pope was important for the stability of the European political system.[72] Catholicism would collapse if the remaining territory of the Papal States was to disappear, he explained, which would in turn lead to the fall of Christianity and, ultimately, also to the destruction of Judaism.

Cohen's comments were a puzzle to his contemporaries. In August Nefftzer's liberal daily *Le Temps*, the journalist Adrien Hébrard expressed his surprise in satirical terms: "We quickly perused the signature with curiosity [. . .]. Oh merriment! We expected a church father and stumbled upon a Jew."[73] Others were equally dismayed. Cohen's change of heart was understandably surprising to observers. Not only had *Les Deïcides* represented an affront to the church, as the article in *Le Temps* did not fail to mention, Cohen had also written in unambiguously negative terms about Catholicism in his own newspaper. In fact, just a year before issuing his defense of the Vatican, he had described Catholicism as a form of "universal domination in the spiritual realm under the conditions of centralization, unity, coercive power, and dogmatic infallibility," while also calling the pope the archenemy of liberty.[74]

Cohen faced the most vehement resistance to his unexpected opinions from members of the Jewish community. He was prudent enough not to run again for his position in the Paris Consistory and also declared his resignation as editor of the *La Vérité israélite*, which soon ceased publication. In a parting statement issued from the final issue of his serial, Cohen sought to appease his critics by clarifying that he would never forget Mortara and that he did not consider the papacy a force for good in the world.[75] He merely believed that, in the interest of order, it was politically expedient that the pope not be deposed in a revolution. An exiled pope would merely be more powerful, he furthered. Attempting to explain his infamous article as an exercise in patriotic politics, he insisted that his statements in support of the papacy were also intended as a denunciation of the British, whom he had accused of secretly pursuing a Protestant agenda. Cohen's arguments convinced none of his friends. True, the French Empire supported Rome as part of its approach to the European balance of power, and his statements were patriotic in this sense, but this type of patriotism went over badly with liberals, republicans, and Jews. Concluding his apologia, Cohen explained that he rejected the aggressive anti-Catholic style now *en vogue* in Jewish circles.

No attempt at damage control could save Cohen from the indignation of his fellow Jewish journalists. Bloch declared that it was "not fitting to rest in the camp of Israel while enlisting under the banners of our most implacable enemies."[76] It was even "against the nature of being Jewish" to support the pope.[77] Bloch was particularly upset about Cohen's claims of Jewish aggressiveness toward Catholicism, a position he claimed was a fantasy that existed only in Cohen's "intolerant and ultramontane imagination."[78] Indeed, the affair surrounding Cohen's statements did not prove that Jews were particularly antagonistic to the majority religion; instead it demonstrated that a Jewish supporter of papal power was a paradox that was more difficult to comprehend than a Jew with almost any other opinion.[79] Ludwig Wihl (1807–1882), an eccentric German Jewish émigré then living in France, expressed this problem in unmistakable terms to his fellow expatriate Moses Hess (1812–1875): "The politics of Mr. de Lagueronnère [a journalist in the service of Napoleon III] smells strongly from his behind, and I don't understand how Mr. Joseph Cohen, the editor of the *La Vérité israélite*, can find an appetite in this."[80]

These sentiments were shared in Germany, where Philippson and various correspondents for the *Allgemeine Zeitung des Judenthums* expressed their outrage at Cohen's comments. Philippson argued that Cohen's opinion was completely unacceptable for someone who was publicly identified with Judaism because of his membership in the Paris Consistory.[81] Cohen's positions were outright "un-Jewish and anti-Jewish," according to Philippson.[82] Jewish tradition gave up priesthood and had always rejected priestly power in worldly matters, he continued, suggesting that any statements in favor of the pope thus necessarily injured the cause of Judaism.[83] Now that the Mortara affair had turned Judaism and the papacy into irreconcilable enemies, Cohen had committed treason in Philippson's eyes.[84] After this impassioned diatribe, Philippson also clarified that it was unseemly for Jews to speak about the question of Rome and that Cohen had also infringed on that rule (which, of course, Philippson had just ignored in the process). In a later article, Philippson also used the affair to promote the seventh volume of Heinrich Graetz's (1817–1891) magnum opus, the *History of the Jews* (1853–1875), which had just appeared with Philippson's publishing venture, the Institut zur Förderung der israelitischen Literatur.[85] Offering further arguments against Cohen, Philippson printed a long excerpt from Graetz's book concerning the anti-Jewish policies of the medieval popes.[86]

Articles from the German Jewish newspaper's Paris correspondent complemented Philippson's polemics. The correspondent pointed out that Cohen's piece was published on the day he had represented the Paris Consistory at *Rosh Hashanah* ceremonies—the very day that Edgardo Mortara's parents were present.[87] The scandal also reached the nonconfessional press. In Breslau's *Morgenzeitung*, an anonymous Jewish author condemned Cohen by arguing that "a Jew could not honestly identify the interests of his religion with the temporal rule of the papacy."[88]

The scandal surrounding Cohen's comments illustrate the extent to which antagonism to the pope was becoming ingrained into the fabric of an increasingly transnational Jewish public sphere. Cohen was able to recover from the blow—becoming, in 1868, a delegate for the Algerian Central Consistory and later chief editor of the newspaper *Liberté*—but the scandal was not easily forgotten. When he died in 1899 his obituaries still mentioned the affair. Although the *Archives israélites* merely noted that Cohen's consistorial career had ended due to "sensational incidents" [*incidents retentissants*], the *Univers israélite* continued to question how it was that a Jew could have said something that was so counterintuitive to his Jewish contemporaries.[89]

Anti-Catholic Insults and Intra-Jewish Conflicts

The depiction of ultramontanism as the epitome of nefarious religious politics was further reinforced by the use of anti-Catholic tropes in intra-Jewish strife. Increasingly, the opposition to conservative Catholicism supplied the leading metaphors for conflicts within the Jewish communities. By the 1860s, "ultramontanism" and "Jesuitism" had become common insults in debates about Jewish religious practice and communal organization.

In France, it was mostly Simon Bloch who used anticlerical language in his polemics against the Jewish Consistory and Reform Judaism. Bloch argued, for example, that Reform rabbis lacked natural authority and thus had to revert to the superficial authority that one could also identify in Roman Catholicism.[90] Anti-Catholic tropes also appeared in Bloch's angry reaction to the increase of consistorial control over rabbinic appointments as a result of an imperial decree of August 29, 1862. Sarcastically, he described the Catholic system of appointments as preferable to the Jewish system employed by the Consistories, suggesting that at least in the church knowledgeable people rather than laymen chose the priests. Bloch also insulted the Consistory by calling its members financiers, businessmen, and artists who treated the rabbis they now had the power to appoint as would-be patriarchs, high priests, bishops, and infallible popes.[91] Invoking the idea of (papal) infallibility in his polemics, Bloch repeatedly taunted the consistorial rabbinate and satirized its claims to authority.[92]

In Germany, the more vicious conflicts between the different strands of reformers and anti-reformers created a situation in which comparisons to non-Jewish religious groups became more common. Although this had already been true in the case of the debates about similarities between Jewish reformers and the Deutschkatholiken in the 1840s, in the aftermath of the Mortara affair and in response to the increasing Jewish antagonism to the Catholic Church, intra-Jewish insults evolved. German Reform Jews employed anti-Catholic insults against Jewish Orthodoxy in a way that did not necessarily mark the speaker as anti-Catholic. Talk of a "Rabbinical encyclical" or "Jewish Jesuits" normalized the language of denominational conflicts without making an explicit statement about the role of Catholicism in society.[93] Although these terms were unmistakably associated with popular suspicions about Catholic backwardness, secrecy, and disloyalty, for liberal Protestants and Jews—much as for most historians—they remained a rather unremarkable, innocent part of intracommunal squabbles.

Yet the fusion of different enemies in the minds of liberals could go beyond rhetoric. It was a slippery slope from taunting one's Jewish opponents by alluding to their similarity to the most popular metaphor of religious pathology to claiming that Jewish Orthodoxy and ultramontanes were in fact in league with each other. One of the earliest and most elaborate claims of such an Orthodox–ultramontane conspiracy appeared in the Jewish press in reports about a court case in Vienna, which had been instigated by the Catholic *Wiener Kirchenzeitung* of Sebastian Brunner (1814–1893). In 1863, Brunner had sued Leopold Kompert (1822–1886), the editor of the Viennese *Jahrbuch für Israeliten*, for publishing an article by Heinrich Graetz entitled "Die Verjüngung des jüdischen Stammes" [The Rejuvenation of the Jewish Tribe]. According to Brunner, Graetz denigrated the Jewish belief in a personal messiah and thus committed the criminal act of libel against a recognized religious community.[94]

Part of the libel charge, according to §303 of the Austrian criminal code, was based on the notion that Graetz, as a Reform Jew, had denigrated Orthodox Jewry as a separate confession. The Austrian court found Kompert guilty of libeling Judaism but rejected the latter charge on the basis of testimony given by two Orthodox Viennese rabbis, Lazar Horwitz and Isaac Noah Mannheimer, who argued in court that Judaism constituted only one single confession.

Early on, contributors to the *Allgemeine Zeitung des Judenthums* attacked Brunner's attempt to split Judaism in two and expressed their dismay at the ultramontanes' celebration of their partial victory in court.[95] The affair took a new turn, however, when Orthodox groups in Hungary began to collect signatures under the aegis of Ezriel Hildesheimer (1820–1899) for a petition against Horwitz and Mannheimer. The association of Jewish Orthodoxy with conservative forces from other religions finally seemed to be substantiated by a real-life alliance. The *Allgemeine Zeitung des Judenthums*'s Vienna correspondent argued that there existed schemes "to impose a schism on Judaism from two sides. I am talking about the party of the *Kirchenzeitung* [. . .] and a *Jewish* party, which purports to be orthodox, and which gladly allies itself with our enemies, if this will help them promote their self-interest and ambition."[96]

Several of the *Allgemeine Zeitung*'s other correspondents from the Habsburg Empire similarly attacked the activities of Neo-Orthodox Jews by denouncing their "campaign against the unity of Judaism" and the "Jesuitical tone" of their petition.[97] The affair acquired an international touch when false rumors circulated that Chief Rabbi Ulmann of France had signed the petition.[98] A correspondent from Paris seized the opportunity to criticize the hierarchical structure of the French consistorial system, using an anticlerical gibe to make his point: "It is rumored here that Mr. Ulmann behaves this way because of the empress' interest in the clergy—Mr. Ulmann, after all, also belongs to the clergy. Perhaps he will write for the pope or in favor of the Jesuits within a couple of years. Just wait!"[99]

The agitation surrounding the lawsuit soon died down, yet accusations against the Jewish Orthodox for their divisive activities continued to be associated with the similarly feared influence of ultramontanes. In the context of criticism of the First Vatican Council, Philippson wrote: "It is obvious that this modern-orthodox party wants to create an *ecclesia militans* following the example of the ultramontanes [. . .]. Whereas Christian ultramontanism draws on everything—church, state, Christendom, the whole world—Jewish ultramontanes on the contrary are content with ripping away pieces from existing communities and taking control of them."[100]

Although the appearance of anti-Catholic tropes in intra-Jewish disputes did not fundamentally change the nature of such disputes, the use of such terms as "Jewish ultramontane" reinforced the sense that ultramontanism was indeed the irreconcilable enemy of Jews and one that could serve as a benchmark for other opponents. By reusing the metaphors drawn from the field of liberal–Catholic battles, the Jewish press deepened its commitment to a dichotomizing logic.

Imagining a Clash of Cultures in the 1860s

Given the pervasiveness of this dichotomizing logic in the Jewish press, it is remarkable that certain journalists—including Isidore Cahen, whose first career had been foiled by ultramontane campaigns—remained cautious in their polemics against the Catholic Church. To some degree, this reluctance to offend was the result of financial and political pressures. Historians writing about Jewish periodicals frequently fail to mention that freedom of the press in France was seriously limited by law through 1881. Jewish papers during the Second Empire had to take into consideration the law of February 17, 1852, which enabled greater censorship and created a distinction between political newspapers and those serving primarily the arts and sciences. Because only the former had to face increased stamp duties, a reclassification of Jewish weeklies from the latter to the former category had the potential to destroy them financially. Only in 1869 did the *Archives israélites* dare change its status, declaring that it was ridding itself of an artificial distinction between the interests of *israélitisme* (a notion combining Jews and Judaism) and politics. For Isidore Cahen, who took over the editorship of the *Archives israélites* in 1859, this meant that he and his collaborators would, from that point on, write like the Jewish journalists in Germany, England, and the United States. Doing so would involve confronting head on—as Cahen put it—the "politico-religious organs" of Catholicism, ultramontanism, and Protestantism on a level playing field.[101] During the decade after the Mortara case, Jewish newspaper editors in France were thus careful to write about politics in a way that would fly under the censors' radar. In fact, because Napoleon III had only a small surveillance apparatus at his disposal, his entire censorship regime relied, to a great extent, on self-censorship.[102] Unlike in Germany, censorship was quite aggressive—with a system of three warnings that eventually resulted in the temporary closure of a periodical—when the infraction concerned a critique of the papacy. A year before the Mortara affair, in 1857, the French Ministry of the Interior threatened to close down *La presse* for serializing George Sand's novel *La Danielle*, which was openly anti-papal.[103] Even though the events of 1858 brought about the French government's realignment in favor of Piedmont and Italian nationalism, aggressive anti-papal rhetoric remained a risky venture.

Jewish newspapers repeatedly suggested that their readers should interpret their contributors' often superficial insistence that they were apolitical as the result of legal pressure. A quote in the *Univers israélite* from a long, friendly review of an indisputably political book by a Jewish republican, Ernest Hendlé's *Questions politiques et sociales*, illustrates this pattern. Bloch explained: "The title of this book [. . .] indicates sufficiently that our newspaper cannot touch it but with the most delicate precaution due to legal restraints. Our Decalogue admonishes the *Univers israélite*: 'Honor the press laws, and thou shall have a long life.'"[104]

Given these constraints, it is surprising how explicit many Jewish periodicals were in their comments on the Catholic Church during this period. Their critiques tended to be strongest when the policies or statements they censured did not directly concern Jews. Thus, although Jewish antagonism to the Catholic Church was most impassioned in light of events like the Mortara affair, Jews articulated their opposition to the church most vocally when they could claim to have no special stakes in the matter at hand. A number of events that aroused anticlerical sentiments throughout the 1860s and 1870s consequently put Jewish journalists and activists in the more comfortable position of belonging to a larger liberal camp that stood in opposition to the Catholic Church.

Jewish writers assumed this disinterested air, for example, when Pope Pius IX promulgated the Syllabus of Errors as an attachment to an encyclical in December 1864. This document listed eighty errors of modern society that all Catholics were instructed to reject. Among these errors were the belief that Catholicism should not be the religion of state and the position that non-Catholics should be allowed to live according to the precepts of their religion.[105] Though it also threatened Jewish emancipation, the document was primarily intended to condemn liberal platforms more broadly as well as ideas associated with modernism and the Enlightenment. The Syllabus became one of the symbols of so-called Catholic intransigence among Jewish and non-Jewish liberals alike. Fighting against it proved a cause that allowed Jews to defend themselves against an institution they perceived as an enemy of Jewish interests without taking up the fight for Jewish reasons.

A consensus soon arose in Jewish newspapers in Germany and France that the Syllabus proved that Judaism was fundamentally different from Catholicism. Whereas Catholicism had now openly attacked modernity, Judaism embraced it.[106] Whereas Catholicism was the religion of absolutist and mind-numbing priestly rule, Judaism had a healthy relationship to science.[107] In the French case, Jewish periodicals additionally contrasted Catholic tenets with the values of the French Revolution, which—they claimed—Jews embraced wholeheartedly.[108]

The vision of liberalism and Catholicism engaged in a conflict between different principles also inspired Bloch to use one of his favorite tropes—God meting out punishments against political enemies of the Jews—in relation to Rome. Bloch's response to the entrance of Italian forces into papal Rome in 1870—which opened the current chapter—offers just one example of many. Elsewhere Bloch detected moral justice in the fact that the Asian plague had hit the Papal States particularly hard. According to Bloch's rendering, the pope's domains were struck by God's anger as the lands of the pharaoh of Exodus had been struck, with the only difference being that the pharaoh had understood that the Ten Plagues were divine signs.[109] Philippson expressed similar sentiments about the fatefulness of disaster hitting the pope's domains, although he added a superficial disclaimer to his analysis: "Any type of feeling of revenge or *Schadenfreude* is far from our heart!" He nonetheless continued: "At the same time, we cannot close our eyes to the obvious ways in which divine retribution is acting in the fate of the nations."[110]

Starting in the late 1860s, Jewish papers increasingly came to treat ultramontanism as an enemy both in the national and international arena.

Regular reports from neighboring countries but also from far-flung places such as Mexico or Chile gave the sense that the same clashes were unfolding across the globe according to the same script, each time pitting the forces of liberalism and ultramontane Catholicism against each other.[111] According to various Jewish commentators from the late 1860s, Jews now formed part of a transnational brotherhood, and sisterhood, of progressives engaged in a worldwide battle with the forces of obscurantism.

Once the Vatican Council assembled in 1869 to discuss and subsequently declare the dogma of papal infallibility, the readers of the *Allgemeine Zeitung des Judenthums* in Germany and the *Univers israélite* in France found reports about the problem of ultramontanism in every other issue.[112] Criticism now focused on the pope and his alleged self-divinization.[113] In the *Univers israélite*'s Passover issue of 1870, Bloch noted that while Jews were celebrating their deliverance by God's hand on their holiday, Catholics were fashioning a new God in Rome.[114] In another instance, Bloch mocked a ceremony involving the kissing of the pope's shoes as a form of sexual fetishism.[115]

In the wake of the broad debates between liberals and political Catholics in the press, certain official Jewish representatives also dared to adopt liberal anti-Catholic polemics openly for the first time. In Württemberg, Jewish petitioners used the Catholic Church as a foil to demand a more democratic structure for their own religious institutions. In their campaign to abrogate a law of 1828, which allowed the state to appoint the members of the Jewish consistory—the Israelitische Oberkirchenbehörde—without consulting members of the Jewish community, Jewish activists invoked the privileges given to the Catholic Church in the predominantly Protestant kingdom: "The state does not fear dangers from the autonomy of the Catholic Church even though it is elaborately organized around the world and has a foreign sovereign, who has great power over a third of the inhabitants of Württemberg. But the state cannot give freedom to the handful of utterly isolated Jews!"[116]

Similarly bold language appeared in the official statements of Aristide Astruc (1831–1905), one of the founders of the Alliance israélite universelle and, though a French citizen, also the chief rabbi of Belgium between 1866 and 1879.[117] Astruc was a controversial reformer whose textbook *Histoire abrégée des Juifs* [A Brief History of the Jews] was hotly debated in the French Jewish press around the time of the Vatican Council due to its rejection of divine miracles.[118] A representative of Franco-Judaism, Astruc also demanded that Jewish history should become the basis of a French republican education.[119] Astruc found much support for his liberal positions among Jewish communal elites in Brussels and made a name for himself there after he fought against an ultramontane procession commemorating the 500th anniversary of the alleged profanation of a host by Jews.[120] Given his clashes with ultramontanes in Belgium, it should be no surprise that Astruc emerged as an outspoken enemy of the Vatican Council. He expressed his disagreement with the council's position in a sermon that contrasted what he described as the true Mosaic religion with the proclamations made in Rome as well as the Catholic intolerance that bolstered anti-Jewish processions. The members of the Belgian Consistory were so impressed by their French rabbi's pronouncements that they decided to print his anticlerical sermon and send a copy to every Jewish household in Belgium.[121]

Rome, New Jerusalem, and Paris

The first wave of Jewish nationalists and proto-Zionists emerged in the 1860s, just as Jewish interest in the fate of Rome was at its most intense. This development also affected the language employed by this small group of Jewish thinkers whose politics departed from the liberal mainstream. The example of these early Jewish nationalists illustrates how the theologized dichotomy between liberals and Catholics that appeared prominently in the Jewish press engendered new alliances as well as new political languages. Most importantly, the struggle against the alleged intolerance of Catholicism helped Jewish nationalists and proto-Zionists articulate their vision of a New Jerusalem.

A politically and theologically motivated form of anti-Catholicism had been central also for the Christian Zionism that preceded the interventions of Jewish nationalists. This was the case, for example, in the works of Abram-François Pétavel (1791–1870), a key figure in the Evangelical Alliance who had maintained close relations with Bloch and his organ, the *Univers israélite*, since the 1850s.[122] For a thinker like Pétavel, the demise of Rome announced the imminent reestablishment of a Jewish commonwealth in the ancient homeland of the Hebrews.[123]

The anti-Catholic thrust of such evangelical Christian Zionist visions remained alive in the writings of individual Jewish writers who made this project their own. The small number of Jews who began to imagine and describe their vision of a New Jerusalem in less metaphorical terms, as the national regeneration of the Jews, developed their own brand of anti-papal theology that paralleled the models their Protestant predecessors had developed. Central to the new form of Jewish nationalist politics was the distinction between Rome and Jerusalem as the symbols of antagonistic principles (rather than the distinction between Rome and liberal progress). The use of Rome and Jerusalem as symbols was not new, of course. Yet, in the 1860s, after Mortara and in the face of Italian unification, these two cities came to stand for a fresh vision of national renewal and universalistic redemption. Among the best-known proponents of this invocation of New Jerusalem as a foil to Rome were Moses Hess, Heinrich Graetz, and Joseph Salvador. Each of these authors identified Jerusalem not only with the existing city of that name but also with a new world-historical age.

Salvador, the most senior of the group, explained his ideas in his work *Paris, Rome, Jérusalem* (1860) and in a revised edition of his *Histoire des institutions de Moïse* entitled *Idée sur l'avenir de la question religieuse* [Idea on the Future of the Religious Question] (1862).[124] Salvador argued that the original aim of his previous works had been to show how pagan Rome and Christianity had created a strong alliance after Jerusalem was defeated in the first and second century. With the "opening of the Orient" due to the weakening of the Ottoman Empire and the demise of Christian Rome in the mid-nineteenth century, he had started to reconsider his approach, he explained. He now claimed that France, which still protected the city of Rome, would soon become the vehicle for the reestablishment of a New Jerusalem.[125] Rome had not won, after all.

In 1862, Moses Hess published his theory of a New Jerusalem in a work with the similar title *Rome and Jerusalem*. As was true in the case of Salvador, Hess's depiction of the concrete (rather than abstract) Jerusalem meant that he was also interested in the fall of the city, and not simply the idea of Rome.[126] Whereas Salvador's views emerged from his earlier historical work, Hess had taken a more circuitous path to Jewish messianic politics. Although Hess received a traditional Jewish education, he also grew up in a Catholic environment in Bonn and Cologne.[127] Even though he never attended university or even a German high school (*Gymnasium*), he identified with the academic milieu of Left Hegelians and was, for a while, close with Karl Marx.[128] Fleeing to Paris in 1849 after the defeat of the revolution in Baden, Hess remained in the French capital most of his life. He briefly returned to Germany in 1861 when the Prussian king declared an amnesty for convicted revolutionaries but settled in Paris again permanently after two years. Although Hess had already issued a rhetorical call for a New Jerusalem in his works of the 1830s, he had not meant it in a national Jewish sense.[129] This changed when Hess slowly discovered his Judaism in the course of the 1850s and 1860s.[130] With his publication of *Rome and Jerusalem* his idea of a New Jerusalem emerged as a national vision that reflected his self-reinvention as a Jew.

Hess expected that Jews would follow in the footsteps of the Italians, another ancient nation that had lost its sovereignty. After Italian unification in 1860, the ancient Israelites could also hope for their reestablishment as a nation-state. The fall of the pope's temporal power was a central inspiration to these ideas, as the work's opening paragraph shows:

> From the time that Innocent III hatched the diabolical plan to destroy the moral stamina of the Jews [. . .] by forcing them to wear a badge of shame, until the audacious kidnapping of a Jewish child from the house of his parents [. . .], papal Rome symbolized to the Jews an inexhaustible poison. It is only with the drying-up of this source of poison that Christian-Germanic antisemitism will die from lack of nourishment. [. . .] with the liberation of the Eternal City on the banks of the Tiber, begins the liberation of the Eternal City on the slopes of Moriah; the renaissance of Italy heralds the rise of Judah.[131]

This double identification of Rome as a theological and political enemy also appealed to Heinrich Graetz, one of the most important and controversial historians of Jewry at the time. Graetz had been an internal reviewer of Hess's *Rome and Jerusalem* for the Institut zur

Förderung der israelitischen Literatur and gave the manuscript his enthusiastic approval.[132] After Philippson's Institut nonetheless rejected the publication, Graetz contacted Hess directly. The two became friends and stayed in epistolary contact until Hess's death in 1875. Their correspondence exhibits the hopes that these early Jewish nationalists invested in the fall of Rome. In the letters he wrote Hess throughout the 1860s, Graetz referred to Rome only as Babylon and regularly lamented the fact that it had not yet fallen.[133]

The theologizing of Rome's demise, an approach championed by the mainstream and more traditional Jewish publicist Simon Bloch, was thus also present among more radical Jewish thinkers who did not share Bloch's basic outlook. The disappearance of Papal Rome encouraged both mainstream hopes for the seamless integration of Jews and Judaism into society and proposals for the renewal of Judaism in a biblically inspired, national utopia. The conquest of the Papal States and its interpretations in the framework of anticlerical polemics offered a variety of Jewish journalists and intellectuals with different outlooks an opportunity to promote a secular political platform with a religious language.

Conclusion

The initial question of this chapter was how the focus on Rome came to take on such an importance in the works of Jewish activists and journalists to the point that it offered them consolation in the midst of a devastating war. The examples explored here demonstrate how Jewish opposition to ultramontanism and the temporal rule of the papacy became an integral part of the Jewish public spheres that emerged beginning in the mid-nineteenth century in both Germany and France. Anti-ultramontanism was more than just a political position for the Jews who contributed to the periodicals of Reform and Conservative Judaism. It assumed a theological dimension and became part of their interpretation of Judaism's role as a catalyst of modernity. Rome had to fall for modernity—understood as a secular project as well as the realization of eternal Jewish tenets—to come into its own.

More than ever before, Jewish intellectuals articulated their secularist expectations of religion by explaining their difference from Catholics. The Mortara affair, often described as a moment of transnational Jewish solidarity, also offered Jews an incentive to further confessionalize Judaism and to prove that Jews, unlike Catholics, were ideal citizens who were capable of transcending their religious interests. Thus we find a situation that appears as the exact inverse of the argument recently made by Lisa Leff that the institutionalization of transnational solidarity in nineteenth-century France was the result of national conflicts between republican anticlericals and Catholics.[134] National divisions indeed shaped foreign policy outlooks. The opposite is just as true, however: A transnational invocation of a global clash of principles with Rome as the capital of anti-liberalism reinforced Jewish support for the secular state at home.

Although Jews encountered opposition to their integration from Protestant conservatives and certain groups on the left, ultramontane Catholicism and the papacy nonetheless remained their principal opponents at least in part because rejecting them made for the simplest story.[135] The complex world of politics could be rendered navigable when reduced to the level of a conflict between two camps: moderate progress on one side and its enemies—fanatical religious reaction as well as fanatical revolutionary atheism—on the other. Many Jewish commentators with a centrist political outlook and religious inclinations found Rome to be the most tangible symbol of the reactionary camp they sought to defeat.

The expected fall of Rome was also the occasion for great politico-religious hopes among politically engaged Jews in mid-nineteenth century Europe. Whereas various contributors to the Jewish press agreed that the Franco-Prussian War was by no means a Jewish war, they happily declared the destruction of the pope's temporal rule a victory of Judaism—although not just for the Jews. When Bloch quipped that Judaism had been delivered from the pope, he expressed a sentiment that was as much religious as it was political. The conquest of Rome inspired many other Jewish commentators to imagine the hand of God behind events. The hubris of the pope had led to his downfall just as he declared himself infallible.[136] For Philippson, the Divine Judge had reacted to the church's blasphemous declaration that the pope incorporated parts of the divine within his person.[137]

Due to the symbolism that many religious Jewish publicists attributed to the idea of Rome and the pope's treatment of Jews, the events of 1870 appeared to vindicate both progress and divine justice. The Roman Question was one of the issues that made it easy to be a French or German patriot and cosmopolitan citizen at the same time; it was in this realm that the universal mission of the Jews (much vaunted by reformers) and the strengthening of the secular state appeared to overlap in a particularly uncomplicated way. Among national-religious thinkers such as Salvador, Hess, Graetz, and their evangelical Christian counterparts, the preoccupation with the pope also took the form of a sacred history of secularism. Rome became part of a story of the rise and fall of sacredness that would ultimately lead to a moral order based on religion while fulfilling universal human goals. The symbol of Rome brought integrationists and Jewish nationalists into a common discussion, within German and French Jewish public spheres that remained connected to a large degree by their shared concern with the fate of Roman Jewry.

Six Representative Secularism
Jewish Members of Parliament and Religious Debate

The comparison between German and French debates undertaken in previous chapters has highlighted not only the points of intersection but also the differences in the forms of secularism that developed in each national context starting in the late eighteenth century. Secularism did not only mean different things across political and linguistic borders, however. It also varied across different arenas of activity within each country. Secularist interpretations of religion at home did not have the same implications as secularist interpretations of religion in a synagogue, newspaper, or political meeting. Claims about the anti-modernity of the Catholic Church—the key theme of secularist polemics throughout Europe's long nineteenth century—were similarly meaningful only within specific contexts.

By focusing our attention on the ways in which secularism emerged and was negotiated in the German and French parliaments, this chapter is meant to sharpen our understanding of relational and shared histories, while exploring how secularism took shape in one distinct arena. European parliamentarians have historically *enacted* secularism in both meanings of the term. In the first sense, nineteenth-century French and German parliaments passed multiple laws regulating the relationship of religion and state. They debated and voted on new bills concerning issues such as obligatory civil marriage and the clergy's role in national education. Yet parliaments have also served as *stages* on which different ideas about the public expression of religious and communal identities have been enacted. From the start, deputies clashed in a highly public manner during debates, both over the issues at hand and over the ways they believed different positions should be articulated. Such debates constituted one of the central arenas for the dissemination of legal norms and social expectations about religion in modern Europe.

Using the concept of an arena can also remind us that the parliament was never a monolithic institution. Although modern parliaments were often touted as symbols of the nation's unity, they also represented the nation at its most divided. Unlike bureaucracies, modern parliaments publicly split into factions, demonstrating just how fragmented their respective nations were. In the face of these divisions, observers and parliamentarians came up with competing theories to distinguish between those divisions they deemed acceptable and those they did not. Among the issues that emerged was the question of whether the deputies represented their particular constituencies or the whole nation. When and in which contexts was it acceptable for deputies elected in Hamburg or Marseille to make demands in the name of their constituents? Similar questions appeared concerning the representation of workers as well as national and religious minorities.[1] When a Jew spoke about equity for other Jews, whom was he (and, much later, she) representing?

Many of the disagreements about these questions were reflected in the terminology deputies used to address one another. This was no small matter, as we can glean from the fact that revolutions sometimes brought about new forms of address in parliament. During the French Second Republic, for example, all deputies were required to refer to each other as *citoyen* (citizen), as they had done in the parliaments of the French revolutionary era. Most conflicts about forms of address did not coincide with tectonic changes in political life, however, but were rather part of the minutiae of everyday parliamentary politics.

One such disagreement ensued in a debate over the North German Constitution in May 1867, in the Prussian lower chamber—the Abgeordnetenhaus. Eduard Lasker (1829–1884), at the time a newly elected Jewish deputy for the National Liberal party, reacted to an independent deputy who had called him and two other members of parliament "unreliable."[2] In his riposte, Lasker twice called his opponent, Friedrich Michelis (1818–1886)—a Catholic theologian and priest—the "clerical member [of parliament] for [the district of] Allenstein."[3] Lasker's inconspicuous aside was well chosen. Only two months earlier, Bismarck had ridiculed Michelis in the North German Reichstag for using theological language in his speeches. In this context, the chancellor had spoken of

Michelis as a "Catholic cleric." When Michelis attempted to abuse his right to speak on another issue in an effort to defend himself from this charge, he ended up in a conflict with the Reichstag's president. This affair had humiliated Michelis to such a degree that he had publicly laid down his mandate in that very session.[4] When Lasker referred to Michelis as "the clerical member" of the Prussian parliament, therefore, he adroitly played on his opponent's weakness. Lasker's anticlerical antics also clearly offended Michelis. During a separate sitting reserved for personal comments at the end of the session, Michelis retaliated by referring to Lasker as "the Jewish deputy from Berlin."[5] While nobody had objected to Lasker's comment about his clerical opponent, Michelis's description of Lasker led to an immediate intervention by the parliament's president, Forckenbeck, who declared that Michelis's expression was "not [fit for] parliamentary [use]."[6] Challenged by Michelis on his ruling, Forckenbeck explained that Michelis had denounced another man's religion, which was not acceptable, whereas Lasker's comment was permissible because it had mentioned only Michelis's occupation or social position [*Stand*].[7]

This decision elicits a number of questions. Did Forckenbeck believe his own claim that Lasker had merely pointed to a colleague's social status when he had called Michelis a "clerical" member of parliament? Was it perhaps more insulting to be called a Jew than a priest and thus less acceptable in such forums? Were the debate and the ruling based on a larger theory of representation that assumed representatives could be divided according to occupation but not on the basis of religion? Put another way, was a secularist framework that defined a person's religion as a private matter and thus not a proper subject of public debate at work in this debate? A second example of a discussion that arose in the German Reichstag only a few years later indicates that none of these questions can be easily answered.[8] In a heated debate over the budget of the Protestant Central Consistory, the president's ruling about the use of personal epithets pulled in a different direction. This time the conflict involved two Protestants. In this case, Deputy Strosser, known mainly for his unusual civil occupation as the director of a state penitentiary, called another deputy "Pastor Müller."[9] The first time Strosser used this form of address the parliament's president interrupted him and admonished him to use only "deputy" and not his opponent's official title. Departing from the earlier ruling in Lasker's case, the president indicated that referencing someone's *Stand* was not a permissible form of address in parliament. When Strosser stubbornly continued to address his fellow deputy as "Herr Pastor," the president threatened disciplinary measures against him. If this threat alone did not suffice to stop Strosser, the anonymous interjection *"Zuchthausaufseher!"*—prison guard—certainly did. Whether due to these official warnings or a fear of being ridiculed because of his own occupation and title, Strosser referred to his opponent simply as "Deputy Müller" from that point on.

Analyzed together, these two incidents unsettle established notions about secularism, Jewish identity politics, and anticlericalism in the parliamentary arena. First, they remind us that official politics were not just about the representation of interests, the exchange of ideas, or the creation of alliances. Parliamentary statements also aimed at affirming a deputy's own legitimacy to speak about an issue and—whenever possible—to delegitimize his enemies' right to speak. When Jewish parliamentarians' relationships to their own Jewishness or to Jewish constituents became an issue of debate, they understood that they could be subject to the same types of backhanded insults that other deputies experienced in other contexts. A Jewish deputy was thus forced to work with the knowledge that he might be addressed as a Jew, whether explicitly or implicitly, just as others knew they might be publicly ridiculed for being a priest or a prison warden. Parliament was, in this sense, a decentered space, where Jews were merely one potentially vulnerable group among many. It was also a place where Jews were not simply members of a minority but also sometimes of *the* minority (in the electoral or political sense)—a place, in other words, where the essentialized identities of Jews and their often fluid political alliances overlapped.

The two incidents concerning the permissibility of pointing out deputies' occupational or religious difference on the floor of parliament also highlight the fluid quality of secularism, which can be grasped neither with the traditional methods of intellectual history nor in terms of distinct German and French models alone. Members of parliament certainly invoked their attachment to lofty ideas and venerable national traditions at various instances, but they often did so in an inconsistent manner and for pragmatic reasons. I do not mean to suggest here that there were no discernable patterns in the rhetoric of German and French deputies but rather that we explore them with a full awareness of their often elusive and always contingent nature. Parliamentary oratory was neither merely an expression of an individual deputy's personal opinion nor a function of rigid rules of behavior—it was also a rhetorical performance.[10] Understanding the dynamic nature of parliamentary speech in this way can enrich the study of Jews in modern politics as well as the ultimately polemical nature of secularism. The identification of Jewish deputies as Jews in the parliamentary arena meant that they had to permanently negotiate multiple expectations, many of which were articulated only as polemical opportunities arose and not the result of preconceived theories of political representation.

This fluidity returns us to one of the basic dilemmas of this book, which is the question of how debates on Catholicism influenced modern secularism broadly and the way Jews articulated politicized expectations about religion in particular. The traditional master narrative of modern German and French Jewish political life has tended to parallel received wisdom about the secularization process in Europe as a whole. While the secularization thesis portrayed an increasing differentiation between religious and political spheres, Jewish historians have often described how Jews aimed to fit into their surrounding societies by giving up their Jewish particularity when in public. According to this view, even if Jews retained social ties with other Jews or kept religious traditions alive in their homes, Jewish men in particular attempted to project a secular or nondenominational public persona.[11] According to this reading of Jewish history, when Jewish men became politicians, they adopted the accepted language of liberal universalism in the hopes of appearing "on the streets" as Germans or Frenchmen rather than members of a religious minority.[12] It is no coincidence that Clermont-Tonnerre's famous sentence in the French National Assembly in December 1789—"We must refuse everything to the Jews as a nation and accord everything to Jews as individuals"— has so often been repeated. Turned into an emblematic statement since the Holocaust, as David Sorkin has shown, Clermont-Tonnerre's statement also fit perfectly the larger narrative of secularism developed in twentieth-century scholarship.[13] The vision he articulated exemplifies the received narrative about the pressure European Jews faced to abandon their Jewish public personas so well that the quote even appears in histories of countries with completely different political and parliamentary traditions.[14]

As the Introduction of this book explains, the twin narratives of European secularization and Jewish assimilation have come under scrutiny in recent years. Newer works have underscored that Jews in nineteenth-century France and Germany felt compelled to emphasize what they might contribute to the nation *as Jews* in response to claims that their citizenship was a reward rather than a right.[15] In taking this approach, such studies show how Jews sought to earn their civic and social status by highlighting their particularity. None of the recent interventions into the scholarship have fully unraveled the narrative of assimilatory pressures, however, particularly with regard to the sphere of national politics. Certain works that have attempted to rethink the relationship between Jews and liberalism have instead reinforced the idea of the homogenizing logic of modernity. In an attempt to challenge the idea that liberalism should be understood as universally emancipatory, such studies adopted the received notion that even those non-Jewish liberals who were sympathetic to Jewish integration demanded that Jews abandon their specificity.[16] This chapter suggests that parliamentary debate broadly understood and Jewish participation in debates on the Catholic Church in particular can help us revise widely held assumptions about the pressures Jewish men felt to become unmarked, generic citizens in the realm of high politics.[17] An analysis of Jewish parliamentary rhetoric points to the existence of alternative values that countervailed against universalist pressures. Abandoning a chronological thrust, the present chapter draws our attention to a field of political debate rather than a particular period. Most examples are chosen, however, from the first four decades of Jewish participation in European parliaments from roughly the 1840s to the 1880s—a period that witnessed the rise of organized liberal politics. Although this chapter also draws on a few examples from the late nineteenth century, which saw the rise of political antisemitism, this later period is covered in more depth in the final chapter of this book.

Beyond Universalism and the Culture of Generality

There are good reasons that some of the most influential works on political representation have come out of France. Whereas the history of representation in Germany is complicated by the wider practice and acceptance of decentralization and federalism, leading politicians of the French Revolution and the Third Republic tended to defend a simpler, purer, and more radical model of unmediated representation. Pierre Rosanvallon, one of the most influential recent critics of this tradition, has referred in this context to a French "culture of generality," which he defines as a belief in the direct relationship between the nation and the individual, the possibility of a collective expression of the nation, and a vision of the law as universal.[18] For Rosanvallon, the lower chambers of parliament (Chambre des députés, or Assemblée nationale) in particular symbolize this culture of generality. While both Rosanvallon and others have explored debates in which important political players broke with the traditions of both the ancien régime and the Jacobins by demanding decentralization, advocates of a strict interpretation of generality nonetheless remained dominant for much of the nineteenth century, according to Rosanvallon's reading.[19] The notion that workers might have the right to represent their fellow workers in legislative bodies, for example, gained traction only slowly, beginning in the 1860s, as Rosanvallon notes.[20]

Given this general assessment of French politics, it is remarkable that several Jewish deputies in France were deeply and publicly involved in Jewish communal politics, in particular in the state-mandated representative bodies of French Jewry—the consistories. This was true as early as the 1840s, when Adolphe Crémieux and Théodore Cerfberr (1792–1876) were simultaneously deputies in the Chambre des députés and presidents of the Central Consistory. The duality of their public personas was evidenced in the reporting of the French state's official periodical, the *Moniteur universel*, which printed both their statements in parliament and their New Year's addresses to the king on behalf of the Jewish community in 1845 and 1846. In the same paper, Jewish deputies could thus appear either as representatives of the French nation as a whole or as Jewish communal leaders, depending on the context. Later in the century, Jewish parliamentarians like Théodore Reinach (1860–1928) were similarly active in Jewish institutions such as the Société des études juives, although most of the overlap in this period of mass politics occurred between the French Jewish consistorial leadership and the governmental administration, where a career was not dependent on elections.[21]

While the elected representatives of the state were less likely to be involved in communal matters than unelected administrators, as Pierre Birnbaum has noted, elected Jewish representatives were arguably more likely to highlight their Jewishness while exercising their official function.[22] Indeed, in some contexts, Jewish deputies even advertised their background as an asset. This approach is made evident in the political maneuvers of Bénédict or Benoît Fould (1792–1858), the first Jewish deputy in a French parliament and, for that matter, in any Western or Central European parliament. Serving since 1834, Fould was typical of the French Jewish deputies who followed in his footsteps in later decades: He was a centrist and came from the wealthiest stratum of society.[23] The oldest son of an important banker, Fould maintained his role in the family business while sitting in parliament.

During the time of his first, if unsuccessful, bid for a parliamentary seat, Fould published an official statement of his political aims, a so-called *profession de foi*. Fould's *profession* is remarkable for its explicit discussion of his religious background. It reads:

> It appears to me that one can see in my person the development of two of the most precious conquests of our revolution: religious liberty and equality among citizens. Indeed, I belong to a religion practiced by a hundred thousand French individuals who support all the responsibilities of the state and contribute approximately three per cent to the [national] budget. They have nevertheless not taken part in national representation, even though everyone agrees to recognize that all interests and all rights deserve to have their own representatives [*mandataires*] and their own organs.[24]

Attempting to preempt the accusation that a Jewish representative would remain wedded to his particular affiliation, Fould instead presented his Jewishness as a boon to the larger national project. In Fould's view, it was precisely his particular identity that made him the perfect example of the universalism of the new era. Indeed, he addressed this message to an electoral college that in all likelihood did not include a single Jew. Only 244 voters were eligible in this seat representing Saint-Quentin *intra-muros*, which had no historical Jewish community.[25] Fould was therefore hardly suggesting that he planned to be a "representative of the Jews" in any straightforward sense. Although he did imply that he hoped to give French Jews a voice, Fould's main argument was that his own voice would make the representation of the French nation more complete. While this advertisement of his theory of representation did not get Fould elected, there is no indication that his contemporaries perceived his arguments as a transgression.

Even though Fould's call for diversity was rarely echoed in parliament, other types of Jewish advocacy were common. Many deputies who were also active in Jewish communal organizations openly made demands on behalf of French Jews. During budget debates held in the years before 1848, for example, Crémieux demanded that the state increase the salary of rabbis on multiple occasions.[26] A lawyer who made his name with, among other things, a prominent case against the *more judaico*—the special oath that Jews had to swear in some French courts until 1846—Crémieux was the longest-serving Jewish deputy in France, holding a parliamentary seat under five different political regimes. A committed republican, Crémieux framed the issue of budgetary allocations for Jewish clergymen in universalistic terms, describing Jewish rights as a matter of equity that concerned the entire nation. He also buttressed his claim with the suggestion that he was an expert on the subject, declaring that members of the budget committee had believed they could cut funding to Jewish clergymen in part because so "few people in France have a precise understanding of the situation of this religion."[27] As concerned rabbis, Crémieux regularly complained that they received less than Protestant religious leaders and, unlike the clergy of the three Christian denominations, did not have access to additional benefits from donations connected with particular services. At times, he even dared to claim a special relationship with the rabbis he sought to protect. In one such instance, Crémieux explained his position thus: "The rabbis, like your priests, have to give to charity."[28] If the priests belonged to the Christian deputies, did the rabbis belong to him and the other Jewish deputies?[29] Crémieux may have articulated his position in terms of universal values, but his use of personal pronouns illustrates that he was not willing to simply play the role of a neutral observer in matters touching Jewish communal affairs.

As in France, we can also find clear expressions of public Jewish identity in nineteenth-century Germany, where—at least in theory—there was hardly more love for the representation of religious interest.[30] Secularism in Germany meant primarily the transcendence of denominational differences in a rational political body, making the representation of religious groups a particularly touchy issue. It is no coincidence that the liberal Karl von Rotteck defined the early nationalist term "*Gemeingeist*" (loosely translatable as "spirit of unity") by distinguishing it from "*kirchliches Partikularinteresse*" (particular, ecclesiastical interests).[31] Secularism in education and other fields of governance for the most part meant the absence of confession—*konfessionslos*—whereas confessionalism was understood as the paradigmatic case of particularism. Whatever terms Jews used to define their particularism—religion, denomination, race, or ethnic group [*Stamm*]—they used them carefully so as not to appear as a different nation. As a consequence, German Jews did not draw on ideas about ethnic representation in the way that deputies of the Polish and Danish faction in the German and Prussian parliaments did.[32] We might expect, therefore, that the representation of Jewish opinions and interests would have collided with the demands of universalism famously championed by secularist liberals.

Yet, as in France, several nineteenth-century German Jewish deputies became known for their willingness to speak on behalf of Jewish rights. Although these individuals frequently used universalistic language in their advocacy, they left no doubt that they were speaking for the particular religious group to which they belonged. In the Prussian parliament and the German Reichstag, Raphael Kosch (1803–1872) was the most famous Jew to pursue this course.[33] Kosch, a physician from Königsberg, started his career in the Prussian Landtag of 1848, acting for a short period as the body's vice president.[34] Representing Königsberg in the Prussian diet between 1862 and 1872, his politics were consistently left of center. He was also one of the founding members of the left-liberal Fortschrittspartei (Progress Party). Kosch was at his most vocal during a debate over the petition of sixteen Jewish assistant judges—the highest judicial position Jews in Prussia could then attain—who demanded the abrogation of limitations on their advancement at court.[35] Kosch explicitly went beyond a universalistic argument in his speech on the subject:

> My aim when I rose to speak here was only to object to these violations of our rights in front of the whole country, as a Jew, in my name, and in the name of all my coreligionists. I demand from parliament that it finally help establish our legal and constitutional rights. Gentlemen, when I say our rights I speak not only of the right of the Jews but also of your rights. You seek a legal state [*Rechtsstaat*]; in a legal state the violation of the rights of an individual or of a minority [*Minorität*] is also a violation of [the rights of] all.[36]

Like most Jewish parliamentarians who claimed to speak "in the name of" the Jews, Kosch did not elaborate on the precise type of representation he envisioned.[37] Many others more explicitly referenced a culture of universalism and explained why they did not believe it applied in their particular case. Jewish deputies' public reflections on their reluctance to speak as Jews usually signaled the beginning of an attempt to move beyond their role as abstract, unmarked representatives of the nation.

Eduard Lasker, who became one of the leading politicians of the German national liberals during the 1870s, offers several examples of such behavior. On a theoretical level, Lasker repeatedly expressed his adherence to a code of universalism. Around the time of Kosch's statement, Lasker explained his position in the North German Reichstag in the following manner: "As a matter of principle I do not speak up regarding such motions, which concern me and my coreligionists so intimately. It might seem as if I were speaking at the same time for my own person."[38] Yet it was precisely such a comment that marked Lasker as a man whose interests might overlap with those of his coreligionists.[39] This tension has led scholars to interpret such statements as evidence of a split consciousness, in which individuals were emotionally torn between their solidarity with other Jews and their desire to become unmarked citizens.[40] Contrary to these attempts to read the contradictory statements of Jewish parliamentarians as evidence of their psychological states, I propose that we treat them as rhetorical devices meant to bolster the legitimacy of their speaking position at a given moment.

Unlike in France, German Jewish parliamentarians frequently felt compelled to discuss Jews' basic rights, which made it nearly unavoidable to point out one's personal involvement in the matter under discussion. Perhaps the most difficult position was that of David Morgenstern (1814–1882), a Jewish lawyer in the Bavarian Landtag, who gave a speech in 1855 opposing proposals to a change to the Bavarian constitution that would have taken both active and passive voting rights away from Jews. Forced to discuss his own future right to speak in the house as a member of the relevant parliamentary commission, Morgenstern likened his situation to an officer who had to listen to rehearsals of the march to be played at his own funeral.[41]

It should be added, however, that Morgenstern's choice of rhetorical strategy was not restricted to German deputies fighting for their very right to speak. Many of the most prominent defenders of Jewish rights made a habit of articulating general principles by pointing to their own situation as Jews. Crémieux used this tactic in French debates, for example, when he complained that the Swiss government discriminated against French Jews. The two countries had agreed in an accord to treat each other's citizens as their own. In Switzerland's interpretation this meant that it could deal with French Jews as if they were Swiss Jews, making them subject to humiliating and highly restrictive legislation on a cantonal level. According to Crémieux, as well as the majority of French liberals in parliament, equal treatment meant that French citizens irrespective of their religion had to be given the rights of full citizens on all levels. He argued:

> In France, legally speaking, are there Jews, Catholics, Protestants? Religiously speaking yes but legally they don't exist. There are only citizens; there is no difference between us and the proof for this is that I have the honor to be here just like everybody else; in Switzerland, I want to arrive just like you, with the same rights as you.[42]

To underline the injustice suffered by Jews, Crémieux decided to use a fictive scenario illustrating how he might be treated differently than French Christians while abroad to make his point. Rather than obscure his stakes in these debates, he highlighted them.

Both in Germany and France, Kosch's and Crémieux's style of politics became rarer with a new generation of deputies. In Germany, prominent Jewish deputies of the 1870s like Ludwig Bamberger (1823–1899) and Leopold Sonnemann (1831–1909), were, for example, less inclined to speak of Jews as "my coreligionists." Even these later deputies were often willing to address issues that were understood as falling into the category of Jewish interests, however—thus risking being seen as particularistic or even unpatriotic. Sonnemann, for his part, made an interpellation in the Prussian parliament for the benefit of the Jewish school of Frankfurt am Main in 1871.[43] While he did not talk about his own religion at this moment and might have claimed that this was simply another issue of his electoral district in Frankfurt, there was little doubt that such advocacy had its risks. The ability to remain silent about one's religion while advocating for the rights of its adherents was as telling about the expectations of German secularism as was the ability (or need) to make one's religion explicit.[44]

Polite Conversation, Honor, and Expertise

What made Jewish deputies speak about their coreligionists and, more importantly, highlight their own Judaism in particular contexts? Three interrelated explanations emerge from an analysis of parliamentary debates. First, deputies found that their speeches were measured not only against the yardstick of liberal or conservative theories of representation but also according to notions of polite conservation. Although parliament was undoubtedly a public institution, deputies were expected to follow accepted forms of speech that fit middle-class notions of propriety in their debates. The parliamentary arena thus shared elements with other partially public venues such as the academic disputation or the literary salon. Although the epithets Lasker and Michelis exchanged in parliament make clear that "parliamentary language" implied greater demands than the minimum standards of civilized dialogue, it was also unthinkable without them.

The most powerful regulative ideas in this context were decency and honor. Composed of a collective of men admitted because of their status in society, nineteenth-century parliaments accepted the notion that deputies had to defend their reputation, which was in turn closely connected with their claims to personal autonomy and rationality.[45]

Scholars have long highlighted the German obsession with honor, a social value that explains both the popularity of dueling and the explosion of honor litigation in courts in late nineteenth-century Germany.[46] This respect for the demands of honor also created the phenomenon of the official "private comment" in German parliaments. When Michelis responded to Lasker, he did so during this final part of the session reserved strictly for the resolution of private matters. After the official debate on a bill or report had closed, these final minutes of each session allowed individuals to set the record straight about concerns that pertained solely to their person. Injuries to the good name of a parliamentarian could be rectified even if these comments had nothing to do with the political order of the day. (In fact, when deputies did try to say something relating to a bill during this period, the president was obliged to silence them.) While such a formal arrangement did not exist in France, normative ideas about polite conversations affected French parliaments as well. In both countries, the regulative ideas of honor sometimes existed in tension with the culture of universalism because they very often transcended the public/private divide. Upholding one's reputation commonly connected the space of politics with the world of duels, where honor was regularly challenged and reestablished.[47]

We can see this logic at work in one of the most famous speeches made by a German Jewish member of parliament in the nineteenth century. In August 1848, the deputy Robert von Mohl proposed to limit the rights of Jews who had just been fully emancipated by the revolution half a year earlier. The Jewish lawyer and deputy Gabriel Riesser repudiated Mohl in a well-received speech in favor of Jewish equality. Rather than avoiding any reference to his particular investment in the issue, Riesser underscored it:

> Gentlemen! In the earlier discussion concerned with the preferred estates, an honorable speaker justly made claim to his right to speak in front of you in the name of the preferred estate to which he belonged, and to defend it. I claim the same right to appear here in the name of a class [*Klasse*] that had been suppressed for millennia, to which I belong through birth, and to which I—because personal religious convictions do not belong here—continue to belong through the principle of honor, which made me reject the acquisition of disdainfully refused rights by religious conversion. I claim the right to rise to speak in

front of you against hateful slander in the name of this oppressed class [*Volksklasse*].[48]

Like many Jewish deputies after him, Riesser defined his relationship to Jewish rights by invoking a universalistic notion of honor and by emphasizing his rights as a respectable male citizen. Parliamentarians did not voice any critique of this approach. Indeed, it is unlikely that Riesser's colleagues were surprised by his invocation of his Jewish background. He had been elected to parliament based on his fame as the champion of Jewish rights since the 1830s, after all.[49] Now, for the second time, Riesser's defense of the rights of his coreligionists brought him to the forefront of parliamentary politics, leading to his appointment as second vice president of the Frankfurt Parliament in October 1848.[50]

Honor also motivated and legitimized the reaction of speakers who were generally less inclined to identify publicly as Jews. This was especially true in the final decades of the nineteenth century, when anti-Jewish demands were discussed with increasing frequently in parliament. In 1895, the French Assemblée nationale discussed two antisemitic interpellations: one asking what the government intended to do to stop the "predominance of the Jews in various branches of the French administration" and the other concerning "the dangers of the incessant infiltration of the Jewish race" into French society.[51] The first deputy to speak was Alfred Naquet, a politician with many contradictory commitments: Scion of a famous Jewish family and a self-declared anarchist and freethinker, he had also been one of the few Jewish supporters of General Boulanger's attempt to create an authoritarian regime in France.[52] Naquet, who was disinterested in Judaism earlier in his career, eventually rediscovered his Jewish background in reaction to the rising tide of antisemitism that emerged in France during the Dreyfus affair.[53] In 1895, he explained to parliament why somebody like him would speak as a Jew to defend the Jews:[54]

> Gentlemen, somewhat earlier I hesitated to speak in the current debate. You all know the reason for this hesitation: If there are indeed Semites, then I am a Semite, and in that respect it might seem as if I was pleading *pro domo med*, which always creates a difficult situation for the speaker. [. . .] I always preached to my coreligionists—if you permit

me to use this word, which does not relate to anything, because if one does not have a religion one cannot have coreligionists; but this helps me avoid another circumlocution—so, I always preached to my co-religionists the fusion into the grand mass of French citizens. I myself am setting an example with my marriage to a Catholic and I have to say that for more than thirty years, I have frequented [the homes of] mostly non-Jews. If I have been moving closer to my coreligionists in the past decade, it is a result of the hate campaign [. . .]. In the face of threats it seemed to me an act of cowardice [*lâcheté*] not to declare my solidarity with those who have the same origin as I do. Incidentally, it would perhaps be difficult for me not to speak.[55]

With these words, Naquet not only explained his ambivalent private sentiments about his own Jewishness; he also described his simultaneous attachment to secularist universalism and honor, a situation that made it both difficult for him to speak and difficult not to speak as a Jew at the same time. Integrating into the French nation meant for Naquet the end of Jewish particularity—something he claimed to embody in his personal life through his marriage to a Catholic—but it also demanded that he should act like an honorable man who would not retreat under attack. A commitment to secularism—from a freethinker and republican—might imply that one should not speak of one's own particular or communal interests, but the threat of being seen as a coward was strong enough to push Naquet in the other direction. Although they were absent from theories of political representation in modern Europe and sometimes went against the integrationist intentions of the speaker, notions of honor profoundly shaped the tension-ridden way secularism was lived in parliament.

Apart from the demands of honor, parliament's need for experts on difficult issues also created opportunities for Jews to move beyond the confines of a narrowly understood culture of generality. Jewish deputies sometimes consciously adopted the role of experts on Jewish matters. (We might recall the example of Crémieux in his advocacy of budget increases for rabbinic salaries, which were based on his knowledge of a group that he claimed was perennially misunderstood.) Just as often, Jews were forced into this role, or they received an invitation to explain the nature of the Jewish community and its religion that they could not refuse without disappointing their interlocutors' expectations of honorable conduct. We can see this pattern at work, for example, in a parliamentary debate on the employment of Jews in Prussian courts and schools that took place in 1860. Early in the debate, the anti-Jewish deputy Moritz von Blankenburg (1815–1888) told the house that he was pleased that the Jewish deputy Moritz Veit (1808–1864) was slated to speak after him as this would give Veit, a successful publisher and former president of Berlin's Jewish community, the possibility of correcting him with regards to any of the claims he was about to make about the Jews.[56] Blankenburg then proceeded to deliver a speech spiked with quotes from the Talmud, taken out of context, and aimed at proving that Jews could not be integrated into civil society.[57] In his speech, Blankenburg explicitly addressed Veit as an observant Jew [*gläubigen Juden*].[58] Veit, in his response, claimed he did not wish to enter into any theological debates, but he nevertheless corrected Blankenburg's statements about the nature of the Talmud.[59] Taking the opportunity to explain to the non-Jewish deputy—as well as the rest of parliament—that the Talmud was a mere collection of opinions, Veit implicitly accepted the role of a specialist on Judaism, even while he explicitly denied any interest in adopting such a position.

When the same debate continued in a later session, Veit again played the role of expert on Jewish affairs, as he offered his non-Jewish audience insights into the Jewish mind. In response to a cabinet minister's argument that the Jews should not demean themselves by demanding positions that they were not eligible to hold, Veit declared: "I believe I can assure you, gentlemen, that the Jews will be too proud to push their way into such positions—the moment that they are convinced that they are [indeed] *not qualified* [. . .] to hold them. I also believe that the *honor of a man* demands that he defend rather than give up his rights."[60] In the months and years that followed, Veit and other Jewish deputies were regularly invited to speak in this manner about the general opinions of Jews. They appear to have rarely declined the offer. In general, Jewish deputies considered it an "honorable" thing to speak as experts about their coreligionists.[61]

The importance of Jews as simultaneous experts and native informants capable of explaining Judaism to non-Jews also appeared in the debates on the legal regulation of rest periods for laborers in France. As in many other countries, laws meant to protect workers mandated that particular groups of laborers were not to be employed on certain holidays or on Sundays. In the German and French case, champions of labor protections often argued for such regulations without any references to Christianity.[62] In such cases, Jewish politicians faced the question of whether they would endorse such bills or insist on laws that would be more neutral on the question of a mandated day of rest.

One such debate in the French Chamber of Deputies in December 1840 is particularly instructive, as it shows the immense power a single Jewish deputy could wield to end the discussion on these matters. In the course of deliberations on a bill intended to afford women and children a mandatory rest on Sundays and holidays, the liberal deputy Sébastien Luneau, who was famous for his attacks against the size of state subsidies for the high clergy, attacked the bill as a contradiction to the legal guarantees of the *Charte* of 1830. In Luneau's view, the bill raised Catholicism above all other religions and thus broke the promises of the *Charte* to treat Catholicism merely as the religion of the majority of the French people rather than the religion of the state. Pointing to Alsace, where several villages had large Jewish populations, Luneau proposed a minor amendment: Jews should be allowed not to work on Saturday instead of Sunday. As all involved understood Luneau's intervention as anticlerical—rather than merely a friendly gesture toward France's Jews—his critics accused him of being anti-religious.[63]

The short and heated debate took a different turn when Benoît Fould took the rostrum. Opening his remarks with the clarification that he belonged "to a minority to which one has alluded," Fould thanked Luneau for his well-meant proposal but rejected it in his own name as well as that of his coreligionists.[64] To the right of Luneau on the political spectrum and disinclined to allow for special laws for Jews, Fould argued that the individual rights guaranteed by the *Charte* were sufficient. Jews could celebrate their festivals privately whenever they wanted and did not need additional protections. He explained that the 300,000 Jews of France (a number he made up) were accustomed to the fact that thirty million non-Jews celebrated their day of rest on Sunday. It was not so much Fould's arguments per se but rather that someone others judged to be a legitimate expert on the interests of Jews in parliament had spoken that immediately ended the debate—thus removing the question of Jewish rights from the agenda. The fact that Fould had no Jewish mandate whatsoever—as the German Jewish paper *Sulamith* pointed out with dismay—seemed to have disturbed nobody in parliament.[65] On the contrary, his statements were later used far beyond their immediate context in discussions of similar laws. When the Jewish deputy Edouard Bamberger protested against new labor laws thirty-two years later because they protected Sunday rest specifically instead of mandating a six-day work week, his detractors cited Fould's expertise and statements in the name of the Jews, using the reputation of the deceased Jewish expert to undermine the critiques of the living one.[66]

Speaking as a Jew in an Period of Secularist Conflict

The desire of Jewish deputies to highlight and deemphasize their Judaism in turn, as well as the tendency of their interlocutors to do so, was not always the result of particular attitudes toward Jews. In an age of liberal–Catholic conflict, the way Jews spoke about themselves was inevitably shaped by the politics of anti-Catholicism. Crémieux's speeches in favor of increased salaries for rabbis are once again instructive. In his 1850 speech on the subject, Crémieux argued that, although Judaism was an ancient religion, it remained poorly understood. He thus felt compelled to clarify certain details about the historic organization of the Jewish religion by explaining that Jews—unlike Catholics—had no traditional clerical hierarchy, which was only later introduced into the French Jewish communal structure by Napoleon. The state was thus primarily responsible for the survival of the institutions it had invented.[67] In moments such as these, Jewish deputies drew on tropes from the language of polemical secularism to seek support for their religion from anticlerical deputies.

In other cases, the politics of Jewish representation intersected with anticlerical concerns more directly. One example from the Reichstag demonstrates this trend in the German case, where the debates on Jews and Catholics as religious minorities were often closely related. In May 1872, the national liberal deputy Ludwig Bamberger proposed that parliament express its gratitude to Bismarck's government for pressuring the state of Romania to take steps to halt violence perpetrated against Jews there. In the debate, Bamberger and Lasker, whom everybody knew to be Jewish, spoke about foreign Jews without any reference to them as their own coreligionists or to their potentially personal relationship to the issue.[68]

The fact that Bamberger, who was reluctant to speak as a Jew in political forums before the intensification of antisemitism in the late 1870s, took a leading role in this initiative is striking. It speaks again to the low barriers keeping Jewish members of parliament from speaking on behalf of other Jews. In this case, the discussion was remarkable because of its timing. Barely more than a year had passed since the famous debate over parliament's response to Wilhelm I's "Speech from the Throne," the so-called *Adreßdebatte* of March 30, 1871. In an attempt to curb the authoritarian militarism they associated with the Prussian state, the majority of national liberals used the opportunity to demand that the monarch declare Germany's commitment to noninterference in other nations' affairs. Afraid that this would dash any hope of a German initiative to reestablish papal sovereignty over Rome, the Catholic faction rejected such a provision. When important Catholic representatives demanded that the monarch should—at the very least—avoid excluding all possibility of German intervention abroad, the liberals denounced the Catholic faction as unpatriotic.[69] The general aversion to the politics of religious interests resonated with contemporary rumors that German Catholics were pawns in the hands of French conspirators who sought to lure Germany into a war on the Italian peninsula. Reverberations of the 1871 debate could thus still be felt during the discussion of Bamberger's bill, even if none of the participants explicitly mentioned the connection.

Instead of addressing the issue directly, those engaging in the 1872 debate performed a tightrope act in political rhetoric. The keyword of the *Adreßdebatte* had been "intervention," meaning military intervention to restore the new Italian capital to the pope's control. Ludwig Windthorst, a leading figure in the Catholic Center Party, used this term strategically when he declared his support for Bamberger's initiative to celebrate Germany's "intervention" in Romania for the sake of the Jews. After this provocation, most of the debate on Bamberger's bill revolved around the controversial term. Lasker and Bamberger were now faced with a problem: If they accepted Windthorst's endorsement and allowed the bill to pass with the help of Center Party deputies, they would implicitly be acknowledging that liberal criticism of the Center Party the year before was nothing less than hypocrisy. If Jews could ask for intervention for their coreligionists in Romania, it seemed reasonable to assume Catholics could legitimately demand intervention for the pope. Reacting to the challenge, Lasker threatened to ask Bamberger to withdraw the bill in the case that "only a significant part of the house shares Windthorst's interpretation."[70] The increasingly charged debates between Catholics and liberals made it necessary for liberal Jewish deputies to carefully consider the wording of their statements so as to avoid playing into the hands of the Center Party. Although the identity of the two Jewish deputies was never explicitly mentioned during these discussions, it was permanently in the background. The challenge in such cases was not how to follow a single rule of secularist or universalist representation but rather the complicated ways in which the politics of one group could be used as a paradigm—as well as a litmus test—in the debates about another community.

Jews, Catholics, and Secularism in Prussia

While the tides of anticlericalism and anti-Catholicism that swept German and French parliaments did little to limit Jewish deputies' ability to advocate for the rights of other Jews, they did affect the way Jewish members of parliament could speak about Catholics and the Catholic Church. Debates on the churches often motivated, or forced, Jewish deputies to highlight their background, just as they had done in discussions of their own civil rights. In periods such as the 1870s in Germany and 1879–1882 and 1895–1905 in France, when political debates about a variety of topics seemed to boil down to questions of religion, such a move had a significant effect on the strategies and possibilities of Jewish self-representation.

The central question facing Jewish deputies in these debates was not so much which positions they should take on the topic of church and state but instead when, where, and how they should articulate them. We can see these dilemmas clearly in the German *Kulturkampf* of the 1870s, when liberals engaged in a failed attempt to unite the country socially—after it had been united politically—by eliminating the Catholic

Church and its clergy as a political force.[71] When Jewish deputies began to speak about the Catholic Church in the beginning of that decade, they faced new pressures to legitimize their own role in politics as Jews. With tensions rising, the unwritten rules of proper speech—that is, expectations about what type of issue a Jew could address without appearing indecent or out of place—became an explicit topic of debate.

Such revealing conflicts concerned Eduard Lasker more than any other Jewish parliamentarian in Germany. One of the most active parliamentarians of his day, and also a central figure within the National Liberal faction both in the Reichstag and the Prussian Landtag, Lasker was more outspoken on issues of religion and politics than any other Jewish deputy. His personal nemesis in debates on religion was the Center Party deputy Hermann von Mallinckrodt (1821–1874), a descendant of a noble family from Westphalia who had been among the founders of the Catholic faction in the Prussian parliament and the Center Party in the Reichstag. The ongoing debates between Lasker and Mallinckrodt are particularly rich sources for an analysis of the complex workings of secularism and anticlericalism in the parliamentary arena.

A brief exchange of insults in an early debate of the *Kulturkampf* set the tone for the series of conflicts that erupted between the two deputies in later periods. On January 16, 1871, Mallinckrodt gave one of his many speeches defending German Catholicism in the Prussian lower chamber. Calling on the house to consider a speech of the national liberal deputy Rudolf Virchow as evidence of sinister motives, Mallinckrodt asked: "Was not the greatest part of his speech nothing but an extremely fierce, hostile attack against the convictions of the Catholics? The most hostile attacks constituted the larger part of his speech." At this point, Eduard Lasker interjected from the bench: "Ultramontane!" Mallinckrodt, reacting to the Jewish deputy's comment, quipped: "I thank the deputy Mr. *Lasker* that he corrects me regarding [the use of] the term Catholic." Mallinckrodt's comment led to "great amusement on the right and with the Center [Party]," according to the stenographic protocol of the session.[72] Depicting Lasker as a Jew who instructed a Catholic about Catholicism, Mallinckrodt had managed to ridicule his opponent's very right to speak in parliament, even without mentioning Lasker's religion explicitly. In doing so, Mallinckrodt nonetheless insinuated that the Jewish deputy's comment had touched on the Catholic religion itself, something that Lasker, as an outsider to that religion, had no right to critique.

We can see the impact of Mallinckrodt's insult in Lasker's response. At the end of the debate, Lasker used the period reserved for personal comments to clarify that his interjection had merely been intended to correct a factual mistake in Mallinckrodt's representation of Virchow's speech. He had hoped to point out that Virchow had criticized only ultramontanism and not Catholicism per se, Lasker explained. Apparently embarrassed by Mallinckrodt's remark and the laughter it had elicited among his opponents, Lasker emphasized repeatedly that he had had no intention of instructing Mallinckrodt about the nature of Catholicism before closing with an uncharacteristically defensive statement: "It was a joke and nothing more."[73] Lasker, the victim of a cruel joke, was in the end the one apologizing for a joke that he never made.

Despite the discomfort this moment brought him, Lasker continued to speak out vociferously when it came to issues of religion and politics. Rather than back down after his temporary defeat, he improved his strategies for self-legitimization and attacked the legitimacy of his opponents more effectively. We can see this in a debate on the influence of local priests on elections—one of the most explosive topics of German parliamentary polemics in the early 1870s. In a seminal speech in parliament, Lasker took a position entirely in accord with his national liberal orientation on this subject by attacking priests' abuse of the pulpit for political purposes.[74] For Lasker, this was an issue of principle on multiple levels. He now rejected not only the arguments of his opponents of the Center Party but also their very claim to represent Catholics and Catholicism. The Center Party's alarmism concerning nonexistent threats to the Catholic religion undermined the peace in the Empire, Lasker argued, because the state's stability was predicated on the understanding that religious disagreements should not be transformed into political disputes. At the same time, Lasker argued that the Center Party had mixed the two spheres of religion and politics, as its members had falsely made political questions appear to be religious issues: "If you lay claim to the pulpit, you make it seem as if the pulpit was an internal affair of the Catholic religious community; as if it had no political relevance. That is not true. All of us, regardless of our beliefs, have a right to have every house of God protected against desecration by citizens as well as against defacement by bad priests."[75] In this statement, Lasker expressed a dominant secularist position, demanding the regulation of religion in the name of an ideal notion of rational politics and societal peace.

While Lasker's speech serves as a good indication of his personal rejection of ultramontanism, perhaps more importantly, it also illuminates how a Jewish deputy who held such opinions and saw fit to express them publicly decided to position himself in the process. Aware of the potential pitfalls of his stance, Lasker emphasized at multiple points throughout his speech that his topic of discussion was not of a religious nature and could thus be treated by any deputy independent of his confession. He also anticipated the arguments of those who might have planned to challenge his right to speak on the topic as he spoke the following words: "Gentlemen, far be it for me to touch anything that even remotely concerns any business of the Catholic religion; you will certainly not want to attribute to me any indecent meddling [*in irgend einer Weise indecent mich einmische*] in something which falls somehow in the domain of the Catholic religion."[76]

The notion of "indecent" meddling and of indecency in general is crucial here because it marks Lasker's efforts to overcome what he understood to be a taboo among his fellow deputies. Aware that it was a delicate matter for Jews to speak on Catholic issues, Lasker preempted some of the potential objections to his position by defensively indicating that he accepted the notion that there were indeed certain religious boundaries one was not meant to overstep. In this case, Lasker's self-positioning and his polemical arguments were intimately entangled. His secularist reasoning suggested that politics and religion should have remained separate and that it was the Center Party's fault for introducing politics into spaces reserved for religious worship. Once the religious sphere had been tainted in this way, religion became a political problem. As a result of this development, Lasker had the right, as a citizen and a politician—independent of his religious affiliation—to comment on the issue.

This interpretation of Lasker's speech as a transparent exercise in self-legitimation is supported by Mallinckrodt's response.[77] The Center Party deputy claimed that he had accepted Lasker's behavior until that point but now felt compelled to reverse his opinion: "At this moment,

I am changing my judgment, when I hear that the deputy Lasker assumes the role of judge and teacher who explains to us what belongs to the content and the character of the Catholic Church."[78] This comment led to some disturbance in the house, which demanded an intervention by the parliament's president. Mallinckrodt then attacked Lasker for commenting on questions relating to the pulpit, the confessional, and bad priests. He also asked if Lasker would not also think God's law higher than humanity's law if the state demanded from him to give up his Judaism.[79] The Catholic deputy thus hinted at the sense of honor that made somebody like Lasker a defender of a religion he hardly practiced.

Lasker did not leave the matter alone but instead responded to Mallinckrodt's polemics at the end of the debate with a personal statement.[80] Rejecting Mallinckrodt's claims that he had spoken about Catholic priests, Lasker objected with the following words: "I was not only speaking about Catholic clergy but about 'every priest' who abuses the pulpit for political aims, so that he—as I had added—will be condemned by a secular court; such a person I am entitled to call a bad priest. [. . .] You don't have to be a Catholic—and I have to call this a superficial gimmick, if Mr. von Mallinckrodt always says that I as a Jew have no right to talk about this or that because he declares it to be part of the Catholic religion. Precisely this I will not put up with."[81] Similar to the earlier example of Mallinckrodt's challenge to Lasker's speaking position, Lasker had once again been pushed to further legitimize himself after the closing of the main debate. This time he did not claim that he was merely joking but rather insisted on his legal and social entitlement to speak on the matter of "bad priests," however defined.

Finding a more self-assertive opponent in Lasker this time around, Mallinckrodt responded with a personal statement of his own, in which he made explicit something he had only insinuated until this point. Now distinguishing between Lasker's formal rights and the unwritten rules of parliamentary and general political discourse, Mallinckrodt explained: "I never challenged Mr. Lasker's right [*Befugniß*] to say whatever he wants concerning civic matters; I also don't want to deny his right to express himself on the religious concerns of one or the other confession. Whether I also consider this to be appropriate [*angemessen*] is another question."[82]

Mallinckrodt's remark does not indicate that Lasker overstepped boundaries of proper speech in the eyes of all present. Indeed, in this case, parliament was divided between a majority, which had applauded Lasker and expressed its discontent with Mallinckrodt's criticism, and a minority, which supported Mallinckrodt's critiques of Lasker. At the same time, the fact that Lasker had the overwhelming support of the house and the visitors' benches does not mean that Mallinckrodt's tactics had no effect. In the end, Mallinckrodt succeeded in distracting the public from Lasker's criticism of political Catholicism by involving him in a debate about the decency and appropriate nature of his statements on the topic as a Jewish deputy.

Perhaps as a reaction to his difficulties in avoiding Mallinckrodt's attacks, Lasker appears to have adopted a new strategy by 1873, when the right of the churches to use coercive means was on the table in parliament. Once again the debates that ensued can help us understand how secularist assumptions were exposed in times of conflict. As in the other cases discussed, Lasker once again sided with the majority of liberals in parliament by supporting a bill intended to prohibit religious institutions from using excommunication as a disciplinary measure. Rather than wait for Mallinckrodt's predictable attacks, Lasker now proactively established his legitimacy to speak on the matter by drawing a comparison with Judaism. These were Lasker's opening words, which deserve to be cited in full:

> In the past I have refrained from participating in [discussions of] bills, not because I thought I had [no] right to participate in those debates that concerned the church; [. . .] the entirety of the people is represented by each deputy. Nevertheless I make it a rule, where the necessity—[and] I mean the subjective one—does not demand it, not to rise to speak about questions that deal exclusively with the church. This is not the case with the current law, which is of interest to all religious communities, not only in form but also with regard to its content.
> In order to strengthen my legitimacy [*um meine Legitimation zu verstärken*] I am compelled to present facts which will make clear that the religious community to which I belong [also] makes substantial use of the measures that are to be prohibited.[83]

To the strong disapproval of the Jewish press, Lasker claimed the right to speak on Catholic clerical abuse because, he claimed, rabbis were just as guilty in such matters.[84] Lasker's remarks did not help his case, however. In fact, they apparently facilitated Mallinckrodt's attack, as he took the opportunity to criticize Lasker's now avowedly open identity as a Jew in parliament. Mallinckrodt again emphasized his suggestion that, while Lasker might be legally entitled to offer such comments about Catholic practices, they were nonetheless socially unacceptable. According to Mallinckrodt, the rules of proper speech made it appropriate for Lasker to speak about the transgressions of Jewish clerics alone.[85] In this instance as well, Mallinckrodt managed to have the last word.

As much as they disagreed about the boundaries of proper speech and the relevance of a speaker's religious identity to the issue at hand, Lasker and Mallinckrodt did agree on one issue: Such matters would have to be decided bearing in mind the distinction between politics and religion, or between outer (political) and inner (purely religious) questions of religious organization. Implicitly, both deputies concurred that purely religious statements about another denomination were indecent. The legitimacy to speak on a topic was thus dependent on the speaker's religious identity, whereas political statements were the equal right of any citizen. Lasker and Mallinckrodt's exchange of insults and accusations can be understood as a negotiation over the boundaries of proper speech, which brought to the fore not only their irreconcilable political differences but also many shared assumptions about the way in which public debates should be regulated.

Jews, Catholics, and Secularism in France

Conflicts similar to those that emerged between Mallinckrodt and Lasker also appeared in France. As in Germany, French Catholic members of parliament did not tend to complain when Jews defended other Jews but challenged deputies with a Jewish background when they spoke about anything involving the Catholic Church—including some of the most important legislation passed in parliament. Several famous incidents followed this German pattern: In one debate on schools for children of soldiers, for example, French republican and Catholic deputies clashed over the role chaplains should play in these educational institutions. In an interjection during the speech of the Jewish deputy Camille Dreyfus, a Catholic deputy called from the benches: "We are not talking about rabbis here."[86] The incident ended with the president's rebuke of the deputy who had interrupted Dreyfus.

Another incident from 1891, which once again involved Camille Dreyfus, led to a more elaborate exchange that recalls Lasker and Mallinckrodt's skirmishes, despite the fact that the Jewish deputy took a completely different position in this case. The debate revolved around a bill Dreyfus had submitted in the name of several other deputies calling for the separation of church and state. In his speech against the bill, the right-wing nationalist Paul Déroulède (1846–1914) argued that the proposal was an attempt to de-Christianize France.[87] Déroulède had been a sworn enemy of parliamentary democracy for some time and had scandalized parliament with his outlandish behavior on various occasions.[88] Just one year before his clash with Dreyfus, he had been censured along with two other members of parliament for preventing another deputy from speaking—a situation that had escalated to the point that the president had Déroulède and his friends removed from the session by force.[89] In his opposition to Dreyfus, Déroulède once again showed his ability to sow dissention with the following statement: "I should add, gentlemen, that I am surprised that such a debate has been opened not by one of the thirty-six million Catholics in question but rather by one of the 500,000 or 600,000 Jews."[90] In reaction, Dreyfus explained that he was not a Jew but a freethinker. After Déroulède continued to insist on the relevance of Dreyfus's Jewish background, the president intervened, declaring: "Here there are no distinctions based on religion."[91] To which Déroulède responded: "Well fine, I will declare my religion openly: I am a Christian republican and I protest when I see that one wants to de-Christianize France, perhaps in order to Judaize it!"[92]

Dreyfus, unlike Lasker, explained his dissociation from Judaism, based on his personal commitments, which were very different from those of the German deputy.[93] Although their responses were different, however, the challenge they faced was similar, as were their implications for a culture of universalism. It is unlikely that the president would have explained to Dreyfus that there "are no distinctions based on religion" in parliament if he had claimed some expert knowledge about Jewish issues or defended the honor of Jews under attack. The president chose to defend Dreyfus's right to speak in universalistic terms rather than to denounce a deputy for speaking in particularistic terms. Indeed, Déroulède provoked the left with his declaration of his Christian republicanism, but he remained unchallenged by the president. In this regard, this episode was typical of nineteenth-century parliamentary culture in Germany and France more generally: Deputies rarely censured each other for speaking explicitly about their own religious or communal identity and more often denounced each other as false universalists. The defenders of secularism did not insist on a space that was devoid of positive representations of particular interests. Multiple values and necessities existed that allowed individuals to speak legitimately about their group of origin on the floor of parliament. Nor did self-described secularists undermine speakers when diverse traditions were invoked to defend their understanding of religious regulation as a neutral, rational endeavor. The opponents of liberal and republican secularism—like Mallinckrodt and Déroulède—were equally happy to accept the prospect that Jews would speak as Jews but rejected the notion that secularism was a disinterested, political position that existed outside of religious strife. Ultimately, Jewish deputies faced opposition as Jews not because of the expectations of a culture of generality that left no room for their particularity but rather because their particularity was understood to either limit or enhance their ability to speak on the floor of parliament depending on the topic at hand.

Conclusion

Parliamentary debates involving Jewish or Catholic interests allow us to reframe a number of assumptions that underlie scholarship on secularism, liberal politics, and Jewish identity in modern Europe. First, the rules and practices of liberal parliamentarism often left Jews freer to speak publicly as Jews than existing scholarship would have us think. In the era of high liberalism, secularist expectations did not necessarily motivate Jewish deputies to hide their background but instead often compelled them to highlight it. The rhetoric of secularism did not follow liberal theories of representation in this regard. In many cases, it even appears to have run counter to such theories. The fact that both German and French Jewish deputies were expected to emphasize their Jewishness in debates more often than they were encouraged to obscure it should also give us pause in reproducing the claim of contemporaries that Jews acted courageously when they stood up for their coreligionists in parliament. Such an interpretation is misleading because it suggests implicitly that Jewish deputies who spoke as Jews about Jews in parliament did so in the face of the pressures of assimilatory universalism. As this chapter has shown, the pressures to speak as Jewish experts, act as native informants, or defend one's honor provided a countervailing force to the universal call to become unmarked citizens in public.

At the same time, these debates also force us to rethink our understanding of the way secularism operated in the parliamentary arena. We can either follow the self-description of the historical actors themselves or look for the unspoken shared assumptions that defined their worldview. The first approach will lead us down a familiar road, even if the deputies involved clearly expressed a wide range of positions that can be understood as secularist. Taking this view, we discover secularist deputies who focused on the disestablishment of churches and demanded that the state police religious spaces. On the other side of these debates, we find outspoken anti-secularists who imagined that religion should be unencumbered by the state or who demanded that religious interests should be involved in the formation of political opinion.

Taking the second approach and thinking about the rhetorical commonalities and shared assumptions of these individuals leads us to discover that the diverging positions outlined in the preceding pages were often established on similar foundations. Many anti-secularists claimed that secularist boundary making was denominational in nature. Jews and Protestants had, in their view, invented secularism as a ruse to implement their anti-Christian or anti-Catholic project. Motivated by Jewish or Protestant ideas and commitments, this secularist fight against Catholicism and the Catholic clergy was thus, according to its detractors, also a type of religious position. Paradoxically, by claiming that Jewish secularists were acting as false universalists, various self-declared enemies of liberal secularism reinforced a larger consensus concerning the way politics and religion should remain compartmentalized in the public arena. In this sense, self-styled anti-secularists *enacted* (in the sense of staging) secularism in parliament just as much as their self-declared secularist opponents did. Even the accusation of antisemitic and otherwise anti-secularist conservatives that Jews spoke for their own nation or race reinforced the secularist consensus that politics and religion were distinct fields of action with different rules. Mallinckrodt and Déroulède were, in this sense, secularists *à contrecœur*.

Jewish deputies' use of anticlerical themes was, under these circumstances, a tool, a limitation, and a gauge of the ability of Jews to transcend suspicions of their particularist interests. In contrast to the acceptance they met when they advocated for Jewish rights, Jewish deputies found it more difficult to invoke their own expertise or their injured honor when they spoke about the rights (or obligations) of the Catholic Church. Skilled politicians like Lasker nevertheless attempted to do just this: He even sought to legitimize his speaking position by claiming that Jewish religious leaders might potentially be just as bad as Catholic priests when it came to abusing their right to excommunicate dissenters.

Clearly, the stories of nineteenth-century French and German Jewish parliamentarians are not identical. German deputies and parliamentary candidates no doubt experienced greater difficulties for much of the nineteenth century. As early as 1880, German Jewish deputies faced an unambiguously hostile parliament when the Prussian Lower House discussed the antisemites' petition, which sought to disenfranchise Jews less than ten years after their emancipation in Germany.[94] In the following decade, the number of Jewish deputies—which had constituted 2 to 3 percent of the lower house in the 1860s and 1870s—dwindled in the face of antisemitic election campaigns.[95] Even Lasker, who had been immensely popular during the 1870s, lost his seat in the face of antisemitic agitation. Eventually, most liberal election committees simply stopped putting Jews on the ballot. The situation for Jewish parliamentary hopefuls was not as dramatic in France, in spite of the substantial antisemitic campaigns against prominent Jewish politicians by the end of the century.[96] Nor can we forget that parliaments are national institutions in countries with different traditions, a fact that establishes certain roadblocks to any attempt to write a transnational, entangled history of the German and French parliaments. While the few legislators who created the rules for parliamentary conduct used other parliaments as

models, deputies rarely referenced other national parliamentary traditions in their speeches.

For the period between 1840 and 1880, and in many respects even for
later periods, the rhetorical similarities between debates that emerged
in the French and German parliaments can nonetheless serve as barom-
eters of the limitations of Western and Central European secularism.
The differences between the pragmatics of representation in nineteenth-
century Germany and France were never as stark as predominant depictions of national models suggest. As different as the role of parliament
was within each state's political system—with governments depending
on parliamentary majorities in France but not in Germany—parliaments in both countries operated according to similar rules and trans-
mitted their debates through similar channels. Expectations about the
nature of polite debate and public propriety were shared across both
national contexts to a greater degree than previously recognized. More
than differences in philosophical or political traditions, expectations of
proper conduct influenced Jewish deputies' decisions to emphasize or
deemphasize their Jewishness in similar terms in Germany and France.

Seven Nationalism, Antisemitism, and the Decline
of Jewish Anti-Catholicism

The *Kaiserreich* (1871–1918) and the Third Republic (1871–1940) are
the periods most commonly scrutinized by historians of Germany and
France for traces of Jewish anticlericalism and anti-Catholicism. This
interest in Jews' opinions on the Catholic Church was born in the very
period historians seek to describe, as conservative Catholics and antisemites alleged that their political opposition to Jews was an outgrowth of the disproportionate role Jews had played in anti-Catholic
and anticlerical campaigns. Several scholars have framed their work as a
response to these accusations. Some have attempted to prove that Jews
were not as anti-Catholic as their antisemitic interlocutors claimed,
while others have argued that the anticlericalism of certain prominent
Jews in the late nineteenth century was indeed a decisive factor in the
rise of Catholic antisemitism.[1] Most historians have tended to come
down somewhere in the middle of these two extremes, arguing that
Jews were, on the whole, willing to embrace many of the liberal and
republican critiques of the Catholic Church but nonetheless rejected
the attempts of secularist republicans and liberals to limit religious
freedoms.[2]

The present chapter engages with this scholarship on various levels.
First, it aims to shift the discussion away from earlier debates over the
intensity and extent of Jewish anti-Catholicism. Such a discussion always threatens to frame the anti-Catholicism of Jews through their detractors' accusations, rather than as an aspect of Jewish politics that was
related only indirectly to Catholic antisemitism. As previous chapters
have done, this chapter seeks to understand what Jews did and could
do with anticlericalism. How important was it for the articulation of

their political ideas? What types of opportunities did it give them and at what price?

Second, the comparative approach pursued here shows that Jewish criticism of the Catholic Church has been underestimated as a political option for Jews in the first years after the founding of the German Empire while it has been overstated for the period of republican dominance in France starting in 1877. Equally important it argues that Jewish anticlericalism dwindled in Germany and France at different times and at a different pace. Only in Germany did anti-Catholicism function briefly as a sign of patriotic dedication to the new empire, and only in Germany did Jewish anti-Catholicism become a potential marker of Jews' status as outsiders to the nation, even among their (mostly Protestant) allies. In Germany, where anti-Catholicism proved a more potent tool for Jewish intellectuals than in France, it thus also disappeared as a viable political option earlier. By the 1880s, most German Jews distanced themselves from aggressive anticlerical rhetoric and were eager to forget their involvement in the *Kulturkampf*. In France during the same period, many Jews were more reluctant to embrace radical rhetoric but found a moderate anticlericalism plausible for much longer. By the early twentieth century, the majority of politically active Jews in both countries came to reject the overtly anticlerical polemics they had entertained in earlier decades. Contrary to the position advanced by nineteenth-century antisemites, as well as many historians who have focused on Jewish anti-Catholicism only in the late nineteenth century, I maintain that the popularity of polemics against Jesuits, ultramontanism, and "clericalism" among Jewish community builders and intellectuals in 1870s Germany and in France between 1898 and 1902 mark the end, rather than the beginning, of the long history of modern Jewish anticlericalism.

Third, this chapter seeks to challenge the perception that Jews were predisposed to reject anti-Catholicism on account of their own marginal position and cultural sensitivity as members of a religious minority. This claim, which depicts Jews as the better liberals who were immunized against anti-pluralistic measures by their experiences of persecution, appears in particular in German historiography.[3] The debates of the *Kulturkampf* suggest that these claims are difficult to prove, however, as they tell us more about the commentators who described Jews in such terms than about the sensibilities of late nineteenth-century Jewish intellectuals themselves. Ultimately, the best explanation for the demise of Jewish anticlericalism in late nineteenth-century Europe is not Jews' innate sensitivity to the marginalization of religious groups but rather the fact that it became politically inopportune. The prevalence of anti-Catholic polemics in various Jewish circles for nearly a century by this time offers powerful support for this interpretation.

Finally, a word about the dramatis personae of this chapter. Many of the public debates over Jewish anticlericalism in the final decades of the nineteenth century revolved around the question of whether communal officials and Jewish journalists represented the larger collectives of German and French Jews. The more antisemites accused Jews of having a particular penchant for anti-Catholicism, the more charged the question became. In this context, the public representatives of Judaism in both countries sought to distance themselves from Jews they considered too radically anticlerical. In the pages that follow, I work with the understanding that the politics of those individuals who referenced their Jewish identity overtly in their polemics can also tell us something about the stakes and challenges confronted by those who experienced their Jewish background principally as an obstacle to the expression of their political identity. These self-consciously Jewish intellectuals illuminate the opportunities and challenges Jews faced in these conflicts, even if they cannot tell us with certainty what the vast majority of Jews thought about the Catholic Church.

Jewish Intellectuals and Nationalist Anti-Catholicism in Germany

In Germany, the most intense period of liberal–Catholic conflict was the *Kulturkampf* of the 1870s, although renewed debates between liberals, the state, and political Catholics had begun earlier in certain German states.[4] For a long time, historians understood the *Kulturkampf* primarily as a conflict between the Bismarckian state and the Catholic Church, motivated in particular by Bismarck's will to assimilate Catholic Poles.[5] More recent scholarship, by contrast, has tended to frame the Catholic–liberal conflicts of the 1870s as part of a longer trajectory of Protestant-dominated liberal nationalism.[6] Such studies have argued persuasively that the anti-Catholic campaigns of the *Kulturkampf* were intimately intertwined with German liberals' attempts to promote the values and symbols of middle-class Protestantism as the common national culture of unified Germany.[7]

German Jews' political imaginaries were shaped through both an affiliation and a struggle with this Protestant-oriented form of nationalism. Those who wanted to establish Judaism as a viable option for modern citizens had to negotiate between the fantasy of a Judeo-Protestant nation and the increasing sense that liberal visions of a Protestant-centered German culture also gave rise to an exclusionary form of nationalism. As in the past, liberal Jews expressed their ambivalent identification with the project of nation building through polemics against conservative Catholics, whom they considered disruptive to their visions for a liberal nation.

In the years immediately following the founding of the German *Kaiserreich* in 1871, a new style of nationalist anti-Catholicism appeared attractive to many Jews in Germany. Although this development was short-lived, it shows the possibilities anti-Catholic alliance building offered German Jews at the height of denominational conflict. In the pages that follow, I illustrate the different ways German Jews found to employ this new version of polemical anti-Catholicism through various examples drawn from the German Jewish press, a case study of two prominent German Jewish intellectuals, and the positions of Germany's largest Jewish community organization.

The new qualities of this nationalist approach to the Catholic Church come into focus through the case of Leopold Zunz (1794–1886), who is often hailed as the founder of modern scholarship on Jewish history and thought, the *Wissenschaft des Judentums* or Science of Judaism. By the time the *Kulturkampf* overtook German politics in the 1870s, Zunz had already enjoyed a long career as a scholar of international Jewish fame. In the early 1820s, he had established the Verein für Cultur und Wissenschaft der Juden, which aimed to investigate Jewish traditions with the new tools of critical historical study. He also served as the editor of its periodical, the *Zeitschrift für die Wissenschaft des Judenthums*, in 1822–1823 and subsequently published multiple seminal scholarly volumes—starting with his groundbreaking 1832 study on the history of the Jewish sermon and rabbinic exegesis.[8] Although his most important works had appeared earlier in the century, he remained a productive scholar of the history of Jewish thought well into the 1870s.

Like many of the first generation of Jewish historians, Zunz was a committed anticlerical. Whereas Graetz had mobilized ideas about the end of the age of Rome toward Jewish nationalist ends, Zunz's anticlericalism was more in line with mainstream liberalism, even if his politics were to the left of the majority of liberals.[9] For Zunz, as for other Jewish progressives since the 1840s, the Catholic "reaction against Protestantism" was closely connected with the fight against liberalism and Jewish emancipation.[10] As conflicts between the self-identified political representatives of Catholicism and Protestantism intensified in the 1860s, he increasingly introduced anticlerical themes into his political speeches, both as a member of the left liberal Fortschrittspartei and in other, less common genres of agitation.[11] An 1864 essay he wrote on early modern Jewish manuscripts in Italy, for example, ends with a call to liberate these documents from the Vatican: "Go ahead, people of Italy! You have snatched the reins from the spiritual jailers in Florence, Bologna, Parma, Turin, and Milan; now liberate Rome and, with it, the Hebrew manuscripts from the dragon. As thought longs for the living word, so Europe longs for the liberating deed and Italy, for the fall of the Papal States."[12]

After the Italian occupation of Rome and the unification of Germany in 1870 and 1871, Zunz began to frame his anticlericalism in more overtly nationalistic terms in a small booklet entitled *Deutsche Briefe* [German Letters].[13] Written as an imaginary epistolary exchange between two friends, the work dealt with a staple of nationalist cultural criticism: the purification of the German language. In Zunz's hands, the theme became a platform from which to address both the menace of Catholicism and threats to the Jews.

In the pages of Zunz's *Deutsche Briefe*, the first reference to the Catholic Church appears in the fictional letter penned by a physician named August, who reports that one of his patients had claimed that the supremacy of the pope had its origin in the first verse of the Bible, which distinguishes between the heavens and the earth. Because of this, his patient argued, the Jesuits were closer to heaven and would thus always be the legitimate rulers of worldly administrators.[14] In August's professional opinion, the ultramontane ideas expressed by his patient were a form of mental illness; they were nothing but delusional ideas cloaked in the language of rational thought.

In another letter from *Deutsche Briefe*, August's interlocutor Julius returns to the issue of Catholicism.[15] Julius reports that he had been treating his own insomnia through medication and the reading of pastoral letters. This combination allowed him to sleep but caused intense dreams. In one such dream, which he recounts in detail, a giant appeared to him and introduced himself as the conjunction *and*. The giant blamed himself for creating the conflict between the states of the world and the papacy, as he was responsible for putting the clergy next to the state and humanity. Many parliamentarians continued to work with the word *and*, the giant furthered, believing that it was possible to allow the Jesuits to flourish because this conjunction suggested the possibility of separating church *and* state. All the while the clergy destroyed the bonds that kept the state together, the giant lamented. In his view, there was only one remedy: "Abolish the papacy and all priestly orders; prohibit the monasteries, monkhood, and nunhood as well."[16]

The rest of Zunz's chapter brings home this point in unambiguous terms. After delivering the report of the curious dream, Julius expresses his sympathy for the giant's diatribe. According to Julius, the Catholic clergy was simply pursuing its innately destructive course because naturally "worms and popes must gnaw and devour."[17] Because the clergy cunningly manipulated the passions of the people, he was not optimistic that the fight against them could be won: "Just like you won't manage to purge the foreign words [from German], I will not be able to drive out the priests [*Pfaffen*]," Julius states baldly.[18] French words and the clergy were equally alien to the German national body in Zunz's account.

Later in the same work, Zunz also has his characters draw a connection between the Catholic Church and anti-Jewish politics. The clergy not only undermined the power of the state, it was also behind the campaigns against Jews—although he was careful to add that conservative Protestants could be just as bad in this respect. Both characters in the work emphasize the deviant psychology of clericalism, thus allowing Zunz to hint at the equally pathological and manipulative character of anti-Jewish sentiments. Although it drew on many older tropes, *Deutsche Briefe* combined an articulation of Jewish interests, liberal polemics against the church, and German nationalism in a way that was unknown even a decade earlier.

Younger authors such as Adolf Kohut (1848–1916) shared Zunz's willingness to view Jewish and German predicaments through the lens of the *Kulturkampf*.[19] Kohut was the son of a Talmud teacher in Hungary and attended the Breslau Jewish Seminary from 1866 to 1869. Instead of becoming a rabbi like his older brother Alexander—who became one of the founders of the Jewish Theological Seminary in New York—Kohut turned to journalism and biographical writing. Over the course of a long and successful career, he worked for a number of major liberal newspapers in Germany, including the *Berliner Zeitung*, and also published over 100 works of biography and fiction as well as numerous popular anthologies.

Kohut's first major publication appeared during the Franco-Prussian war and signaled his definite break with his teachers. In his *Memoiren eines jüdischen Seminaristen* [Memoirs of a Jewish Seminarian], Kohut wrote a scathing and insulting critique of the Breslau Seminary.[20] According to Kohut, it was necessary to excise the cancer of the seminary from the body of Judaism. His satire was meant to facilitate this effort by proving to the world that the rabbis of this institution were "Jesuits" and the seminary a "Jewish Jesuit College."[21] Kohut used the language of the *Kulturkampf* to amplify his personal attacks against Zacharias Frankel, the institute's director. At the same time, he also participated in the larger liberal anti-Catholic campaign by reproducing its major tropes.

Much like Zunz, Kohut linked Jewish and universal liberal themes in his polemics. He also followed in Zunz's footsteps as he combined anti-Catholicism with an idealization of German humanistic culture. Two years after his first publication, Kohut published *Unsere drei Dichterheroen und das Pfaffenthum* [Our Three Poet-Heroes and the Priesthood], which collected the negative statements Lessing, Schiller, and Goethe had issued on the topic of the priesthood.[22] Kohut viewed his anthology as his contribution to the German battle against Jesuitism, which he believed to conspire secretly against the states of the world.[23] In a more explicit show of support for Bismarck's policies, he also wrote a pamphlet extolling the work of Adalbert Falk, the Minister of Religious Affairs responsible for many of the measures of the *Kulturkampf*.[24] Falk had been instrumental, for example, in the passing of the so-called May Laws that made the training and appointment of clergy a prerogative of the state (May 1873), allowed the state to expel priests who resisted the state's authority (May 1874), and prohibited all religious congregations not involved in sick care (May 1875).

Zunz and Kohut were not isolated voices among German Jews during this period.[25] The contributors to the (non-Orthodox) German Jewish press expressed similar opinions. This was particularly true of the *Allgemeine Zeitung des Judenthums*, where Philippson found new occasions to elaborate the anticlerical nationalism he had embraced since the late 1860s. Explaining that "the adherents of ultramontanism now appear openly as enemies of the German Empire," he suggested they fought the empire with "any form at their disposal."[26] At least the true supporters of Germany could be glad that the enemies of progress had finally taken off their mask. The plan Philippson repeatedly ascribed to the Catholic hierarchy was, in fact, nothing other than a conspiracy to restore the church to a position of absolute power.[27] As part of this scheme, Philippson alleged, the pope had already turned the clergy into a "great and powerful army."[28] Although he was critical of policies that discriminated against Catholics or undermined his understanding of religious pluralism, Philippson remained committed to the isolation of political Catholicism, which he believed threatened both the social standing of Jews and the unity of Germany.

Such ideas appeared in other Jewish periodicals as well, including the journal of Abraham Geiger (1810–1874), one of the founders of modern Jewish historical studies alongside Zunz and Graetz. Although his paper rarely commented on current affairs, at the height of the *Kulturkampf* he also briefly appropriated the nationalist rhetoric of unity in the face of a clerical threat, declaring that "the new national movement of the united German tribes, which belong together, [*geeinten zusammengehörigen Volksstämmen*] must revolt against the ecclesiastical imperiousness that feeds fragmentation everywhere, so that it alone can take control, as a single power."[29] The same language appeared in the *Israelitische Wochen-Schrift*, which had also written enthusiastically about the fall of papal Rome. Bismarck's fight was also a Jewish one, according to the *Wochen-Schrift*.[30] The enemies of Judaism and liberalism were to be blamed for their own situation as targets of discriminatory legislation.

Had they not caused confessional discord, they would not have been attacked.[31]

During the early years of the *Kulturkampf*, various Jewish observers expressed a similar sense of optimism that the campaigns against ultramontanism entailed a vindication of Judaism's path. Indeed, until 1873, Judaism was hardly touched by the new restrictive legislation. The fact that ultramontane Catholics rather than Jews were the target of new discriminatory policies appeared to some like a late affirmation of Judaism—both as a belief-system and as an institutional reality.[32] Even the progressive deputy Rudolf Virchow, whom the *Allgemeine Zeitung des Judenthums* had castigated in 1868 for discriminating against a Jewish candidate for an assistantship in his medical laboratory, seemed to have found a new appreciation for Judaism.[33] In his famous speech of January 1873, in which he popularized the term *Kulturkampf*, Rabbinic Jewry became a positive model and a foil to the Catholic Church against which he campaigned.[34] According to Virchow, the nonhierarchical structure of Judaism demonstrated unambiguously that centralized clerical authority was not necessary for the survival of a religion. In Virchow's rendering, Jews thus appeared as more progressive and in tune with liberal assumptions about middle-class religiosity than did Catholics—even if it remained unclear whether they were more German because of it.[35]

Under these circumstances, Jewish publicists could finally give the century-old debates over the modernity and progressiveness of Judaism a plausibly triumphalistic spin. For those Jewish activists who argued that Jews were well disposed toward modernity while Catholics resisted it, Virchow had vindicated their position by suggesting that Catholics could learn a thing or two from the Jews. Perhaps the most poignant expression of this sentiment was an article in the *Wochen-Schrift*, which returned the dubious favor of a century's worth of Christian advice to Jews on how to reform Judaism, by pointing out to Catholics how they might seek to regain favor in the eyes of the state:

> What [Catholicism] calls [. . .] God's law, is priests' law. It is founded on [. . .] forged documents [. . .] and it serves: authority, churchly power, worldly property. We also have priests. Don't give them more power, authority, property, than our *kohanim* have, then all will be fine.

> Elect and appoint your teachers and clerics as we do; do not ask for
> privileges and preferential treatment from the state. Then the state will
> also have no reason to interfere in your affairs.[36]

Of course, the principal reason for Judaism's alleged progressiveness
in this regard was not the foresight of German legislators but rather the
unwillingness of various German states to fund Jewish religious institutions.[37] Rather than complain about this reality, however, certain Jewish intellectuals suggested that it was simply a historic irony that earlier
discrimination had pushed Judaism into the position of a role model.[38]

Jewish Communal Organizations in the Kulturkampf

More than any other Jewish institution, the Deutsch-Israelitische Gemeindebund [Federation of German-Jewish Communities], stood for
Jewish identification with a Protestant-dominated national project and
its antagonism to the Catholic Church. The organization was founded
in 1871 in an attempt to overcome the fragmentation of Jewish communal structures. Some administrative diversity was common in a federal
empire. Even after German unification, all religious groups remained
largely bound by old dynastic borders because the regulation and funding of religion remained the prerogative of particular German states.
In the case of Judaism, the situation was more complicated, however,
because not even the Jews of Prussia—by far the largest of the German states—had an umbrella organization to represent them. The Gemeindebund set out to change this. Its aim was both to create a united
infrastructure for Prussian Jews and to fulfill the more ambitious goal
of unifying all of German Jewry.

Comparing his organization to the Gustav-Adolph-Verein and the
Protestantenverein, which were the two most active Protestant associations of their day, the author of the Gemeindebund's first official history of 1879 revealed both the Gemeindebund's self-positioning within
German confessional conflicts and its members' self-understanding as
a vital part of the German political landscape.[39] All three organizations
expressed a nonpartisan but politicized vision of religious unity represented largely by their lay leaders. In the first years of its existence,
the Gemeindebund, much like the Protestantenverein, presented it-

self as part of a contested liberal and national consensus that had to be defended against ultramontane Catholicism.[40] This is reflected in the speech that the association's president, Moritz Kohner (1818–1877), gave at the founding conference of the organization. Inventing his personal Jewish version of mythical German nationalism, Kohner spoke of a medieval Jewish myth that predicted that the German Empire, once "independent of Rome and France, will have the mission to bring into being the messianic age."[41] Expressing his hope that the "spirit of the nation" would eliminate all reactionary attempts to exclude Jews in the future, Kohner explained that already "in the German parliament even our arch-enemies (the ultramontanes) invoke the principle of freedom and equality of all confessions."[42] In his underhanded compliment to the ultramontanes, Kohner did not alter his position that conservative Catholics remained Jews most serious foe.

The Deutsch-Israelitische Gemeindebund's opposition to ultramontanism made another prominent appearance in the association's official address to Bismarck of 1872. The lawyer Emil Lehmann came up with the idea of paying tribute to the man who had united Germany and granted Jews full civil rights. The members of the acting committee of the association, as well as Ludwig Philippson and the Berlin Professor Moritz Lazarus, drafted the document in its final version.[43] After commending Bismarck for achieving unity and equality, the address read, "Your Highness, with the same energy you have victoriously fought the battle against the internal enemies of the empire. To the best of our abilities we also stand by your and the empire's side in this battle— because it was precisely the former omnipotence of this enemy, which made many generations of our co-religionists suffer persecution, pressure, and exclusion."[44] The Gemeindebund thus expressed its patriotism by officially endorsing the *Kulturkampf* against political Catholicism. This form of anticlerical citizenship, which resonates with the statements of various Jewish intellectuals during the French Revolution, did not go unchallenged within the Jewish community, however. Whereas the reform-oriented Jewish press simply reproduced the text of the letter and Bismarck's polite if terse reply without further comment, the Orthodox paper *Der Israelit* rejected this meddling in religious politics from a supracommunal Jewish body.[45]

Indeed, Orthodox Jews were the only Jewish group within Germany that repeatedly sought alliances with Catholics and defended their interpretation of religion and politics during this period.[46] On several occasions, Orthodox Jews supported Catholic candidates in different parts of Germany, including Hannover, various south German cities, and cities with Catholic majorities such as Mainz and Cologne.[47] Orthodox Jews' outrage over the anti-Catholicism of reform-dominated Jewish institutions was not merely the result of Orthodoxy's pragmatic cooperation with Catholic politicians, however. It also afforded Orthodox constituents the opportunity to criticize their ideological opponents within Judaism. Many German Jews did not have an ax to grind with the reformers who controlled institutions such as the Deutsch-Israelitische Gemeindebund, however, and thus appear to have accepted the association's support for the *Kulturkampf* as a legitimate strategy of Jewish political integration.

The Myth of Minority Sensitivity

Such prominent and varied examples of Jewish anti-Catholicism should not obscure the fact that a large number of Jews were uncomfortable with the public statements of radical Jewish anti-Catholics. Even Philippson, who was convinced that the intolerant and divisive forces in society had to be excised, was worried that National Liberal policies might soon turn against other religious minorities.[48] The central political question for many Jews concerned the price of competing visions of secularism. How much pressure and what type of pressure should the state exert in the name of confessional peace and unity against those they believed to be causing discord? Given the opportunities Jews had to express their anti-Catholicism for much of the nineteenth century, we might wonder whether their reluctance to turn to more aggressive rhetoric was due to their own sensibilities as a persecuted minority. This position, which has received much attention among historians of Germany, has relied in particular on the reaction of several prominent Jews to an 1872 law that expelled the Jesuits from Germany.[49] An exploration of the facts and mythmaking that surround this moment can illustrate the problems with the notion that Jews qua Jews had a heightened sensibility to repressive secularist measures.

The anti-Jesuit law, more than any other legislation during the *Kulturkampf*, stands as a monument to the will of the liberals in the Reichstag to destroy a force that they perceived as hostile to the nation, even if they had to undermine constitutional guarantees in the process. The anti-Jesuit law did not just dissolve the order in Germany, it also deprived German citizens of their basic civil rights because it forced German Jesuits to leave their country of citizenship. When the bill came before the German Reichstag, none of the four Jewish deputies voted for the law, a position that contrasted with that of non-Jewish members of their respective parliamentary factions.[50] After the vote, Jewish periodicals chimed in and denounced the government's overreach, explaining the Jewish deputies' vote as a result of their collective historical experiences as a persecuted minority as well as a particularly Jewish sensitivity to religious coercion.[51] Scholars have cited the voting patterns of the Jewish deputies as well as the responses of the Jewish press to illustrate Jews' tendency to defend a more pluralistic vision of religious coexistence than the anti-Catholic and state-centered view held by the majority of representatives of the National Liberal and Progressive parties.

Several aspects of this unusual vote call for caution, however, and ultimately cast doubt on this narrative. In the wake of the passing of the law expelling the Jesuits, only the Jewish deputies Eduard Lasker and Ludwig Bamberger explained their opposition. Neither spoke about their religious background as a motivating factor.[52] Complicating matters further, Bamberger appeared in his public pronouncements as a true *Kulturkämpfer*, a man who wholeheartedly embraced the campaigns against ultramontane Catholicism.[53] In Lasker's case, even though Catholic deputies acknowledged his reluctance to go as far as other members of his faction had during the vote, his followers continued to cite his anti-Catholic credentials.[54] Indeed, when he competed against the democratic deputy Sonnemann to represent Frankfurt am Main in the Reichstag in the 1874 elections, Lasker's supporters produced a flysheet advertising him as somebody who (unlike Sonnemann) "stands with those [. . .] who are willing to fight most emphatically the great *Kulturkampf* of our time."[55]

Table 7.1. Voting behavior of Jewish deputies on selected *Kulturkampf* bills.

Bill	Bamberger	Lasker	Sonnemann	National Liberal Faction
Pulpit Law (1871)	For	Against	Against	For
Anti-Jesuit Bill (1872)	Against	Against	Against	For
Expatriation Bill (1874)	For	For	Against	For
Rescinding the law against unwarranted use of clerical positions (1884)	Abstained	For	—	For

Note: Vote in second reading, RT, November 25, 1871, 544–545; Vote in second reading, RT, June 17, 1872, 1094–1095, vote in third reading RT, June 19, 1872, 1149–1150. Sonnemann was absent in the third reading; Vote in third reading, RT, April 25, 1874, 1145–1147; RT, January 12, 1882, 589–592. The last bill was submitted by Windthorst to end a crucial law of the *Kulturkampf*: "Gesetzentwurf betreffend die Aufhebung des Gesetzes über die Verhinderung der unbefugten Ausübung von Kirchenämtern vom 4.5.1874." Lasker was one of six deputies who first voted for a bill to ignore Windthorst's bill to abolish the law (RT, January 12, 1882, 587–589) and then nevertheless voted in favor of Windthorst's bill.

Once we include other anti-Catholic legislation into our purview, we can see more clearly that the track records of the three most prominent German Jewish deputies of the era—Lasker, Bamberger, Sonnemann—do not indicate any single "Jewish" position on the *Kulturkampf* (see Table 7.1).

The case of the Jewish press's opposition to the Jesuit Bill of 1872 is also more complicated than scholars have allowed: Before the vote on the bill, most Jewish newspapers either remained silent on the topic of anti-Jesuit policies or gave space to both friends and enemies of the anti-Jesuit legislation.[56] Only after the bill, once it became clear that the two most famous Jewish deputies, Lasker and Bamberger, had dissented from the majority of their party (the National Liberals) to oppose the law, did Jewish newspapers state their position clearly. Only now did they claim that Jews were natural enemies of laws that allowed the state to infringe on an individual's civil rights because of his or her belief. Their analysis of Jewish motives was no longer meant to mobilize Jews but rather to explain a development they had neither caused nor predicted.

Given the extant sources, the claim that German Jews opposed exclusionary practices due to their marginal status is difficult to prove. The better-documented story concerns the historical construction of a narrative of Jewish opposition, not Jewish opposition itself. This narrative began to emerge already in 1872. The Jewish journalists who tried to explain the actions of their coreligionists in parliament were not the only ones who began to theorize about Jews' special sensitivities. Certain defenders of the Jesuit Bill also noticed the apparent anomaly of Jewish dissent from the liberal mainstream in this critical anti-Catholic initiative.[57] In particular, Bismarck, the bill's original sponsor, tried to use the vote to blacken the name of the Jewish deputies and give the impression that support for his bill was even broader than it appeared once one subtracted those who had voted as Jews rather than as Germans. On this subject, he sent the following note to his secretary: "Plant an article, which should say [. . .], that 'the Jews [and] the former Jews in the Reichstag, Lasker, Bamberger, Friedenthal, [. . .] and others who can perhaps still be discovered most likely opposed the Jesuit law because they had a dark premonition that a general indignation will rise also against their coreligionists [*Stammesgenossen*] and that one could also demand exceptional laws against them and their activities.'"[58] Bismarck and the Jewish press were thus in agreement on this point, as various later scholars have also been. To different ends, they have theorized that the German Jewish deputies acted out their historical sensitivity to religious persecution: Bismarck, to denounce Jews and the Jewish deputies; the Jewish press, to explain the surprising fact that Jews had gone against mainstream liberal opinion; and recent scholars, to celebrate the critical potential inherent in Jewish marginality.

During and immediately after the *Kulturkampf*, by contrast, the enemies of the Jews denounced the anti-Catholic campaigns of the 1870s as a Jewish invention, ignoring the voting patterns of the Jewish deputies in 1872 as well as the responses they had elicited.[59] Jews had the opposite tendency. With the failure of the *Kulturkampf* by the end of the decade, Jewish authors tended instead to overemphasize their earlier opposition to liberal anti-Catholicism. Once the anti-Catholic campaigns of the 1870s had become an embarrassment to German Jews, they searched for examples of Jewish resistance to the now unpopular policies. As they continued to tell this story to themselves and the world, they often used references to the vote of four Jewish deputies on a single day in 1872 as their principal proof.[60]

This is not to say that there is not much that is plausible in this narrative. Contrary to the accusations of Catholic antisemites, Jews did not distinguish themselves from non-Jewish liberals in anti-Catholic campaigns or legislative initiatives. Different Jewish liberals did express their discomfort with the new legislation at various points. Yet we miss an important part of the story of modern German Jewish history if we allow ourselves to view the events of the early 1870s through the lens of the subsequent rise of political antisemitism. In contrast to French Jews' limited engagement with anti-Catholic anticlericalism during this period, certain German Jews employed anti-Catholicism as part of a new type of Protestant-inflected German nationalism that emerged in the first years of the *Kaiserreich*. Many central Jewish figures remained willing to experiment with this new option during the early period of the *Kulturkampf*, even if later Jewish observers preferred to forget this.

Anti-Catholicism and Opposition to Religious Pluralization

When scholars analyze Jews' reluctance to endorse the campaigns of the *Kulturkampf*, they usually point to Jewish resistance toward the state's overreach of its authority as well as their fears of a police state.[61] To some degree, the search for special Jewish sensibilities has obscured the fact that liberal Jews often worried in equal measure about the threat that the pluralization caused by some *Kulturkampf* policies represented to their communal structures. The major conflict in this regard revolved around the so-called *Austrittsgesetz*, which plagued parliament between 1873 and 1876. Initially, the May Laws of 1873, which, among other things, put the Christian clergy under stronger state supervision, did not elicit any protests in the Jewish public sphere.[62] This soon changed with the passing of a bill Lasker had introduced, demanding that one of the new laws facilitating withdrawal from a religious community without conversion to another should be applied also to Jews. Orthodox Jews were the greatest supporters of this initiative. It promised to allow them to leave their mostly reform-oriented local communities to create their own state-recognized religious communities without legally leaving the Jewish religion—a right demanded prominently by the Orthodox leader Samson Raphael Hirsch (1808–1888).

As a consequence, a heated conflict between Reform and Orthodox Jews ensued, with eighty-eight petitions reaching the responsible commission of the Prussian parliament.[63] Turning the tables on the Jewish reformers who had attacked Orthodox authoritarianism, Orthodox Jews invoked the liberal value of religious freedom in their petitions as they explained that at present the law coerced them to fund the services in Reform synagogues, which contradicted their religious beliefs. Reform Jewish leaders countered that dividing the Jewish communities of Germany would ruin them financially. To their embarrassment, these arguments sounded increasingly like those of conservative Catholics and Protestants who defended the autonomy of their churches. As it turns out, their arguments also resembled those French Jewish liberals had been making for a long time. As French Jewish journalists during the Terquem affair had done some decades earlier, Reform Jews in Germany now focused on Jews' collective contribution to the secular nation rather than on the individual freedoms that a secular order should grant to individuals.

Arguments about the applicability of the secession law to Jews pivoted around the question of whether Reform and Orthodox Jewry constituted two different Jewish confessions—an issue that had also arisen earlier in the libel case against Leopold Kompert in 1863–1864. If Judaism was, like Christianity, a vaguely defined religious group made up of different denominations, then the new legislation would allow Jews to withdraw from their communities and create their own separate, recognized Jewish communities. If Judaism instead constituted a tightly knit organizational unit comparable to individual Christian churches, then each Jewish community had to be treated as equivalent to a parish. In this case, Jews only had two options: They could choose to leave Judaism altogether or remain within their parish, because each recognized denomination had a state-guaranteed monopoly on a specific territory.

The Gemeindebund, in its capacity as an umbrella organization of mostly reform-oriented Jewish communities, argued for the latter viewpoint. Aiming to bolster the legitimacy of this position, the organization solicited expert opinions on the issue from Jewish institutions such as the Hochschule für die Wissenschaft des Judentums in Berlin and the Jewish Theological Seminary in Breslau.[64] Backed by Germany's principal institutions of Jewish learning, the Deutsch-Israelitische Gemeindebund argued that the differences within Judaism were not as deep as those among Christian churches and instead merely entailed questions of "external rites."[65] Suggesting that Lasker's bill should be rejected because it promised to further the separation of church and state, the association's official petition sought to appeal to centrist liberals who remained leery of further weakening the churches.[66] This argument apparently impressed few liberal deputies, however, as it soon became clear that the parliamentary committee planned to recommend the passing of the bill and that the majority in the Reichstag supported it. The members of the Gemeindebund may have been at a disadvantage from the start, however: This was not the only time that the parliament had disregarded calls to protect the integrity of religious groups to enforce laws that protected individuals from the influence of religious institutions.

Jewish liberals' reactions to their looming defeat illustrate some of the paradoxes of anticlerical rhetoric in this context. Jewish representatives tried to undermine separationist secularism with the very anti-Catholic rhetoric that others regularly used to argue for it. Once Kohner learned that the parliamentary committee was likely to vote against the position of his organization, he drafted a confidential letter to the committee's president, Rudolf von Gneist, in a last-minute attempt to turn the tide in parliament. In an interpretation that is perhaps overly generous to its author, Ismar Schorsch has described Kohner's letter as "a moving affirmation of Jewish solidarity."[67] A renewed reading quickly reveals that the letter was anything but that. Kohner, who was known for overstepping his authority as president of the Deutsch-Israelitische Gemeindebund, clearly drafted the piece with the help of other members of his organization in the hopes of tarnishing the reputation of his Orthodox opponents with every possible accusation he could muster.[68] Well aware that Gneist vocally advocated laws restricting the rights of the Catholic clergy, Kohner had prepared his letter based on the plausible assumption that Gneist would be susceptible to anti-Catholic rhetoric. Kohner's semiprivate plea thus denounced Jewish Orthodoxy in a language that drew on anti-Catholic polemics and also far exceeded any public text in the Jewish press in its aggressive polemics.[69]

The document contained ad hominem attacks against the neo-Orthodox leaders Samson Raphael Hirsch, Ezriel Hildesheimer, and Marcus Lehmann (1831–1890) and suggested that all three individuals sustained close ties with Catholicism. According to Kohner,

All three [. . .] gentlemen have the peculiar fate of having left Germany, ending up in Austria, and exhibiting a certain Catholicizing tendency. Mr. Hirsch served for twenty years as chief rabbi [*Landes-Rabbiner*] in Moravia but was ultimately too rigorous even for the Austrian Jews. Mr. Hildesheimer was a rabbi for several years in Eisenstadt and leader of the ultras of this country.[70]

Kohner also described Marcus Lehmann, the editor of *Der Israelit*, as the publisher of a Jewish newspaper modeled on the kind to be found among the "small Bavarian ultramontane press."[71] Kohner further claimed that Lehmann was "not unperturbed by the monetary support of Bishop Kettler [of Mainz]," thereby insinuating that the Orthodox Jewish publicist had received bribes from one of the most powerful Catholic clergymen in Germany.[72]

Kohner took the comparisons between Jewish Orthodoxy and conservative Catholicism further still, as he suggested that Orthodox Jews' insistence on preserving references to the Jews' longing for Palestine in Jewish prayer books—something Reform Jews in Germany had done away with—made them no better than ultramontanes. In Kohner's portrayal, Orthodox Jews who yearned for the Land of Israel were just as disloyal to the German nation as were Catholics who obeyed a pope "beyond the mountains." Such "fanatics" are thus "justly called Jewish ultramontanes," Kohner concluded.[73]

Although Reform Jews had already attempted to conflate Orthodox Judaism with ultramontanism during the Kompert affair, Kohner's approach was even bolder, as he denounced his Orthodox coreligionists to a non-Jewish politician with the claim that they were disloyal to the state. Pointing out the extended periods of time German neo-Orthodox leaders spent in Austria and suggesting that "one can find nearly no truly Prussian group among the petitioners" were together meant to insinuate the foreign origins of the initiatives he sought to combat.[74] In Kohner's portrayal, liberal Jews and liberal Protestants were the only truly authentically Prussian and German groups, both of which constituted a bulwark against fanaticism from Jewish and Christian circles alike. Jewish Orthodoxy, by contrast, was—like ultramontane Catholicism—ultimately something foreign and un-Prussian. It came from Austria, Hungary, or at best, from Catholic regions in Germany, such as Bavaria.

Although Kohner's letter is by no means typical of the approach Jewish communal representatives adopted when dealing with the authorities, its language is nonetheless characteristic of the ways that Jews in Germany—particularly in Protestant-dominated Prussia—found ways to appropriate anticlerical tropes as they sought to inscribe themselves into the nation. It also shows how anti-Catholicism could serve multiple functions, sometimes giving Jews the opportunity to celebrate liberal religious policies and, in other instances, allowing them to contest some of the effects of the anti-Catholic *Kulturkampf*.

Antisemitism and the Demise of Jewish Anti-Catholicism in Germany

With the rise of antisemitic parties and campaigns by the late 1870s, statements such as those made by the Gemeindebund increasingly became a liability for politically engaged Jews in Germany. Antisemitism destroyed the raison d'être of modern Jewish anti-Catholicism: to make Jews seem like an uncomplicated part of a progressive, nationalist project. Although writers in the ultramontane press had already identified Jews with liberalism earlier, suggesting that they were responsible for the *Kulturkampf*, the late 1870s saw a spate of antisemitic attacks that emphasized these accusations against Jews in more threatening ways.[75] The idea of a Jewish conspiracy against Catholicism, once merely a marginal position, now surfaced even in parliament. In the infamous debate over the Antisemites' Petition in the Prussian Diet in 1880, Catholic deputies accused Jews of having been the principal supporters of the *Kulturkampf*.[76]

Equally important, as the popularity of the policies of the *Kulturkampf* began to wane, the claim that Germany was experiencing a clash of civilizations between liberal Protestants and Jews, on the one side, and conservative Catholics on the other became harder and harder to sustain. By the early 1880s, the National Liberal Party, the political home of most German Jews in the 1860s and 1870s, increasingly turned toward a narrower interpretation of nationalism and consistently excluded Jews from their parliamentary electoral lists.[77] The government also began relying less on national and progressive liberals for parliamentary votes, thus ending the liberal era of German and Prussian politics—even though liberals remained dominant for several decades in many municipalities.[78] Further complicating the political scene, various members of the Catholic Center Party regularly opposed political anti-semitism in parliament.[79] All this meant that the perceived dichotomy between patriotic, progressive liberals and intolerant, anti-loyalist Catholics, which had driven many Jews' politics in earlier eras, no longer made sense.

By the mid-1880s, all public Jewish figures ostensibly rejected the *Kulturkampf*. Anti-Catholic polemics no longer facilitated Jewish political and social integration as they had for nearly a century, even if assumptions about Catholic backwardness continued to appear in the social commentaries of many Jews.

Ambivalent Anti-Catholicism under the French Third Republic

As was the case in Germany throughout much of the 1870s, many French Jews in the French Third Republic continued to define anti-liberal Catholicism as their principal political foe. The Ferry laws on secular public schooling (1882, 1883) and the separation of church and state (1905) were—like the secularizing laws in Germany—the result of intense struggles with conservative Catholicism. As in Germany, Jews' political alliances with those who created such legislation based on anti-clerical polemics were ambivalent. Those Jews who were interested in sustaining Jewish communal life knew that certain advocates of secularizing laws were less welcoming of religious pluralism than others. Like German Jews, French Jews thus found themselves between different political fault lines and had to answer two basic sets of questions about their relationship to Catholicism: (1) How did they feel about new laws on church–state relations? Did such laws undermine the position of their political enemy—conservative political Catholicism—or did they constitute an attack against all recognized religions? (2) How should they understand antisemitism? Was it mainly Catholic in origin or rather a complex phenomenon that transcended simple religio-political divisions?

In their responses to both sets of questions, we might expect French Jews to have subscribed to the dominant republican line and to have associated their political enemies with Catholicism more than German Jews had. First, French anticlericalism appeared less coercive than German anti-Catholicism: French republicans did not infuse their campaigns against the Catholic Church with an exclusive, ethnic nationalism that could target Jews, as was the case in Germany by this period. Second, antisemites in France were much more clearly associated with political Catholicism than was true in Germany, left-wing antisemitism and individual Protestant antisemites notwithstanding.[80]

To a certain extent, an analysis of the Jewish press and the texts penned by Jewish authors during this period confirms these expectations: Before World War I, Jews in the Third Republic were, on the whole, more likely to embrace the dichotomy between political progressives and conservative Catholics than their German counterparts. Yet, at the same time, French Jews remained surprisingly reluctant to go beyond a condemnation of "clericalism" in general terms. The nationalist anticlerical polemics that Zunz and Kohut pursued in Germany at this time found no equivalent in the French Third Republic, nor did the official positions of institutions like the Deutsch-Israelitische Gemeindebund. Indeed, the few radical anticlericals with a Jewish background active in France during these years tended to highlight their distance from Judaism, while Jewish representatives similarly attempted to distances themselves from such individuals.

Overall, French Jews remained more ambivalent about anticlericalism under the Third Republic than their critics at the time allowed. Three interconnected problems can explain their ambivalence: growing agitation against Germany as a new national enemy, the pressures the state put on institutional Jewry, and pragmatic considerations concerning the most effective strategy for fighting antisemitism.

The first set of challenges affected all republicans but played a special role for Jewish republicans, a category that included nearly all publically active Jews in France after 1871.[81] French Jewish patriotism under the Third Republic was affected by the fact that Germany—widely understood to be a Protestant power—had now become a national enemy of France.[82] French Jewish intellectuals thus joined other French political thinkers of the era in mourning the loss of its eastern provinces to Germany and contemplating their country's "German crisis" after France's defeat in the Franco-Prussian War of 1870–1871.[83] These new developments also affected French Jews' depictions of Catholicism. In some instances, Jewish journalists adopted the general line of anticlerical republicans, who blamed Catholicism for France's defeat. In one such article, Simon Bloch of the *Univers israélite* claimed that modern life was not to be held responsible for France's stunted population growth, as the ultramontane and antisemitic journalist Veuillot had previously argued. The low birthrates that weakened France in its recent war were rather caused by the unnatural Catholic tradition of maintaining a celibate priesthood.[84] Bloch's position was, for the most part, indistinguishable from other republican diatribes against Catholicism in the wake of the war. The only difference was his conclusion that Judaism was the key to France's regeneration.[85]

Yet the antagonism sustained between Germany and France during this period also had the potential to undermine this interpretation of anticlericalism as a patriotic exercise. Resentment of the Catholic conservatives who dominated the early French Third Republic from 1871 to 1877 conflicted with national sentiments against "Protestant" Germany. Isidore Cahen explained this dilemma in a series of articles he published in the 1870s.[86] Although he suggested that ultramontanes constituted a threat to all religious minorities, Cahen was also torn because the ultramontanes who had come under German control in the region of Alsace were now claiming devotion to their former French homeland. In this context, Cahen suggested, political Catholics deserved their country's support in their struggle against their German oppressors. The situation had grown all the more complicated, Cahen claimed, because the Germans had begun collecting examples of French liberals' attacks against ultramontanes to use them to slander France as the home of clericalism. Was it not antipatriotic to attack conservative Catholicism under these circumstances? Cahen asked this question several times, and each time he decided that winning the battle against ultramontanism, the country's internal enemy, was more important for the future of France than was protecting the country against outside threats. Ultimately, Cahen concluded, "secular [*laïque*] France does not need compromised alliances to defend herself."[87]

The tensions between republican anticlericalism and the dedication to a nation made up mostly of Catholics emerged again in the 1874 celebrations for children of families exiled from Alsace. At the event, Amélie Crémieux, Adolphe Crémieux's wife, who had converted to Catholicism four decades earlier, served as an official host.[88] Isidore Cahen praised her participation in "this celebration, which is Christian in name and form but patriotic in its goals."[89] Yet Christian form and patriotic aim sometimes came as a package that could not be separated. The fact that Alsace was predominantly Catholic but also home to the largest Jewish population of pre-1870 France did not lessen this tension.

Similar dilemmas affected Cahen's attitude toward the German *Kulturkampf*. The German government's engagement in a struggle against the Catholic Church just as the newly unified country annexed French territory made any straightforward sympathy for German anti-Catholic policies difficult. Yet, the conflict with ultramontanism nevertheless remained one of the elements that bound contributors to the Jewish press together in Germany and France, just as it had in the 1860s. Cahen, for example, explained German events with references to domestic conflicts in France: The Catholic newspaper *Germania* was for him a German version of France's antisemitic Catholic *Univers*. By making this comparison Cahen implied that the Jews of both countries faced similar challenges.[90] According to Cahen, "those who defended [the principles of the secular state] in Prussia did not have our sympathy, but those who attacked them have them even less!"[91]

Bloch's paper was similarly split in its reports. Unlike the *Archives israélites*, the *Univers israélite* remained critical of the anti-Catholic statements of the Deutsch-Israelitische Gemeindebund. Bloch even translated an article from the German Orthodox *Israelit* that condemned the German Jewish organization for meddling in the affairs of other religious groups and for pushing patriotism in a direction that was unbecoming to Jews.[92] Despite his opposition to Reform Jews' anti-Catholicism in this instance, at other moments Bloch praised the anticlericalism of the *Kulturkampf* and even issued his own anticlerical attacks. In 1871, he applauded the Bavarian Minister of Religious Affairs, Johann von Lutz, for claiming that representatives of the Catholic Church believed that the church stood above the state's law. According to Bloch, this speech—which was one of the clarion calls to initiate anti-church legislation in Germany—was well-supported by the fact that the anti-modern papacy was also anti-Jewish.[93] Bloch also argued that German Catholics simply imagined their own persecution in the face of the *Kulturkampf* and that any real suffering they may have experienced was divine retribution for Catholic anti-Jewish aggression.[94] Indeed, Bloch wrote about the Catholic Church in France in a way that resembled the *Kulturkampf* rhetoric of many of his German coreligionists. Blaming the church for organizing collections for the pope, for example, he suggested that the funds collected were lost to patriotic projects such as the "deliverance of the fatherland," that is, the liberation of the provinces annexed by Germany.[95]

The second complication involved the debates on *laïcité*, starting with the first initiatives to reform the educational system during the so-called Republic of Republicans, which emerged after the defeat of the Regime of Moral Order in 1877. Unlike in Germany, there were substantial pragmatic reasons for Jews associated with French Jewish community bodies to engage in what Zvi Jonathan Kaplan has called a Jewish form of "soft clericalism" during these years.[96] Whereas the *Kulturkampf* was widely interpreted as a conflict between different denominations, the French anticlerical campaigns aimed at creating a form of nondenominational secularism. While this avowedly "neutral" form of secularism may have made the initiatives of Education Minister Jules Ferry to create a secular school system more appealing for Jews in general, they also immediately threatened to affect French Jews more directly than the laws of the *Kulturkampf* had affected German Jews. In Germany, although laws establishing and expanding non-confessional schools concerned Jews, as did the *Austrittsgesetz*, for the most part their institutions were not threatened by the renegotiation of church–state relations.[97] Jewish communities already lacked financial support in most German states. In France, things were different. The suppression of the budget for religious groups, which a radical minority demanded during debates over the Ferry laws in the 1880s, clearly put Jewish communal institutions in jeopardy.[98] As a result, the contributors to Jewish press in France made a point to argue that Jews—and the Judaism they claimed to represent—opposed both clericalism and atheistic freethinking. French Jewish leaders' self-positioning as moderates in religious matters became part of their emphatic centrism in the political realm during this period.

Anticlericalism, Anti-Catholicism, and Antisemitism in France

French Jews' ambivalence toward both conservative Catholicism and anticlericalism continued to characterize the positions expressed in the Jewish press even after the rise of antisemitism in France in the mid-1880s. Unlike in Germany, antisemitism did not completely undermine Jewish anticlerical polemics. Nor did it radicalize Jewish positions before the Dreyfus affair in the late 1890s. The number of articles issued by Jewish papers on the topic of ultramontanes, the pope, and Jesuits remained steady in the 1880s and for much of the 1890s, yet few Jewish authors appealed to anticlericalism in an attempt to build coalitions against antisemites. Indeed, as in Germany, most Jews in France did not explain antisemitism in terms of an exclusively ultramontane threat.[99] Unlike in Germany during the early *Kulturkampf*, those French Jewish individuals who turned to aggressive anticlerical rhetoric before the Dreyfus affair remained on the margins of the Jewish community and of political debate.

This was in part because French Jews tended to externalize antisemitism as a German phenomenon and thus allayed their fears by depicting the new movement as foreign to France. Taking this approach also proved a rhetorical boon because it allowed Jews—whom antisemites denounced as un-French—to portray antisemites as utterly un-French in response.[100] Even after French antisemitism became an undeniable phenomenon with the publication of Drumont's notorious *La France juive* in 1886, Jewish activists stood fast to their position that antisemitism was a foreign import.[101] This interpretation, the result of nationalist boundary making against a German foil, made anticlerical positions more complicated, as it did in debates on Jewish opposition to political Catholicism in the 1870s. If antisemitism was indeed genuinely German and thus part of the heritage of Protestant nationalism, then it could hardly also be primarily an expression of an inherently Catholic tradition. Faced with rising antisemitism from a new political right that

combined old monarchists, conservative Catholicism, and integral republican nationalists, French Jews acknowledged the complicated, and
seemingly multiple, origins of the movement that sought to undo their
place in society.

The increasing accusations French conservatives and antisemites lev-
eled against Jews, whom they charged with being agents of an atheist,
materialist form of state secularism, additionally undermined the appeal
of public anticlericalism for politically engaged Jews in France. This
pattern was reinforced by the example of the *Kulturkampf* in Germany,
which had demonstrated that such polemics could become a liability
to Jews. Unlike non-Jewish republicans in France, who were not asked
to prove their belonging, Jews found it increasingly difficult to show
their loyalty to the nation through radical anticlericalism because doing
so made them a target for polemics that had the potential to undermine any policies they sought to promote. Even those Jews who rose in
the republican administration during this period tended to distinguish
themselves primarily by their attempts to avoid close association with
anticlerical policies, as Pierre Birnbaum has shown.[102] Jewish prefects
charged with enforcing secularizing and anticlerical laws made an effort
to maintain good relations with the high clergy of their departments.

The responses that the few Jewish authors who chose a more radical
approach to secularist rhetoric elicited offer a useful gauge for understanding the decreasing appeal of vocal anticlerical polemics for French
Jews during an era of rising anti-Semitism. One such case is that of
Héber Marini, an engineer by profession, who penned one of the rare
Jewish rebuttals to Drumont's *La France juive*. Written when Marini
was seventy-two years old, his *Le fin mot sur la question juive* [The Truth
behind the Jewish Question] received an unenthusiastic response from
representatives of the Jewish community.[103] In his work, Marini decided to speak for those who were not "under the yoke of the Catholic
Church" and to explain to Catholics why Jews were superior.[104] According to Marini, Jews were not inherently different from others—they
were merely better educated. Unlike Catholics, who exposed their children to fanaticism and superstition early on, Jews offered their children
an exclusively secular education, Marini continued. Apparently extrapo-
lating from a narrow set of upper and middle-class urban French Jews,
Marini argued that no Jews had ever been illiterate and that under no

circumstances were Jewish children taught by rabbis.[105] In a manner that resembled the approach of the *Israelitische Wochen-Schrift* during the *Kulturkampf*, Marini turned the debates on the regeneration of the Jews on their head by advertising Jews as a model for the reform of Catholicism.

Marini's pamphlet was mostly ignored by the Jewish press. Only Cahen reviewed his work, explaining that he disagreed with Marini's political strategy even if he approved of his intentions.[106] Cahen argued that Marini had been correct in ridiculing "superstitious aberrations" among the lower classes but that he was wrong to mock them openly.[107] Non-Jews perceived Jews as partisan in this conflict, Cahen objected. They should leave the improvement of Christians to other Christians and not exacerbate the situation. Under current conditions, Cahen recommended that Jews remain silent and keep their ideas about the transformation of religious education to themselves. According to Cahen, all persons directly attacked by Drumont had already understood this and had wisely kept a low profile in the debates.

Cahen was not quite correct, in fact. Alexandre Weill, a Jewish author whom Drumont had attacked by name in his *La France juive*, had also responded to the antisemitic publication. Weill's response to Drumont offers another glimpse into the self-marginalizing qualities of some of the most aggressive anticlerical polemics among Jews in late nineteenth-century France.[108] After spending his early childhood in Alsace, Weill had moved to Frankfurt at the age of thirteen to become a rabbi. After eleven years as a yeshiva student, however, he decided to become a novelist and feuilleton writer instead.[109] Throughout his long career, he published several dozen works in German and French, often translating his own texts into both languages.

In the 1840s, Weill settled in Paris, where he became a republican political commentator. In a pamphlet of 1845, he attacked ultramontanism as a principle defined by its opposition to democracy and freedom. Curiously, Weill fashioned himself a defender of true Catholicism against ultramontanism, which he also described as the continuation of the strand of Judaism responsible for the death of Jesus.[110] The peculiar nature of Weill's politics is also reflected in his short friendship with the anti-Jewish agitator Louis Veuillot. The two became close in 1849 and later parted ways because Weill idealized a type of Catholicism that did not interest Veuillot.[111] Weill continued to present himself as a defender of true Christianity in the years after the 1848 Revolution.[112]

After the Mortara affair Weill rediscovered Judaism—or rather his own brand of Judaism—and, with it, a new religious form of anticlericalism. From this point on Weill endorsed a revival of the Jewish nation and became a regular contributor to the *Archives israélites*, where he also reviewed Moses Hess's *Rome and Jerusalem*. His first major work of this period, *Moïse et le Talmud*, stood in the tradition of Salvador's and Astruc's writings by embracing Mosaic Judaism as a genuine republican tradition.[113] Others, like James Darmesteter, developed their own attempts to fuse republicanism and Jewish prophetic traditions—an approach often referred to as Franco-Judaism—around the same time.[114] The main difference between Weill and these other authors was that Weill was not merely interested in salvaging the prophetic tradition of ancient Judaism; he also believed himself to be a prophet.[115]

Weill's later work combined French patriotism, Jewish nationalism, and a vocal rejection of Catholicism as anti-religious, anti-French, and anti-Jewish. His response to *La France juive* shows Weill at his most polemical in this regard.[116] He was apparently doing his best to beat Drumont at his own game of slanderous polemics. According to Weill, the religion of Jesus, as exemplified in particular by Catholicism, was nothing but an offspring of a degenerate form of Judaism. The true Mosaic tradition found its home in Judaism and in the French Revolution, Weill argued boldly.[117] Ultramontane Catholicism was ultimately nothing but "the poisoned source of all evil, [and of] all civil and international wars that afflicted humankind for more than a thousand years."[118]

For Weill, there was no longer anything redeeming about Catholicism. It had emerged from the clerical tradition of Ezra combined with the barbarism of the Aryans. Weill excluded only the Immaculate Conception of Mary—which had been declared as a dogma by the Catholic Church in 1854—from this claim. In Weill's view, this dogma constituted a purely pagan part of the degenerate tradition of Christianity, or, as he put it in his colorful language, it was "like a gnawing worm emerging from a gangrenous cancer."[119] Putting a spin on Gustav Tridon's antisemitic claims about Judaism as the tradition of Moloch cannibalism, Weill argued that Catholics who thought of Jesus as a god persecuted members of other religions and sacrificed them to the "Moloch Jesus."[120]

To a certain extent, the Jewish press had tolerated Weill's eccentricity, and they reviewed his work favorably up to this point. In their comments on his 1858 collection of letters to Veuillot, which documented his break with the famous antisemite, they gave him credit for being an original writer and for his sharp polemics against ultramontanism.[121] This approach slowly gave way to a more critical attitude. When non-Jewish papers wrote enthusiastic reviews of his *Moïse et le Talmud* in the 1860s, Cahen saw it necessary to clarify that he supported Weill's views on Moses but not his rejection of rabbinic tradition.[122] Cahen also eventually began to distance himself from Weill's tendency to denigrate his opponents as a transhistorical source of evil.[123] Up to 1886, when Weill published his response to Drumont, reviews in Jewish papers in France and Germany had either been friendly or at least expressed some polite interest in Weill's musings. Now, his latest diatribe provoked no reaction at all. His approach was apparently beyond the pale of the polemics that contributors to the Jewish press wished to consider.

Before the Dreyfus affair, the majority of publicly active and politically engaged Jews in France remained reluctant to employ anticlerical rhetoric in response to antisemitism. Those who did so were marginal and were further marginalized through their polemics.

The Dreyfus Affair: Anticlericalism as a Weapon against Antisemitism

It was only during the height of the Dreyfus affair that a broad consensus emerged among the representatives of French Jewry that antisemitism was a form of clericalism.[124] Although Alfred Dreyfus (1859–1935) was convicted as a German spy in 1894, his case became a national affair only in 1897, when the Alsatian senator Scheurer-Kestner (1833–1899) began to campaign for a retrial, based on his conviction that Dreyfus was in fact innocent. The national affair then turned into an international scandal when Emile Zola (1840–1902) went on trial for making accusations of wrongdoing against the military in his famous January 1898 article in favor of Dreyfus, "J'accuse." This is also when contributors to the Jewish press began to speak more about the affair and to campaign actively for the captain's exoneration.[125] Shortly before this shift in coverage, they started to depict antisemitism more frequently as "the ancient fight of clericalism against Judaism," as the editor of the *Archives israélites* put it.[126] This was due in large part to the antisemitism of the Catholic right in France, which was reinvigorated through the first conviction of Dreyfus.[127] Events such as the congress of Christian Democrats in Lyon in 1896, which dedicated a whole day to pronouncements of antisemitism, made the association between antisemitism and "clerical reaction" easier, even before the Jewish newspapers addressed the Dreyfus affair in full.[128]

The timing of Jewish polemics suggests that the turn to anticlerical frames of interpretation and polemics was the result not just of greater pressure but also, more important, of Jewish intellectuals' increasing ability to find allies by using anticlerical language. During the first two years of the affair's intensive phase (1897–1898), articles railing polemically against clericalism still appeared only irregularly in France's principal Jewish periodicals.[129] This is all the more remarkable because anticlericalism took center stage in the French socialist and liberal press as well as in the writings of individual Dreyfusards beginning as early as 1897.[130] The rhetoric of the Jewish press and other Jewish public figures became radicalized mainly after the government of Réné Waldeck-Rousseau (1846–1904) was formed in June 1899. Waldeck-Rousseau was a moderate republican who tried to reign in the Catholic congregations of France with the support of wide parts of the republican left.[131] Only with this change in policy and the broad use of anticlericalism as an integrative force among republicans of all shades did the Jewish press—particularly the *Univers israélite*—put Jesuits, clericalism, and clerical cabals front and center.[132] The anti-congregationalist laws of Waldeck-Rousseau's government for the "defense of the republic" were widely popular among Dreyfusards, in particular its legal initiatives to limit access to positions in the state's bureaucracy to graduates of schools unaffiliated with the church. Jewish newspapers followed the arguments of the government and of anticlerical Dreyfusards, who extolled these initiatives as a necessary reaction to clerical attempts to take over society.[133]

In the 1901 debates over new laws limiting the Catholic congregations but codifying extended rights for all other associations, most Jews who spoke publicly on the subject supported the republican side as well as its anticlerical arguments.[134] When, in a parliamentary speech, Waldeck-Rousseau hinted that the law could be understood as retaliation for the antisemitism espoused by Catholic congregations, the *Archives israélites* and the *Univers israélite* responded enthusiastically.[135] These moments guaranteed Jewish journalists' long-standing admiration for Waldeck-Rousseau and reinforced their interpretation of the Dreyfus affair as part of a war between republicans and clericals in France.[136]

Other prominent Jews who were less involved in communal matters followed similar arguments. In the process, they created a new anticlerical master narrative that seemed attractive once debates revolved around an alleged anti-republican clerical conspiracy, rather than the culpability of Jews. This pattern emerges clearly in Joseph Reinach's (1856–1921) seminal history of the Dreyfus affair, the first volume of which appeared in 1901, the same year that the Associational Laws were passed.[137] Reinach, a Jewish politician and public intellectual whose father was involved in the Panama scandal of 1892, was among those who had suffered personally from the defamations of Drumont and other antisemitic journalists.[138] Although he intended his history of the affair to legitimize the anticlerical campaigns of the government of the Third Republic, it has since become the standard Dreyfusard account of the affair and remains influential until today.[139] Reinach argued that Drumont had been a puppet of Jesuits and that his antisemitic campaign had been orchestrated by clerics.[140] The Jewish press applauded Reinach's work, focusing on those passages that dealt with the Jesuit involvement in the affair.[141] This narrative made it easier for Jews to leave behind their moderate positions of the early Third Republic and to instead throw their support behind anticlerical legislation that would soon also begin to take a financial toll on Jewish institutions.

Whereas French Jewish periodicals had reported about the antisemitism of the years 1886–1897 with relatively few references to ultramontanism or Jesuits, by the turn of the century the combination of an actively anticlerical government and the Dreyfus affair helped make pronounced anticlericalism productive once again as a monocausal ex-planatory framework and a political tool for Jewish authors and activ-ists alike. Even though public figures who claimed to speak for French Jewry often remained skeptical of the policies that radical anticlericals envisioned, as the historian Zvi Jonathan Kaplan has noted, the po-litical language of anticlericalism experienced a last renaissance in the French Jewish public sphere for a few years.[142]

Jewish Anticlericalism in Algeria

The enthusiasm for anticlerical rhetoric in this period also spread to some Jewish intellectuals in Algeria during this period, the French departements with the most active antisemitic movement. In Algeria, however, any attempt to think of challenges to the Jews' position in society as a clerical cabal proved much more difficult, as the case of a Jewish anticlerical author active in Algiers in the late 1890s illustrates. Henri, or Henry, Tubiana was a Jewish left-wing journalist who briefly contributed to the Algerian socialist publication *Solidarité* as well as the often antisemitic, Paris-based *Revue socialiste*.[143] Having previously attempted to establish his own newspaper—the *Gazette de Algérie* (1884–1886)—in 1898 Tubiana founded the only Jewish periodical ever dedicated exclusively to anticlericalism.[144] His short-lived publication consisted of broadsheets with subsequent numbering and changing titles: *Le paria juive*, *L'anticléricale juif*, and *À bas les jésuites*.[145] Tubiana's paper was primarily a reaction to the devastating antisemitic campaigns that allowed the antisemite Max Régis to become the mayor of Algiers and brought four antisemitic deputies, including Edouard Drumont, into parliament from the Algerian departments.

Like Salvador, Weill, and many other Jewish authors in nineteenth-century Germany and France, Tubiana created a large world-historical and theological narrative meant to defend Judaism against its detrac-tors. In an article he published for the *Revue socialiste*, he focused on the revolutionary potential of the Algerian Jewish working class and highlighted how Judaism could be part of a socialist vision.[146] Among Judaism's innate characteristics was its long history of anticlericalism, Tubiana posited:

Contrary to the clichés foolishly reproduced by our adversaries, Israel is in good standing when it comes to revolutionary service. Our secular [*laïque*] pioneers never stopped fighting against clericalism and suffered a thousand deaths for their universal solidarity. No nation, not even the courageous Gauls, resisted so obstinately against the egoistical domination of Rome. It is among us that the first dawn of the modern world arose, which eventually destroyed the empire of the Caesars.[147]

Tubiana's polemics against ancient Rome, which he sometimes connected with papal Rome, are reminiscent of the anticlerical writings of other nineteenth-century Jewish authors such as Heinrich Heine. In the Algerian context, however, they were particularly forceful, as the vanguard of Algerian antisemitism played with images of ancient Rome as a Latin life force around the Mediterranean. In the theories of Cardinal Charles Lavigerie and Louis Bernard, Roman colonial activity in the region served as a model and a precedent that—in Bernard's secular version—were destined to lead to the creation of a new Mediterranean race in Algeria.[148] European colonists of diverse origin, including the mass of Italian and Spanish immigrants, would thus be united at the exclusion of Jews. In this context, Tubiana not only aimed his anticlerical statements at antisemites, whom he associated with the rise of "clerical supremacy in Europe until the Renaissance";[149] he also attempted to counter racialized notions of European colonial unity with a socialist vision that had a place for both historical Judaism and the Algerian Jewish workers of his day as its vanguard.[150]

In the 1880s, Tubiana had started an initiative that was more revolutionary than his socialist rhetoric at the time. He wanted to change the status quo of French colonial policy in Algeria. The Jews of Algeria had received French citizenship en masse with the Crémieux decree of 1870, unlike their Muslim neighbors who collectively remained colonial subjects. The rise of antisemitism in Algeria was closely tied to Jews' collective enfranchisement at this time: Antisemites argued that Jews did not deserve their new status as equals and that they abused their new powers in electoral politics.[151] By the 1880s and 1890s, antisemitic activists spearheaded broader campaigns to demand the abrogation of the Crémieux decree. Tubiana sought to unhinge this fateful connection as he unsuccessfully petitioned the Chamber of Deputies to extend full citizenship to Algeria's Muslim population.[152] Tubiana's *Gazette de*

Algérie was also a platform for this position. It bore the subtitle *republic-aine et assimilateur*, which was meant to indicate his desire to assimilate both Jews and Muslims into French culture and legal structures.[153]

By the time Tubiana published his anticlerical journal in 1898, he had radicalized his language. Similar to Weill, he began to engage in theo-logically inspired symbolic politics that are at times difficult to follow. In this later work, he claimed, for example, that the Jews were the only true Aryans and, as such, the true defenders of the proletariat. Within the pages of his paper he similarly tried to depict antisemites' attacks on his person as anti-Aryan and anti-proletarian—including their alleged calls of "Down with Tubiana" at a rally held in Algiers during a visit Drumont paid to the city.[154] By comparison, his anticlericalism emerges as among his least eccentric positions.[155]

Tubiana's attempt to fight antisemitism with anticlericalism was nev-ertheless bound to fail. Most importantly, it was, in fact, rather difficult to equate Algerian antisemitism and the political camp of those Tubiana called clericals. On the contrary, although many lower clergy were ac-tive in the antisemitic movement, most antisemites of Algeria consid-ered themselves as republicans. Here, more than in any other French region, one could find political agitators who were both passionately anticlerical and antisemitic at the same time. Indeed, Algerian social-ists and freemasons were among the most dynamic elements within the broad antisemitic movement among European colonists in Algeria.[156] Even Tubiana had to admit that the socialists he endorsed for the up-coming parliamentary election were also antisemites. He merely main-tained that they would sit in parliament with other socialists who were not as prejudiced and that their antisemitism would thus be silenced by other members of their own faction.

Tubiana's anticlericalism in Algeria was thus a strange experiment in socialist and republican politics combined with attempts to coun-ter the antisemitism of his day. His claim that antisemitism was merely the latest ruse drawn from a clerical toolbox clashed with a much more complicated reality. This made any attempt to associate anticlericalism exclusively with progressive and liberal political platforms difficult in Algeria.

Tubiana was not the only or last person in Algeria to neverthe-less seek to simplify political alliance building in Algeria through an anticlerical interpretation.[157] One indicator of this comes from the massive archive of congratulatory messages that Prime Minister Émile Combes (1835–1921, in office 1902–1905), a radical anticlerical and free-thinker, received for his initiatives to curb the power of the Catholic Church. Among the hundreds of official declarations of support from freemasons' lodges and republican and socialist groups, few notes from Jewish groups appear.[158] The only avowedly Jewish missives came from Algeria, where a number of Jews in Oran—the center of Algerian anti-semitism—penned telegrams of support for the prime minister.[159] The chief rabbi of Algiers, Abraham Bloch, also paid homage to the repub-lican politician in the name of the local consistory, a mere two weeks before Combes resigned from his position as prime minister and min-ister of the interior and religion.[160] Although none of these declarations expressed the radical anticlerical sentiments that could be found in the missives of other French political groups, and although Bloch was no friend of the separation law, they nonetheless conveyed a clear political message.[161] Besides the small group of Jews who sent congratulatory letters to Combes from Algeria, no other non-Jewish religious repre-sentatives from the departments of the Seine (which included Paris) or Algeria expressed their support for the vocally anticlerical prime minis-ter in this form.

The Demise of Jewish Anticlericalism in France

By 1902, the Combes government's radical religious policies and its move toward separation convinced many of the official and self-appointed representatives of French Jewry to be more wary of their anticlerical allies.[162] As a consequence, the Jewish intellectuals closest to Jewish communal politics changed their rhetoric. They now largely abandoned the language of anticlericalism in the face of growing con-cerns about shifting church–state relations, even if they remained sup-portive of republican politics. Anticlerical polemics continued to lose their luster for Jewish community builders once the separation law of 1905 passed, after which time Jewish relations to the Catholic Church slowly began to improve in France.

The final blow to anticlericalism as a political language came with World War I and the evocation of the *union sacré*—the notion of a unified France without party or religious divisions—across the political spectrum. In this context Jewish anticlericalism lost much of its political rationale. With the outbreak of the war, Jews followed a general trend of putting national union above all else as they emphasized their national bonds with French Catholics in the conflict against Germany and its allies.

One small incident from the trenches that made the rounds in newspapers during the Great War illustrates this shift. According to one popular version the story, in the very first month of the war, a Jewish military chaplain attended to a seriously wounded Catholic soldier. Asked for his last wish, the soldier demanded a crucifix. Obliging his dying compatriot, the rabbi was killed just as he attempted to fulfill the Catholic soldier's request.[163] Although such stories of shared sacrifice were hardly unique to this war, or to the French side, journalists and readers frequently looked for such narratives of cross-denominational charity as their nation went to war. The Jewish press regularly returned to such anecdotes to highlight Jews' dedication to the nation. In this case, the story was powerful enough to cross some of the deepest political divisions. Even the old anti-Dreyfusard Maurice Barrès referenced it with great admiration in his irenic *Les diverses familles spirituelles de la France* [The Faith of France: Studies in Spiritual Differences & Unity] (1917).[164] For our purposes, the identity of the chaplain who allegedly died while serving a Catholic compatriot is also interesting: He was none other than the former chief rabbi of Algiers, Abraham Bloch, who had expressed his support for Combes at the height of the country's conflicts over the separation of church and state.

The broad popularity of the story and its ecumenical message are symbolic of a climate in which anti-Catholicism no longer appeared to be a patriotic position, even in the eyes of republicans. This is not to say that the *union sacré* of the World War I permanently mended all divisions. Even the most optimistic political commentators would have conceded its limited power and legacy in the civil war atmosphere of the mid-1930s, under the impression of the antisemitic campaigns of the Action française, or in light of the policies of the Vichy government a decade later. Yet, despite these vicissitudes in intercommunal relations and governmental policies, the simplest narratives of the anticlerical culture wars—with a convenient world-historical Catholic enemy—were never again as effective for non-Jews and Jews as they were in the long nineteenth century.

German Jews during the Dreyfus Affair and Beyond

When German and French Jewish journalists discussed the fate of their coreligionists across the border with an eye to similarities they were usually concerned not with "clericalism" but rather with antisemitism. This was the case, for example, in the 1898 elections to the French Chamber of Deputies and the German Reichstag, when the Jewish press gave a great deal of space to the political successes and failures of antisemitic candidates.[165] In that year, French Jewish journalists found it increasingly difficult to speak of a purely German problem of antisemitism because the majority of antisemitic deputies failed in Germany but succeeded in France.[166]

By the end of the nineteenth century, Catholic challenges to Jewish civic equality appeared, in contrast to antisemitism in general, to be limited to Catholic countries. In Germany during the late 1890s, Jewish periodicals noted the involvement of the so-called clerical party in enflaming French antisemitism while drawing comparisons with the situation in Austria, which had just experienced the rise of the antisemitic Christian Socialists under Karl Lueger.[167] Whereas just a few decades earlier certain contributors to the Jewish press had wondered whether Catholic antisemitism was the result of strategic decisions made in the Vatican, many Jewish observers in Germany now saw antisemitic mobilization as a consequence of local conditions combined with uncoordinated processes of transmission. Fewer and fewer articles now made reference to a clerical cabal. Instead, articles in the Jewish press described the spread of antisemitism in the biologized language of contagion. Jewish journalists thus spoke of the "pest of antisemitism" or suggested that the French had now been "infected" with antisemitism as well.[168]

When contributors to the German Jewish press discussed Jesuit support for Drumont's newspaper or the alliance that had emerged between the clericals and the military, they often pointed to what they considered different in Germany. According to German Jewish writers, clericals no longer constituted a major political opponent of Jewish civic rights in Germany.[169] Indeed, even the Catholic Center Party now rejected the activities of conservative Catholics in France, as both German and French Jewish periodicals noted.[170] Once the Center Party began to fight for new laws guaranteeing religious freedom in Germany in 1900, Jewish–Catholic relations in the two countries appeared ever more distinct.[171] Many Jews also applauded the Center Party's opposition to legislation that promised to limit the religious freedom of observant Jews, including laws that threatened to forbid kosher slaughtering in the name of the protection of animal rights.[172]

Certainly, there was much that continued to divide Catholics and Jews in Germany. A vibrant culture of Catholic antisemitism still persisted, and, at the universities, Jewish university students remained, on the whole, closer to their Protestant peers than to their Catholic fellow students.[173] As Lisa Zwicker has shown, there were even times when Jewish students supported liberal student unions with the aim of excluding Catholics, during the so-called academic *Kulturkampf* of 1902–1907.[174] Such examples notwithstanding, Jews and Catholics in turn-of-the-century Germany clearly experienced a rapprochement that did not develop among Jews and self-declared Catholic forces in France. The historian Jacob Toury has even claimed that significant numbers of Jews voted for Germany's Center Party as they began to shift their support away from National Liberals, who now excluded Jewish candidates and were reluctant to oppose antisemites.[175] By the time Chancellor Bernhard von Bülow created an electoral block including conservatives, National Liberals, and Left Liberals against Catholics and Socialists in 1907, many Jews no longer found such calls to unity compelling.[176] Instead, as they increasingly confronted the choice between antisemitic and Catholic candidates, many German Jews chose the latter.[177]

Between the period of the *Kulturkampf* and the Dreyfus affair, the alliance politics of German Jews had been completely remade. The belief that Protestant and Jewish liberals could together form the foundation of the empire flagged and, with it, so too did the notion that Catholicism was a major political problem. Fewer and fewer Jewish publicists were now willing to defend Protestantism as the core of the German idea. A new generation of Jewish activists and thinkers instead moved toward accommodation with Catholic political positions during the period of the Weimar republic. Indeed, as the republic was threatened by the rise of Nazism, many Jews put their faith in the tenacity and steadfastness of the Catholic parties. By the interwar era, anticlericalism disappeared as a major theme of Jewish politics in both countries. The vast majority of politically active Jews from both countries continued to look beyond their national borders to gauge the shifting relationship between religion and mass politics that they now rightly perceived as one that transcended any simplistic scenarios of civilizational conflict.

Conclusion
Rethinking European Secularism from a Minority Perspective

"I regularly came to talk about Luther's antisemitism, a dilemma for me, because Protestantism was, after all, enlightened compared to Catholicism, because a Protestant pastor had helped us on the run, and because the young Luther was a man of deeds and a hero among the poets and writers," Ruth Klüger wrote in her memoir of a childhood spent between survival in Theresienstadt and Auschwitz and in hiding in Germany.[1] These observations about conversations she had in Regensburg during the years after her liberation suggest the staying power of the anti-Catholic images nurtured in the crucible of nineteenth-century European secularism. Even after the Holocaust—often depicted as the apocalyptic outcome of the racial antisemitism that emerged among Germany's Protestant middle classes—many European Jews continued to associate Catholicism with backwardness and Protestantism with progress.[2]

There has been no dearth of conflicts between self-identified Jews and the Catholic Church since World War I, several of which have revolved around themes that were prevalent already earlier. Tensions between Jews and the church during the twentieth century arose, for example, over the fate of Jewish children who had survived the Holocaust by hiding in Catholic households or institutions. In the most famous case, the Finaly affair of 1953, the church supported a French woman who kept custody over two Jewish siblings in spite of demands by relatives to return the children at war's end.[3] For many, the church's arguments about its obligations to keep within its fold Jewish children who had been baptized were redolent of the Mortara affair of 1858. Other tensions were even more long lasting. In 1963 Rolf Hochhuth's drama *The Deputy* highlighted the failings of Pius XII in the face of the

Nazi genocide. The play sparked an international debate about the actions of the Catholic Church during the Holocaust that remains with us to this day.[4]

Yet, even though certain nineteenth-century clichés about Catholicism have survived among Jews, and in spite of the periodically fraught relations between the Vatican and Jewish representatives, Catholicism no longer forms a constitutive Other of Jewish politics. Many historically minded Jews now highlight the fact that Catholics were less likely than Protestants to vote for Hitler during his party's meteoric rise to power, while many leftist Jews celebrate the activities of Catholic lay activists, clergy, and theologians in civil rights movements around the world. Ruth Klüger's remarks are thus typical not because of the anti-Catholic sentiments she described feeling in the late 1940s but because she implicitly distanced herself from her former views by describing them as part of a learning process. It is also unlikely any Jew—or non-Jew for that matter—after the Second Vatican Council (1962–1965) would suggest that Catholic despotism offers a typical pathology of political religion, as Mendelssohn did in the late eighteenth century. Nor is it likely that a liberal Jewish group would compare conservative Catholicism with Orthodox Judaism to denounce the latter. Jewish anti-Catholicism as a constitutive element of political thought was specific to the period of Jewish emancipation and liberal ascendance in Western and Central Europe.

In this unique constellation of Europe's long nineteenth century, Jewish anti-Catholicism served as a gauge of Jews' political and social integration. As soon as German and French Jews started speaking publicly about modern European politics, they commented openly on the Catholic Church. Jews could show their personal ability to transcend their allegedly backward background by denouncing fanaticism among their own, but they could do so equally in polemics against the Catholic Church. Perhaps most striking of all was the freedom Jews found to participate in such debates. Indeed, although the first generations of Jewish enlighteners in France and Germany had numerous detractors—among both Enlightenment thinkers and their enemies—none took exception to Jews' anti-Catholicism. Nor did the governments that ruled over these Jewish thinkers usually take issue with their anticlericalism or anti-Catholicism. When judged from the vantage point of later periods,

Jews' critiques of the Catholic Church during the late Enlightenment were surprisingly unproblematic in their ability to make Jews seem like everyone else.

This pattern gradually changed throughout the nineteenth century, ultimately leading to an inverse situation in which Jews' critiques of the Catholic Church appeared to threaten Jewish integration. Indeed, by the last quarter of the nineteenth century, antisemites used Jewish anti-Catholicism to highlight Jews' inability to identify with the German and French nation and their compatriots' Christian or Catholic traditions. By this point, most German and French Jews alike understood that vocal anti-Catholic anticlericalism no longer served their interests. A century after Mendelssohn penned his anti-Catholic remarks in *Jerusalem*, taking such a position made Jews vulnerable to accusations of partisanship and even helped inspire conspiracy theories. As a result, Jewish criticism of the Catholic Church was muted in public debates during the era of mass politics, when accusations against Catholics, but also Jews, became particularly vicious.

These opportunities and limitations Jews encountered as they employed anti-Catholic polemics at different moments throughout Europe's long nineteenth-century speak to broader debates on the relationship between minorities and secularism. They allow for a reevaluation of the three most common scholarly critiques of secularism. The first critique rests on claims that secularism is a case of false universalism. In the nineteenth century, this argument was put forward mostly by conservatives of different hues who opposed what they saw as the godless materialism of the secularist anticlericals in their midst. In Germany, Catholic conservatives denounced the universalistic arguments of liberals as merely Protestantism in new clothes. In twentieth- and twenty-first-century academic discussions, a left-wing version of this critique—which also has its origins in the nineteenth century—is particularly popular: Many of today's critics accuse secularism of continuing rather than breaking with the legacy of Christianity. Some of them even view secularism and modern forms of Christianity as mutually constitutive in Western contexts. Critics of secularism's false universalism point to the American and European celebration of Christian holidays such as Christmas as purely "secular" vacations. Such a development, they rightly suggest, forces non-Christians to explicitly invoke religious traditions to be able get time away from work or school to celebrate non-Christian holidays, whereas Christians (of the majority denominations) have the freedom to celebrate holidays from their own tradition in secular form. Since the nineteenth century, critics of the false universalism inherent in secularist arrangements have similarly noted that Sunday rest laws, which frequently appear under the guise of workers' protection, in fact reproduce in a secularized form a Christian rhythm of dividing the week. Such accusations of a surreptitiously Christian secularism have gained new currency in debates on Islam in Europe in recent years.[5]

In their critique of secularism's false universalism many scholars have also gone beyond an analysis of legal restrictions, looking instead at the tacit assumptions motivating powerful social institutions and discourses. Talal Asad, whose essays have come to shape much of the field, describes secularism as a reflection of power relations in a nation-state framework.[6] In Asad's account, the modern distinction between religion and the secular is itself part of a secularist framework, based on Western narratives and assumptions, in which religion is always under suspicion. Secularism is ultimately problematic because its practitioners do not understand that their seemingly universalistic judgments are based on assumptions about human nature that emerge from specific historical contexts and power asymmetries.[7]

A second set of critiques associates secularism with anti-religious policies and radical individualism. While conservative enemies of atheism and materialism had already put forward such arguments in the nineteenth century, twentieth-century thinkers have adopted them to their own ends. According to this critique, the secular nation-state might have brought about the blessings of civic equality but it did so at the expense of communal rights and thus also damaged the integrity of historical communities of believers.[8] Proponents of this approach argue that secularism, with its pressures to assimilate, limits religious freedom in general, and particularly that of marginalized religious communities whose detractors denounce them as reactionary fanatics.

A clear sign of secularism's many forms can be found in the fact that its critics have also come to the opposite conclusion, offering a third set of critiques of the phenomenon. Various scholars posit that secularism reinvigorated and radicalized religious divisions by politicizing them.

According to this view, the modern state's emphasis on the primacy of secular citizenship has resulted in the formation of new distinctions among citizens. Rather than simply destroying expressions of particular identities, in other words, secularism also inspired new ones. In the work of Zygmunt Bauman, for example, racism figures among those modern secular inventions that produced more entrenched, and even more dangerous, boundaries where old boundaries were erased.[9] In the eyes of many critics of secularism, the violence of the religious conflicts the modern state promised to heal paled in comparison to the violence engendered in its attempts to reinforce modern distinctions among citizens. These new, more violent distinctions could also take explicitly religious forms. German historians have spoken about the nineteenth century as a second confessional age in which religious differences between Catholics and Protestants acquired renewed urgency.[10] Other scholars have highlighted how European powers fostered religious divisions and created religious conflict through their colonial projects.[11]

Nineteenth-century Jews in Germany and France struggled with all these aspects of secularism. Some Jews complained about the bias of laws mandating Sunday rest, while others made it their business to protect their community's shrinking social role against competing nonreligious communities. Western and Central European Jews also suffered from the new racist antisemitism, which was infused with religious tropes even when it appeared in a secular guise.

An analysis of Jewish anticlerical polemics also illuminates other, previously unrecognized challenges European Jews faced, however, allowing for a reevaluation of these three common scholarly critiques of secularism. First, Jewish politicians and intellectuals in both France and Germany often struggled less with the false universalism of Christian secularists than with accusations that they themselves were false universalists. Parliamentary debates on religion and churches illustrate Jews' dilemmas in this respect. Most critics have suggested that secularism forces members of religious minorities to obscure interests they share with their coreligionists when speaking in political contexts. The experiences of Jewish parliamentarians in nineteenth-century France and Germany show a more complicated picture, however. They were not so much under pressure to hide their Jewishness in public debates as to remain silent on policies toward the Catholic Church. Whenever Jewish deputies took the floor to speak about church–state relations, they risked being attacked as infringing on unwritten rules prohibiting individuals from one religious community from interfering in the internal affairs of another. Reflecting the narrowing of opportunities for Jewish anti-Catholic anticlericalism in other arenas during the second half of the nineteenth century, Jewish deputies also found that their opponents increasingly portrayed their comments on the church as Jewish anti-Christian attacks hidden behind a mask of general politics. The critique of the secularists' false universalism was thus itself part of a potentially exclusionary logic.

To some degree, this challenge was specific to the particular status of Catholicism as the main—but also Christian—Other of nineteenth-century European secularist politics. Although discussions of religious policies and secularist ideals regularly charged Catholics with being backwards and even disloyal to the nation, they were still simultaneously seen as internal Christian Others. The status of Jews within these different national and European contexts was, by comparison, much more tenuous. Jews' adoption of secularist polemics, which were inevitably articulated in relation to the Catholic Church throughout the long nineteenth century, was thus from the start a problematic proposition. Jews remained limited in their ability to express a secularist vision because secularism was, in the end, articulated not merely by Christians but also against certain Christians.

In this context, Jews' attacks against clerics in their own religion could become a means of proving the neutrality of their anticlericalism. This was the case when the Jewish deputy Eduard Lasker initiated a speech against the right of churches to excommunicate their members with a diatribe against rabbis who excluded Jews from their communities. Attacking their own "fanatics" could suggest that Jewish deputies were in fact rightful interlocutors within general debates on secularism. Intra-Jewish debates on religious and moral reform and Jewish participation in broader debates on modernity's other Others were thus often intimately connected.

Second, as an expression of diverse expectations about religion's role in society, Jewish anticlericalism helps us rethink current critiques of secularism that treat it as either limiting religious expression or as reinforcing intergroup boundaries. Anticlericalism was central for nineteenth-century secularism because it allowed liberals and republicans to explain the need for a strong constitutional state with the power to keep problematic religious groups and institutions in check. In this respect, Jewish anticlericals were not different from their non-Jewish peers. Like most Protestant German liberals or French republicans of their day, nineteenth-century Jews attacked the Catholic Church because they believed it worked against the pluralistic but unified state they championed.

At the same time, anti-Catholic polemics could also serve Jews who sought to bolster the boundaries of their own community. During the Terquem affair in the mid-1840s, French Jewish journalists attempted to reinforce communal cohesion, for example, by suggesting that conniving priests had been working to convert Jews to Catholicism. In other instances, Jewish liberals found that anticlerical tropes allowed them to highlight the usefulness of Jewish religious traditions within the liberal order. This was the case, for example, when nineteenth-century Jewish authors projected the eighteenth-century claim that they were in society but not from society—*in civitate* but not *de civitate*—onto the church. According to Jewish writers like Sigismund Stern or Simon Bloch, the Catholic Church was by nature foreign to the state, whereas Jews were willing to submit to the state's authority. Jews thus elaborated a polemical view of secularism in a way that both critiqued the disunity of the nation and articulated their religion's political raison d'être.

Third, Jewish anticlericalism highlights the importance of understanding the multiplicity of secularisms that emerge from different foils. Secularists defined their expectations about proper religion against a variety of Others. Focusing solely on a single foil of secularist thought thus assures that we miss a large part of the story. A comparative perspective shows us that European Jews were capable critics of certain aspects of secularism but poor observers of others. Both Catholics and Jews reserved their critique primarily for the aspect of nation-state thinking most harmful to them: Jews were great critics of anti-pluralistic nationalism, while Catholics offered a succinct critique of an interventionist, secular state. The study of polemics about religion and politics between different marginalized groups thus reveals unique positions of critique and affirmation alike. At the same time, these different foils are always interconnected. As I have argued in Chapter One concerning the case of antisemitism and anti-Catholicism, and as others have shown for Jews and Muslims, different European Others were historically entangled in popular depictions of pathological religion, even as these groups' attempts to formulate political visions usually obscured these connections.[12]

A focus on the interconnected nature of different targets of secularist critique also helps expose the lacunae of existing studies of Jewish secularism. This scholarship can be divided into two different schools of thought: The first, older tradition sees Jewish secularism as the imitation of a Christian model and Jewish secularization as the result of Jews' entrance into either a Christian or postreligious world. Secularization and assimilation are thus similar or parallel processes for Jews, according to this line of thought. While this position is mostly implicit in older studies, Shmuel Feiner's work offers the most sustained and explicit example of this approach. His book on the origins of Jewish secularization traces the many stories of hedonistic consumption and personal doubt that led eighteenth-century Jews to abandon Judaism's legal prescriptions.[13] The second approach seeks the origins of Jewish secularism not in the abandonment of Jewish laws and life but as emerging from a long genuinely Jewish tradition of secularism. The most prominent representative of this line of inquiry is David Biale, who has probed deep into the history of Jewish thought, going back as far as biblical sources to find the roots of Jewish secularism.[14] His account also aims to offer an intellectual foundation to attempts to define Judaism in cultural rather than religious terms.

As different as these two approaches are, they share a focus on intra-Jewish debates. For both Feiner and Biale, the history of Jewish secularism is the result of an ideological conflict, or *Kulturkampf*, between Jewish traditionalists and Jewish secularists.[15] Such portrayals are illuminating but remain incomplete, for they absolve readers from engaging with the full range of polemical positions that made Jewish secularism powerful in the modern period. Contrary to the received story of Jewish thought, modern Jewish secularism did not emerge out of efforts to imitate or adopt a single dominant model of Christian secularism; nor did it emerge primarily out of a Jewish tradition of secular thinking. Instead, modern Jewish secularism emerged both in conversations with particular Christian allies and with other particular Christian enemies as a foil. Eighteenth- and nineteenth-century Jewish secularism was never only a fight against rabbis or the strictures of Jewish law but also part of European debates about other religious groups.

In their attempts to become modern citizens and gain acceptance in different national contexts, French and German Jews had little choice but to judge the relative modernity of modern secularism's other principal Other, namely Catholicism. In today's Europe, the religion that inspires the language of secularism by serving as its main foil is undoubtedly Islam. While I venture that the current debates on Islam underscore the urgency of inquiring into the polemical roots of secularism, I do not mean to suggest that there is a direct line that leads from the nineteenth century to today's debates. The entangled history of European anti-Catholicism and antisemitism shows that the foils of secularism are not exchangeable, even if they are intricately connected. In this sense the phenomenon analyzed in this book does not offer simple lessons. Islam today has not merely assumed the position that either Catholicism or Judaism held in previous eras.[16] The history of Jewish anti-Catholicism nevertheless draws our attention to a constellation that complicates our understanding of minoritarian secularism at large. In spite of the different experiences and pressures that shaped each group's history at different times, there is one constant: Religious minorities continue to be invited to demonstrate their willingness to integrate, not only by reforming themselves but also by demanding the reformation of other marginalized groups.

Reference Matter

Abbreviations in the Endnotes

ADBR	Archives départementales du Bas-Rhin
ADHR	Archives départementales du Haut-Rhin
AI	*Archives israélites*
AN	Archives nationales de France
AIU	Alliance israélite universelle
AZJ	*Allgemeine Zeitung des Judenthums*
BArch	Bundesarchiv Berlin
CAHJP	Central Archive for the History of the Jewish People
DHA	Düsseldorfer Heine-Ausgabe: Heinrich Heine, *Historisch-kritische Gesamtausgabe der Werke*, ed. Manfred Windfuhr (Hamburg: Hoffmann und Campe, 1973–1997)
GStPK	Geheimes Staatsarchiv Preußischer Kulturbesitz
HSA	Heinrich Heine, *Säkularausgabe: Werke, Briefwechsel, Lebenszeugnisse*, ed. Nationale Forschungs- und Gedenkstätten der klassischen deutschen Literatur and Centre National de la Recherche Scientifique (Berlin: Akademie-Verlag, 1970–)
IWS	*Israelitische Wochen-Schrift*
LBIYB	*Leo Baeck Institute Yearbook*
PHdA	Preußisches Haus der Abgeordneten, *Stenographische Berichte*
RT	Deutscher Reichstag, *Stenographische Berichte*
RTNDB	Reichstag des Norddeutschen Bundes, *Stenographische Berichte*
UI	*Univers israélite*

Notes

Introduction

1. For a transnational survey of nineteenth-century anti-Catholicism, see Christopher Clark and Wolfram Kaiser, eds., *Culture Wars: Secular–Catholic Conflict in Nineteenth-Century Europe* (Cambridge, UK: Cambridge University Press, 2003).

2. Among the exceptions, see Till van Rahden, *Juden und andere Breslauer: die Beziehungen zwischen Juden, Protestanten und Katholiken in einer deutschen Grossstadt von 1860 bis 1925* (Göttingen: Vandenhoeck & Ruprecht, 2000) and the contributions to *Juden, Bürger, Deutsche: zur Geschichte von Vielfalt und Differenz 1800–1933*, ed. Andreas Gotzmann, Rainer Liedtke, and Till van Rahden (Tübingen: Mohr, 2001), especially Till van Rahden, "Von der Eintracht zur Vielfalt: Juden in der Geschichte des deutschen Bürgertums," 9–31, and Olaf Blaschke, "Bürgertum und Bürgerlichkeit im Spannungsfeld des neuen Konfessionalismus von den 1830er bis zu den 1930er Jahren," 33–66. Van Rahden has been an important proponent of the type of critique I describe here.

3. On the notion of fanaticism, see Werner Conze and Helga Reinhart, "Fanatismus," in *Geschichtliche Grundbegriffe: historisches Lexikon zur politisch-sozialen Sprache in Deutschland*, ed. Otto Brunner, Werner Conze, and Reinhart Koselleck (Stuttgart: Klett, 1975), 2:203–327; Thomas Schleich, "Fanatique, Fanatisme," in *Handbuch politisch-sozialer Grundbegriffe in Frankreich 1680–1820*, ed. Rolf Reichardt and Eberhard Schmitt (Munich: Oldenbourg, 1986), 4:51–115; and Dominique Colas, *Civil Society and Fanaticism: Conjoined Histories* (Stanford, CA: Stanford University Press, 1997).

4. On the concept, see Hannah Arendt, "The Jew as Pariah: A Hidden Tradition," *Jewish Social Studies* 6, no. 2 (1944), 99–122.

5. *Orientalism and the Jews*, ed. Ivan Davidson Kalmar and Derek J. Penslar (Hanover, NH: University Press of New England, 2005).

6. For other attempts to rethink these dichotomies, see David Biale, *Power & Powerlessness in Jewish History* (New York: Schocken Books, 1986); and *Insider/Outsider: American Jews and Multiculturalism*, ed. David Biale, Michael Galchinsky, and Susannah Heschel (Berkeley: University of California Press, 1998).

7. See, for example, Aamir Mufti, *Enlightenment in the Colony: The Jewish Question and the Crisis of Postcolonial Culture* (Princeton, NJ: Princeton University Press, 2007); Susannah Heschel, *Abraham Geiger and the Jewish Jesus* (Chicago: University of Chicago Press, 1998); and Michael Brocke, Margarete Jäger, Siegfried Jäger, Jobst Paul, and Iris Tonks, *Visionen der gerechten Gesellschaft: Der Diskurs der deutschen Publizistik im 19. Jahrhundert* (Cologne: Böhlau, 2009).

8. See, for example, Olaf Blaschke, *Offenders or Victims? German Jews and the Causes of Modern Catholic Antisemitism* (Lincoln: University of Nebraska Press, 2009). There are some exceptions to this rule. Richard Millman in "Jewish Anticlericalism and the Rise of Modern French Antisemitism," *History* 77, no. 250 (1992), 220–236, argues that the perceived anticlericalism of the Jews and the actual anticlericalism of individual Jews was one factor in the rise of antisemitism in France. He bolsters this argument by a somewhat problematic chronology: He claims that antisemitism came mostly from the left before the 1880s and only then from the church in reaction to Jewish anticlericalism. This argument is not fully persuasive in light of the history of Catholic, politicized anti-Judaism in France since the Revolution. See Julie Kalman, *Rethinking Antisemitism in Nineteenth-Century France* (New York: Cambridge University Press, 2010).

9. Blaschke, *Offenders or Victims*.

10. Manuel Borutta, *Antikatholizismus: Deutschland und Italien im Zeitalter der europäischen Kulturkämpfe* (Göttingen: Vandenhoeck & Ruprecht, 2010); Michael B. Gross, *The War against Catholicism: Liberalism and the Anti-Catholic Imagination in Nineteenth-Century Germany* (Ann Arbor: University of Michigan Press, 2004); and Helmut Walser Smith, *German Nationalism and Religious Conflict: Culture, Ideology, Politics, 1870–1914* (Princeton, NJ: Princeton University Press, 1995).

11. Blaschke, *Offenders or Victims*.

12. Uriel Tal, "'Milchemet-Hatarbut' Vema'amad ha-yehudim be-germania," *Zion* 29 (1964), 208–242; reprinted in Uriel Tal, *Christians and Jews in Germany: Religion, Politics, and Ideology in the Second Reich, 1870–1914* (Ithaca, NY: Cornell University Press, 1975), 81–120; Jacob Toury, *Die politischen Orientierungen der Juden in Deutschland; von Jena bis Weimar* (Tübingen: Mohr Siebeck, 1966), 246–294; Lisa Moses Leff, *Sacred Bonds of Solidarity: The Rise of Jewish Internationalism in Nineteenth-Century France* (Stanford, CA: Stanford University Press, 2006); Zvi Jonathan Kaplan, *Between the Devil and the Deep Blue Sea? French Jewry and the Problem of Church and State* (Providence, RI: Brown Judaic Studies, 2009); and Jeffrey Haus, *Challenges of Equality: Judaism, State, and Education in Nineteenth-Century France* (Detroit, MI: Wayne State University Press, 2009). See also Abigail Green, "Nationalism and the 'Jewish International': Religious Internationalism in Europe and the Middle East, c.1840–c.1880," *Comparative Studies in Society and History* 50, no. 2 (2008), 535–558, which focuses on Jewish–Catholic competition in international relations and foreign policy.

13. On the concept, see J. G. A. Pocock, "The Concept of a Language and the *métier d'historien*: Some Considerations on Practice" in *The Languages of Political*

Theory in Early-Modern Europe, ed. Anthony Pagden (Cambridge, UK: Cambridge University Press, 1987), 19–38. For an attempt to show the variety of images, see René Rémond, *L'anticléricalisme en France de 1815 à nos jours* (Paris: Fayard, 1976), who prefers to speak of anticlericalism as a positive political ideology, however.

14. Gauri Viswanathan, *Outside the Fold: Conversion, Modernity, and Belief* (Princeton, NJ: Princeton University Press, 1998), 47.

15. Talal Asad, *Formations of the Secular: Christianity, Islam, Modernity* (Stanford, CA: Stanford University Press, 2003).

16. Jean-Marie Mayeur, in *La question laïque: XIXe–XXe siècle* (Paris: Fayard, 1997), 30–34, dates the transition to antireligious secularism among French republicans to the 1860s. Even after that point the representatives of organized militant atheism remained a minority among republicans. On the small number of freethinkers in France, see Jacqueline Lalouette, *La Libre pensée en France: 1848–1940* (Paris: Albin Michel, 1997). In many contexts, especially in Germany, a shift to an antireligious position never happened.

17. George L. Mosse, *Nationalism and Sexuality: Respectability and Abnormal Sexuality in Modern Europe* (New York: H. Fertig, 1985).

18. On the notion of multiple secularisms, see Janet R. Jakobsen and Ann Pellegrini, "Introduction: Times Like These," in *Secularisms*, ed. Janet R. Jakobsen and Ann Pellegrini (Durham, NC: Duke University Press, 2008), 1–38.

19. Geoffrey Brahm Levey, "Secularism and Religion in a Multicultural Age," in *Secularism, Religion and Multicultural Citizenship*, ed. Geoffrey Brahm Levey and Tariq Modood (Cambridge, UK: Cambridge University Press, 2009), 5. This distinction corresponds roughly to what Charles Taylor terms "common ground" and "independent ethic" strategies. See Charles Taylor, "Modes of Secularism," in *Secularism and its Critics*, ed. Rajeev Bhargava (Delhi: Oxford University Press, 1999), 31–53.

20. See Michael Stolleis, "'Konfessionalisierung' oder 'Säkularisierung' bei der Entstehung des frühmodernen Staates," *Ius Commune* 20 (1993), 1–23, for a nuanced account of this process that brings secularization theory in dialogue with the confessionalization thesis that sees religious competition and the policing of religious boundaries as central.

21. This distinction between public and private preceded the notion of toleration. Even before the popularization of the concept as an ideal during the Enlightenment, lived toleration was based on the will to accept the presence of religious communities other than those associated with the state as long as they practiced their religion in private; Benjamin J. Kaplan, *Divided by Faith: Religious Conflict and the Practice of Toleration in Early Modern Europe* (Cambridge, MA: Belknap, 2007). For a review of literature on toleration, see Jeffrey R. Collins, "Redeeming the Enlightenment: New Histories of Religious Toleration," *Journal of Modern History* 81, no. 3 (2009), 607–636.

22. On the diverse schools of thought on civil religion, see Ronald Beiner, *Civil Religion: A Dialogue in the History of Political Philosophy* (New York: Cambridge University Press, 2011).

23. On police science, see Hans Maier, *Die ältere deutsche Staats- und Verwaltungslehre* (Munich: dtv, 1986); on religion: Dirk Fleischer, "Kirchenverständnis aus polizeiwissenschaftlicher Sicht: Johann Heinrich Gottlob von Justis Verständnis der Kirche," in *Christentum im Übergang: Neue Studien zu Kirche und Religion in der Aufklärungszeit* (Leipzig: Evangelische Verlagsanstalt, 2006), 71–83.

24. See Jean Baubérot, *Histoire de la laïcité en France*, 5th ed. (Paris: Presses universitaires de France, 2010), 49–54. On the debates on the Bible as a source of national culture and a textbook of secular morality, see Jonathan Sheehan, *The Enlightenment Bible: Translation, Scholarship, Culture* (Princeton, NJ: Princeton University Press, 2005). On the similarity of the moral ideas of anticlericals and Catholics, see Theodore Zeldin, "The Conflict of Moralities: Confession, Sin and Pleasure in the Nineteenth Century," in *Conflicts in French Society: Anticlericalism, Education and Morals in the Nineteenth Century: Essays*, ed. Theodore Zeldin (London: Allen & Unwin, 1970), 36–47.

25. Levey, "Secularism and Religion," 5.

26. This was true especially for liberal Catholics in the tradition of Lammenais and Montalembert. See Bernard M. G. Reardon, *Liberalism and Tradition: Aspects of Catholic Thought in Nineteenth-Century France* (Cambridge, UK: Cambridge University Press, 1975); and Georg Schwaiger, "Liberaler französischer Katholizismus im Vormärz (1830–1848)," in *Kirchen und Liberalismus im 19. Jahrhundert*, ed. Martin Schmidt and Georg Schwaiger (Göttingen: Vandenhoeck und Ruprecht, 1976), 143–154.

27. See, for example, Wilhelm Emmanuel Ketteler, *Freiheit, Autorität und Kirche* (Mainz: Kirchheim, 1862).

28. On the term *fanaticism*, see note 3 of this chapter.

29. The more unacceptable retributive, ritualistic, or apocalyptic violence became in German and French politics, the more effective stories of religious bloodshed became. On the role of stories of violence for nineteenth-century French politics, see Alain Corbin, *The Village of Cannibals: Rage and Murder in France, 1870* (Cambridge, MA: Harvard University Press, 1992).

30. Voltaire, *Treatise on Tolerance* (Cambridge, UK: Cambridge University Press, 2000), 3–11.

31. On Europe as an exception, see Grace Davie, "Patterns of Religion in Western Europe: An Exceptional Case," in *The Blackwell Companion to Sociology of Religion*, ed. Richard K. Fenn (Oxford, UK: Blackwell Publishers, 2001), 264–278; and Grace Davie, *Europe—The Exceptional Case: Parameters of Faith in the Modern World* (London: Darton Longman & Todd, 2002). For an example of essays that largely affirm the notion of distinct French and German models of religious politics even as it questions them, see *Religionskontroversen in Frankreich und Deutschland*, ed. Matthias Koenig and Jean-Paul Willaime (Hamburg: Hamburger Edition, 2008).

32. David Martin, *A General Theory of Secularization* (Oxford, UK: Blackwell, 1978).

33. David Jan Sorkin, *The Religious Enlightenment: Protestants, Jews, and Catholics from London to Vienna* (Princeton, NJ: Princeton University Press, 2008); and Jonathan Irvine Israel, *Radical Enlightenment: Philosophy and the Making of Modernity, 1650–1750* (New York: Oxford University Press, 2001).

34. Hans Kohn, *The Idea of Nationalism: A Study in its Origins and Background* (New York: Macmillan, 1944).

35. See Rogers Brubaker, *Citizenship and Nationhood in France and Germany* (Cambridge, MA: Harvard University Press, 1992). For a different view, see Patrick Weil, *How to be French: Nationality in the Making since 1789* (Durham, NC: Duke University Press, 2008), 179–193.

36. *Paths of Emancipation: Jews, States, and Citizenship*, ed. Pierre Birnbaum and Ira Katznelson (Princeton, NJ: Princeton University Press, 1995); *Assimilation and Community: The Jews in Nineteenth-Century Europe*, ed. Jonathan Frankel and Steven J. Zipperstein (Cambridge, UK: Cambridge University Press, 1992); and *The Emancipation of Catholics, Jews and Protestants: Minorities and the Nation State in Nineteenth-Century Europe*, ed. Rainer Liedtke (Manchester, UK: Manchester University Press, 1999).

37. Shulamit Volkov, "Comparing Germany with the French Republic," in *Germans, Jews, and Antisemites: Trials in Emancipation* (New York: Cambridge University Press, 2006), 145–155.

38. *German-Jewish History in Modern Times*, ed. Michael Brenner, Stefi Jersch-Wenzel, and Michael A. Meyer (New York: Columbia University Press, 1996), 2:38–42.

39. On this preoccupation, see Michael Jeismann, *Das Vaterland der Feinde: Studien zum nationalen Feindbegriff und Selbstverständnis in Deutschland und Frankreich, 1792–1918* (Stuttgart: Klett-Cotta, 1992).

40. Gareth Stedman Jones, "Religion and the Origins of Socialism," in *Religion and the Political Imagination*, ed. Ira Katznelson and Gareth Stedman Jones (Cambridge, UK: Cambridge University Press, 2010), 171–189.

41. On France, see George Armstrong Kelly, *The Humane Comedy: Constant, Tocqueville, and French Liberalism* (Cambridge, UK: Cambridge University Press, 1992); on Germany, see Wolfgang Altgeld, *Katholizismus, Protestantismus, Judentum: Über religiös begründete Gegensätze und nationalreligiöse Ideen in der Geschichte des deutschen Nationalismus* (Mainz: M.-Grünewald-Verlag, 1992).

42. See also Jens Neumann-Schliski, *Konfession oder Stamm?: Konzepte jüdischer Identität bei Redakteuren jüdischer Zeitschriften 1840 bis 1881 im internationalen Vergleich* (Bremen: Edition Lumière, 2011); and Heidi Knörzer, "Ludwig Philippson et Isidore Cahen: Deux journalistes, deux pays, un discours politique commun?" *Archives juives* 43, no. 2 (2010), 121–131.

43. Kaiser, "Clericalism."

44. For a minor exception, see the failed attempt to create a Jewish party in the Prussian province of Posen; Toury, *Politischen Orientierungen*, 276–294.

45. Phyllis Cohen Albert, "Ethnicity and Jewish Solidarity in Nineteenth-Century France," in *Mystics, Philosophers, and Politicians: Essays in Jewish Intellectual History in Honor of Alexander Altmann*, ed. Jehuda Reinharz and Daniel Swetschinski (Durham, NC: Duke University Press, 1982), 249–274; Lisa Moses Leff, "Self-Definition and Self-Defense: Jewish Racial Identity in Nineteenth-Century France," *Jewish History* 19, no. 1 (2005), 7–28; Michael Brenner, "Religion, Nation oder Stamm: Zum Wandel der Selbstdefinition unter deutschen Juden," in *Nation und Religion in der deutschen Geschichte*, ed. Heinz-Gerhard Haupt and Dieter Langewiesche (Frankfurt a. M.: Campus, 2001), 587–601; and Till van Rahden, "Germans of the Jewish Stamm: Visions of Community between Nationalism and Particularism, 1850 to 1933," in *German History from the Margins*, ed. Neil Gregor, Nils H. Roemer, and Mark Roseman (Bloomington: Indiana University Press, 2006), 27–48. For a critique of earlier models of assimilation, see also Pierre Birnbaum and Ira Katznelson, "Emancipation and the Liberal Offer," in Birnbaum and Katznelson, *Paths of Emancipation*, 3–37; and Jay R. Berkovitz, *The Shaping of Jewish Identity in Nineteenth-Century France* (Detroit, MI: Wayne State University Press, 1989).

46. For a reevaluation of Napoleonic policies toward the Jews, see also Jay R. Berkovitz, *Rites and Passages: The Beginnings of Modern Jewish Culture in France, 1650–1860* (Philadelphia: University of Pennsylvania Press, 2004), 115–143.

47. Christopher Clark, "The Napoleonic Moment in Prussian Church Policy," in *Napoleon's Legacy: Problems of Government in Restoration Europe*, ed. David Laven and Lucy Riall (Oxford, UK: Berg, 2000), 217–235.

48. Baubérot, *Histoire de la laïcité*, 5–23; Jean Baubérot, "The Two Thresholds of Laïcization," in *Secularism and its Critics*, ed. Rajeev Bhargava (Delhi: Oxford University Press, 1999), 94–136.

49. Henri Plard, "Anticlérical, anticléricalisme: évolution de ces termes," in *Aspects de l'anticléricalisme du Moyen Age à nos jours: hommage à Robert Joly: colloque de Bruxelles, juin 1988*, ed. Robert Joly and Jacques Marx (Bruxelles: Éditions de l'Université de Bruxelles, 1988), 15–22.

50. In Germany, there were no equivalents to anti-socialist associations like the Reichsverband gegen die Sozialdemokratie that would identify as anti-Catholic. Even the most anti-Catholic associations, such as Paul Hoensbroech's Antiultramontaner Reichsverband (est. 1906), recoiled from calling themselves anti-Catholic. German liberals did, however, speak of themselves as *anti-ultramontane*, as the last example illustrates. Much like the terms *anticlerical*, *antisemitic*, and *anti-socialist*, the term *anti-ultramontane* implied that the enemy had political motives and could thus be legitimately challenged by political means. For a list of associations in Germany, see Dieter Fricke, *Lexikon zur Parteiengeschichte: die bürgerlichen und kleinbürgerlichen Parteien und Verbände in Deutschland (1789–1945)* (Leipzig: VEB Bibliographisches Institut Leipzig, 1986), 4:692–731. I thank Helmut Walser Smith and David Blackbourn for drawing my attention to these examples.

51. Borutta, *Antikatholizismus*. Another transnational study that focuses on anti-Catholicism specifically is Timothy Verhoeven, *Transatlantic Anti-Catholicism: France and the United States in the Nineteenth Century* (New York: Palgrave Macmillan, 2010).

52. On republicans and institutional Judaism, see Leff, *Sacred Bonds*.

53. For reflections on this from the perspective of a Catholic region of Germany, see Ian Farr, "From Anti-Catholicism to Anticlericalism: Catholic Politics and the Peasantry in Bavaria, 1860–1900," *European Studies Review* 13, no. 2 (1983), 249–269.

54. Wolfram Kaiser, "'Clericalism—That is our Enemy!': European Anticlericalism and the Culture Wars," in *Culture Wars*, 47–76.

55. The most provocative expression of this idea is Olaf Blaschke, "Das 19. Jahrhundert: Ein Zweites Konfessionelles Zeitalter?" *Geschichte und Gesellschaft* 26 (2000), 38–75. Among the vast literature see, for example, *Konfessionen im Konflikt: Deutschland zwischen 1800 und 1970: ein zweites konfessionelles Zeitalter*, ed. Olaf Blaschke (Göttingen: Vandenhoeck & Ruprecht, 2002); Smith, *German Nationalism*; and Thomas Nipperdey, *Religion im Umbruch: Deutschland 1870–1918* (Munich: Beck, 1988).

56. On Jews in the context of denominational conflicts, see Altgeld, *Katholizismus*; Andreas Gotzmann, *Eigenheit und Einheit: Modernisierungsdiskurse des deutschen Judentums der Emanzipationszeit* (Leiden: Brill, 2002); and Keith H. Pickus, "Native Born Strangers: Jews, Catholics and the German Nation," in *Religion und Nation, Nation und Religion: Beiträge zu einer unbewältigten Geschichte*, ed. Michael Geyer and Hartmut Lehmann (Göttingen: Wallstein, 2004), 141–156.

57. See August-Hermann Leugers, "Latente Kulturkampfstimmung im Wilhelmistischen Kasierreich: Konfessionelle Polemik als konfessions- und innenpolitisches Kampfmittel," in *Die Verschränkung von Innen-, Konfessions- und Kolonialpolitik im Deutschen Reich vor 1914*, ed. Johannes Horstmann and Winfried Becker (Schwerte: Katholische Akademie Schwerte, 1987), 13–37.

58. Claudia Lepp, *Protestantisch-liberaler Aufbruch in die Moderne: der Deutsche Protestantenverein in der Zeit der Reichsgründung und des Kulturkampfes* (Gütersloh: Kaiser, 1996), 358–359.

59. This approach is closest to what Kocka and Haupt have called "comparisons in comprehensive arguments"; Jürgen Kocka and Heinz-Gerhard Haupt, "Contents: Comparison and Beyond: Traditions, Scope, and Perspective of Comparative History," in *Comparative and Transnational History: Central European Approaches and New Perspectives*, ed. Heinz-Gerhard Haupt and Jürgen Kocka (New York: Berghahn Books, 2009), 9–10.

60. Reinhart Koselleck, "Einleitung" in *Geschichtliche Grundbegriffe*, 1:xv.

Chapter One

1. Anatole Leroy-Beaulieu, *Les doctrines de haine: l'antisémitisme, l'antiprotestantisme, l'anticléricalisme* (Paris: C. Lévy, 1902).

2. Patrick Cabanel, "Antisémitisme et anticléricalisme selon Anatole Leroy-Beaulieu: un essai d'approche structuraliste de l'extrémisme politique (1893–1902)," *Jean Jaurès: Cahiers trimestrielles*, no. 142 (1996), 65.

3. Leroy-Beaulieu, *Doctrines*, 73.

4. On Leroy-Beaulieu's approach, see Antoine Compagnon, "Antisémitisme ou antimodernisme? Anatole Leroy-Beaulieu, Bernard Lazare, Léon Bloy," in Ilana Y. Zinguer and Sam W. Bloom, ed., *L'antisémitisme éclairé: Inclusion et exclusion depuis l'Epoque des Lumières jusqu'à l'affaire Dreyfus/Inclusion and Exclusion: Perspectives on Jews from the Enlightenment to the Dreyfus Affair* (Leiden: Brill, 2003), 423–446.

5. Jean Réville, review of *Les doctrines de haine* by A. Leroy-Beaulieu, *Revue de l'histoire des religions* 46 (1902), 125–126; and review of *Les doctrines de haine* by A. Leroy-Beaulieu, *Revue des deux mondes*, May 15, 1902, 480.

6. See, for example, the excerpts chosen in A. Leroy-Beaulieu, "Quelques spécimens de l'esprit juif," *AI 62* (September 26, 1901), 307–308; and *AI 62* (October 3, 1901), 316.

7. Cabanel, "Antisémitisme et Anticléricalisme"; and Jean Baubérot and Valentine Zuber, *Une haine oubliée: l'antiprotestantisme avant le "pacte laïque" (1870–1905)* (Paris: Albin Michel, 2000), part 4. Baubérot has also sought to introduce the term *doctrines of hatred* into current debates on laicism and Islam; see Jean Baubérot, "Identité nationale: pour une laïcité de sang-froid," *Le Monde*, December 21, 2009.

8. On Germany: Manuel Borutta, *Antikatholizismus: Deutschland und Italien im Zeitalter der europäischen Kulturkämpfe* (Göttingen: Vandenhoeck & Ruprecht, 2010); Michael B. Gross, *The War against Catholicism: Liberalism and the Anti-Catholic Imagination in Nineteenth-Century Germany* (Ann Arbor: University of Michigan Press, 2004); and Róisín Healy, *The Jesuit Specter in Imperial Germany* (Boston: Brill, 2003). On France: Geoffrey Cubitt, *The Jesuit Myth: Conspiracy Theory and Politics in Nineteenth Century France* (New York: Oxford University Press, 1993); Michel Leroy, *Le mythe jésuite: de Béranger à Michelet* (Paris: Presses universitaires de France, 1992); and René Rémond, *L'anticléricalisme en France de 1815 à nos jours* (Paris: Fayard, 1976).

9. Among these are most notably Léon Poliakov, *La causalité diabolique: essai sur l'origine des persécutions* (Paris: Calmann-Lévy, 1980), 53–85; and Wolfgang Altgeld, *Katholizismus, Protestantismus, Judentum: Über religiös begründete Gegensätze und nationalreligiöse Ideen in der Geschichte des deutschen Nationalismus* (Mainz: M.-Grünewald-Verlag, 1992).

10. Bauman did not invent the term but popularized it most successfully. On allosemitism, see Zygmunt Bauman, "Allosemitism: Premodern, Modern, Postmodern," in *Modernity, Culture, and "the Jew,"* ed. Bryan Cheyette and Laura Marcus (Stanford, CA: Stanford University Press, 1998), 143–156.

11. Manuel Borutta, "Der innere Orient: Antikatholizismus als Orientalismus in Deutschland," in *Religion und Grenzen in Indien und Deutschland: Auf dem Weg zu einer transnationalen Historiographie*, ed. Monica Juneja (Göttingen: Vandenhoeck & Ruprecht, 2009), 245–274.

12. The notion that rabbinic power was responsible for Jews' lack of will to convert was, however, central in the early modern literature. See Gerhard Lauer, *Die Rückseite der Haskala: Geschichte einer kleinen Aufklärung* (Göttingen: Wallstein, 2008), 59.

13. On the affair, see David I. Kertzer, *The Kidnapping of Edgardo Mortara* (New York: Alfred Knopf, 1997).

14. I have also chosen the unequal spelling of antisemitism and anticlericalism on the one hand and anti-Judaism and anti-Catholicism on the other. "Semitism" and "clericalism" are ascribed categories. They were invented only shortly before the terms *antisemitism* and *anticlericalism* became popular. "Catholicism" and "Judaism," on the other hand, were self-descriptions that existed independently of the coining of the terms "anti-Catholicism" and "anti-Judaism."

15. E. H. Müller and C. F. Schneider, *Jahresbericht des Statistischen Amtes im Kgl. Polizei-Präsidio zu Berlin im Jahre 1852* (Leipzig: Huebner, 1853), 70, lists 13,372 Catholics (3.15 percent) and 11,835 Jews (2.79 percent) among 423,864 inhabitants. The Catholic population grew more quickly and was significantly larger within a decade. By 1861 there were 28,150 Catholics and 18,953 Jews registered in Berlin. See Georg von Hirschfeld, *Religionsstatistik der Preussischen Monarchie* (Arnsberg: W. von Schilgen, 1866), 71, 78.

16. For Germany, see *Exclusionary Violence: Antisemitic Riots in Modern German History*, ed. Christhard Hoffmann, Werner Bergmann, and Helmut Walser Smith (Ann Arbor: University of Michigan Press, 2002). For an example of Catholic violence against evangelical Protestants, see Daniel Koehler, "Contested Enchantments: Evangelical Revival and the Global Dimensions of National Religious Conflict in the German Empire, 1870–1914" (Ph.D. dissertation, University of Chicago, 2010), 149–153. There is still little scholarship on different targets of riots or simultaneous outbreaks of violence in different countries.

17. Pierre Birnbaum, *La France aux français: Histoire des haines nationalistes* (Paris: Ed. du Seuil, 1993), 20–22.

18. Stefan Rohrbacher, "The 'Hep Hep' Riots of 1819: Anti-Jewish Ideology, Agitation, and Violence," in *Exclusionary Violence*, 24–42; Daniel Gerson, *Die Kehrseite der Emanzipation in Frankreich: Judenfeindschaft im Elsass 1778–1848* (Essen: Klartext, 2006) 76–87, 229–297; Manfred Gailus, "Anti-Jewish Emotion and Violence in the 1848 Crisis of German Society," in *Exclusionary Violence*, 43–65; Zosa Szajkowski, "French Jews during the Revolution of 1830 and the July Monarchy," in *Jews and the French Revolutions* (New York: Ktav, 1970), 1017–1042; and Natalie Isser, *Antisemitism during the French Second Empire* (New York: P. Lang, 1991), 13–20.

19. Helmut Walser Smith, *The Butcher's Tale: Murder and Anti-Semitism in a German Town* (New York: Norton, 2002).

20. Pierre Birnbaum, *Jewish Destinies: Citizenship, State, and Community in Modern France*, trans. Arthur Goldhammer (New York: Hill and Wang, 2000), 178–188. Jews were, however, threatened with murder several times during the riots in Alsace in 1848; Gerson, *Kehrseite*, 235–249.

21. Pierre Birnbaum, *The Anti-Semitic Moment: A Tour of France in 1898*, trans. Jane Marie Todd (New York: Hill and Wang, 2003).

22. On anticlerical violence see, for example, Alain Corbin, *The Village of Cannibals: Rage and Murder in France, 1870* (Cambridge, MA: Harvard University Press, 1992).

23. See Nigel Aston, *Religion and Revolution in France, 1780–1804* (Washington, DC: Catholic University of America, 2000), 220–243; Robert Tombs, *The Paris Commune, 1871* (London: Longman, 1999), 178–179.

24. Birnbaum, *Jewish Destinies*, 183. It depends on our analytic categories and thus ultimately on heuristics if this should count as anti-Catholic violence. Birnbaum's account of this anti-immigrant violence disproves his own argument against Leroy-Beaulieu that violence against Catholics was always merely the state defending laws that the majority of citizens had passed; Birnbaum, *La France aux français*, 22.

25. Werner Giesselmann, *"Die Manie der Revolte": Protest unter der Französischen Julimonarchie (1830–1848)* (Munich: Oldenbourg, 1993), 474–507.

26. Borutta, *Antikatholizismus*, 249–254; with a greater focus on its representation: Gross, *War*, 170–184.

27. The latter approach has been more popular in recent studies on anti-Jewish violence. See David Nirenberg, *Communities of Violence: Persecution of Minorities in the Middle Ages* (Princeton, NJ: Princeton University Press, 1996).

28. Miriam Bodian, "Jews in a Divided Christendom," in *A Companion to the Reformation World*, ed. R. Po-chia Hsia (Malden, MA: Blackwell, 2004), 471–485; and Miriam Bodian, "The Reformation and the Jews," in *Rethinking European Jewish History*, ed. Jeremy Cohen and Murray Jay Rosman (Oxford, UK: Littman Library of Jewish Civilization, 2009), 112–132. On the new proximity between Jews and mostly Protestant Christians, see Richard H. Popkin, "Christian Jews and Jewish Christians in the 17th Century," in *Jewish Christians and Christian Jews: From the Renaissance to the Enlightenment*, ed. Richard H. Popkin and Gordon M. Weiner (Dordrecht: Kluwer, 1994), 57–72. On the impact of confessionalization on seventeenth- and eighteenth-century Jewry, see Gerhard Lauer, *Die Rückseite der Haskala: Geschichte einer kleinen Aufklärung* (Göttingen: Wallstein, 2008).

29. Early works in favor of Jewish toleration by French or Dutch Calvinists and British Protestants in particular emerged in this context. See, for example, Jonathan Karp, *The Politics of Jewish Commerce: Economic Thought and Emancipation in Europe, 1638–1848* (Cambridge, UK: Cambridge University Press, 2008), 61–66, on the anti-Catholic motives behind John Toland's *Reasons for Naturalizing the Jews in Great Britain and Ireland* (1714).

30. On the Huguenots and Jews, see Myriam Yardeni, *Huguenots et juifs* (Paris: Editions Honoré Champion, 2008).

31. Lynn Hunt, Margaret C. Jacob, and Wijnand Mijnhardt, *The Book that Changed Europe: Picart & Bernard's Religious Ceremonies of the World* (Cambridge, MA: Harvard University Press, 2010).

32. Jacques Basnage, *Histoire des Juifs depuis Jesus-Christ jusqu'à present: Pour servir de continuation à l'Histoire de Joseph* (La Haye: H. Scheurleer, 1716), first published in a shorter version in 1706.

33. Gerald Cerny, *Theology, Politics, and Letters at the Crossroads of European Civilization: Jacques Basnage and the Baylean Huguenot Refugees in the Dutch Republic* (Dordrecht: Nijhoff, 1987).

34. Jonathan M. Elukin, "Jacques Basnage and the History of the Jews: Anti-Catholic Polemic and Historical Allegory in the Republic of Letters," *Journal of the History of Ideas* 53, no. 4 (1992), 603–630.

35. Adam Sutcliffe in *Judaism and Enlightenment* (Cambridge, UK: Cambridge University Press, 2003), 85, challenged Elukin's claim that Basnage's anti-Catholicism is a central feature of the work. In spite of this disagreement, Elukin's and Sutcliffe's positions are quite compatible. Basnage's anti-Catholicism can be a useful key to the work even if anti-Catholic comparisons were not systematic and merely very frequent.

36. Basnage's work remained one of the most reliable sources on Jewish history into the early nineteenth century and thus exerted a strong influence on later accounts of the Jewish past, including those of Christian Dohm and Léon Halévy. Some Berlin Jews in the 1780s were sufficiently convinced of Basnage's message that they commissioned the radical Jewish enlightener Moses Maimon to translate the *Histoire des Juifs* into Hebrew for the benefit of their Polish coreligionists. See Salomon Maimon, *Solomon Maimon: An Autobiography*, trans. John Clark Murray (Urbana: University of Illinois Press, 2001), 266; and Michael A. Meyer, "The Emergence of Jewish Historiography: Motives and Motifs," *History and Theory* 27, no. 4 (1988), 164.

37. Dominique Bourel, "Le marquis d'Argens à Berlin," in *Le Marquis d'Argens: colloque international de 1988*, ed. Jean Louis Vissière (Aix-en-Provence: Université de Provence, 1990), 31–39.

38. The use of Jews for such a critique has historical precedents. Christopher Oncker, for example, reports about a Corpus Christi play from 1479 in which the Jews denounce the Christians as monkeys who follow their greedy clergy, in spite of being exploited. Christopher Ocker, "Contempt for Friars and Contempt for Jews in Late Medieval Germany," in *Friars and Jews in the Middle Ages and Renaissance*, ed. Steven J. McMichael and Susan E. Myers (Leiden: Brill, 2004), 146. For a completely different use of the form invented by Montesquieu by an enemy of the Enlightenment, see Heinrich Ernst Teuthorn, *Briefe eines reisenden Juden über den gegenwärtigen Zustand des Religionswesens unter den Protestanten und Catholicken, und über die Auferstehung Jesu*, 4th ed. (n.p.: 1781). Teuthorn depicted the Jews as secretly celebrating the divisions between different Christian denominations.

39. Jean-Baptiste de Boyer marquis d'Argens, *Lettres juives* (La Haye: Paupie, 1738), 282.

40. Ibid., 283.

41. Friedrich Nicolai, *Beschreibung einer Reise durch Deutschland und die Schweiz, im Jahre 1781 nebst Bemerkungen über Gelehrsamkeit, Industrie, Religion und Sitten* (Berlin: n.p., 1783–1796). On the anti-Catholic descriptions in this work and the ensuing debate around it, see Horst Möller, *Aufklärung in Preussen: der Verleger, Publizist und Geschichtsschreiber Friedrich Nicolai* (Berlin: Colloquium Verlag, 1974), 99–120.

42. See Sigrid Habersaat, *Verteidigung der Aufklärung: Friedrich Nicolai in religiösen und politischen Debatten* (Würzburg: Königshausen & Neumann, 2001). On his anti-Catholicism, see also Roger Kirscher, *Théologie et Lumières: les théologiens éclairés autour de la revue de Friedrich Nicolai, Allgemeine deutsche Bibliothek, 1765–1792* (Villeneuve d'Ascq: Presses universitaires du Septentrion, 2001), 160–176.

43. On English travelers and anti-Catholicism, see Jeremy Black, *The Grand Tour in the Eighteenth Century* (New York: St. Martin's Press, 1992), 238–251.

44. On the depiction of Catholics, Nicolai's larger opposition to Catholicism, as well as, his rejection of projects for the reunification of Catholicism and Protestantism, see Christopher Spehr, *Aufklärung und Ökumene: Reunionsversuche zwischen Katholiken und Protestanten im deutschsprachigen Raum des späteren 18. Jahrhunderts* (Tübingen: Mohr, 2005), 374–408.

45. Nicolai, *Beschreibung*, 1:67–68 and 306–307.

46. Ibid., 3:10.

47. Arthur Hertzberg, *The French Enlightenment and the Jews: The Origins of Modern Anti-Semitism* (New York: Schocken Books, 1970), 280–308.

48. See Sutcliffe, *Judaism and Enlightenment*, 231–246. Hertzberg notes much of the evidence about positive depictions of Jews in Voltaire but ultimately decided to stress the enlightener's anti-Judaism over the ambivalence found in his works.

49. For an analysis of this argument on Jewish and Christian fanaticism, see Allan Arkush, "Voltaire on Judaism and Christianity," *AJS Review* 18, no. 2 (1993), 223–243.

50. The quote is from Voltaire's *Philosophical Dictionary*, cited in Arkush, "Voltaire," 239.

51. Ronald Schechter, *Obstinate Hebrews: Representations of Jews in France, 1715–1815* (Berkeley: University of California Press, 2003), 49–50.

52. Voltaire, *La Hendriade*, canto 5.

53. Protestants were more important as paradigmatic victims. See Voltaire, *Treatise on Tolerance* (Cambridge, UK: Cambridge University Press, 2000).

54. On romantic antisemitism, see *Romantischer Antisemitismus: von Klopstock bis Richard Wagner*, ed. Wolf-Daniel Hartwich (Göttingen: Vandenhoeck & Ruprecht, 2005); and Paul L. Rose, *Revolutionary Antisemitism in Germany from Kant to Wagner* (Princeton, NJ: Princeton University Press, 1990).

55. Novalis, "Christianity or Europe: A Fragment" in *The Early Political Writings of the German Romantics*, ed. Frederick C. Beiser (Cambridge, UK: Cambridge University Press, 1996), 59–80.

56. See Richard Littlejohns, "Everlasting Peace and Medieval Europe: Romantic Myth-Making in Novalis's *Europa*," in *Myths of Europe*, ed. Richard Littlejohns and Sara Soncini (Amsterdam: Rodopi, 2007), 171–181.

57. See Jeffrey S. Librett, *The Rhetoric of Cultural Dialogue: Jews and Germans from Moses Mendelssohn to Richard Wagner and Beyond* (Stanford, CA: Stanford University Press, 2000), 300n65.

58. On the depiction of Jews as foreign and Asiatic see, for example, Johann Gottfried Herder, "Bekehrung der Juden," *Adrastea* 4 (1802), 145.

59. Herder also believed that some Jews could be educated by modern Christianity, however. See Liliane Weissberg, "Juden oder Hebräer? Religiöse und politische Bekehrung bei Herder," in *Johann Gottfried Herder: Geschichte und Kultur* (Würzburg: Königshausen & Neumann, 1994), 191–211.

60. Johann Gottfried Herder, "Ueber National-Religionen," *Adrastea* 4 (1802), 113.

61. Altgeld, *Katholizismus*, is one of the exceptions.

62. Arnold Ages, "Bonald and the Jews," *Revue de l'Université d'Ottawa* 44, no. 1 (1974), 32–43; and Pierre Birnbaum, *L'aigle et la synagogue: Napoléon, les Juifs et l'état* (Paris: Fayard, 2007), 99–102.

63. See Julie Kalman, "The Unyielding Wall: Jews and Catholics in Restoration and July Monarchy France," *French Historical Studies* 26, no. 4 (2003), 661–686.

64. See George Armstrong Kelly, *The Humane Comedy: Constant, Tocqueville, and French Liberalism* (Cambridge, UK: Cambridge University Press, 1992).

65. Ceri Crossley, *French Historians and Romanticism: Thierry, Guizot, the Saint-Simonians, Quinet, Michelet* (London: Routledge, 1993).

66. We can see this among thinkers who drew on the Gospels and early Christianity as models for revolutionary politics such as Auguste Comte and Felicité de Lamennais. On Comte, see Helena Rosenblatt, "Re-Evaluating Benjamin Constant's Liberalism: Industrialism, Saint-Simonianism and the Restoration Years," *History of European Ideas* 30, no. 1 (2004), 23–37. On Lamennais, see Bernard M. G. Reardon, *Liberalism and Tradition: Aspects of Catholic Thought in Nineteenth-Century France* (Cambridge, UK: Cambridge University Press, 1975), 62–112. See Arnold Ages, "Lamennais and the Jews," *Jewish Quarterly Review* 63 (1972), 158–170, on his position on the Jews, albeit with a focus on his preliberal phase.

67. Edward Berenson, *Populist Religion and Left-Wing Politics in France, 1830–1852* (Princeton, NJ: Princeton University Press, 1984); and Edward Berenson, "A New Religion on the Left: Christianity and Social Radicalism in France, 1815–1848," in *The French Revolution and the Creation of Modern Political Culture*, ed. Keith Michael Baker et al. (Oxford, UK: Pergamon Press, 1989), 3:543–560.

68. On the implications of the rediscovery of both Protestants and Jews by the "generation of 1820" (as Alan Spitzer called this group of thinkers) for Jews, see Leff, *Sacred Bonds*, 81–116.

69. Madame de Staël, *De la littérature* (Paris: Flammarion, 1991), 202–203. On her work in the context of suggestions to Protestantize France, see Helena

Rosenblatt, *Liberal Values: Benjamin Constant and the Politics of Religion* (Cambridge, UK: Cambridge University Press, 2008), 80–85.

70. P.-J. Proudhon, *De la justice dans la révolution et dans l'église* (Paris: Garnier frères, 1858), 1:445, cited in Robert S. Wistrich, "Radical Antisemitism in France and Germany (1840–1880)," *Modern Judaism* 15, no. 2 (1995), 117.

71. Ibid. Proudhon, *Carnets*, 2:52, cited in Wistrich, "Radical Antisemitism," 118. A similar combination of anticlericalism and racist antisemitism appears in Louis-Auguste Blanqui's works of the 1840s. Wistrich, "Radical Antisemitism," 119–120.

72. Gustave Tridon, *Du molochisme juif: études critiques et philosophiques* (Brussels: Maheu, 1884). On the trope of Molochism see also Rose, *Revolutionary Antisemitism*, 251–262.

73. There is a vast scholarship on the Wandering Jew in literature. One of the best historical overviews remains George Kumler Anderson, *The Legend of the Wandering Jew* (Providence, RI: Brown University Press, 1965). See also Marie-France Rouart, *Le mythe du juif errant dans l'Europe du XIXe siècle* (Paris: Corti, 1988).

74. Eugène Sue, *The Wandering Jew* (New York: The Modern Library, n.d.), 2:664.

75. On the theme of Jesuit self-submission and its interpretation as an attack on individuality, see Cubitt, *Jesuit Myth*, 280–283.

76. Dagmar Herzog, in *Intimacy and Exclusion: Religious Politics in Pre-Revolutionary Baden* (Princeton, NJ: Princeton University Press, 1996), 53–84, argued that the realignment was motivated by liberals' opposition to conservative Catholicism and their support for legal equality for liberal religious movements. Brian E. Vick, in *Defining Germany: The 1848 Frankfurt Parliamentarians and National Identity* (Cambridge, MA: Harvard University Press, 2002), 83–109, has challenged this claim and argued that the rise of conservative Catholicism motivated only a few radicals in Baden to change their minds about Jewish legal equality.

77. Vick, *Defining Germany*, 83–109.

78. See Wolfgang Schieder, "Kirche und Revolution: Sozialgeschichtliche Aspekte der Trierer Wallfahrt von 1844," *Archiv für Sozialgeschichte* 14 (1974), 419–454; idem, *Religion und Revolution: Die Trierer Wallfahrt von 1844* (Vierow bei Greifswald: SH-Verlag, 1996); and Borutta, *Antikatholizismus*, 77–88.

79. *Staats-Lexikon oder Encyklopädie der Staatswissenschaften*, ed. Carl von Rotteck and Karl Theodor Welcker, 15 vols. (Altona: Hammerich, 1834–1843).

80. H. E. G. Paulus, "Hebräer und heilige Schriften des alten Testaments: Die Bibel und die biblische Geschichte aus dem staatsrechtlichen Gesichtspuncte betrachtet," *Staats-Lexikon* (1839), 7:543–573.

81. Franz Bopp, "Judenschutz und Judenabgabe," *Staats-Lexikon* (1839), 8:677–697.

82. Ibid., 678.

83. Hirscher, "Katholizismus," *Staats-Lexikon* (1840), 9:226–238. Herzog, in *Intimacy and Exclusion*, describes how Hirscher was part of the conservative Catholic campaign against mixed marriages between Catholics and Protestants and opposed

proposals for Jewish equality in 1846. He was, however, in other respects eager to reform Catholic pedagogical practices.

84. Hirscher, "Katholizismus," 9:235.

85. Q., "Kirchenverfassung, katholische," *Staats-Lexikon* (1840), 9:310–327.

86. Ibid., 318.

87. Friedrich Kolb, "Klöster," *Staats-Lexikon* (1840), 9:416–451, here cited from p. 446. For another anti-Catholic article see, for example, Q., "Ohrenbeichte," *Staats-Lexikon* (1841), 11:755–760.

88. S. Jordan, "Jesuiten," *Staats-Lexikon* (1839), 8:437–538.

89. Ibid., 538.

90. Protestants were even more frequently the victims of Inquisition stories in Germany; only Jewish authors consistently described Jews as the main victims. See Jonathan M. Hess, *Middlebrow Literature and the Making of German-Jewish Identity* (Stanford, CA: Stanford University Press, 2010), 132–135.

91. On Freytag's anti-Catholicism and his depiction of Luther, see Larry L. Ping, *Gustav Freytag and the Prussian Gospel: Novels, Liberalism, and History* (Oxford, UK: Peter Lang, 2006), 209–232. See Martin Gubser, *Literarischer Antisemitismus: Untersuchugen zu Gustav Freytag und anderen bügerlichen Schiftstellern des 19. Jahrhunderts* (Göttingen: Wallstein, 1998), on the development of Freytag's antisemitism.

92. Gustav Freytag, "Der Streit über das Judenthum in der Musik," *Grenzboten* 22 (1869), 321–326, is his reaction to Wagner.

93. Gustav Freytag, *Bilder aus der deutschen Vergangenheit* (Leipzig: Insel Verlag, n.d.), 2:524–525.

94. Ibid., 526.

95. Blaschke, *Katholizismus und Antisemitismus*, 42–56.

96. For an analysis of these accusations and the development of antisemitism in a "confessional system," see Todd H. Weirr, "The Fourth Confession: Atheism, Monism and Politics in the *Freigeistig* Movement in Berlin 1859–1924" (Ph.D. dissertation, Columbia University, 2005).

97. Otto Glagau, *Des Reiches Noth und der neue Culturkampf* (Osnabrück: Wehberg, 1879); Otto Glagau, *Der Kulturkämpfer. Zeitschrift für öffentliche Angelegenheiten* (Berlin: Likhardt, 1880–1888). On Glagau, see Daniela Weiland, *Otto Glagau und 'Der Kulturkämpfer': Zur Entstehung des modernen Antisemitismus im frühen Kaiserreich* (Berlin: Metropol Verlag, 2004).

98. Eugen Karl Dühring, *Die Judenfrage als Racen-, Sitten-und Culturfrage* (Karlsruhe: Reuther, 1881), 107. See, for a similar parallel argument, Moritz Busch, *Israel und die Gojim: Beiträge zur Beurtheilung der Judenfrage* (Leipzig: Grunow, 1880), 309.

99. Dühring, *Die Judenfrage,* 107.

100. Ibid., 97.

101. See, for example, Helmut Walser Smith, "Religion and Conflict: Protestants, Catholics, and Anti-Semitism in the State of Baden in the Era of Wilhelm II," *Central European History* 27, no. 3 (1994), 283–314.

102. For a detailed account of the internal conflicts that led to the downfall of German political antisemitism, see Richard S. Levy, *The Downfall of the Anti-Semitic Political Parties in Imperial Germany* (New Haven, CT: Yale University Press, 1975).

103. Heinrich Class, *Wenn ich der Kaiser wär: Politische Wahrheiten und Notwendigkeiten* (Leipzig: Dietrich, 1912), 192–200. The book was first published anonymously.

104. Schönerer's version was "Ohne Juda, ohne Rom, bauen wir den Deutschen Dom." ["Without Judah without Rome, we will build the German dome."] On the Alldeutscher Verband before World War I, see Michael Peters, *Der Alldeutsche Verband am Vorabend des Ersten Weltkrieges (1908–1914): ein Beitrag zur Geschichte des völkischen Nationalismus im spätwilhelminischen Deutschland* (Frankfurt a. M.: P. Lang, 1992); and Roger Chickering, *We Men Who Feel Most German: A Cultural Study of the Pan-German League, 1886–1914* (Boston: Allen & Unwin, 1984).

105. On Schönerer, see Andrew Gladding Whiteside, *The Socialism of Fools: Georg Ritter von Schönerer and Austrian Pan-Germanism* (Berkeley: University of California Press, 1975).

106. Geoffrey G. Field, *Evangelist of Race: The Germanic Vision of Houston Stewart Chamberlain* (New York: Columbia University Press, 1981), 235–237.

107. One of the earliest such works is O. Beta, *Darwin, Deutschland und die Juden oder der Juda-Jesuitismus: Dreiunddreißig Thesen nebst einer Nachschrift über einen vergessenen Factor der Volkswirtschaft* (Berlin: Selbst-Verlag, Expedition der Eisenbahn-Zeitung, 1876). See also Healy, *Jesuit Specter*, 126–128, and for an overview that includes Nazism, see Poliakov, *Causalité diabolique*, 53–85.

108. Shulamit Volkov, "Antisemitism as Cultural Code: Reflections on the History and the Historiography of Antisemitism in Imperial Germany," *LBIYB* 23 (1978), 25–46.

109. The concept of four milieus that shape Germany was introduced by Rainer Lepsius, "Parteiensystem und Sozialstruktur: Zum Problem der Demokratisierung der deutschen Gesellschaft," in *Wirtschaft, Geschichte und Wirtschaftsgeschichte: Festschrift zum 65. Geburtstag von F. Lütge*, ed. Wilhelm Abel (Stuttgart: Fischer, 1966), 371–393.

110. For a narrative that goes back to the French Revolution, see Claude Langlois, "Catholics and Seculars," in *Lieux de mémoire: Realms of Memory: Rethinking the French Past*, ed. Lawrence D. Kritzman (New York: Columbia University Press, 1996), 109–143.

111. For this comparative argument see also Johannes Heil, "Antisemitismus, Kulturkampf und Konfession—die antisemitischen 'Kulturen' Frankreichs und Deutschlands im Vergleich," in *Katholischer Antisemitismus im 19. Jahrhundert: Ursachen und Traditionen im internationalen Vergleich* (Zurich: Orell Füssli, 2000), 195–228. I do not follow Heil in his distinction between a more religious French and a more racist German antisemitism. As Vicki Caron has shown in a recent article, secular and religious antisemitism could be seamlessly integrated within the Catholic camp; Vicki Caron, "Catholic Political Mobilization and Antisemitic Violence in

Fin de Siècle France: The Case of the Union Nationale," *Journal of Modern History* 81, no. 2 (2009), 294–346. See also Birnbaum, *Jewish Destinies*, 101–115.

112. Stephen Wilson, *Ideology and Experience: Antisemitism in France at the Time of the Dreyfus Affair* (Rutherford, NJ, and London: Fairleigh Dickinson University Press and Associated University Presses, 1982), 231; Zosa Szajkowski, "Socialists and Radicals in the Development of Antisemitism in Algeria (1884–1900)," *Jewish Social Studies* 10, no. 3 (1948), 257–280; and Geneviève Dermenjian, *La crise anti-juive oranaise, 1895–1905: l'antisémitisme dans l'Algérie coloniale* (Paris: L'Harmattan, 1986).

113. Several historians have suggested in this context that we read the Dreyfus affair as a result of republican alliance building and not just antisemitism. See, for example, Robert Kaplan, "A Brief Political History of France in the 1890s and a Hypothesis for Future Investigation," in *L'antisémitisme éclairé*, 295–312.

114. There were some notable exceptions to this pattern among Jewish Orthodoxy.

Chapter Two

An earlier version of this chapter appeared in the following article: "Jewish Anticlericalism and the Making of Modern Jewish Politics in Late Enlightenment Prussia and France," *Jewish Social Studies* 17, no. 3 (2011), 40–77. Reprinted with permission from Indiana University Press.

1. Allan Arkush, *Moses Mendelssohn and the Enlightenment* (Albany: SUNY Press, 1994), 167.

2. Moses Mendelssohn, *Jerusalem, or, On Religious Power and Judaism*, ed. and trans. Allan Arkush (Hanover, NH: University Press of New England, 1983), 34.

3. Ibid.

4. Ibid.

5. For surveys of works on the religious character of the Enlightenment, see Charly Coleman, "Resacralizing the World: The Fate of Secularization in Enlightenment Historiography," *Journal of Modern History* 82, no. 2 (2010), 368–395; Jonathan Sheehan, "Enlightenment, Religion, and the Enigma of Secularization: A Review Essay," *American Historical Review* 108, no. 4 (2003), 1061–1080; and Robert Sullivan, "Rethinking Christianity in Enlightened Europe," *Eighteenth-Century Studies* 34, no. 2 (2001), 298–309. Most of the works that have reintroduced religion to the study of the Enlightenment have not attempted to revise our view of Enlightenment anticlericalism or avoided the topic altogether; see David Sorkin, *The Religious Enlightenment: Protestants, Jews, and Catholics from London to Vienna* (Princeton, NJ: Princeton University Press, 2008); Dale Van Kley, *The Jansenists and the Expulsion of the Jesuits from France, 1757–1765* (New Haven, CT: Yale University Press, 1975); and Catherine-Laurence Maire, *De la cause de Dieu à la cause de la nation: le jansénisme au XVIIIe siècle* (Paris: Gallimard, 1998). On the religious character of the Enlightenment in Germany, see, for example, Hans Erich Bödeker, "Die Religiosität der Gebildeten," in *Religionskritik und Religiosität in der deutschen Aufklärung* (Heidelberg: Schneider, 1989), 145–149.

6. David Sorkin, *Moses Mendelssohn and the Religious Enlightenment* (Berkeley: University of California Press, 1996); and idem, *Religious Enlightenment*.

7. On the continuing consensus that the Enlightenment was anticlerical (if not necessarily anti-religious) see *Religion and Politics in Enlightenment Europe*, ed. James E. Bradley and Dale Van Kley (Notre Dame, IN: University of Notre Dame Press, 2001); S. J. Barnett, *The Enlightenment and Religion: The Myths of Modernity* (Manchester, UK: Manchester University Press, 2003); and L. Jean Mondot, "Klerikalismus/Antiklerikalismus," in *Lexikon der Aufklärung: Deutschland und Europa*, ed. Werner Schneiders (Munich: Beck, 1995), 212–213. There are some exceptions to this lacking interest in anticlericalism; see, for example, S. J. Barnett, *Idol Temples and Crafty Priests: The Origins of Enlightenment Anticlericalism* (New York: St. Martin's Press, 1999).

8. The Jewish thinkers discussed here hailed from five cities: Berlin, Breslau, Paris, Metz, and Bordeaux. They were a small minority in each of these places. During the French Revolution, Paris is estimated to have had approximately 500 Jewish inhabitants and Berlin 3,500; Steven M. Lowenstein, *The Berlin Jewish Community: Enlightenment, Family, and Crisis, 1770–1830* (New York: Oxford University Press, 1994), 3–4; and Esther Benbassa, *The Jews of France: A History from Antiquity to the Present* (Princeton, NJ: Princeton University Press, 1999), 70. Although the two royal capitals, which were major centers of the Enlightenment, both had fairly small numbers of Jews, Jews were more important in Berlin; see Reinhard Rürup, "Jüdisches Großbürgertum am Ende des 18. Jahrhunderts," in *Europa und die Europäer: Quellen und Essays zur modernen europäischen Geschichte*, ed. Hartmut Kaelble et al. (Stuttgart: Steiner, 2005), 134–140.

9. Haim Hillel Ben-Sasson, "The Reformation in Contemporary Jewish Eyes," *Proceedings of the Israel Academy of Sciences and Humanities* 4 (1971), 239–327. For a more recent evaluation of Ben-Sasson's contribution, see Miriam Bodian, "The Reformation and the Jews," in *Rethinking European Jewish History*, ed. Jeremy Cohen and Murray Jay Rosman (Oxford, UK: Littman Library of Jewish Civilization, 2009), 112–132; and Elisheva Carlebach, "Jewish Responses to Christianity in Reformation Germany," in *Jews, Judaism, and the Reformation in Sixteenth-Century Germany* (Leiden: Brill, 2006), 451–480.

10. Archiwum Państwowe we Wrocławiu, Księstwo Wrocławskie, sygn. 555, "Acta von einer durch einen polnischen Juden in Breslau herumgetragenen öffentlich zum Schimpf der Katholischen Religion geprägten Münze."

11. On the related differentiation between early *maskilim* and the mature Jewish Enlightenment articulated by a coherent group between 1778 and 1797, see Shmuel Feiner, *The Jewish Enlightenment* (Philadelphia: University of Philadelphia Press, 2002).

12. See, for example, Horst Möller, "Nicolai und Mendelssohn: Zwei Repräsentanten der Berliner Aufklärung," *Menora: Jahrbuch für deutsch-jüdische Geschichte* 16 (2005), 97–114.

13. Alexander Altmann, *Moses Mendelssohn: A Biographical Study* (Philadelphia: Jewish Publication Society of America, 1973), 24–26, mentions Mendelssohn's acquaintance with d'Argens via Gumperz. More important, however, was the connection through Nicolai, who claims to have introduced the Berlin Jew and the French nobleman to each other. Nicolai also was the first to report that d'Argens helped Mendelssohn acquire a *Schutzprivileg* from Fredrick II in 1763; Friedrich Nicolai, *Anekdoten von König Friedrich II. von Preussen, und von einigen Personen, die um Ihn waren: Nebst Berichtigung einiger schon gedruckten Anekdoten: Erstes Heft* (Berlin: n.p., 1788), 61–69.

14. Mendelssohn was associated with a group of Berlin Jews—including Dr. Bloch, Isaac Daniel Izig, David Friedländer, and Samuel Levy—that commissioned Moses Maimon to translate Basnage's *Histoire des Juifs* into Hebrew for the benefit of unenlightened Polish Jews; Altmann, *Mendelssohn*, 363.

15. Wolfgang Altgeld, *Katholizismus, Protestantismus, Judentum: Über religiös begründete Gegensätze und nationalreligiöse Ideen in der Geschichte des deutschen Nationalismus* (Mainz: M.-Grünewald-Verlag, 1992), 89–91. In 1783, the same year that Mendelssohn published *Jerusalem*, Johann Salomo Semler, the most influential theologian of the Protestant Enlightenment, also argued against attempts at reunification of the Christian denominations; Johann Salomo Semler, *Freimütige Briefe über die Religionsvereinigung der dreien streitigen Theile im römischen Reiche* (Leipzig: Weygandsche Buchhandlung, 1783). On Semler's position in these debates, see Christopher Spehr, *Aufklärung und Ökumene: Reunionsversuche zwischen Katholiken und Protestanten im deutschsprachigen Raum des späteren 18. Jahrhunderts* (Tübingen: Mohr, 2005), 338–373.

16. Ibid, 86. On the anti-Catholic rhetoric in Nicolai's *Allgemeine deutsche Bibliothek*, see Roger Kirscher, *Théologie et Lumières: les théologiens éclairés autour de la revue de Friedrich Nicolai, Allgemeine deutsche Bibliothek, 1765–1792* (Villeneuve d'Ascq: Presses Universitaires du Septentrion, 2001), 160–176.

17. On the conflicts on crypto-Catholicism after 1785, see Jean Blum, *J.-A. Starck et la querelle du crypto-catholicisme en Allemagne 1785–1789* (Paris: F. Alcan, 1912); and Roland Mortier, *Diderot en Allemagne, 1750–1850* (Paris: Presses universitaires de France, 1954), 375.

18. Mendelssohn, *Jerusalem*, 72.

19. The first two terms appear in a letter to Homberg, September 22, 1783, in Mendelssohn, *Gesammelte Schriften (Jubiläumsausgabe)*, ed. Fritz Bamberger et al. and continued by Alexander Altmann (Stuttgart–Bad Cannstatt: Frommann, 1971–), 8:134; the last term in a letter to Homberg, March 1, 1784, Mendelssohn, *Gesammelte Schriften (Jubiläumsausgabe)*, 8:178. "Heucheley und Pfaffenlist" appears also in *Jerusalem*, 116. See also Mendelssohn's "Preface to Manasseh Ben Israel," where he wrote that Dohm, "rightly ignored the inhuman accusations against the Jews, which show the mark of the times and monks' cells in which they were devised"; Mendelssohn, "Vorrede zu Manasseh Ben Israel," in *Jerusalem*, 11.

20. Mendelssohn, *Jerusalem*, 14. On anti-Jewish measures by the Catholic Church, see Gershon David Hundert, *Jews in Poland-Lithuania in the Eighteenth Century: A Genealogy of Modernity* (Berkeley: University of California Press, 2004), 57–78; and Jonathan Irvine Israel, *European Jewry in the Age of Mercantilism, 1550–1750* (Oxford, UK, and New York: Clarendon Press and Oxford University Press, 1998), 220–222. For a depiction of anti-Jewish blood libel accusations written a decade after Mendelssohn's account, see Salomon Maimon, *Solomon Maimon: An Autobiography*, trans. John Clark Murray (Urbana: University of Illinois Press, 2001), 14–17. Maimon noted that the accusation originated with a Russian (Orthodox) clergyman, but he attributed the tradition of such denunciations to "Catholic Christians" (p. 21).

21. On the Lavater affair, see Altmann, *Mendelssohn*, 194–263.

22. Carlebach, "Jewish Responses," 452.

23. Mendelssohn, *Gesammelte Schriften (Jubiläumsausgabe)*, 8:136.

24. On the larger context of this debate, see Altmann, *Mendelssohn*, 529–531. On Michaelis and his anti-Judaism, see Dominique Bourel, "La Judéophobie savante dans l'Allemagne des Lumières: Johann David Michaelis," in *L'antisémitisme éclairé: inclusion et exclusion depuis l'époque des Lumières jusqu'à l'affaire Dreyfus*, ed. Ilana Zinguer and Sam W. Bloom (Leiden: Brill, 2003); Anna-Ruth Löwenbrück, *Judenfeindschaft im Zeitalter der Aufklärung: eine Studie zur Vorgeschichte des modernen Antisemitismus am Beispiel des Göttinger Theologien und Orientalisten Johann David Michaelis (1717–1791)* (Frankfurt a. M.: P. Lang, 1995); and Jonathan M. Hess, *Germans, Jews and the Claims of Modernity* (New Haven, CT: Yale University Press, 2002), 51–89.

25. Mendelssohn, *Gesammelte Schriften (Jubiläumsausgabe)*, 8:223.

26. Mendelssohn to Nicolai, November 12, 1783, in Mendelssohn, *Gesammelte Schriften (Jubiläumsausgabe)*, 13:156.

27. Benedikt Stattler, *Wahres Jerusalem oder, Ueber religiöse Macht und Toleranz in jedem und besonders im katholischen Christenthume, bey Anlass des Mendelssohn'schen Jerusalems und einiger Gegenschriften nebst einem Nachtrage an Hr. Nikolai in Berlin* (Augsburg: Mattäus Reigers sel. Söhnen, 1787).

28. On Kuh's biography see M. Kayserling, *Der Dichter Ephraim Kuh: Ein Beitrag zur Geschichte der deutschen Literatur* (Berlin: Julius Springer, 1864).

29. See, for example, the poem entitled "The Polish Jew who was a Christian," *Deutsches Museum*, January 1784, 38, reprinted in Ephraim Moses Kuh, *Hinterlassene Gedichte* (Zurich: Orell, Gessner, Fuessli, 1792), 157.

30. Kuh, *Hinterlassene Gedichte*, 224.

31. *Deutsches Museum*, September 1784, 194. This poem was not included in *Hinterlassene Gedichte*.

32. Isaschar Falkensohn Behr, *Gedichte von einem polnischen Juden* (Göttingen: Wallstein, 2002).

33. Indeed, even Kuh's marginality had a classical model: In 1784, Kuh translated the Latin poet Martial, who was known for his vivid description of ancient

Rome's dark side. Kuh's highlighted position as an outsider raised his appeal as a comical critic of society for readers who could recognize the underlying literary paradigm. See review of *Hinterlassene Gedichte* by Ephraim Moses Kuh, *Allgemeine Literaturzeitung*, June 25, 1793, 729, 733.

34. Kuh, *Hinterlassene Gedichte*, 7–8.

35. Kuh had serious differences with Jewish traditionalists, however. On him and the Breslau Jewish context more generally, see Anne-Margarete Brenker, *Aufklärung als Sachzwang: Realpolitik in Breslau im ausgehenden 18. Jahrhundert* (Hamburg: Dölling und Galitz, 2000), 250–257.

36. The most comprehensive biography is Gerda Heinrich, "Moses Hirschel–Biographie," available at www.haskala.net/autoren/hirschel01/biographie.html.

37. Moses Hirschel, *Kampf der jüdischen Hierarchie mit der Vernunft* (Breslau: Korn, 1788).

38. Ibid., 16.

39. Moses Hirschel, *Apologie der Menschenrechte: Oder philosophisch kritische Beleuchtung der Schrift: Ueber die physische und moralische Verfassung der heutigen Juden* (Zurich: Orell, Gressner, Füssli & Co., 1793). The work was prominently referenced by the anti-Jewish romantic philosopher Jakob Friedrich Fries, among others.

40. Ibid., 119.

41. Ibid., 3; Voltaire, *La Henriade*, in *Œuvres complètes*, vol. 8 (Paris: Garnier Frères, 1877), chant 2, lines 268–272. The translation follows Caroline Weber, "Voltaire's Zaïre: Fantasies of Infidelity, Ideologies of Faith," *South Central Review* 21, no. 2 (2004), 60n20.

42. David A. Bell, *The Cult of the Nation in France: Inventing Nationalism, 1680–1800* (Cambridge, MA: Harvard University Press, 2001), 30–32. On the *longue durée* story of these memories in Germany, also in the context of the history of Jews in Germany, see Helmut Walser Smith, *The Continuities of German History: Nation, Religion, and Race across the Long Nineteenth Century* (Cambridge, UK: Cambridge University Press, 2008), 74–114. Voltaire's epos was particularly popular and controversial in Germany; H. A. Korff, *Voltaire im literarischen Deutschland des XVIII. Jahrhunderts: ein Beitrag zur Geschichte des deutschen Geistes von Gottsched bis Goethe* (Heidelberg: Winter, 1917–1918), 37–70.

43. Hirschel might have also appreciated the piece due to Voltaire's positive depiction of Jewish victims of the Inquisition.

44. Feiner, *Jewish Enlightenment*, 173–176; idem, *The Origins of Jewish Secularization in Eighteenth-Century Europe* (Philadelphia: University of Pennsylvania Press, 2010).

45. Moses Hirschel, "Vier Briefe über Schlesien," in Johann Joseph Kausch, *Erste Fortsetzung seiner Nachrichten über Schlesien, Böhmen und das vormalige Polen* (Breslau: Gehr und Co., 1796), 199–236.

46. See P. G. M. Dickson, "Joseph II's Reshaping of the Austrian Church," *Historical Journal* 36, no. 1 (1993), 89–114, on the impact of Josephinian monastery policies.

47. Ibid., 217–226.

48. Ibid., 200.

49. Ibid., 225–226.

50. [Johannes Aloysius Martyni-Laguna], review of *Kausch's erste Fortsetzung seiner Nachrichten über Schlesien, Böhmen und das vormalige Polen*, in *Neue allgemeine deutsche Bibliothek* 45 (1799), 168–176.

51. Perhaps the most ironic twist in Hirschel's own life story was his conversion to Catholicism in 1804; Heinrich, "Moses Hirschel."

52. Jay R. Berkovitz, *Rites and Passages: The Beginnings of Modern Jewish Culture in France, 1650–1860* (Philadelphia: University of Philadelphia Press, 2004), chs. 1 and 2.

53. In the biographical information as well as the identification of most of the anticlerical works of Hourwitz, I have relied on Frances Malino's meticulous study, *A Jew in the French Revolution: The Life of Zalkind Hourwitz* (Cambridge, MA: Blackwell Publishers, 1996).

54. *Courier de l'Europe*, October 7, 1783, 225–226.

55. *Courier de l'Europe*, October 31, 1783, 287–288.

56. Malino, *A Jew in the French Revolution*, 11.

57. Zalkind Hourwitz, *Apologie des juifs en réponse à la question: Est-il des moyens de rendre les Juifs plus heureux & plus utiles en France?* (Paris: Gattey and Royer, 1789), 73–74.

58. Ibid., 74.

59. Ibid., 74–75. The annates were payments made for the upkeep of the papacy. The National Assembly abolished them without resistance as early as August 1789. They had also figured prominently in Luther's polemics against Church abuses and the early reformation; Nigel Aston, *Religion and Revolution in France, 1780–1804* (Washington DC: Catholic University of America, 2000), 143.

60. Malino, *A Jew in the French Revolution*, 46. See also David Feuerwerker, *L'Émancipation des Juifs en France: de l'ancien régime à la fin du Second Empire* (Paris: A. Michel, 1976), 130, 132.

61. Cited in Malino, *A Jew in the French Revolution*, 226n78; the original is in AN M771/no. 15. Camus also made clear that he was in general agreement with Hirschel's argument. Another one of Camus' censorship reports shows that he was at times willing to have works to which he objected published, however. See AN M771/no. 14.

62. David A. Bell, *Lawyers and Citizens: The Making of a Political Elite in Old Regime France* (New York: Oxford University Press, 1994), 183; and J.-R. Suratteau, "Camus, Armand Gaston," in *Dictionnaire historique de le Révolution Française*, ed. Albert Soboul (Paris: Presses Universitaires de France, 1989), 186–188.

63. Aston, *Religion and Revolution*, 161.

64. For the argument that the Civil Oath of the Clergy forms the key to the rupture between Catholicism and Revolution, see Claude Langlois, "La rupture entre l'Eglise catholique et la Révolution," in *The French Revolution and the Creation*

of Modern Political Culture, ed. François Furet and Mona Ozouf (Oxford, UK: Pergamon Press, 1989), 3:375–390.

65. For an argument that anticlericalism rather than de-Christianization was a driving factor for the events of 1793 and 1794, see Clarke Garrett, "The 'Dechristianization of the Year II': Historians' Dilemma," *Consortium on Revolutionary Europe 1750–1850: Selected Papers* (1995), 209–215.

66. Letter to the editor, *Chronique de Paris*, February 11, 1791, 167 ; and Z. H. P., "Avis très pressant donné à l'auteur du Courrier," *Courrier de Paris*, April 12, 1791, 188.

67. Letter to the editor, *Chronique de Paris*, February 11, 1791, 167, translation follows; and Malino, *A Jew in the French Revolution*, 110.

68. Ibid. In another 1791 article, Hourwitz also employed humor to promote his anticlerical platform when he joked about the sexual exploits of friends who were taking advantage of the trust that aristocratic women in particular had in the nonjuring priests; Z. H. P., "Avis très pressant donné à l'auteur du Courrier," *Courrier de Paris*, April 12, 1791, 188.

69. *Le Courrier de Paris* 20 (January 10, 1791), 153. Here I follow the translation of Malino, *A Jew in the French Revolution*, 110.

70. Malino, *A Jew in the French Revolution*, 110.

71. "Italie," *Courrier de Strasbourg*, March 23, 1793 (an 2), 283.

72. *Wochenblatt*, no. 22, March 28, 1793, 286.

73. Registre de correspondance du Directoire du District de Colmar (August 16, 1792–November 20, 1795), ADHR L833, 94–95.

74. ADHR L645, item 70.

75. Ronald Schechter, "Translating the 'Marseillaise': Biblical Republicanism and the Emancipation of Jews in Revolutionary France," *Past & Present*, no. 143 (1994), 108–135; and Ronald Schechter, *Obstinate Hebrews: Representations of Jews in France, 1715–1815* (Berkeley: University of California Press, 2003), 185–192.

76. "Naflah naflah malchut ha-resha / cherem hi u-tehi toeva": Bibliothèque municipale, Nancy, 4372, *La-Menatseach Shir le-Moshe Ensheim hushar be-yom gavra yad yoshve erets moledetenu al kol oyevenu mesaviv* [A Song to the Victor by Moïse Ensheim, Sung on the Day when the Hand of the Inhabitants of Our Fatherland Prevailed over All the Surrounding Enemies] (Metz, 1792). Reprinted in *Les Juifs et la révolution française: histoire et mentalités*, ed. Mireille Hadas-Lebel and Evelyne Oliel-Grausz (Louvain: E. Peeters, 1992), 183–187.

77. See entry "Ensheim, Moses" in *Encyclopaedia Judaica*, 2nd ed., ed. Michael Berenbaum and Fred Skolnik (Detroit, MI: Macmillan Reference USA, 2007), 6:447. On Metz as a center of the Haskalah in France and a node of European Jewish developments, see Simon Schwarzfuchs, "La Haskalah et le cercle de Metz à la veille de la Révolution," in *Politique et religion dans le judaïsme moderne: des communautés à l'émancipation*, ed. Daniel Tollet (Paris: Presses de l'Université de Paris-Sorbonne, 1987), 51–59. More pessimistic about the role of the Enlightenment in Metz is Pierre-André Meyer, *La communauté juive de Metz au XVIIIe siècle: histoire*

et démographie (Nancy: Presses universitaires de Nancy and Editions Serpenoise, 1993), 85. See also Richard Ayoun, "L'impact de la révolution sur le rabbinat français: Les rabbins, la communauté de Metz et la révolution française," in *Les Juifs et la révolution française*, 167–187.

78. Among other things, he translated Mendelssohn's most famous philosophical treatise *Phaedon* into French. On Bing, see Jay R. Berkovitz, *The Shaping of Jewish Identity in Nineteenth-Century France* (Detroit, MI: Wayne State University Press, 1989), 67–70; and Berkovitz, *Rites and Passages*, 96–99.

79. Many of his connections might have come via the Abbé Grégoire. Alyssa Goldstein Sepinwall, "Strategic Friendships: Jewish Intellectuals, the Abbé Grégoire, and the French Revolution," in *Renewing the Past, Reconfiguring Jewish Culture: From al-Andalus to the Haskalah*, ed. Ross Brann and Adam Sutcliffe (Philadelphia: University of Philadelphia Press, 2004), 198.

80. Schechter, "Translating," 117.

81. Schechter does, however, point out the ambivalence of another contemporary Jew in this regard. The printer Abraham Spire, who published a Judeo-German periodical from November 1789 to March 1790, combined a reverence for the clergy in general with a complete rejection of "monks." Whereas the integration of the clergy in revolutionary assemblies were for him a sign of the nation's new unity, "monks" were in his depiction the victims of just indignation by "the people"; Schechter, *Obstinate Hebrews*, 179–181.

82. The translation follows Schechter, "Translating the 'Marseillaise,'" 117. I only replaced "cloak of fur" with "hairy mantle," following the New Revised Standard Version's translation of Zachariah 13:4.

83. See Zachariah 13:4–5 (Revised Standard Version): "On that day every prophet will be ashamed of his vision when he prophesies; he will not put on a hairy mantle in order to deceive, but he will say, 'I am no prophet, I am a tiller of the soil; for the land has been my possession since my youth.'"

84. Schechter, *Obstinate Hebrews*, 191; and Schechter, "Translating," 117.

85. References to fur as a sign of status from the late eighteenth century that appears in the ARTFL database refer primarily to the fur as a status symbol within the university. See, for example, Diderot: "J'allais prendre la fourrure et m'installer parmi les docteurs de Sorbonne." Denis Diderot, *Salon de 1767* (first published 1768), ed. Jean Seznec and Jean Adhemar (Oxford: Clarendon Press, 1963), 256. There are various earlier uses in this sense as well, such as this one from 1686: "Le recteur étoit habillé en bachelier, avec sa fourrure de recteur," Philippe de Courcillon, marquis de Dangeau, *Journal* (Paris: Didot, 1854), 1:223, retrieved in September 2012 from www.lib.uchicago.edu/efts/ARTFL/databases/TLF07/. A look at the self-representation of the aristocracy in portraits and of fashion drawings of the eighteenth century can also dispel the assumption that fur was the distinctive marker of the aristocracy. See, for example, André Blum, *Histoire du costume: Les modes au XVIIe et au XVIIIe siècle* (Paris: Hachette, 1928).

86. Daniel Roche, *The Culture of Clothing: Dress and Fashion in the "Ancien Régime"* (Cambridge, UK: Cambridge University Press, 1994), 30–34. On the debates on wigs in the context of a history of modern consumption, see Michael Kwass, "Big Hair: A Wig History of Consumption in Eighteenth-Century France," *American Historical Review* 111, no. 3 (2006), 631–659.

87. This follows from the fact that there was a revolutionary debate on wigs as a possible form of deceit, because the republican-style wig might mask counterrevolutionary identities; Richard Wrigley, *The Politics of Appearances: Representations of Dress in Revolutionary France* (Oxford, UK: Berg, 2002), 239.

88. Isaïe Berr-Bing, "Cantique," reprinted in *Les Juifs et la révolution française*, 185–187. The prophecy of Zachariah contains the prediction of the end of all false prophets; a notion that is close to the idea in this stanza that God will strike those who used "religion as a pretext."

89. Moshe Ensheim, "Al ha-Va'ad Ha-Gadol asher be-Medinat Zarfat," *Hameasef* 7 (1790), 33–37.

90. Not surprisingly, the new text omitted any reference to the enlightened king [*melech ha-maskil*], and, as Schechter has pointed out, Ensheim had a more emphatic identification with France as his homeland, adding *moledetenu* (our homeland) to the title of his work; Schechter, *Obstinate Hebrews*, 190.

91. Ayoun, "L'impact de la révolution sur le rabbinat français," 172–173.

92. See Zosa Szajkowski, *Jews and the French Revolutions* (New York: Ktav, 1970), 388–398; and Daniel Gerson, *Die Kehrseite der Emanzipation in Frankreich: Judenfeindschaft im Elsass 1778–1848* (Essen: Klartext, 2006), 76–87.

93. Ensheim, *Cantique*. See Schechter, *Obstinate Hebrews*, 191.

94. "Il n'est plus, ce temps, où le fanatisme alimenté par quel- / ques Prêtres sanguinaires, sema les haines et les divisions entre / les enfans d'un même père! la bienfaisante philosophie a com- / pris tous les hommes dans les liens de la fraternité."

95. Voltaire also uses the term *bloodthirsty priests* in the Philosophical Dictionary in a section of the entry on "Moses" meant to show the hypocrisy embedded in the Old Testament narrative; Voltaire, *Philosophical Dictionary* (Harmondsworth, UK: Penguin, 1971), 321. There is only one other reference to *"prêtres sanguinaires"* in the ARTFL database, once again from Voltaire.

96. On the importance of the oath for the rhetoric of the Revolution and the creation of national unity, see Jean Starobinski, *1789: The Emblems of Reason*, trans. Barbara Bray (Cambridge, MA: MIT Press, 1988), 101–124; and S. Bianchi, "Serment," in Soboul, *Dictionnaire historique de la Révolution française*, 979–980. Claude Langlois referred to the swearing of oaths, which was a key moment for the visible construction of the unanimous nation through the will of the individual, as the *"sacrament* of the Revolution"; Langlois, "La Rupture," 383.

97. I rely for his biography on Frances Malino, "From Patriot to Israélite: Abraham Furtado in Revolutionary France," in *Mystics, Philosophers, and Politicians: Essays in Jewish Intellectual History in Honor of Alexander Altmann*, ed. Jehuda Reinharz and Daniel Swetschinski (Durham, NC: Duke University Press, 1982), 213–248.

98. Ibid., 217.

99. Ibid., 219, on the dating of the document.

100. Abraham Furtado, "Folie de Jeunesse," Manuscript [1791], AIU Archives, legs de Pascal Themanlys, no. 2, 1.

101. Ibid., 20.

102. Malino, "From Patriot to Israélite," 214–215.

103. Anticlericalism was not high on his agenda by the time he headed the Assembly of Jewish Notables in 1806. See Malino, "Mémoires," 79–80. In his emphasis on the "fanaticism" of the (anti-religious) revolutionaries who come out of a Rousseauian tradition (99–100), Furtado is in fact closer to the growing school of anti-*philosophes*. See Darrin M. McMahon, *Enemies of the Enlightenment: The French Counter-Enlightenment and the Making of Modernity* (New York: Oxford University Press, 2001).

104. Zalkind Hourwitz, "À l'auteur du Babillard," *Le Journal de Paris*, 6 Brumaire, an VI (October 27, 1797), no. 36, 148.

105. Susanne Lachenicht, *Information und Propaganda: die Presse deutscher Jakobiner im Elsass (1791–1800)* (Munich: R. Oldenbourg, 2004), 93, for a summary of his biography. The following biographical information on Lambert comes from Lachenicht.

106. "Ueber ungeschworne Pfaffen," *Republikanischer Wächter*, no. 1, 3 Vendemiaire, an 4 (September 24, 1795), 5–8, here 6. See also, for example; "Aufgepaßt! ruft unser Wächter, die ungeschwornen Herren arretirt, und über den Rhein mit den unsaubern Soldpfaffen des Vatikans!" *Republikanischer Wächter*, no. 2, 6 Vendemiaire, an 4 (September 27, 1795), 28–30. On Lembert's likely participation in this publication and his likely editorship starting in November 1795, see Lachenicht, *Information*, 83–84.

107. "Ein Wort an die Unglaubigen etc." *Der Wahlmann*, 17 Ventos an 5 (March 7, 1797), 113–115; *Wahlmann*, 18 Ventos, an 5 (March 8, 1897), 123–126; "An die deutschen Departements (Aus dem Friedensboten)," *Wahlmann*, 19 Ventos, an 5 (March 9, 1897), 129–130; "Ein Wort an die Unglaubigen etc." *Wahlmann* 1, 19 Ventos, an. 5 (March 9, 1897), 131–135; "An die deutschen Departemente," *Wahlmann*, 21 Ventos, an 5 (March 11, 1897), 147–148; "Einige Beweise, daß alles, was in der bekannten mit dem Namen Albert unterzeichneten Petition steht, erlogen war," *Wahlmann*, 21 Ventos, an 5 (March 11, 1897),148–150; "Kann ein zur Deportation verurtheilter Priester vor die Anklage-Geschwornen gebracht warden," *Der Wahlmann*, 25 Ventos, an 5 (March 15, 1797), 169–171; and "Anekdote," *Wahlmann*, 27 Ventos, an 5 (March 17, 1797), 191–192. See also Susanne Lachenicht, "Die Revolutionierung des Diskurses: Begriffs- und Kulturtransfer zur Zeit der Französischen Revolution," in *Historische Diskursanalysen: Genealogie, Theorie, Anwendungen*, ed. Franz X. Eder (Wiesbaden: VS Verlag für Sozialwissenschaften, 2006), 333–335 on his milieu and the *Wahlmann*.

108. For example, *Wahlmann*, 4 Venos, an 5 (February 22, 1797), 18. Lambert's claim resonates with arguments by Darrin McMahon that the radical opposition

between religion and (atheist) philosophy was popularized to a large degree by enemies of the Revolution; McMahon, *Enemies of the Enlightenment*, 90–120.

109. "Nachtrag über die Verträglichkeit eidscheuer Priester (Eingesandt)," *Wahlmann*, 7 Floreal, an 7 (April 26, 1797), 465–466.

110. *Rheinische Kronik*, February 24, 1797, 4; also cited in Lachenicht, *Information*, 178.

111. Lachenicht, *Information*, 116.

112. Ibid., 121. The only evidence I found for his conversion is the Kirchenbuch of the Evangelical Church in Mannheim, Baden, which lists him as a Protestant marrying another Protestant, Christina Elisabetha Augsburger, on May 25, 1807. See "Germany, Marriages, 1558–1929," index, FamilySearch; retrieved on January 7, 2013, from https://familysearch.org/pal:/MM9.1.1/J4RL-9JQ); citing FHL microfilm 1192143.

113. Abraham Lembert, *Essai sur une meilleure organisation des écoles primaires dans les campagnes: présenté au conseil général du Département du Mont-Tonnerre, lors de la session de l'an 10* (Mainz: C. F. Pfeiffer, 1801–1802).

114. For a synthetic summary of this view, see Yosef Hayim Yerushalmi, *Servants of Kings and Not Servants of Servants: Some Aspects of the Political History of the Jews* (Atlanta, GA: Tam Institute for Jewish Studies, Emory University, 2005).

115. The most elaborate work on French-Jewish attempts to create vertical and horizontal alliances and the risks of and failures involved in this transformation is Pierre Birnbaum, *Prier pour l'état: Les Juifs, l'alliance royale et la démocratie* (Paris: Calmann-Lévy, 2005). Birnbaum also analyzes Ensheim's *Cantique* as a key moment of transformation but does not elaborate on the role of anticlericalism, 49–51.

116. This does not mean that denominational polemics did not at times become part of revolutionary debates. In Catholic circles a form of "anti-Judeo-Protestantism" emerged for the first time. See Patrick Cabanel, *Juifs et protestants en France, les affinités électives: XVIᵉ-XXIᵉ siècle* (Paris: Fayard, 2004), 73–82; and Szajkowski, *Jews and the French Revolutions*, 388–398. On Protestants, see also Jacques Poujol, "Le changement d'image des protestants pendant la Révolution," *Bulletin de la Société de l'histoire du protestantisme français* 127 (1989), 500–541.

117. There is, however, also a debate about the sincerity of Mendelssohn's orthodoxy in regard to revelation. See Allan Arkush, *Mendelssohn*; and Allan Arkush, "The Questionable Judaism of Moses Mendelssohn," *New German Critique* (1999), 29–44. For the counterposition, see David Sorkin, "The Mendelssohn Myth and Its Method," *New German Critique*, no. 77 (1999), 7–28.

Chapter Three

1. Irene Fozzard, "The Government and the Press in France, 1822 to 1827," *English Historical Review* 66, no. 258 (1951), 54–55; and Mary S. Hartman, "The Sacrilege Law of 1825 in France: A Study in Anticlericalism and Mythmaking," *Journal of Modern History* 44, no. 1 (1972), 21–37.

2. On anticlerical violence see, for example, J. Michael Phayer, "Politics and Popular Religion: The Cult of the Cross in France, 1815–1840," *Journal of Social History* 11, no. 3 (1978), 346–365.

3. Julie Kalman, *Rethinking Antisemitism in Nineteenth-Century France* (New York: Cambridge University Press, 2010).

4. See Wolf-Daniel Hartwich, *Romantischer Antisemitismus: von Klopstock bis Richard Wagner* (Göttingen: Vandenhoeck & Ruprecht, 2005).

5. *German-Jewish History in Modern Times*, ed. Michael Meyer et al. (New York: Columbia University Press, 1996–1998), 2:31.

6. Stefan Nienhaus, *Geschichte der deutschen Tischgesellschaft* (Tübingen: Niemeyer, 2003).

7. Jean Baubérot, *Histoire de la laïcité en France* (Paris: Presses universitaires de France, 2007), 27.

8. Jacques-Olivier Boudon, *Napoléon et les cultes: les religions en Europe à l'aube du XIXe siècle 1800–1815* (Paris: Fayard, 2002).

9. Darrin M. McMahon, *Enemies of the Enlightenment: The French Counter-Enlightenment and the Making of Modernity* (New York: Oxford University Press, 2001), 128–133.

10. Pierre Birnbaum, *L'aigle et la synagogue: Napoléon, les Juifs et l'état* (Paris: Fayard, 2007). For a subtle analysis of the opportunities French Jews had in the mythopoetic project of Napoleonic self-representation, see Ronald Schechter, *Obstinate Hebrews: Representations of Jews in France, 1715–1815* (Berkeley: University of California Press, 2003), 194–234.

11. Jacques-Olivier Boudon, "Les fondements religieux du pouvoir impérial, " in *Voies nouvelles pour l'histoire du premier empire: territoires, pouvoirs, identités: Colloque d'Avignon, 9–10 mai 2000* (Paris: Bibliothèque de l'histoire, 2003), 204–205.

12. Ibid., 225–247.

13. Julie Kalman, "The Unyielding Wall: Jews and Catholics in Restoration and July Monarchy France," *French Historical Studies* 26, no. 4 (2003), 661–686; and Kalman, *Rethinking Antisemitism*, 46–70.

14. AN F7 6769 dossier 15, letter from Cabinet of the Prefect of Landes to the Minister of the Interior, Mont-de-Marsan, August 24, 1829. Various letters from the prefect report the persistent fears. See also the letter from the Prefecture of Landes to Mont-de-Marsan, September 29, 1829, which points again to the special tensions in St. Esprit.

15. On such fears among the peasantry and anticlericalism, see Alain Corbin, *The Village of Cannibals: Rage and Murder in France, 1870* (Cambridge, MA: Harvard University Press, 1992). On the Jewish community in Saint-Esprit, see Anne Bénard-Oukhemanou, *La communauté juive de Bayonne au XIXe siècle* (Anglet, France: Atlantica, 2001).

16. Berr Isaac Berr, *Réflexions sur la régénération complète des Juifs en France* (Paris: Giguet et Michaud, 1806).

17. Ibid., 11.

18. *Courrier français*, May 14, 1831.

19. Paul D'Hollander, "Processions et liberté sous la monarchie de Juillet," in *L'église dans la rue: les cérémonies extérieures du culte en France au XIXe siècle*, ed. Paul D'Hollander (Limoges: Presses universitaires de Limoges, 2001), 57–90.

20. Lisa Moses Leff, *Sacred Bonds of Solidarity: The Rise of Jewish Internationalism in Nineteenth-Century France* (Stanford, CA: Stanford University Press, 2006), 234–235.

21. Ruth Harris, *Dreyfus: Politics, Emotion, and the Scandal of the Century* (New York: Picador, 2010), 9.

22. Letter of the Jews of Lauterbourg to the Subprefect of the Arrondissement of Wissembourg, May 27, 1831, and letter of the mayor of Lauterbourg to the Subprefect of the Arrondissement of Wissembourg, May 28, 1831, ADBR V23, Lauterbourg.

23. On the Jews of Lauterbourg, see Serge Braun, *Le Dernier Testament: Chronique de la communauté juive de Lauterbourg* (Strasbourg: Editions Coprur, 1997).

24. The mayor suggested that those who had denounced the local Catholics for their Corpus Christi processions could be found instead among low-ranking officers from the local army garrison who staffed France's easternmost fortress along the German border. He thus conveniently put the blame on outsiders to the village community.

25. Letter of the Jews of Lauterbourg to the Subprefect, May 27, 1831, ADBR V23, Lauterbourg.

26. Letter of the Prefect of Bas-Rhin to the Subprefect of the Arrondissement of Wissembourg, May 30, 1831, ADBR V23, Lauterbourg.

27. Letter of the Minister of Public Instruction and Religion to the Prefect of Bas-Rhin, June 11, 1831, ADBR V23, Lauterbourg.

28. Alan B. Spitzer, *The French Generation of 1820* (Princeton, NJ: Princeton University Press, 1987).

29. Leff, *Sacred Bonds*, 81–116.

30. On Salvador's historical narratives and his views on Judaism, see Paula E. Hyman, "Joseph Salvador: Proto-Zionist or Apologist for Assimilation?" *Jewish Social Studies* 34 (1972), 1–22. Hyman generally underlines the fact that he leaves little room for the future mission of modern Judaism in spite of his apology of ancient Mosaic traditions. Michael Graetz, in *The Jews in Nineteenth-Century France: From the French Revolution to the Alliance Israélite Universelle* (Stanford, CA: Stanford University Press, 1996), 161–193, sees him as typical of the freedoms that Jews could have on the margins of traditional frameworks. See also Jacques Eladan, "Joseph Salvador et la Jérusalem nouvelle," *Pardès* 15 (1992), 194–207.

31. Gabriel Salvador, *J. Salvador, sa vie, ses œuvres et ses critiques* (Paris: Calmann-Lévy, 1881), 22–23.

32. Graetz, *Jews in Nineteenth-Century France*, 173.

33. Hyman, "Joseph Salvador," 4. The chief rabbi at the time was Abraham Hai de Cologna.

34. Salvador, *Histoire des Institutions*, 2:80–90. On the contemporary debate on Salvador's views on Jesus' trial, see James Darmesteter, "Joseph Salvador," *Annuaire de la Société des Études Juives* 1 (1881), 23–26; and Eladan, "Joseph Salvador," 198–199.

35. Salvador, *Histoire des Institutions*, 1:109.

36. Ibid., 3:170–171.

37. Ibid., 3:171–172.

38. Ibid., 3:157.

39. Ibid., 1:12.

40. Ibid., 3:419.

41. Ibid., 1:253.

42. Ibid., 1:55, 1:252, 1:263.

43. Eugène Fleischmann, *Le christianisme mis à nu: la critique juive du christianisme* (Paris: Plon, 1970), 56.

44. Ceri Crossley, *French Historians and Romanticism: Thierry, Guizot, the Saint-Simonians, Quinet, Michelet* (London: Routledge, 1993).

45. Corinne Pelta, *Le romantisme libéral en France, 1815–1830: la représentation souveraine* (Paris: Harmattan, 2001); and F. W. J. Hemmings, *Culture and Society in France 1789–1848* (Leicester, UK: Leicester University Press, 1987), 163–172.

46. Pierre Rosanvallon, *Le moment Guizot* (Paris: Gallimard, 1985), 163–169; and Biancamaria Fontana, *Benjamin Constant and the Post-Revolutionary Mind* (New Haven, CT: Yale University Press, 1991), 108–109.

47. Immanuel Wolf, "Ueber den Begriff einer Wissenschaft des Judenthums," *Zeitschrift für die Wissenschaft des Judenthums*, no. 1 (1823), 1–24. See also Ismar Schorsch, *From Text to Context: The Turn to History in Modern Judaism* (Hanover, NH: University Press of New England, 1994), ch. 11.

48. Anticlerical arguments found their way into the criticism of the rabbinate and the wealthy lay leadership of Jewry in "Aus dem Archiv des Vereins, für die Correspondenz (Polen betreffend.) Nebst einem Nachworte," *Zeitschrift für die Wissenschaft des Judenthums*, no. 3 (1823), 533–539.

49. See the letters from John Stuart Mill to Gustave d'Eichthal, January 10, 1842 and July 23, 1863, as well as the letter from Mill to Frederick Denison Maurice, September 9, 1842; John Stuart Mill, *Collected Works* (Toronto: University of Toronto Press, 1963–1991), 13:496–497, 15:870, 17:1997–1998. D'Eichthal had introduced Salvador to Mill. See also Gustave d' Eichthal, *A French Sociologist Looks at Britain: Gustave d'Eichthal and British Society in 1828*, ed. Barrie M. Ratcliffe and W. H. Chaloner (Manchester, UK, and Totowa, NJ: Manchester University Press and Rowman and Littlefield, 1977), 126. On the Bible in German and French romanticism, see Abraham Albert Avni, *The Bible and Romanticism: The Old Testament in German and French Romantic Poetry* (The Hague: Mouton, 1969).

50. Salvador, *Salvador*, 13–68, described these debates in detail. See ibid., 56–59, on the positive review from the *Globe*, April 19, 1829.

51. *Le Constitutionnel*, February 20, 1823, 2–3.

52. Michel Nicolas, review of *Institutions de Moïse et du peuple hébreu* by Joseph Salvador, 3rd edition (Paris 1862), *Revue germanique* 20 (1862), 439–441.

53. This use of religious narratives for politics also found many inspired readers among Jewish Saint-Simonians of the 1830s, who believed the "New Christianity" their movement embraced had been built on Jewish (or Mosaic) foundations; Graetz, *Jews in Nineteenth-Century France*, 133–134. Indeed, later writers sometimes understood Salvador mainly as an apostle of Saint-Simonism. See, for example, a series that Moses Hess—publishing under his Gallicized forename, Maurice—wrote for the *Archives Israélites* in 1864 under the title "Lettres sur les missions d'Israël dans l'histoire de l'humanité."

54. Georges Weill, "Les Juifs et le Saint-Simonisme," *Revue des Études Juives* 31, no. 62 (1895), 261; idem, *L'école Saint-Simonienne: son histoire, son influence jusqu'à nos jours* (Paris: F. Alcan, 1896), 2.

55. Léon Halévy, "Souvenirs de Saint-Simon," *La France littéraire* 1 (1832), 541.

56. Ruth Jordan, in her biography of Fromental Halévy, claims that Léon did not just marry a Catholic but also converted; Ruth Jordan, *Fromental Halévy: His Life & Music, 1799–1862* (New York: Limelight Editions, 1996), 43–44. Jordan gives no sources for this claim, and Diane Hallman has compellingly challenged this; Diana R. Hallman, *Opera, Liberalism, and Antisemitism in Nineteenth-Century France: The Politics of Halévy's La juive* (Cambridge, UK: Cambridge University Press, 2002), 105.

57. Eric C. Hansen, *Ludovic Halévy: A Study of Frivolity and Fatalism in Nineteenth-Century France* (Lanham, MD: University Press of America, 1987), 17–18.

58. On these works, see Aron Rodrigue, "Leon Halévy and Modern French Jewish Historiography," in *Jewish History and Jewish Memory: Essays in Honor of Yosef Hayim Yerushalmi* (Hanover, NH: University Press of New England, 1998).

59. Léon Halévy's *Résumé de l'histoire des juifs modernes* (Paris: Lecointe, 1828) was printed a year before its official publication date; see the permit of April 21, 1827, AN F/18*II/14, no. 2218.

60. Félix Bodin, *Résumé de l'histoire de France jusqu'à nos jours*, 5th ed. (Paris: Lecointe, 1823).

61. *Défense des résumés historiques* (Paris: Lecointe et Durey, 1824), 17. The anonymous pamphlet was appended to various of the publishing house's *résumés* and is frequently misattributed to the author of the main work in library catalogues.

62. Ibid., 19.

63. Ibid., 21.

64. Léon Halévy, *Résumé de l'histoire des juifs modernes* (Paris: Lecointe, 1828), vii–viii. Halévy mentions in the autobiography he wrote of his brother that their father was not directly involved in their education; Léon Halévy, *F. Halévy, sa vie et ses œuvres*, 2nd ed. (Paris: Heugel et Cie, 1863), 8.

65. AN F/18*II/12, no. 2057 and no. 5450. The histories of Russia, Brazil, or the Reformation in this series were printed in similar runs, usually of 2,000 copies.

66. Halévy, *Résumé de l'histoire des juifs anciens*, 17–18.

67. Cf. Rodrigue, "Leon Halévy," 420.

68. Frank Edward Manuel, *The New World of Henri Saint-Simon* (Cambridge, MA: Harvard University Press, 1956), 356–357, on the discussion in *Le nouveau christianisme*.

69. Crossley, *French Historians*, 117.

70. *Opinions littéraires*, 62–63.

71. The book was originally published anonymously. On its authorship, see Manuel, *Saint-Simon*, 346.

72. Léon Halévy, *Résumé de l'histoire des juifs anciens*, 2nd ed. (Paris: Lecointe et Durey, 1827), 337–338.

73. His last article in the movement's journal, *Le Producteur*, appeared in early 1826.

74. Halévy, *Résumé de l'histoire des juifs modernes*, 148.

75. Ibid., 386.

76. Weill, *L'école Saint-Simonienne,* 18 and 88. The poem was published in 1831.

77. Diane Hallman argues that similar concerns also influenced Fromenthal Halévy to focus on Jan Hus in his opera *La juive* and Giacomo Meyerbeer to use a Lutheran chorale in *Les Huguenots* (1836); Hallman, *Opera*, 136–139. Showing a similar interest, Jules Michelet published his compilation *Mémoires de Luther* in 1835.

78. Léon Halévy, *Luther: poème dramatique en 5 parties* (Paris: Dépôt central de la librairie, 1834), foreword. His *Luther* was also republished in a revised version without the foreword in the 1860s; Léon Halévy, *Martin Luther, ou La diète de Worm: drame historique en 4 actes, en vers, imité de Zacharias Werner* (Paris: A. Le Chevalier, 1866).

79. Halévy, *Luther* (1834), foreword.

80. Ibid.

81. Jean Bauberot, "Les principaux thèmes antiprotestants et la réplique protestante," *Revue d'histoire et de philosophie religieuse* 53, no. 2 (1973), 177–223.

82. See Nils Roemer's comment, in *Jewish Emancipation Reconsidered: The French and German Models*, ed. Michael Brenner, Vicki Caron, and Uri R. Kaufmann (Tübingen: Mohr Siebeck, 2003), 50. There was also a non-Jewish readership of his work; see Friedrich Wilhelm Carové, *Der Saint-Simonismus und die neuere französische Philosophie* (Leipzig: Hinrich, 1831), 68–107.

83. Joseph Salvador, *Jésus-Christ et sa doctrine: Histoire de la naissance de l'église: de son organisation et de ses progrès pendant le premier siècle* (Paris: A. Guyot et Scribe, 1838).

84. A. Weill, "Salvador," *AZJ* 3 (September 14, 1839), 471–472.

85. Eduard Gans, *Naturrecht und Universalrechtsgeschichte: Vorlesungen nach G.W.F. Hegel*, ed. Johann Braun (Tübingen: Mohr Siebeck, 2005), 299.

86. Eduard Gans, *Vermischte Schriften, juristischen, historischen Staatswissenschaftlichen und ästhetischen Inhalts* (Berlin: Duncker und Humblot, 1834), 151–159.

87. Joseph Salvador, *Geschichte der mosaischen Institutionen und des jüdischen Volks*, trans. Dr. Essena, intr. by Gabriel Riesser (Hamburg: Hoffmann und Campe, 1836), x.

88. Ibid., xiv.

89. Ibid.

90. His great-grandfather had been among the leaders of the Berlin community. Walter Grab, "Saul Ascher, ein jüdisch-deutscher Spätaufklärer zwischen Revolution und Restauration," *Jahrbuch des Instituts für Deutsche Geschichte* 6 (1977), 137.

91. Ibid., 138.

92. In German-Jewish historiography, Ascher had been nearly forgotten until Walter Grab published an article on his biography and political outlook in 1977. See ibid.; Christoph Schulte, "Saul Ascher's Leviathan, or the Invention of Jewish Orthodoxy in 1792," *LBIYB* 45 (2000), 25–34; idem, *Die jüdische Aufklärung: Philosophie, Religion, Geschichte* (Munich: Beck, 2002); and Jonathan M. Hess, *Germans, Jews and the Claims of Modernity* (New Haven, CT: Yale University Press, 2002), 137–167. On *Leviathan* and Reform Judaism, see also Ellen Littmann, "Saul Ascher: First Theorist of Progressive Judaism," *LBIYB* 5 (1960), 107–121. Toury claimed Ascher was the first Jew in the nineteenth century who produced political theory; Jacob Toury, *Die politischen Orientierungen der Juden in Deutschland: von Jena bis Weimar* (Tübingen: Mohr, 1966), 31.

93. Wolfgang Altgeld, *Katholizismus, Protestantismus, Judentum: Über religiös begründete Gegensätze und nationalreligiöse Ideen in der Geschichte des deutschen Nationalismus* (Mainz: M.-Grünewald-Verlag, 1992), 193.

94. Saul Ascher, *Ideen zur natürlichen Geschichte der politischen Revolutionen* (Kronberg/Ts.: Scriptor, 1975). The *Ideen* were suppressed because they were seen as expressing Jacobin sentiments; Grab, "Saul Ascher," 148.

95. Dw., review of *Skizzen philosophische, zur natürlichen Geschichte des Ursprungs, Fortschritts u. Verfalls der gesellschaftlichen Verfassungen*, in: *Neue allgemeine deutsche Bibliothek* 81 (1803) 1. St., 223–331. This was an alternative title of Ascher's *Ideen*.

96. Ascher, *Ideen*, 108.

97. Ibid., 139.

98. Reprint of Saul Ascher, *Napoleon oder: Über den Fortschritt der Regierung* in *Vier Flugschriften* (Berlin: Aufbau-Verlag, 1991), 81–190.

99. The pamphlet was discussed before the *décret infâme* was published with detrimental effects not just on the Jews of Alsace but also of many German states; *German-Jewish History* 2:20–21. Ascher was a supporter of the idea of a Sanhedrin; *Vier Flugschriften*, 155.

100 *Vier Flugschriften*, 153.

101. Ibid., 153–155.

102. On the centrality of new perceptions of history for German romanticism, see Theodore Ziolkowski, *Clio the Romantic Muse: Historicizing the Faculties in Germany* (Ithaca, NY: Cornell University Press, 2004).

103. Friedrich Rühs, "Ueber die Ansprüche der Juden an das deutsche Bürger-recht," *Zeitschrift für die neueste Geschichte, die Staaten- und Völkerkunde* 3 (1815), 129–161. Published in English as: Friedrich Rühs, *The Claims of the Jews for Civil Rights in Germany*, trans. Jakob Weil (Cincinnati, OH: Hebrew Union College-Jewish Institute of Religion, 1977).

104. On Rühs see Gerald Hubmann, "Völkischer Nationalismus und Antisemitismus im frühen 19. Jahrhundert: Die Schriften von Rühs und Fries zur Juden-frage," in *Antisemitismus, Zionismus, Antizionismus, 1850–1940*, ed. Renate Heuer and Ralph-Rainer Wuthenow (Frankfurt a. M.: Campus, 1997), 9–34.

105. Ascher, *Vier Flugschriften*, 197.

106. Ibid., 198.

107. Ibid.

108. Ibid., 239, 198.

109. Ibid., 204–205.

110. Ibid., 205.

111. George S. Williamson, "What Killed August von Kotzebue? The Temptations of Virtue and the Political Theology of German Nationalism, 1789–1819," *Journal of Modern History* 72, no. 4 (2000), 924 (on Fries), 942 (on Kotzebue). Kotzebue's assassin, Karl Sand, shared a dislike of Catholicism as corrupting German society with his victim; see p. 922.

112. Ibid., 918; *Literarisches Wochenblatt* 3, no. 20 (1819), 153.

113. Review of *Almanach für die israelitische Jugend auf das Jahr der Welt 5579* in *Literarisches Wochenblatt* 2, no. 12 (1818), 92–94.

114. W. von Kotzebue, *August von Kotzebue: Urtheile der Zeitgenossen und der Gegenwart* (Dresden: Baensch, 1881), 164–165, letter of February 1, 1818. See also Walter Grab, "Saul Ascher," 172.

115. "Pudenda eines Geistlichen," *Literarisches Wochenblatt* 2, no. 37 (1818), 295.

116. Saul Ascher, *Idee einer Preßfreiheit und Censurordnung: Den hohen Mitgliedern des Bundestages vorgelegt* (Leipzig: Achenwall, 1818), 27.

117. DHA, 6:103.

118. On his complex relationship to romanticism, see Herbert Clasen, *Heinrich Heines Romantikkritik: Tradition, Produktion, Rezeption* (Hamburg: Hoffmann und Campe, Heinrich-Heine-Verlag, 1979); Herbert Gutjahr, *Zwischen Affinität und Kritik: Heinrich Heine und die Romantik* (Frankfurt a. M.: P. Lang, 1984); and *Heinrich Heine und die Romantik*, ed. Markus Winkler (Tübingen: Niemeyer, 1997).

119. DHA, 10:238–248.

120. Galley/Estermann, *Heines Werk im Urteil*, 1:345–346.

121. Ibid., 354.

122. Hans-Joachim Teuchert, *August Graf von Platen in Deutschland: Zur Rezeption eines umstrittenen Autors* (Bonn: Bouvier, 1980).

123. Ibid., 34–35.

124. Heine to Moses Moser, September 6, 1828, HSA, 20:341 (no. 282). Heine made similar comments about being one-sided and choosing nobility and clergy as

enemies for tactical reasons in his later letter to Karl August Varnhagen von Ense, November 19, 1830, HSA, 20:422 (no. 357).

125. Gerhard Höhn, *Heine-Handbuch: Zeit, Person, Werk* (Stuttgart: Metzler, 1997), 249–250. The complete version was published in 1831.

126. DHA, 7/1:194.

127. DHA, 7/1:167; see Jost Hermand, *Der frühe Heine: Ein Kommentar zu Heines Reisebildern* (Munich: Winkler, 1976), 168–180. Hermand's analysis is contradictory on this point. He argues that Heine criticized Jews less than Protestants and Protestants less than Catholics (170–175); in other instances, however, he claims that they are all equally targets of Heine's criticism (168).

128. DHA, 7/1:166–167.

129. DHA, 7/1:166.

130. Ibid.

131. DHA, 7/1:175.

132. Ibid.

133. Ibid. The fact that this kiss takes place in front of a Madonna underlines that Franscheska is a personification of Catholic tradition. See Olaf Briese, "Venus–Madonna–Maria: Über Heines Marienverständnis," in *Internationaler Heine-Kongress: Aufklärung und Skepsis*, ed. Joseph A. Kruse, Bernd Witte, and Karin Füllner (Stuttgart: Metzler, 1999), 436–449, especially 441.

134. DHA, 7/1:175. The law that Heine refers to punished the theft of Church property more severely than other theft under certain circumstances. Its passing in 1825 served as the occasion for a famous anticlerical campaign in France. See Hartman, "The Sacrilege Law."

135. DHA, 7/1:175–176.

136. Heine claimed this explicitly toward the end of his life in his *Geständnisse* (1854) DHA, 15:51. On Heine's artistic appreciation of Catholicism, see Joseph A. Kruse, "'Der Dichter versteht sehr gut das symbolische Idiom der Religion': Über Heines kritisch-produktives Verhältnis zu religiösen Traditionen," *Zeitschrift für Religions- und Geistesgeschichte* 58, no. 4 (2006), 289–309.

137. On Heine's concept of secularization as the movement between different religions, see Willi Goetschel, "Heine's Critical Secularism," *boundary 2*, vol. 31, no. 2 (2004), 151. On sensualism in the *Reisebilder*, see Olaf Hildebrand, *Emanzipation und Versöhnung: Aspekte des Sensualismus im Werk Heinrich Heines unter besonderer Berücksichtigung der 'Reisebilder'* (Tübingen: Niemeyer: 2001).

138. See Galley/Estermann, *Heines Werk im Urteil*, 1:476–478, 488, 534.

139. I differ here with earlier interpretations that saw Heine's theories about priestly deception mainly in the context of an abstract political critique. Cf. Günter Oesterle, *Integration und Konflikt: die Prosa Heinrich Heines im Kontext oppositioneller Literatur der Restaurationsepoche* (Stuttgart: Metzler, 1972), especially 8–12.

140. Edgar Quinet, "De l'avenir de l'art. De l'art en Allemagne," *Revue des deux mondes* (June 1, 1832), 512–513, reprinted in *Französische Heine-Kritik* 1:82–83. Hans Hörling showed in a quantitative analysis of French reviews on Heine between 1830

and 1841 that only 0.4 percent of all reviews in major newspapers referred to Heine as Jewish; *Die französische Heine-Kritik*, ed. Hans Hörling (Stuttgart: Metzler, 1996–2002), 1:20–25; and Hans Hörling, *Heinrich Heine im Spiegel der politischen Presse Frankreichs von 1831–1841: Ansatz zu einem Modell der qualitativen und quantitativen Rezeptionsforschung* (Frankfurt a. M.: Lang, 1977), 233–240.

141. Galley/Estermann, *Heines Werk im Urteil*, 1:33.

142. *Französische Heine-Kritik*, 2:107–109.

143. *Französische Heine-Kritik*, 1:319–323.

144. *Französische Heine-Kritik*, 2:128–129.

145. Ibid.

146. For similar comments, see DHA, 6:351 and *Französische Heine-Kritik*, 1:297.

147. *L'Europe littéraire* 1, no. 4 (March 8, 1833), 17n. This sentence is also cited in DHA, 8/2:1578.

148. DHA, 8/1:493.

149. DHA, 8/2:991–992.

150. DHA, 8/1:456.

151. See DHA, 8/2:993.

152. Félicité Robert de Lamennais, *Worte des Glaubens*, trans. Ludwig Börne (Paris: Aillaud, 1834).

153. Ludwig Börne, "De l'Allemagne par Henri Heine," *Réformateur*, May 30, 1835.

154. Frank Paul Bowman, *Le Christ romantique* (Genève: Droz, 1973).

155. Isaac Pereire, *La question religieuse* (Paris: Motteroz, 1878).

156. A. Rebenstein, [pseud. of A. Bernstein], "Rationalismus im Judentum," in *Plan zu einer neuen Grundlage für die Philosophie der Geschichte: Wissenschaftlicher Versuch nebst einigen literarischen Studien* (Berlin: Natorff, 1838), 27–33.

Chapter Four

1. See Volkmar Wittmütz, "Preußen und die Kirchen im Rheinland 1815–1840," in *Preussens schwieriger Westen: rheinisch-preussische Beziehungen, Konflikte und Wechselwirkungen*, ed. Georg Mölich, Meinhard Pohl, and Veit Veltzke (Duisburg: Mercator-Verlag, 2003), 134–161.

2. See Heinrich Schrörs, *Die Kölner Wirren (1837): Studien zu ihrer Geschichte* (Berlin: Dümmler, 1927).

3. James J. Sheehan, *German Liberalism in the Nineteenth Century* (New York: Humanity Books, 1999), 41, on the willingness of liberals throughout the Vormärz to support the state against the Catholic Church.

4. Manuel Borutta, *Antikatholizismus: Deutschland und Italien im Zeitalter der europäischen Kulturkämpfe* (Göttingen: Vandenhoeck & Ruprecht, 2010), 272–273; and Schrörs, *Die Kölner Wirren*, 575–600.

5. Borutta, *Antikatholizismus*, 78–81. Catholics in the western provinces, on the other hand, did not necessarily see this as a fight against liberalism but rather one against Prussian authoritarianism and militarism; Susanne Kill, *Das Bürgertum in*

Münster 1770–1870: bürgerliche Selbstbestimmung im Spannungsfeld von Kirche und Staat (Munich: Oldenbourg, 2001), 106–114.

6. Many later conflicts in nineteenth-century Germany and France also emerged around pilgrimage sites, creating similar debates on superstition and clerical influence. See, for example, David Blackbourn, *Marpingen: Apparitions of the Virgin Mary in Nineteenth-Century Germany* (New York: Knopf, 1994); and Ruth Harris, *Lourdes: Body and Spirit in the Secular Age* (New York: Penguin Compass, 1999).

7. Georges Weill, *Histoire de l'idée laïque en France au XIXe siècle* (Paris: Hachette, 2004), 113–131.

8. Caroline Ford, *Divided Houses: Religion and Gender in Modern France* (Ithaca, NY: Cornell University Press, 2005); and René Rémond, *L'anticléricalisme en France de 1815 à nos jours* (Paris: Fayard, 1976), 68–69.

9. Jules Michelet, *Le prêtre, la femme et la famille* (Paris: C. Lévy, 1878), first published 1845. The work was instantly translated into English as *Priests, Women and Families*, trans. C. Cocks (London: Longman, Brown, Green, and Longmans, 1845). Michelet's gendered vision of social romanticism also appeared in several other works published around the same time. See Arthur Mitzman, "Michelet and Social Romanticism: Religion, Revolution, Nature," *Journal of the History of Ideas* 57, no. 4 (1996), 659–682.

10. Stephen A. Kippur, *Jules Michelet, a Study of Mind and Sensibility* (Albany: SUNY Press, 1981), 96–97.

11. See Róisín Healy, "Anti-Jesuitism in Imperial Germany: The Jesuit as Androgyne," in *Protestants, Catholics and Jews in Germany, 1800–1914,* ed. Helmut Walser Smith (Oxford, UK: Berg, 2001), 153–181, on the implications of this ambivalence.

12. On the notion of Jesuitism, see Geoffrey Cubitt, *The Jesuit Myth: Conspiracy Theory and Politics in Nineteenth Century France* (New York: Oxford University Press, 1993), 275–294.

13. Michelet, *Le prêtre*, 8.

14. Ibid., 14.

15. Ibid., 315–324.

16. See Jens Neumann-Schliski, *Konfession oder Stamm? Konzepte jüdischer Identität bei Redakteuren jüdischer Zeitschriften 1840 bis 1881 im internationalen Vergleich* (Bremen: Edition Lumière, 2011); Simone Lässig, *Jüdische Wege ins Bürgertum: kulturelles Kapital und sozialer Aufstieg im 19. Jahrhundert* (Göttingen: Vandenhoeck & Ruprecht, 2004), 445–504; and Jan Schwartz, "The Origins and the Development of German-Jewish Press in Germany till 1850, Reflections on the Transformation of the German-Jewish Public Sphere in Bourgeois Society," printed lecture from the 66th general conference of the International Federation of Library Associations and Institutions, Jerusalem, 2000; available at www.ifla.org/IV/ifla66/papers/106–144e.htm. On later periods, see Barbara Suchy, "Die jüdische Presse im Kaiserreich und in der Weimarer Republik," in *Juden als Träger bürgerlicher Kultur in Deutschland*, ed. Julius Schoeps (Stuttgart: Burg Verlag, 1989), 167–191.

17. Michael A. Meyer, *Response to Modernity: A History of the Reform Movement in Judaism* (Detroit, MI: Wayne State University Press, 1995), ch. 3. I do not capitalize the word *reform* here to indicate that in this period it had not yet become a unified movement.

18. See, for example, Lässig, *Jüdische Wege*, who analyzes the changing economic and social fortunes of European Jews during this period in detail; Jacob Toury, *Soziale und politische Geschichte der Juden in Deutschland, 1847–1871: zwischen Revolution, Reaktion und Emanzipation* (Düsseldorf: Droste, 1977), 100–118; and Paula Hyman, *The Jews of Modern France* (Berkeley: University of California Press, 1998), 62–63.

19. Lässig, *Jüdische Wege*, 445–504. On Jews and the scholarship on the middle classes, see Till van Rahden, "Von der Eintracht zur Vielfalt: Juden in der Geschichte des deutschen Bürgertums," in *Juden, Bürger, Deutsche: zur Geschichte von Vielfalt und Differenz 1800–1933* (Tübingen: Mohr, 2001), 9–31. Terms such as *forum* are meant to suggest a less isolated and hermetic situation than that implied by the term *subculture*. On the latter, see David J. Sorkin, *The Transformation of German Jewry, 1780–1840* (New York: Oxford University Press, 1987).

20. On Mannheim, see Dagmar Herzog, *Intimacy and Exclusion: Religious Politics in Pre-Revolutionary Baden* (Princeton, NJ: Princeton University Press, 1996), 111–139. On these groups more generally, see Jörn Brederlow, *"Lichtfreunde" und "Freie Gemeinden": religiöser Protest und Freiheitsbewegung im Vormärz und in der Revolution von 1848/49* (Munich: Oldenbourg, 1976); and Peter Bahn, *Deutschkatholiken und Freireligiöse: Geschichte und Kultur einer religiös-weltanschaulichen Dissidentengruppe, dargestellt am Beispiel der Pfalz* (Mainz: Gesellschaft für Volkskunde in Rheinland-Pfalz, 1991).

21. The letter of October 1, 1844, is reprinted in Friedrich Wilhelm Graf, *Die Politisierung des religiösen Bewusstseins: die bürgerlichen Religionsparteien im deutschen Vormärz, das Beispiel des Deutschkatholizismus* (Stuttgart-Bad Cannstadt: Frommann-Holzboog, 1978), 196–199.

22. On the formation of the *Deutschkatholiken*, see Andreas Holzem, *Kirchenreform und Sektenstiftung: Deutschkatholiken, Reformkatholiken und Ultramontane am Oberrhein (1844–1866)* (Paderborn: Schöningh, 1994).

23. On the political aspects of the movement, see Graf, *Politisierung*; G. A. Kertesz, "A Rationalist Heresy as a Political Model: The Deutschkatholiken of the 1840s, the Democratic Movement and the Moderate Liberals," *Journal of Religious History* [Australia] 13, no. 4 (1985), 355–369; and Hans Rosenberg, "Theologischer Rationalismus und vormärzlicher Vulgärliberalismus," *Historische Zeitschrift* 141, no. 3 (1930), 497–541, esp. 529–537.

24. Frank Eyck, "Liberalismus und Katholizismus in der Zeit des deutschen Vormärz," in *Liberalismus in der Gesellschaft des deutschen Vormärz*, ed. Wolfgang Schieder (Göttingen: Vandenhoeck & Ruprecht, 1983), 133–146. According to some scholars, it also contributed to the utopian language of the revolutionaries of 1848. See Michaela Tomaschewsky, "Dress Rehearsal for 1848: Johannes Ronge and the German Catholic Movement," *Consortium on Revolutionary Europe 1750–1850: Se-*

lected Papers (1994), 116–122. This pattern resembles that of the French left: Edward Berenson, *Populist Religion and Left-Wing Politics in France, 1830–1852* (Princeton, NJ: Princeton University Press, 1984).

25. On Auerbach's life, see Anton Bettelheim, *Berthold Auerbach: der Mann, sein Werk, sein Nachlass* (Stuttgart: Cotta, 1907); and Sorkin, *Transformation of German Jewry*, 140–155.

26. Berthold Auerbach, *Briefe an seinen Freund Jakob Auerbach: Ein biographisches Denkmal* (Frankfurt a. M: Rütten & Loening, 1884), 53.

27. In his commemorative speech for Auerbach, Eduard Lasker suggested that the Deutschkatholiken were an inspiration for Auerbach's anticlerical story "Luzifer," which he wrote shortly after his letter to Jacob Auerbach; Eduard Lasker, *Berthold Auerbach: eine Gedenkrede, gehalten im Grossen Berliner Handwerkerverein am 4. März 1882* (Berlin: Auerbach, 1882), 19.

28. Letter to D. Honigmann, Breslau, March 19, 1845, Abraham Geiger, *Nachgelassene Schriften*, ed. Ludwig Geiger (Berlin: Gerschel, 1878), 5:177–178.

29. Ibid.

30. Meyer, *Response to Modernity*; and Samuel Holdheim, *Geschichte der Entstehung und Entwickelung der jüdischen Reformgemeinde in Berlin im Zusammenhang mit den jüdischreformatorischen Gesammtbestrebungen der Neuzeit* (Berlin: J. Springer, 1857). For a recent survey of the Reformgemeinde, see Simone Ladwig-Winters, *Freiheit und Bindung: zur Geschichte der Jüdischen Reformgemeinde zu Berlin von den Anfängen bis zu ihrem Ende 1939*, ed. Peter Galliner (Teetz: Hentrich & Hentrich, 2004).

31. Graf, *Politisierung*, 96–119. The Deutschkatholiken also had a strong presence in Berlin and an impact on organized secularism in the city. See Todd Weirr, *Secularism and Religion in Nineteenth-Century Germany: The Fourth Confession* (New York: Cambridge Univeristy Press, forthcoming).

32. Markus Salomonides Krüger, *Bedenken gegen die neusten Reformbestrebungen im Judenthume* (Berlin: A. Schepeler, 1845); Eduard Kley, *Noch ein Wort zur israelitischen Reformfrage: Eine Stimme aus dem Volke, vielleicht auch eine Stimme in der Wüste* (Hamburg: Vogel, 1845); and the examples in the following discussion.

33. "Berlin, im Februar 1845," *Der Israelit des 19. Jahrhunderts* 6 (March 16, 1845), 88.

34. Ω, "Stern's Vorlesungen und die Kapuzinaden von Sachs," *Der Israelit des 19. Jahrhunderts* 6 (Apr. 13, 1845), 117. On Sachs, see Franz D. Lucas and Heike Frank, *Michael Sachs: der konservative Mittelweg: Leben und Werk des Berliner Rabbiners zur Zeit der Emanzipation* (Tübingen: Mohr, 1992).

35. "Die ersten Regungen einer deutsch-jüdischen Kirche," *Der Orient* 6, no. 16 (April 16, 1845), 128–132.

36. Ibid., 128.

37. "Breslau, 27. Sptbr.," *Der Orient* 6 (October 8, 1845), 321–322.

38. Ibid.

39. "Breslau, 8. April" *Der Orient* 6 (April 23, 1845), 132. For similar arguments, see "Reformen im Judenthum," *Der Israelit des 19. Jahrhunderts* 6 (June 8, 1845), 181–182.

40. *Der Orient* 6 (April 23, 1845), 132.

41. Meyer, *Response to Modernity*, 129.

42. "Die hallenser und marburger Lichtfreunde," *AZJ* 10 (October 26, 1846), 637–640; Ludwig Philippson, *Die Entwickelung der religiösen Idee im Judenthume, Christenthume und Islam* (Leipzig: Baumgartners Buchhandlung, 1847), 163–166. Philippson's lectures of 1847 were also published abroad. They were translated into French as Ludwig Philippson, *Le développement de l'idée religieuse dans le judaïsme, le christianisme et l'islamisme*, trans. L. Lévy-Bing (Paris: Lévy frères, 1856). They also appeared in English and Italian in the 1850s.

43. Ein Candidat der jüdischen Theologie, *Eine deutsch-jüdische Kirche die nächste Aufgabe unserer Zeit* (Leipzig: Wigand, 1845). Herzog (*Intimacy*, 211n122) claims that the work was probably written by Stern. Her argument is based on an article by the author defending his text, -n. "Aus Preußen," *Der Israelit des 19. Jahrhunderts* 6 (July 6, 1845), 210–211. Given that some other names also end with the letter *n*, this remains only a weak indication of Stern's authorship. Stern had published on his general project under his real name for years by this point and had just given a public lecture on the topic. It is unclear to me why he would hide behind a pseudonym, particularly one that would have implied a lower social standing.

44. Ibid., 5.

45. Ibid., 5–6.

46. Ibid., 20.

47. Ibid., 9. See also comments about Jewish women and their inate interiority and emotionalism in the draft program prepared by the Frankfurt Association in 1842; *Zur Judenfrage in Deutschland* 1 (1843), 263–264.

48. Ein Candidat, *Eine deutsch-jüdische Kirche*, 22.

49. "Reformen im Judenthum," *Der Israelit des 19. Jahrhunderts* 6 (June 8, 1845), 181–182. It should be noted that criticism of the term *Kirche* was not common among contemporary commentators. On the contrary, the fact that some bureaucrats seemed to avoid the term *Kirche* when referring to Jews was not so much a sign of respect for Judaism but of their unwillingness to give Jewish institutions equal treatment. See, for example, *Zur Judenfrage in Deutschland* 1 (1843), 120.

50. See, for example, Wilhelm Freund in "Unser Streben," *Zur Judenfrage in Deutschland* 2 (1844), 1–6, who also demands that Jews reject rabbinic "orientalism" to become more German; and S. Stern, "Die Aufgabe der jüdischen Gemeinde zu Berlin für die Gegenwart," *Zur Judenfrage in Deutschland* 2 (1844), 26–41.

51. Certain authors were willing to recognize that Jews and Catholics faced similar challenges on the question of intermarriage, but the comparisons they offered in this regard were cautious. See, for example, Samuel Hirsch, *Die Religionsphilosophie der Juden oder das Prinzip der jüdischen Religionsanschauung und sein Verhältnis zum Heidentum, Christentum und zur absoluten Philosophie* (Hildesheim: Georg Olms

Verlag, 1986 [1842]), vii; Samuel Hirsch, *Das Judenthum der christliche Staat und die moderne Kritik: Briefe zur Beleuchtung der Judenfrage von Bruno Bauer* (Leipzig: H. Hunger, 1843), 99; and Samuel Holdheim, *Das Religiöse und Politische im Judenthum* (Schwerin: C. Kürschner, 1845), 70.

52. Jacob Katz, "The Term 'Jewish Emancipation': Its Origin and Historical Impact," in *Studies in Nineteenth-Century Jewish Intellectual History*, ed. Alexander Altmann (Cambridge, MA: Harvard University Press, 1964), 1–25.

53. On his life, see Arthur Galliner, *Sigismund Stern: Der Reformator und der Pädagoge* (Frankfurt a. M.: Englert und Schlosser, 1930); "Stern, Sigismund," *Encyclopaedia Judaica*, 2nd ed. (Detroit, MI: Macmillan Reference USA, 2007), 19:217; Salomon Wininger, *Grosse jüdische National-Biographie* (Cernauti: Orient, 1925–1936), 6:23; and Meyer, *Response to Modernity*, 125–129.

54. Meyer, *Response to Modernity*, 119–131, describes this as the "revolt of the radical laity."

55. "Aktenstücke des Frankfurter Reform-Vereins," in *Die Judenfrage in Deutschland vom Standpunkte des Rechts und der Gewissensfreiheit* (1843), 257–265.

56. Sigismund Stern, "Das Judenthum als Element des Staats-Organismus," in *Die Judenfrage in Deutschland* (1843), 125–165.

57. When Stern did allude to the French system, in fact, such as in his "Die Aufgabe der jüdischen Gemeinde," he did so only to explain that French and German Jews were utterly different in both their organization and fundamental characteristics (pp. 27–28).

58. *Die Judenfrage in Deutschland* 1 (1843), 153, 158.

59. Klaus Herrmann, "Die jüdische Reformbewegung zwischen Protestantismus und Katholizismus," in *Katholizismus und Judentum: Gemeinsamkeiten und Verwerfungen vom 16. bis zum 20. Jahrhundert*, ed. Florian Schuller, Giuseppe Veltri, and Hubert Wolf (Regensburg: Pustet, 2005), 222–240.

60. On the popularity of the lectures and Stern's diverse audience, which included many women and non-Jews, see Ω, "Berlin," *Der Israelit des 19. Jahrhunderts* 6 (February 23, 1845), 61–62; Ω, "Berlin, im Februar 1845," *Der Israelit des 19. Jahrhunderts* 6 (March 16, 1845), 87–88; and "Berlin, 28. Decbr. 1845," *Der Orient* 7 (January 15, 1846), 13–14.

61. Clark, "The 'Christian' State."

62. Sigismund Stern, *Das Judenthum und der Jude im christlichen Staat (Vorlesung gehalten in Berlin am 26. Februar und auf Verlangen wiederholt am 15. März 1845)* (Berlin: Buchhandlung des Berliner Lesecabinets, 1845), 24. This is the separate publication of his sixth lecture. Other parts of the lecture are cited from the published version of his whole lecture.

63. Stern, *Das Judenthum*, 25.

64. Sigismund Stern, *Die Aufgabe des Judenthums und des Juden in der Gegenwart*, 2nd ed. (Berlin: W. Adolf, 1853), 58.

65. Ibid., 10.

66. Ibid., 11, 12. The question of the role of the state was a central concern of both reformers and the proponents of the Science of Judaism. See Rachel Livné-Freudenthal, "Der 'Verein für Cultur und Wissenschaft der Juden' (1819–1824) zwischen Staatskonformismus und Staatskritik," *Tel Aviver Jahrbuch für Deutsche Geschichte* 20 (1991), 103–126.

67. While Stern's "Protestantizing" tendencies have been noted in the past, scholars have generally glossed over their potential implications as a form of boundary making vis-à-vis Catholicism. See, for example, Ralph Bisschops, "Samuel Holdheim and Sigismund Stern: The Clash between the Dogmatic and Historicist Approach in Classical German Reform Judaism," in *Redefining Judaism in an Age of Emancipation: Comparative Perspectives on Samuel Holdheim (1806–1860)*, ed. Christian Wiese (Leiden: Brill, 2007), 241–277. Stern was careful to stay within the logic of the dynastic state, avoiding the claim that a German-Jewish national church (unlike a Prussian-Jewish national church) was feasible at the time; Stern, *Die Aufgabe*, 289–290. Others had ideas about founding a "Jewish Church" [*Israelitische Kirche*], which was to be granted its authority by the German Confederation, yet those proposals proved to be politically unrealistic and impracticable. See, for example, "Entwurf eines israelitischen Kirchenrechts," *AZJ* 8 (September 9, 1844), 513–517.

68. Meyer, *Response to Modernity*, 125–126.

69. Ibid.

70. Michaelis, *Rechtsverhältnisse*, 277–278.

71. Annegret H. Brammer, *Judenpolitik und Judengesetzgebung in Preussen 1812 bis 1847: mit einem Ausblick auf das Gleichberechtigungsgesetz des Norddeutschen Bundes von 1869* (Berlin: Schelzky & Jeep, 1987), 278.

72. Holdheim, *Geschichte der Entstehung*, 30.

73. On religious language in politics, see Berenson, *Populist Religion*. The small evangelical movement that existed within the two Protestant churches in France remained outside the purview of most Jews until the 1850s and, even then, became interesting as political allies rather than religious models.

74. On the affair and its developments, see Jonathan Frankel, *The Damascus Affair: "Ritual Murder," Politics, and the Jews in 1840* (Cambridge, UK: Cambridge University Press, 1997); and Ronald Florence, *Blood Libel: The Damascus Affair of 1840* (Madison: University of Wisconsin Press, 2004).

75. Lisa Moses Leff, *Sacred Bonds of Solidarity: The Rise of Jewish Internationalism in Nineteenth-Century France* (Stanford, CA: Stanford University Press, 2006), 120–125.

76. Adolphe Crémieux, for example, argued: "Christians are starting to feel the consequences of their influence in these regions [of the Orient]; and behold, the prejudices of the Occident awaken in the Orient!"; "Horrible accusation contre les Juifs de Damas," *AI* 1 (March 1840), 170. Crémieux's letter was also discussed in Germany. See "Damaskus," *Der Orient* 1 (April 25, 1840), 125–128.

77. On his *Catéchisme du culte judaïque* (Metz: Gerson-Lévy, 1818), see Jay R. Berkovitz, *Rites and Passages: The Beginnings of Modern Jewish Culture in France,*

1650–1860 (Philadelphia: University of Pennsylvania Press, 2004), 219–220. On Lambert's role in the Rabbinical Seminary, see Jean Daltroff, "Écoles rabbiniques et séminaires théologiques dans la seconde moitié du XIXe siècle: Un pont ou un fossé entre la France et l'Allemagne?" *Kirchliche Zeitgeschichte* 14, no. 2 (2001), 373–388.

78. Lion Mayer Lambert, *Précis de l'histoire des Hébreux, depuis le patriarche Abraham jusqu'en 1840* (Paris: Créhange, 1840).

79. Ibid., 405.

80. Ibid., 417.

81. Ibid., 406–407.

82. Ibid., 421.

83. Ibid., 423.

84. Ibid., 424.

85. On paranoid politics, see Richard Hofstadter, "The Paranoid Style in American Politics," in *The Paranoid Style in American Politics and Other Essays* (New York: Knopf, 1964), 3–40; for such a political rhetoric in regard to anti-Jesuitism, see Geoffrey Cubitt, *The Jesuit Myth: Conspiracy Theory and Politics in Nineteenth Century France* (New York: Oxford University Press, 1993).

86. On his biography, see Sabine Decup, "Fabius, Auguste," in *Dictionnaire du monde religieux dans la France contemporaine*, ed. Jean-Marie Mayeur and Yves-Marie Hilaire (Paris: Beauchesne, 1995), 6:176. On the Lyon Jewish community more generally, see François Delpech, "La seconde communtauté juive de Lyon (1775–1870)," in *Sur les Juifs: Etudes d'histoire contemporaine* (Lyon: Presses Universitaires de Lyon, 1983), 147–159.

87. Letter from S. Cahen to Central Consistory, Paris, January 5, 1843. Jewish Theological Seminary, FJC, box 19, no dossier, p. 810, seen as a microfilm, CAHJP HM2/4177.

88. See the letters between the Consistoire Centrale and the Consistoire of Marseille, January 8, 1843 and January 25, 1843, in AN F19 11036/j.

89. "Outrages publics à la religion de la majorité des Français par un prédicateur Juif," *Univers religieux* 11 (April 6, 1843).

90. Note on paper with letterhead of Ministre de la Justice et des Cultes, n.d., AN F19 11036/j. Jay R. Berkovitz, *The Shaping of Jewish Identity in Nineteenth-Century France* (Detroit: Wayne State University Press, 1989), 237, attributes this turn toward anti-Christian polemics to the increasing proselytism of Christians. Although this is possible, all of the evidence I have seen suggests that Fabius was primarily concerned with the Damascus affair.

91. Ibid., 23. It is unclear whether Fabius's position on the subject was his independent creation, based on his reading of Lambert, or an adaptation from rumors to which both Jewish authors might have been exposed.

92. August Rohling, *Der Talmudjude: zur Beherzigung für Juden und Christen aller Stände*, 4th ed. (Münster: Adolph Russell, 1872), 27 and 31n55. The French translation of the same work made even more of Fabius's role in fomenting anti-Catholicism; August Rohling, *Le juif selon le Talmud* (Paris: Albert Savine, 1889),

where a long footnote on pp. 218–219 also claims that Jews commonly employed anti-Jesuitism and that Fabius had not come up with the idea on his own. See also Hermann Scharff von Scharffenstein, *Das geheime Treiben: der Einfluss und die Macht des Judenthums in Frankreich seit hundert Jahren (1771–1871)*, 2nd ed. (Stuttgart: Killinger, 1872), 52–66, which noted Fabius's accusations against the Jesuits, 56–57; Constantin Cholewa von Pawlikowski, *Eine Christen-Antwort auf die Judenfrage* (Vienna: In Kommission bei Mayer & Co, 1859), 53–59, 56, also cites the accusation against Jesuits.

93. On the trials: Josef Kopp, *Zur Judenfrage nach den Akten Prozesses Rohling-Bloch* (Leipzig: Klinkhardt, 1886), 37–39; and *Pressprozess Doktor Brunner-Ignaz Kuranda*, ed. Wenzel August Neumann (Vienna: Mayer, 1860), 38, 52. In the earlier trial from 1860, the lawyer for the Jewish defendant seemed to imply that a person by the name of Fabius might have never existed (p. 52). On the Consistory's reactions to an inquiry from Rabbi Bloch in Austria: Hebrew Union College Library, Cincinnati, French Miscellanea Collection, box 4, folder 9/b, Declaration of Consistoire Central des Israélites de France of May 16, 1884.

94. Graetz, *Jews*, 194–248.

95. Philippe-Éfraïm Landau, "Olry Terquem (1782–1862): Régénérer les juifs et réformer le judaïsme," *Revue des Études Juives* 160, no. 1–2 (2001), 169–187; Berkovitz, *Shaping*, 234; and Thomas Kselman, "Turbulent Souls in Modern France: Jewish Conversion and the Terquem Affair," *Historical Reflections/Réflexions historiques* 32, no. 1 (2006), 83–104. Kselman offers the most detailed analysis of the Terquem case to date.

96. Parts of my analysis here have previously appeared in Ari Joskowicz, "The Priest, the Woman, and the Jewish Family: Gender and Conversion Fears in 1840s France," *Jewish Quarterly Review* 101, no. 3 (Summer 2011), 439–457.

97. AN F/19/11025, dossier 2.

98. Ibid.; Lazard Terquem, *Guide du posthétomiste ou mohel, avec l'exposé d'un nouveau procédé pour le second acte de l'opération religieuse des Israëlites, dite circoncision* (Metz: Gerson-Lévy et Alcan, 1843).

99. "Attentat audacieux de deux apostats," *AI* 6 (April 1845), 308.

100. On Olry Terquem, see Landau, "Olry Terquem"; and Berkovitz, *Rites and Passages*, 153–157.

101. Archives municipales de Metz, Tables decénnales, vol. 19.

102. *AI* 6 (June 1845), 454.

103. *AI* 6 (1845), 453–459; Olry Terquem, *Lettre adressée à M. le président et à MM. les membres du Consistoire du département de la Seine au sujet du baptême conféré à son frère, le Dr L. Terquem, 'in articulo mortis'* (Metz: impr. de J. Mayer-Samuel, 1845); and Olry Terquem, *Extrait des "Archives israélites de France," numéro de juin 1845: Lettre à M. l'abbé Ratisbonne, chanoine honoraire* (Paris: impr. de Wittersheim, n.d.). In the following notes, references are to the reprints in the *Archives israélites*, which are more widely available.

104. *AI* 6 (June 1845), 454.

105. Olry himself also lived in a bidenominational household. Once his mother died, Olry married a Catholic, Estelle Gouchon, on September 1, 1824 in Montrouge. The couple already had three children by this time, one of whom had the middle name Marie; Landau, "Olry Terquem," 175.

106. Ibid., 456.

107. Ibid., 455.

108. Ibid., 311.

109. *AI* 6 (April 1845), 310.

110. *AI* 6 (June 1845), 473.

111. Ibid.

112. Ibid., 474. Lazard's son Jules Terquem eventually converted to Catholicism on December 22, 1849. See Archives Historiques de l'Archevêché de Paris, Registre des abjurations 4°rE–6 1807–1878, no. 754.

113. Ben Lévy, "Réaction ultramontaine," *AI* 5 (June 1844), 380–384; and Simon Bloch, "Exposé," *UI* 1 (1844), 2.

114. *UI* 1 (Mar. 1845), 126.

115. See, for example, G. Ben-Lévi, "Œuvre de Notre-Dame de Sion," *AI* 6 (August 1845), 680.

116. G., "Mort de M. le Docteur Terquem," *AI* 6 (Mar. 1845), 189–191. I am presuming here that the abbreviation "G." stands for the long-term contributor of the *Archives*, Gérson-Lévy. Gérson-Lévy and Lazard Terquem were together on the administrative board of the seminary, and both taught there; "Etat de Situation de l'Ecole rabbinique de Metz, au 31 Mars 1831," AN F/19/11025, dossier 2. On Gerson-Lévy, see Berkovitz, *Shaping*, 131–132.

117. Michelet's complex relationship to sexuality, motherhood, and the image of woman has been the subject of various works. See Thérèse Moreau, *Le sang de l'histoire: Michelet, l'histoire et l'idée de la femme au XIXe siècle* (Paris: Flammarion, 1982); Linda Orr, *Jules Michelet: Nature, History, and Language* (Ithaca, NY: Cornell University Press, 1976), 74–93; and Jeanne Calo, *La création de la femme chez Michelet* (Paris: Nizet, 1975).

118. Ford, *Divided House*, shows that the idea of abduction was a much older theme in anticlerical polemics. It did not become central to Jewish–Catholic relations until 1858, however.

119. *AI* 6 (March 1845), 189. On Jewish education efforts for girls in reaction to the targeting of Jewish girls and women by proselytizers, see Berkovitz, *Shaping*, 232–236. Discussions about the importance of educating girls and women had started before the affair with the emergence of romantic ideas of sentimental religiosity in the early 1800s.

120. *AI* 6 (May 1845), 363.

121. *AI* 6 (May 1845), 365

122. Todd M. Endelman, "Gender and Radical Assimilation in Modern Jewish History," in *Gendering the Jewish Past*, ed. Marc Lee Raphael (Williamsburg, VA: Dept. of Religion, The College of William and Mary, 2002), 25–40; and Todd M. Endelman, "Gender and Conversion Revisited," in *Gender and Jewish History*, ed. Marion A. Kaplan and Deborah Dash Moore (Bloomington: Indiana University Press, 2010), 170–186.

123. For a further analysis of the registries, see Joskowicz, "The Priest."

124. My numbers differ from those mentioned by Thomas Kselman in "Turbulent Souls," 89. The most detailed analysis of conversion numbers can be found in Philippe Landau, "Se convertir à Paris au XIXe siècle," *Archives Juives* 35, no. 1 (2002), 27–43. Landau notes that 48 percent of all adult converts to Catholicism in the Archdiocese of Paris between 1807 and 1914 were women (p. 30).

125. This includes all people listed as older than eighteen.

126. See Julie Kalman, "The Unyielding Wall: Jews and Catholics in Restoration and July Monarchy France," *French Historical Studies* 26, no. 4 (2003), 661–686; and idem, *Rethinking Antisemitism in Nineteenth-Century France* (New York: Cambridge University Press, 2010), 46–89.

127. We know very little about the private motivations that drove this conversion. See, for example, Simone Mrejen-O'Hana, "Isaac-Jacob Adolphe Crémieux, Avocat, homme politique, président du Consistoire central et de l'Alliance israélite universelle. (Nîmes, 30 avril 1796–Paris, 10 février 1880)," *Archives Juives* 36, no. 36 (2003), 44–45.

128. See "Est-il utile d'éliminer des fonctions consistoriales les Israélites qui ont des enfants étrangers à notre religion?" *AI* 6 (September 1845), 699–706.

129. See Leff, *Sacred Bonds*, for such an argument regarding Jewish internationalism.

130. "Exposé," *UI* 1 (April 1844), 1–5; and Berkovitz, *Shaping*, 129–130.

131. "Mort du docteur Terquem," *UI* 1 (February 1845), 52.

132. Simon Bloch, "Les jésuites, l'université et la synagogue," *UI* 2 (July 1845), 173–180; *UI* 2 (August 1845), 249–254; *UI* 2 (August 1845), 281–283.

133. On the debates on these reforms among Jews, see Phyllis Cohen Albert, *The Modernization of French Jewry: Consistory and Community in the Nineteenth Century* (Hanover, NH: Brandeis University Press, distributed by University Press of New England, 1977), 66–77.

134. Ibid., 282.

135. Ibid.

136. Ibid., 284. The original distinction from the eighteenth century concerning Jews' position in society was offered by the German legal scholar Johann Ulrich von Cramer. See Jacob Katz, *Out of the Ghetto: The Social Background of Jewish Emancipation* (Cambridge, MA: Harvard University Press, 1973), 16.

137. Bloch, "Les jésuites, l'université et la synagogue," 283.

138. Ibid., 284.

139. Ibid., 286.

140. See also review of A. H. Arnoud, *Les Jésuites: histoire, types, mœurs, mystères,* *AI* 6 (August 1845), 688–689; "Jésuites polonais," *AI* 6 (July 1845), 563–566; and *UI* 2 (August 1845), 334–335.

141. Benjamin Maria Baader, *Gender, Judaism, and Bourgeois Culture in Germany, 1800–1870* (Bloomington: Indiana University Press, 2006); and Lässig, *Jüdische Wege*, 326–61; for the later period, see Marion Kaplan, *The Making of the Jewish Middle Class: Women, Family, and Identity in Imperial Germany* (New York: Oxford University Press, 1991). Some of the results of recent research on the topic have also appeared in *Deutsch-jüdische Geschichte als Geschlechtergeschichte: Studien zum 19. und 20. Jahrhundert*, ed. Kirsten Heinsohn and Stefanie Schüler-Springorum (Göttingen: Wallstein, 2006). On France, see Paula Hyman, *The Emancipation of the Jews of Alsace: Acculturation and Tradition in the Nineteenth Century* (New Haven, CT: Yale University Press, 1991), 50–63; Paula E. Hyman, "The Modern Jewish Family: Image and Reality," in *The Jewish Family: Metaphor and Memory*, ed. David Charles Kraemer (New York: Oxford University Press, 1989), 179–93; and Jennifer I. Sartori, "'Wanted: A Jewish Governess': The Education of Middle-Class Jewish Girls in Nineteenth-Century Paris," *Proceedings of the Annual Meeting of the Western Society for French History* 25 (1999), 24–34.

142. Isaïe Bédarride, *Du prosélytisme et de la liberté religieuse ou le judaïsme au milieu des cultes chrétien dans l'état actuel de la civilisation* (Paris: Michel Lévy Frères, 1875), 46, 47–48.

143. See, for example, "L'église juive allemande," *UI* 2 (1845), 57–63, which mocks the "Protestant Judaism" created in the new *"église juive-allemand"* [German-Jewish Church]. Berkovitz, *Rites and Passages*, 211, at one point contrasts "progressive and conservative traditionalists."

144. "Paris, im April," *AZJ* 9 (April 21, 1845), 253–254; "Paris, 1. Juni," *AZJ* 9 (June 16, 1845), 367–368; "Paris, 7. September," *AZJ* 9 (September 22, 1845), 592–593; and *AZJ* 9 (June 16, 1845), 367.

145. When such cases were reported in Catholic regions of Germany, they led to similar attacks against "Jesuitism" as those that commonly surfaced in France; see "München," *Der Orient* 4 (February 21, 1843), 60.

146. Christopher M. Clark, *The Politics of Conversion: Missionary Protestantism and the Jews in Prussia, 1728–1941* (Oxford, UK, and New York: Clarendon Press and Oxford University Press, 1995), 151–154.

Chapter Five

1. On the situation in Paris, see Victor Debuchy, *La vie à Paris pendant le siège 1870–1871* (Paris: Harmattan, 1999).

2. S. Bloch, "1870," *UI* 26 (January 15, 1871), 196. Joseph Lémann (1836–1915) and Augustin Lémann (1836–1909) were twins who had converted from Judaism to Catholicism in 1854. They were famous for their missionary efforts among Jews. The italics are in the original.

3. "Mutter und Tochter," *IWS* 2 (January 25, 1871), 25–26; and *IWS* 2 (February 8, 1871), 41–42.

4. For a survey of German Jewish reactions to the war, see Christine G. Krüger, *"Sind wir denn nicht Brüder?" Deutsche Juden im nationalen Krieg 1870/71* (Paderborn: Ferdinand Schöningh, 2006).

5. Christine G. Krüger, "'Weil nun der Kampf der Völker die jüdischen Bruch-stücke gegeneinander schleudert . . .' Die deutsch-jüdische Öffentlichkeit im Krieg von 1870/71," *Geschichte und Gesellschaft* 31 (2005), 168.

6. *AI* 31 (August 15, 1870), 483.

7. *AI* 31 (August 15, 1870), 487–488; and *AI* 31 (September 1, 1870), 518.

8. S. Rosenthal, "De coté et d'autre," *AI* 31 (October 15, 1870), 615

9. "Eine neue Befreiung," *AZJ* 34 (September 20, 1870), 738.

10. On France, see Paula Hyman, *The Jews of Modern France* (Berkeley: University of California Press, 1998), 53–76; and Phyllis Cohen Albert, *The Modernization of French Jewry: Consistory and Community in the Nineteenth Century* (Hanover, NH: University Press of New England, 1977), 20–23. On Germany, see Jacob Toury, *Soziale und politische Geschichte der Juden in Deutschland, 1847–1871: zwischen Revolution, Reaktion und Emanzipation* (Düsseldorf: Droste, 1977) 100–118; and Simone Lässig, *Jüdische Wege ins Bürgertum: kulturelles Kapital und sozialer Aufstieg im 19. Jahrhundert* (Göttingen: Vandenhoeck & Ruprecht, 2004).

11. "Die Israeliten im Kirchenstaate," *Israelitische Annalen* 2 (January 3, 1840), 2–3; and *Israelitische Annalen* 2 (January 10, 1840), 13–15, translated and published in France as "Les israélites dans les états du Pape," *AI* 1 (February 1840), 84–86 and *AI* 1 (March 1840), 151–154. More optimistic: "Kirchenstaat: Allgemeine Verhältnisse und Beispiele dazu," *Israelitische Annalen* 3 (November 19, 1840), 370–372.

12. *Der Orient* 8 (June 18, 1847), 200; and "Installation du grand-rabbin de Rome," *AI* 8 (October 1847), 810–812; on Pius IX in his early years, see Owen Chadwick, *A History of the Popes, 1830–1914* (Oxford, UK, and New York: Clarendon Press and Oxford University Press, 1998), 61–94.

13. "Ferrara, Aug." *Der Orient* 7 (September 10, 1846), 292; and *UI* 4 (July 1847), 111.

14. "À Pie IX," *AI* 8 (November 1847), 882.

15. "Émancipation des israélites italiens," *AI* 9 (May 1848), 272–275; and *La Paix* (June 1847), 470.

16. "Nackel (im Gh. Posen), 1. Juli," *Der Orient* 8 (July 16, 1847), 228.

17. "Les israélites à Rome," *AI* 9 (December 1848), 617–619.

18. Chadwick, *History of the Popes*, 92. For an argument that there was more continuity in Pius IX's policies, see Frank J. Coppa, "Pio Nono and the Jews: From 'Reform' to 'Reaction,' 1846–1878," *Catholic Historical Review* 89, no. 4 (2003), 671–695.

19. See also Aram Mattioli, "Das Ghetto der 'ewigen Stadt' im Urteil deutschsprachiger Publizisten (1846–1870)," in *Zwischen Selbstbehauptung und Verfolgung: Deutsch-jüdische Zeitungen und Zeitschriften von der Aufklärung bis zum Nationalsozialismus*, ed. Michael Nagel (Hildesheim: Olms, 2002), 159–188.

20. Hermann Vogelstein and Paul Rieger, *Geschichte der Juden in Rom* (Berlin: Mayer & Müller, 1895), 376; and Frank J. Coppa, *The Papacy, the Jews, and the Holocaust* (Washington, DC: Catholic University of America Press, 2006), 88–89.

21. S. Bloch, "À nos lecteurs," *UI* 5 (September 1849), 3.

22. See, for example, *UI* 5 (November 1849), 137.

23. Georges Weill, *Histoire du catholicisme libéral en France, 1828–1908* (Paris: Alcan, 1909), 91–99.

24. Paul Christophe, *L'Église de France dans la révolution de 1848* (Paris: Éditions du Cerf, 1998), 78–81.

25. Adrien Dansette, *Religious History of Modern France*, trans. John Dingle (Freiburg: Herder, 1961), 1: 265–271.

26. Robert Tombs, *France 1814–1914* (London: Longman, 1996), 385–388.

27. See Georges Cogniot, *La question scolaire en 1848 et la loi Falloux* (Paris: Éditions hier et aujourd'hui, 1948).

28. See Austin Gough, *Paris and Rome: The Gallican Church and the Ultramontane Campaign, 1848–1853* (Oxford, UK, and New York: Clarendon Press and Oxford University Press, 1986); and Weill, *Histoire du catholicisme libéral*, 99–108.

29. Georges Weill, *Histoire de l'idée laïque en France au XIXe siècle* (Paris: Hachette, 2004), 151–176.

30. See the collection *Christianisme et Vendée: la création au XIXe d'un foyer du catholicisme* (La Mothe-Achard: Centre vendéen de recherches historiques, 2000).

31. Ibid., 91.

32. *Liberté de Penser* (December 1849–May 1850), 192.

33. On the Cahen affair: *AI* 10 (November 1849), 557–561; *AI* 11 (February 1850), 59–63; and "Affaire de M. Is. Cahen," *AI* 11 (March 1850), 123–125. Further articles on the church during and after the affair: "Lettre de M. Victor Hugo," *AI* 10 (November 1849), 578–580; "L'enseignement et les minorités religieuses," *AI* 10 (December 1849), 621–628; G. Ben-Lévi, "L'illusion et la réalité," *AI* 10 (December 1849), 665–672; *AI* 10 (December 1849), 680–683; "Les minorités religieuses au commencement de 1850" *AI* 11 (January 1850), 8–22; "Le Judaïsme en France depuis la révolution de février" *AI* 11 (March 1850), 113–117; *AI* 11 (April 1850), 174–175; *AI* 11 (June 1850), 296; *AI* 11 (July 1850), 338–339; and S. Cahen, "Le Ghetto de Rome," *AI* 11 (December 1, 1850), 623–624.

34. Simon Bloch, "Démission du Consistoire Centrale" *UI* 5 (January 1850), 201–211. According to Bloch, the main reason for the Consistory's resignation was a scandal involving the Consistory in Colmar, p. 205; "Assemblée Nationale," *UI* 5 (February 1850), 259–261.

35. "Paris, 13. Januar," *AZJ* 14 (January 28, 1850), 60–61; and "Paris, im Dezember," *AZJ* 14 (January 1, 1850), 9–11.

36. Simon Bloch, "Les Professeurs Juifs," *UI* 5 (November 1849), 119–127.

37. For such a restrained articulation of discontent with the close relationship between the government and the church, see Isidore Cahen, "Situation du judaïsme," *AI* 13 (1852), 3–7. Depicting ultramontanism as a minor danger: Isidore

Cahen, "Les principes et les hommes," *AI* 16 (January 1855), 12–21; and Isidore Cahen, "Chronique du mois," *AI* 17 (January 1856), 42–53.

38. Hans Joachim Schoeps, *Das andere Preussen: konservative Gestalten und Probleme im Zeitalter Friedrich Wilhelms IV* (Honnef am Rhein: Peters, 1957); Hans-Christof Kraus, *Ernst Ludwig von Gerlach: politisches Denken und Handeln eines preussischen Altkonservativen* (Göttingen: Vandenhoeck & Ruprecht, 1994); Ruben Alvarado, *Authority Not Majority: The Life and Times of Friedrich Julius Stahl* (Aalten: WordBridge, 2007); and Wilhelm Füssl, *Professor in der Politik, Friedrich Julius Stahl (1802–1861): das monarchische Prinzip und seine Umsetzung in die parlamentarische Praxis* (Göttingen: Vandenhoeck & Ruprecht, 1988).

39. See, for example, "Der Antrag des Abgeordneten Wagener," *AZJ* 20 (January 28, 1856), 55–57; and "Berlin, 7. April," *AZJ* 22 (April 19, 1858), 233.

40. On the role of affairs in modern Jewish history, see Jonathan Frankel, "Crisis as a Factor in Modern Jewish Politics, 1840 and 1881–82," in *Living with Antisemitism: Modern Jewish Responses*, ed. Jehuda Reinharz (Hanover, NH: University Press of New England, 1987), 42–58. In spite of excellent work on the events of the affair, no study examines it as a wider German, French, European, or Atlantic phenomenon. George Weill pointed out some of the lacunae of previous research in "L'affaire Mortara et l'anticléricalisme en Europe à l'époque du Risorgimento," in *Aspects de l'anticléricalisme du Moyen Age à nos jours: hommage à Robert Joly: colloque de Bruxelles, juin 1988*, ed. Robert Joly and Jacques Marx (Brussels: Éditions de l'Université de Bruxelles, 1988), 103–134. Most of these lacunae still exist.

41. David Kertzer, *The Kidnapping of Edgardo Mortara* (New York: Alfred Knopf, 1997).

42. "Die Angelegenheit in Bologna," *AZJ* 22 (October 4, 1858), 558.

43. "Italien. Bologna, im Juli," *AZJ* 22 (August 30, 1858), 489.

44. See Natalie Isser, "The Mortara Affair and Louis Veuillot," *Proceedings of the Annual Meeting of the Western Society for French History* 7 (1979), 69–78.

45. Isidore Cahen, "L'affaire Mortara," *AI* 19 (November 1858), 617–625.

46. Aron Rodrigue, *French Jews, Turkish Jews* (Bloomington: Indiana University Press, 1990); idem, *Jews and Muslims: Images of Sephardi and Eastern Jewries in Modern Times* (Seattle: University of Washington Press, 2003); and Michael M. Laskier, *The Alliance Israélite Universelle and the Jewish Communities of Morocco, 1862–1962* (Albany: State University of New York Press, 1983).

47. Michael Graetz, *The Jews in Nineteenth-Century France: From the French Revolution to the Alliance Israélite Universelle* (Stanford, CA: Stanford University Press, 1996); and Lisa Moses Leff, *Sacred Bonds of Solidarity: The Rise of Jewish Internationalism in Nineteenth-Century France* (Stanford, CA: Stanford University Press, 2006).

48. Isidore Cahen, "Chronique du mois," *AI* 19 (1858), 519–530.

49. Letter of O. Terquem, Paris, September 6, 1858, "Quelques mots sur les vols d'âmes," *UI* 14 (October 1858), 60–70; see also *AI* 19 (October 1858), 556.

50. *AZJ* 22 (October 4, 1858), 558.

51. "Amsterdam, le 10 août," *AI* 19 (1858), 540–542, translated as "Amsterdam, 10. August," *AZJ* 22 (September 13, 1858), 524–525.

52. "Der religiöse Fanatismus," *AZJ* 22 (September 13, 1858), 516.

53. S. Honel, "Revue mensuelle," *Le Lien d'Israël* 4 (August 1858), 135–136.

54. Isidore Cahen, "La tentative d'Amsterdam," *AI* 19 (October 1858), 586–593. The French report forms the basis for the German one: "Amsterdam, im September," *AZJ* 22 (November 1, 1858), 622–633.

55. O. Terquem, "Correspondance," *UI* 13 (August 1858), 545. See also Isidore Cahen, "Chronique du mois," *AI* 19 (1858), 519–530.

56. Pétavel, *L'époque*, 12–14, reprints the letter of the president of the AIU, Louis Kœnigswarter, to the Spanish minister of justice from 1863. Official histories of the AIU omit this episode. It is not mentioned, for example, in Narcisse Leven, *Cinquante ans d'histoire: L'alliance israélite universelle (1860–1910)* (Paris: Alcan, 1911). Whereas scholarship has repeatedly emphasized the republican origins of the AIU, the model function of liberal evangelicals has been mostly overlooked. Abigail Green suggests that there was a mutual influence of Jewish, Catholic, and Protestant forms of religious internationalism, mostly however as the result of competition; Abigail Green, "Nationalism and the 'Jewish International': Religious Internationalism in Europe and the Middle East, c.1840–c.1880," *Comparative Studies in Society and History* 50, no. 2 (2008), 535–558.

57. Thomas Nipperdey, *Deutsche Geschichte 1800–1866: Bürgerwelt und starker Staat* (Munich: C. H. Beck, 1983), 697–702.

58. *Paths of Emancipation: Jews, States, and Citizenship*, ed. Pierre Birnbaum and Ira Katznelson (Princeton, NJ: Princeton University Press, 1995), 25. Certain exclusions remained, such as restriction on receiving fellowships at Oxford and Cambridge, which only opened up to Jews in 1871.

59. For local interpretations, see Bertram Korn, *The American Reaction to the Mortara Case* (Cincinnati: American Jewish Archives, 1957); W. M. DeLang, "Weerklank van de Mortara-Affaire in Nederland," *Studia Rosenthaliana* 19 (1985), 159–173; and Julius H. Schoeps, "Der Fall Edgardo Mortara: Die Reaktionen in Deutschland auf die vom Vatikan veranlasste Entführung und Zwangstaufe eines jüdischen Kindes in den fünfziger Jahren des 19. Jahrhunderts," *Menora* 14 (2003), 219–227. It should be added that many Jewish children had been forcefully taken from their parents' home in the decade preceding the case of Edgardo Mortara, yet none had caused uproar of the type Mortara did; Kertzer, *Kidnapping*, 33–34. On the history of forced baptisms, see also David Kertzer, *The Popes against the Jews: The Vatican's Role in the Rise of Modern Anti-Semitism* (New York: Knopf, 2001), 38–59.

60. See, for example, "Frankenthal, 16. Februar," *AZJ* 29 (March 7, 1865), 148; *AZJ* 29 (June 20, 1865), 378; "Frankfurt a. M., 25. October," *AZJ* 30 (November 13, 1866), 731; "Berlin, im März," *AZJ* 31 (April 30, 1867), 354–355, where they talk about a "Mortara baptism" of a child; "Die Mortarafälle in Galizien und die Verhandlungen des österreichischen Abgeordnetenhauses darüber," *AZJ* 31 (October 29, 1867), 872–878; "Die Mortarafälle in Galizien," *AZJ* 31 (November 5, 1867), 892–894; "Die

Mortarafälle in Galizien," *AZJ* 31 (November 12, 1867), 912–914; *AI* 21 (January 1860), 59–60; Leone Ravenna, "Deux pendants à l'affaire Mortara," *AI* 21 (February 1860), 74–78; "Chronique du mois," *AI* 23 (January 1862), 45–48; "Un rapt d'un israélite au Pérou," *AI* 30 (1869), 55; "Une affaire Mortara à Jérusalem," *UI* 23 (March 1868), 324–325; *UI* 25 (April 15, 1870), 421; *UI* 31 (October 1, 1875), 91; L. L., "Une nouvelle affaire Mortara," *UI* 55 (March 2, 1900), 747–748; and *UI* 55 (March 9, 1900), 778.

61. S. Bloch, "Bulletin," *UI* 24 (June 15, 1869), 571.

62. Isidore Cahen, "Chronique israélite de la quinzaine," *AI* 24 (1863), 95–96.

63. Kertzer, *Kidnapping*, 258–259.

64. *AI* 19 (November 1858), 653.

65. On his life, see Assan Valérie, "Joseph Cohen, avocat, publiciste (Marseille, 1er novembre 1817–Paris, 22 novembre 1899)," *Archives Juives* 45, no. 2 (2012), 141–142; P., "Nécrologie: Joseph Cohen," *AI* 40 (December 7, 1899), 393–394; and C. B., "Nécrologie: Joseph Cohen," *UI* 55 (December 1, 1899), 342–343.

66. Rodrigue, *French Jews*, 8–9.

67. "Nécrologie: Joseph Cohen," *AI* 40 (December 7, 1899), 393–394.

68. *UI* 17 (August 1862), 552.

69. Joseph Cohen, *Les Déicides: examen de la divinité de Jésus-Christ et de l'église chrétienne au point de vue du judaïsme* (Paris: Michel Lévy frères, 1861).

70. "Une explication," *UI* 17 (December 1861), 183–186. Philippson was similarly acerbic about Cohen's periodical; see the review of *La vérité israélite* in *AZJ* 24 (April 24, 1860), 252.

71. "L'ennemi est à nos portes," *Vérité israélite* 9 (1862), 1–5; "Le rabbinat français," *Vérité israélite* 9 (1862), 5–3; and "Le rabbinat et le rabbinisme," *Vérité israélite* 9 (1862), 121–128.

72. J. Cohen, "La politique anglaise en Italie," *France*, September 25, 1863.

73. A. Hébrard, "Bulletin du Jour," *Le Temps*, October 1, 1862.

74. J. Cohen, "De l'état des croyances religieuses au XIXᵉ siècle: Le Catholicisme", *Vérité israélite* 4 (1861), 145.

75. J. Cohen, "À mes lecteurs," *Vérité israélite* 5 (1862), 145–152.

76. S. Bloch, "Les adieux d'un journaliste," *UI* 18 (November 1862), 123–124.

77. Ibid., 124.

78. Ibid., 125.

79. See also L. Cassoute, "Lettres marseillaises," *UI* 18 (November 1862), 120–123. The *Archives israélites* did not comment on the affair and generally kept a much lower profile in debates on the papacy at the time. Perhaps Cahen did not want to contribute to exacerbating the scandal involving his former contributor.

80. Letter of October 19, 1862, in Moses Hess, *Briefwechsel*, ed. Edmund Silberner ('s-Gravenhage: Mouton, 1959), 412.

81. "J. Cohen und die weltliche Macht des Papstes," *AZJ* 26 (October 21, 1862), 605–608.

82. Ibid., 605.

83. Ibid., 606.

84. Ibid.

85. Heinrich Graetz, *Geschichte der Juden: Von der ältesten Zeit bis auf die Gegenwart* (Leipzig: Leiner, 1897–1908); the original edition was published 1853–1875.

86. "Das Papstthum und das Judenthum," *AZJ* 26 (November 18, 1862), 673–674.

87. "Pariser Briefe," *AZJ* 26 (October 21, 1862), 608–610.

88. "Breslau, 5. Oct.," *AZJ* 26 (October 28, 1862), 633.

89. *AI* 40 (December 7, 1899), 394.

90. S. Bloch, "Les aspirations cléricales dans le judaïsme," *UI* 17 (November 1861), 101–107; similar arguments regarding rabbinic authority were made in Germany and Austria throughout the nineteenth century; see Andreas Brämer, *Rabbiner und Vorstand: Zur Geschichte der jüdischen Gemeinde in Deutschland und Österreich 1808–1871* (Wien: Böhlau, 1999).

91. *UI* 18 (October 1862), 61–62. For similar polemics against the consistory, see S. Bloch and Prosper Lunel, "Consistoire de Paris: Son compte rendu," *UI* 17 (November 1861), 119–123; and *UI* 17 (December 1861), 145–146.

92. *UI* 18 (November 1862), 102.

93. See, for example, the anticlerical tropes in the following articles against orthodoxy: "Aus Unterfranken, im Juli," *AZJ* 29 (August 8, 1865), 491–492; B. N. G., "Aus Unterfranken, in Baiern, im April," *AZJ* 29 (April 18, 1865), 242–243; "Unterfranken, im December," *AZJ* 29 (January 3, 1865), 5–6; and Khm., "Eine rabbinische Encyklika aus dem 19. Jahrhundert," *AZJ* 29 (February 14, 1865), 98–101.

94. Heinrich Graetz, "Die Verjüngung des jüdischen Stammes," *Jahrbuch für Israeliten* 10 (1863–1864), 1–13. The article was inspired by Hess's arguments. For an analysis of the article, see Reuwen Michael, "Graetz and Hess," *LBIYB* 9 (1964), 102–105. On the trial in the context of debates on biblical scholarship, see also Nils H. Roemer, *Jewish Scholarship and Culture in Nineteenth-Century Germany: Between History and Faith* (Madison: University of Wisconsin Press, 2005), 56–57.

95. "Wien, 13. Januar," *AZJ* 28 (January 26, 1864), 69; and "Einige Worte über diesen Prozeß," *AZJ* 28 (January 12, 1864), 36–37. Horwitz insisted on having his statements reprinted in full to avoid misunderstanding: "Einige Nachwehen des Kompert'schen Prozesses "*AZJ* 28 (February 2, 1864), 77–78.

96. "Wien, 19. Januar," *AZJ* 28 (February 2, 1864), 86.

97. "Aus Ungarn, 25. Januar," *AZJ* 28 (February 9, 1864), 102; "Preßburg, 9. März," *AZJ* 28 (March 22, 1864), 195.

98. The rectification of the earlier rumors: "Paris, 25. April," *AZJ* 28 (May 10, 1864), 311.

99. "Paris, im März," *AZJ* 28 (April 12, 1864), 244. See also "Paris, im April," *AZJ* 28 (April 19, 1864), 260–261.

100. "Der Moment und einige Bemerkungen dazu," *AZJ* 33 (December 28, 1869), 1040. Similarly, "Was ist und will der Fanatismus der neueren jüdischen Orthodoxen?" *AZJ* 34 (June 28, 1870), 509–512.

101. Isidore Cahen, "Manifeste," *AI* 30 (1869), 3–14, here 12–13.

102. See Irene Collins, *The Government and the Newspaper Press in France, 1814–1881* (London: Oxford University Press, 1959), 136–146, on press censorship under Napoleon III.

103. Paul Christophe, *George Sand et Jésus: une inlassable recherche spirituelle* (Paris: Éditions du Cerf, 2003), 102.

104. S. Bloch, review of Ernest Hendlé, *Questions politiques et sociales*, in *UI* 23 (April 1868), 367–368.

105. Nos. 77 and 78 of the *Syllabus of Errors*.

106. "Die römische Encyklica und die Lehren des Judenthums," *Illustrierte Monatshefte für die gesammten Interessen des Judenthums* 1, no. 1 (April 1865), 70–76.

107. "Die confessionellen Schroffheiten. Die pästliche Encyclica.—Die Erklärung evangl. Geistlicher in Berlin," *AJZ* 29 (January 17, 1865), 31–34.

108. Isidore Cahen, "Chronique Israélite de la quinzaine," *AI* 26 (January 15, 1865) 2, 49–55; *UI* 20 (January 1865), 197; S. Bloch, "Bulletin," *UI* 20 (February 1865), 241–249; and *UI* 20 (February 1865), 244–245.

109. *UI* 23 (September 1867), 8–9.

110. "Mortara und der Papst," *AZJ* 31 (May 21, 1867), 410.

111. The following are examples from the AZJ, which offered the broadest coverage of these conflicts: "Mexiko, im Januar," *AZJ* 29 (March 14, 1865), 169–170; "Etwas über den Judenhaß," *AZJ* 29 (September 12, 1865), 564–570; and "Aus Amerika, im Aug.," *AZJ* 29 (September 12, 1865), 574–575. On conflicts surrounding the Austrian concordat and constitution, see "Wien, 1. August," *AZJ* 31 (August 13, 1867), 655–657; "Der Sieg," *AZJ* 31 (December 10, 1867), 989–990; "Die Allocution des Papstes," *AZJ* 32 (July 7, 1868), 554–555; and "Des österreichischen Kaiserstaates Aufschwung," *AZJ* 32 (Feb. 18, 1868), 141–143. See also "Das Princip in Preußen," *AZJ* 32 (March 31, 1868), 263–266. On France being the center of conflicts: "Paris, 18. Januar," *AZJ* 29 (January 31, 1865), 71–72; "Paris, 28. Januar," *AZJ* 29 (February 21, 1865), 119–120; "Paris, im Februar," *AZJ* 29 (February 21, 1865), 120; "Paris, 15. Februar," *AZJ* 29 (February 28, 1865), 139–140; "Paris, im Februar," *AZJ* 29 (March 14, 1865), 167–168; "Paris, 15. März," *AZJ* 29 (April 4, 1865), 214–216; "Paris, im Mai," *AZJ* 29 (May 16, 1865), 307; "Paris, im Februar," *AZJ* 30 (March 20, 1866), 182–183; "Paris, 20. September," *AZJ* 31 (October 1, 1867), 799; "Paris, im September," *AZJ* 31 (October 15, 1867), 839–840; "Paris, 10. November," *AZJ* 31 (November 26, 1867), 960; "Paris, 2. December," *AZJ* 32 (January 1, 1868), 12; and "Paris, 23. Sept.," *AZJ* 33 (October 5, 1869), 808–809.

112. "Bonn, 18. Juli," *AZJ* 31 (August 13, 1867), 657–658; "Die päpstliche Bulle," *AZJ* 32 (July 21, 1868), 594–595; "Wien, 16. Juli," *AZJ* 32 (July 28, 1868), 617–618; *AI* 30 (November 15, 1869), 675–678; "Das ökumenische Concil," *AZJ* 33 (December 7, 1869), 980–882; "Bonn, 1. Dec.," *AZJ* 33 (December 12, 1869), 1003–1004; *AI* 31 (January 1, 1870), 3–4; "Die römische Intoleranz," *AZJ* 34 (April 5, 1870), 265–266; "Die römische Anmaßung," *AZJ* 34 (April 26, 1870), 330–331; *AI* 31 (May 1, 1870), 259–261; S. Bloch, "Bulletin," *UI* 25 (November 15, 1869), 166–167; S. Bloch, "La

question du messie et le concile du Vatican, par MM. les abbés Lémann," *UI* 25 (December 1, 1869), 209–214; and S. Bloch, "Bulletin," *UI* 25 (January 1, 1870), 259–270.

113. *UI* 24 (August 1, 1869), 632.

114. *UI* 25 (April 1, 1870), 457.

115. *UI* 25 (February 15, 1870), 357. For a similar comment, see *UI* 27 (March 15, 1872), 423.

116. *Bitte württembergischer Israeliten an die hohe Kammer der Abgeordneten, betreffend die Gewissensfreiheit der Israeliten und die religiöse Autonomie der israelitischen Gemeinden* (Heilbronn: Güldig, 1869).

117. Georges Weill, "Élie-Aristide Astruc, rabbin, écrivain et publiciste (Bordeaux, 12 décembre 1831–Bruxelles, 23 février 1905)," *Archives Juives* 35 (2002), 137–143.

118. Jean-Philippe Schreiber, "Paris-Bruxelles: la polémique suscitée par l'*Histoire abrégée des Juifs* d'Elie Aristide Astruc (1870)," *Archives Juives* 40 (2007), 43–64.

119. Jean-Philippe Schreiber, "Un rabbin dans le siècle. Elie-Aristide Astruc, Grand Rabbin de Belgique de 1866 à 1879," *Bijdragen. Tijdschift voor philosophie en theologie* 52 (1992), 2–22; and Elie-Aristide Astruc, *Enseignement normal de l'histoire des Hébreux* (Paris: Delagrave, 1881).

120. AIU Archives, IAI, Astruc, Grand-rabbin de Belgique, unnamed subfolder. The procession was ultimately stopped by the archbishop of Mechelen after protests from liberals. For German Jewish interest in the affair, see also "Die Blutprozession in Brüssel," *AZJ* 34 (June 21, 1870), 495–497; *AZJ* 34 (June 5, 1870), 535–536; and *AZJ* 34 (June 12, 1870), 552–554.

121. Élie-Aristide Astruc, *Le Décalogue: réponse au Postulatum des évêques du Concile* (Brussels: Ferdinand Claasen, 1870), which includes minutes of meetings, in which the consistory decided to distribute the work.

122. "L'alliance évangélique," *UI* 7 (October 1851), 74–77; S. Bloch, review of *Alliance religieuse universelle: Essai sur les moyens de rapprocher toutes les croyances* by Henri Carle, *UI* 17 (September 1861), 30–33; and S. Bloch, "Bulletin," *UI* 27 (August 15, 1872), 708–716. On further contacts, see Abram-François Pétavel, *L'époque du rapprochement ou entente fraternelle entre l'Alliance Évangélique et l'Alliance Israélite Universelle* (Paris and Neuchâtel: Lévy Frères and Delachaux, 1863).

123. Abram-François Pétavel, *La fille de Sion ou le rétablissement d'Israël: Poème en sept chants avec annotations et études bibliques* (Paris: E. Dentu, 1868).

124. Joseph Salvador, *Paris, Rome, Jérusalem; ou, La question religieuse au XIXe siècle* (Paris: M. Levy, 1860); and Joseph Salvador, *Idée sur l'avenir de la question religieuse* (Paris: Imprimerie Wittersheim, 1862).

125. Ibid., 7–8.

126. On Hess, *Rome and Jerusalem*, see Ken Koltun-Fromm, *Moses Hess and Modern Jewish Identity* (Bloomington: Indiana University Press, 2001).

127. Edmund Silberner, *Moses Hess: Geschichte seines Lebens* (Leiden: Brill, 1966). Silbener calls him a "Jewish child raised in Catholicism" (p. 396).

128. On his education, see Silberner, *Hess*, 6.

129. Moses Hess, *Die heilige Geschichte der Menschheit von einem jünger Spinozas* (Stuttgart: Hallberger, 1837), ch. 3.

130. See Shlomo Avineri, *Moses Hess: Prophet of Communism and Zionism* (New York: New York University Press, 1985), 174, on Hess's complex motives.

131. Moses Hess, *Rom und Jerusalem: Die letzte Nationalitätenfrage* (Leipzig: Wengler, 1862), v; my translation is inspired by Moses Hess, *Rome and Jerusalem: A Study in Jewish Nationalism*, trans. Meyer Waxmann (New York: Bloch, 1918), 35.

132. Reuwen Michael, "Graetz and Hess," *LBIYB* 9 (1964), 94–95. The work was at that point entitled "Die Wiedergeburt Israels" [The Rebirth of Israel]. Graetz helped find the title of the work (ibid., 100).

133. Heinrich Graetz, *Tagebuch und Briefe*, ed. Reuven Michael (Tübingen: Mohr, 1977). See the following letters: Graetz to Hess, Breslau, October 15, 1862, 237; Graetz to Hess, Breslau, March 31, 1868, 287–288; and Graetz to Hess, Breslau, October 16, 1868, 293. Graetz continued his anti-Catholic statements also in the 1870s during the *Kulturkampf*: Graetz to Hess, Breslau, July 10, 1871, 308–310; and Graetz to Karl Marx, February 1, 1877, 336–337.

134. Leff, *Sacred Bonds*.

135. On the left, see Robert S. Wistrich, "Radical Antisemitism in France and Germany (1840–1880)," *Modern Judaism* 15, no. 2 (1995), 109–135.

136. *UI* 26 (October 25, 1870), 109.

137. *AZJ* 34 (September 20, 1870), 739.

Chapter Six

1. For a historical reflection on these questions in the French case, see Pierre Rosanvallon, *Le peuple introuvable: histoire de la représentation démocratique en France* (Paris: Gallimard, 1998).

2. Michelis, PHdA, May 7, 1867, 76.

3. Lasker, PHdA, May 8, 1867, 87–94.

4. Michelis's original speech against the new federal constitution: RTNDB, March 9, 1867, 115–116; Bismarck's comments on him as *"ein katholischer Geistlicher"*: RTNDB, March 11, 1867, 136; the conflict with the president: RTNDB, March 21, 1867, 308; his resignation: RTNDB, March 21, 1867, 312. The hostility to Michelis's use of a religiously inspired rhetoric also colored Michaelis's appearances in the Prussian Abgeordnetenhaus: Michelis opened his speech on the constitutional draft with a wordy rejection of the suspicion that he, as a Catholic and priest, would be unable to vote uninfluenced by "religious and confessional bias"; Michelis, PHdA, May 7, 1867, 74.

5. Michelis, PHdA, May 8, 1867, 98.

6. PHdA, May 8, 1867, 98.

7. This debate was also discussed in the Jewish press: "Berlin, 8. Mai," *AZJ* 31 (May 28, 1867), 437–438. A second disagreement about the use of anticlerical rhetoric ensued between the two. Michelis accused Lasker of appealing to known resentments when he denounced Michelis as giving a "pious comment" [*mit einer*

frommen Bemerkung]. PHdA, May 8, 1867, 98–100. A related debate on the use of "Jewish" [*judaïque*] as a pejorative term occurred also in the French parliament: *Journal officiel*, January 15, 1873, 275.

8. The Reichstag of the German Empire and the Reichstag of the North German League were different institutions. In practice most deputies continued their service in the enlarged institution, and they retained most of the same rules on election (universal male suffrage) and parliamentary procedure.

9. Strosser, PHdA, January 31, 1872, 552.

10. This approach is indebted to the notion of a cultural history of politics. See Thomas Mergel, "Überlegungen zu einer Kulturgeschichte der Politik," *Geschichte und Gesellschaft* 28 (2002), 574–606. There are also attempts to read parliamentary speeches from the perspective of literary studies and linguistics that offer some useful models. See, for example, Armin Burkhardt, *Das Parlament und seine Sprache: Studien zu Theorie und Geschichte parlamentarischer Kommunikation* (Tübingen: Niemeyer, 2003); and Hans-Peter Goldberg, *Bismarck und seine Gegner: Die politische Rhetorik im kaiserlichen Reichstag* (Düsseldorf: Droste Verlag, 1998). On Lasker, from this perspective, see Richard W. Dill, "Der Parlamentarier Eduard Lasker und die parlamentarische Stilentwicklung der Jahre 1867–1884: Ein Beitrag zur Geistesgeschichte des politischen Stils in Deutschland" (PhD dissertation, Universität Erlangen, 1956).

11. See, for example, Marion Kaplan, *The Making of the Jewish Middle Class: Women, Family, and Identity in Imperial Germany* (New York: Oxford University Press, 1991).

12. Jacob Toury, *Die politischen Orientierungen der Juden in Deutschland; von Jena bis Weimar* (Tübingen: Mohr Siebeck, 1966), 149–150, for example, makes this argument based on some of the examples in the following discussion, with different conclusions.

13. David Sorkin, *The Count Sanislas de Clermont-Tonnerre's 'To the Jews as a Nation . . .': The Career of a Quotation*, Jacob Katz Memorial Lecture (Jerusalem: Leo Baeck Institute Jerusalem, 2011).

14. Michael Clark, "Jewish Identity in British Politics: The Case of the First Jewish MPs, 1858–87," *Jewish Social Studies* 13, no. 2 (2007), 101–102, mentions Clermont-Tonnerre to explain British politics, for example.

15. Ronald Schechter, *Obstinate Hebrews: Representations of Jews in France, 1715–1815* (Berkeley: University of California Press, 2003), 150–193. On the notion of citizenship as the equivalent of an occupational or civic status (*Stand*) in Germany, see Rogers Brubaker, *Citizenship and Nationhood in France and Germany* (Cambridge, MA: Harvard University Press, 1992), 62.

16. Marcel Stoetzler, *The State, the Nation, & the Jews: Liberalism and the Antisemitism Dispute in Bismarck's Germany* (Lincoln: University of Nebraska Press, 2008); and Uffa Jensen, *Gebildete Doppelgänger: Bürgerliche Juden und Protestanten im 19. Jahrhundert* (Göttingen: Vandenhoeck & Ruprecht, 2005).

17. I depart here from other work on Jewish deputies, particularly those concerning the German context. I am not interested in asking "whether the component of origins made itself felt in the public activity of Jews," as the first large survey of Jewish politicians by Ernest Hamburger programmatically stated; Ernest Hamburger, *Juden im öffentlichen Leben Deutschlands Regierungsmitglieder, Beamte und Parlamentarier in der monarchischen Zeit 1848–1918* (Tübingen: Mohr [Siebeck], 1968), x. Although authors like Jacob Toury, Uriel Tal, and Peter Pulzer have been cautious not to essentialize the positions of Jews in the German parliaments, it is a slippery slope from the enumeration of opinions that Jewish politicians happened to share to attempts to understand specific opinions as specifically Jewish; Toury, *Die politischen Orientierungen*; and Peter Pulzer, *Jews and the German State: The Political History of a Minority, 1848–1933* (Oxford, UK: Blackwell, 1992).

18. Pierre Rosanvallon, *The Demands of Liberty: Civil Society in France since the Revolution* (Cambridge, MA: Harvard University Press, 2007), 4–6.

19. Pierre Rosanvallon has noted that France would not have managed to function if the political elites of the country had in fact eliminated all intermediary bodies, as Alexis de Tocqueville claimed they had. France was not just the country of the Jacobin tradition but precisely also of liberals like Tocqueville who challenged these very same traditions. On the importance of decentralization debates for the development of democratic traditions in France, see Sudhir Hazareesingh, *From Subject to Citizen: The Second Empire and the Emergence of Modern French Democracy* (Princeton, NJ: Princeton University Press, 1998).

20. Rosanvallon, *Le peuple introuvable*, 68–70.

21. Pierre Birnbaum, *The Jews of the Republic: A Political History of State Jews in France from Gambetta to Vichy* (Stanford, CA: Stanford University Press, 1996), 74–75.

22. Ibid., 76.

23. Ibid., 213. Much as in England but unlike the case in Germany, the most prominent Jewish politicians in France were often financiers up to the 1870s. On England, see Clark, "Jewish Identity," 96.

24. Frédéric Barbier, *Finance et politique: la dynastie des Fould, XVIIIe-XXe siècle* (Paris: Colin, 1991), 118.

25. Ibid.

26. *Moniteur universel*, May 22 and 23, 1846, 1486; and *Moniteur universel*, June 24, 1847, 1712–1713.

27. *Moniteur universel*, June 24, 1847, 1712.

28. Ibid.

29. The same attempt to distinguish between the Judaism he owned and the Christianity his interlocutors owned appeared in Crémieux's plead for a more heavy-handed approach to helping Christians in Lebanon. According to Crémieux, the inactivity of France since 1840 — since the fiasco of the Damascus affair — had allowed other powers to eclipse France. Invoking the Crusader King Louis IX, he spoke both about a humanitarian and a historic mission that should motivate the

government to intervene in Ottoman Syria: "Fine, destroy the work of Saint Louis and of your kings; destroy with one blow these Christian populations who have the same faith, the same God, and the same religion as you [. . .]." *Moniteur universel*, July 4, 1847, 1887.

30. On federalism and German parliaments, see Gerhard Albert Ritter, *Föderalismus und Parlamentarismus in Deutschland in Geschichte und Gegenwart* (Munich: Verlag der Bayerischen Akademie der Wissenschaften, 2005).

31. Cited by Irmline Veit-Brause, "Partikularismus," in *Geschichtliche Grundbegriffe: historisches Lexikon zur politisch-sozialen Sprache in Deutschland*, ed. Otto Brunner, Werner Conze, and Reinhart Koselleck (Stuttgart: E. Klett, 1978), 4:741–742.

32. See Albert S. Kotowski, *Zwischen Staatsräson und Vaterlandsliebe: die Polnische Fraktion im Deutschen Reichstag 1871–1918* (Düsseldorf: Droste, 2007).

33. On Kosch see Hamburger, *Juden im öffentlichen Leben*, 226.

34. On his upbringing and early career, see *AZJ* 31 (February 26, 1867), Feuilleton-Beilage, 182–183.

35. The petition was discussed together with a more far-reaching second one by the chief rabbi of Münster demanding the proper implementation of article 12 of the constitution and thus an end to discrimination against Jews in the state service.

36. Kosch, PHdA, December 7, 1866, 981.

37. Kosch made his intervention for Jewish equality in the state service an annual event. He never received any critiques of his advocacy. Eventually, he met with no responses of any kind to his arguments; Kosch, PHdA, November 27, 1868, 308–309.

38. Lasker, RTNDB, June 16, 1868, 496.

39. Employing a strategy that will be discussed in more detail in the following pages, he then went on to clarify that certain accusations made by another deputy had "made it his duty" to publicly explain why certain statements "injured the feelings" of the Jews; ibid.

40. Toury, *Die politischen Orientierungen*, 150.

41. "Die Rede des Dr. Morgenstern in der bayer'schen Kammer der Abgeordneten," *AZJ* 19 (February 5, 1855), 63–68.

42. *Moniteur universel*, June 11, 1845, 1657.

43. Sonnemann, RT, April 25, 1871, 373.

44. Similarly, Lasker, who was willing to strategically mention his own Jewishness at other points, did not explicitly refer to himself as a Jew when he pleaded the cases of Jews in Palestine, who were demanding or already enjoying Prussian protection. This was the case both in his public advocacy in parliament and in petitions to the ministry of foreign affairs; "Berlin, 20. Februar," *AZJ* 32 (March 3, 1868), 187–188; "Berlin, im März," *AZJ* 32 (April 21, 1868), 235–236; "Berlin, 18. Decbr.," *AZJ* 32 (December 29, 1868), 1051; and BArch N2167/358, 6, 12.

45. For a thick description of parliamentary ideas on honor, see Brian E. Vick, *Defining Germany: The 1848 Frankfurt Parliamentarians and National Identity* (Cambridge, MA: Harvard University Press, 2002), 67–68.

46. Ute Frevert, *Men of Honour: A Social and Cultural History of the Duel* (Cambridge, MA: Polity Press, 1995); Kevin McAleer, *Dueling: The Cult of Honor in Fin-de-Siècle Germany* (Princeton, NJ: Princeton University Press, 1994); and Ann Goldberg, *Honor, Politics and the Law in Imperial Germany, 1871–1914* (Cambridge, UK: Cambridge University Press, 2010).

47. On honor as a code within the French bureaucracy, see William M. Reddy, *The Invisible Code: Honor and Sentiment in Postrevolutionary France, 1814–1848* (Berkeley: University of California Press, 1997), 114–183.

48. Gabriel Riesser, "Rede gegen Moritz Mohl's Antrag zur Beschränkung der Rechte der Juden. 29. August 1848," in *Gesammelte Schriften* (Frankfurt a. M.: Verlag der Riesser-Stiftung, 1868), 4:403–410, here 403–404.

49. Riesser had often spoken about honor as a motive for his and other Jews' actions before. He was also very explicit in private correspondence about his rejection of any universalism that could easily be unmasked as surreptitious particularism. See his letter to Mrs. Haller in Riesser, *Gesammelte Schriften* 1:262–266.

50. On Riesser in 1848, see Hamburger, *Juden im öffentlichen Leben*, 180–183.

51. For the whole debate, see *Journal officiel*, May 28, 1895, 1492–1505.

52. On Naquet, see Birnbaum, *Jews of the Republic*, 234–247.

53. Ibid., 83–84.

54. On the parliamenary debates in 1895 as a turning point in the history of antisemitism, see Laurent Joly, "L'entrée de l'antisémitisme sur la scène parlementaire française: Le débat sur l'*'infiltration juive'* à la Chambre en mai 1895," *Archives Juives* 38, no. 1 (2005), 114–128.

55. *Annales: Débats parlementaires* 45 (1895), session of May 27, 1895, 1492.

56. *Die bürgerliche Gleichstellung der Juden in Preußen: Verhandlungen des Hauses der Abgeordneten vom 24. bis 27. April 1860 und 10. Mai 1860* (Berlin: W. Adolf, 1860), complete speech 20–28, here 20.

57. Ibid., 25.

58. Ibid., 25.

59. Ibid., 28.

60. Ibid., 122.

61. The speech has more references to honor. He also spoke of the noble manly pride (*edlem Mannesstolze*) of those Jews who become teachers out of idealism in spite of the discrimination they experience from the minister.

62. In the United States the laws and statues were more explicitly argued for as a form of Sunday observance; Naomi Wiener Cohen, *Jews in Christian America: The Pursuit of Religious Equality* (New York: Oxford University Press, 1992), 55–64.

63. *Moniteur universel*, December 26 and 27, 1840, 2527.

64. Ibid.

65. *Sulamith*, year 8, vol. 2, no. 1 (1834/1843), 132–133.

66. Eugène Tallon in session of February 5, 1873, *Annales de l'Assemblée Nationale*, 15:559–560. Tallon confused Benoît Fould for his brother Achille. The right-

center deputy defended the new measures claiming that a Jewish deputy had already argued that the Jews only want general laws and no special protections. In response Bamberger challenged Fould's right to speak but explained that he "did not want to enter into the details [of the matter] which would be out of place here, in public" (p. 560). Fould's statements were also remembered later when similar debates took place; *AI* 49 (June 28, 1888), 205.

67. *Le Moniteur universel*, April 4, 1850, 1088. See also the report in the Jewish press, "Assemblée Nationale: Discussion du budget des cultes pour 1850," *AI* 11 (May 1850), 228–231.

68. Like earlier speakers, Lasker and Bamberger focused on universalistic arguments, in this case less with references to civil rights and more emphatically appearing as representatives of European culture. Bamberger spoke of offences to the "European cultural world" [*europäische Kulturwelt*] and Lasker spoke of "acts that are hostile to culture" [*kulturfeindliche Haltungen*]. Bamberger, RT, May 22, 1872, 469; Lasker, RT, May 22, 1872, 473.

69. On the *Adreßdebatte*, see Rudolf Lill, "Der Kulturkampf in Preußen und im Deutschen Reich (bis 1878)," in *Handburch der Kirchengeschichte*, ed. Hubert Jedin (Freiburg, Basel, and Vienna: Herder, 1973), 32–33.

70. Lasker, RT, May 22, 1872, 474.

71. Armin Heinen, "Umstrittene Moderne: Die Liberalen und der preußisch-deutsche Kulturkampf," *Geschichte und Gesellschaft* 29 (2003), 138–156.

72. Mallinckrodt, PHdA, January 16, 1871, 292–293, here 293. Stenographic protocols did not always register all interjections but were particularly meticulous in noting them when they led to a reaction from the main speaker. On the history and theory of the parliamentary interjection, see Armin Burkhardt, *Zwischen Monolog und Dialog: Zur Theorie, Typologie und Geschichte des Zwischenrufs im deutschen Parlamentarismus* (Tübingen: Niemeyer, 2004).

73. Lasker, PHdA, January 16, 1871, 294.

74. Lasker, RT, April 5, 1871, 173–175. Lasker introduced an example, which became one of the more intensively debated cases of clerical influence, the unexpected defeat of Lord Ratibor, a well-known Catholic estate holder, by a politically active Catholic priest, Chaplain Eduard Müller. On the incident and the debate, see Margaret Lavinia Anderson, *Practicing Democracy: Elections and Political Culture in Imperial Germany* (Princeton, NJ: Princeton University Press, 2000), 70–71.

75. Lasker, RT, April 5, 1871, 175. The minutes note the reaction from the benches as: "Too true! Dissent with the Center [Party]."

76. Lasker, RT, April 5, 1871, 174.

77. Präsident [des Reichstags], ibid., 175.

78. Mallinckrodt, ibid.

79. Mallinckrodt, ibid., 176.

80. Lasker, ibid., 180. Emphasis in original.

81. Ibid.

82. Mallinckrodt, ibid., 180.

83. Lasker, PHdA, January 21, 1873, 684. It is interesting that the official protocol erroneously omitted the second "not" in the first sentence, letting Lasker imply that he actually had no right to speak on Church issues: "Ich habe bei den bisherigen Gesetz-Entwürfen mich der Theilnahme enthalten nicht etwa, weil ich gemeint hätte, es stünde mir das Recht zu [sic!], auch an solchen Debatten mich zu betheiligen, welche die Kirche betreffen."

84. "Die neuen kirchlichen Gesetze für Preußen," *IWS* 4 (February 5, 1873), 41–42; "Die neuen preußischen Religionsgesetze und das Judenthum," *AZJ* 37 (February 4, 1873), 83–87.

85. Mallinckrodt, PHdA, January 21, 1873, 683. Many contemporary and later interpreters, who did not otherwise have an interest in parliamentary rhetoric easily identified Lasker's attempt as strategic. Whereas in the past Jewish newspapers had ignored these conflicts, they now intervened as Lasker's strategy seemed to help establish his position in parliament at the expense of Judaism. According to Philippson, Lasker's attacks against Judaism were completely unnecessary given his speaking position: "We don't believe that deputy Lasker needed to adduce these particular cases to legitimize his speech." "Die neuen preußischen Religionsgesetze und das Judenthum," *AZJ* 37 (February 4, 1873), 87. On Lasker's strategy in this case, see also Johannes Baptist Kissling, *Geschichte des Kulturkampfes im Deutschen Reiche* (Freiburg i. Br.: Herder, 1911–1916), 2:176; James F. Harris, "Eduard Lasker: The Jew as National German Politician," *LBIYB* 20 (1975), 156; and James F. Harris, *A Study in the Theory and Practice of German Liberalism: Eduard Lasker, 1829–1884* (Lanham, MD: University Press of America, 1984), 13.

86. *Journal officiel*, February 19, 1884, 460. See also H. Prague, "Débats parlementaires: Le culte israélite au Sénat et à la Chambre," *AI* 45 (February 28, 1884), 67–68.

87. *Journal officiel*, session of October 29, 1891, 2013.

88. Bertrand Joly, *Déroulède: l'inventeur du nationalisme français* (Paris: Perrin, 1998), 184.

89. *Dictionnaire des parlementaires français: notices biographiques sur les ministres, députés et sénateurs français de 1889 à 1940*, ed. Jean Jolly (Paris: Presses universitaires de France, 1966), 4:1397.

90. *Journal officiel*, session of October 29, 1891, 2012.

91. Ibid.

92. Ibid.

93. On this incident, see also Birnbaum, *Jews of the Republic*, 119.

94. The complete debate: PHdA, November 20, 1880, 226–251, and November 22, 1880, 253–300.

95. On these campaigns, see Toury, *Die politischen Orientierungen*, 192–201. For some time after 1886 not a single Jews sat in the Prussian or German lower chamber.

96. Birnbaum, *Jews of the Republic*, 287–300 et passim.

Chapter Seven

1. Emphasizing Jews' reluctance to attack Catholics: Olaf Blaschke, *Offenders or Victims? German Jews and the Causes of Modern Catholic Antisemitism* (Lincoln: University of Nebraska Press, 2009). Focusing on the influence of Jewish or allegedly Jewish critiques on the rise of Catholic antisemitism: Richard Millman, "Jewish Anticlericalism and the Rise of Modern French Antisemitism," *History* 77, no. 250 (1992), 220–236; and Albert S. Lindemann, *Esau's Tears: Modern Anti-Semitism and the Rise of the Jews* (Cambridge, UK: Cambridge University Press, 1997), 122–123.

2. Zvi Jonathan Kaplan, *Between the Devil and the Deep Blue Sea? French Jewry and the Problem of Church and State* (Providence, RI: Brown Judaic Studies, 2009); Uriel Tal, *Christians and Jews in Germany: Religion, Politics, and Ideology in the Second Reich, 1870–1914* (Ithaca, NY: Cornell University Press, 1975), 81–120; and Jacob Toury, *Die politischen Orientierungen der Juden in Deutschland: von Jena bis Weimar* (Tübingen: Mohr Siebeck, 1966), 246–294.

3. See note 49 for examples of this claim.

4. The clashes in 1860s Baden became the model for many later anticlerical campaigns. On Baden, see Josef Becker, *Liberaler Staat und Kirche in der Ära von Reichsgründung und Kulturkampf: Geschichte und Struktur ihres Verhältnisses in Baden 1860–1876* (Mainz: M.-Grünewald-Verlag, 1973).

5. For such a view, see especially Erich Schmidt-Volkmar, *Der Kulturkampf in Deutschland, 1871–1890* (Göttingen: Musterschmidt, 1962).

6. Armin Heinen, "Umstrittene Moderne: Die Liberalen und der preußisch-deutsche *Kulturkampf*," *Geschichte und Gesellschaft* 29 (2003), 138–156. Pflanze integrated both perspectives in Otto Pflanze, *Bismarck and the Development of Germany* (Princeton, NJ: Princeton University Press, 1990), especially 179–206. On the role of the state, see Ronald J. Ross, *The Failure of Bismarck's Kulturkampf: Catholicism and State Power in Imperial Germany, 1871–1887* (Washington, DC: Catholic University of America Press, 1998).

7. Helmut Walser Smith, *German Nationalism and Religious Conflict: Culture, Ideology, Politics, 1870–1914* (Princeton, NJ: Princeton University Press, 1995).

8. Leopold Zunz, *Die gottesdienstlichen Vorträge der Juden, historisch entwickelt: Ein Beitrag zur Alterthumskunde und biblischen Kritik, zur Litteratur- und Religionsgeschichte* (Berlin: Ascher, 1832).

9. In 1848, Zunz spoke at the funeral of fallen democrats and eventually campaigned as a democratic politician in February 1849; Nahum N. Glazer, "Leopold Zunz and the Revolution of 1848: With the Publication of Four Letters by Zunz," *LBIYB* 5 (1960), 122–139; and Leopold Zunz, *Den Hinterbliebenen der Märzhelden Berlin's: Ein Wort des Trostes* (Berlin: Lassar, 1848). See also his lectures on democracy in the Berliner Volksverein, "Die Prinzipien der Demokratie," in Leopold Zunz, *Gesammelte Schriften* (Berlin: Gerschel, 1875), 1:308–316.

10. "Die jüdische Literatur" (1845), reprinted in *Gesammelte Schriften*, 1:55.

11. The best short summary of his opinions on the Catholic Church is Luitpold Wallach, *Liberty and Letters: The Thoughts of Leopold Zunz* (London: East and West Library, 1959), 62–67; see also Glatzer, "Leopold Zunz and the Revolution," 127–128. On his speeches, see Zunz, *Gesammelte Schriften*, 1:231–232.

12. *Die hebräischen Handschriften in Italien: Ein Mahnruf des Rechts und der Wissenschaft* (Berlin: W. Adolf & Co. 1864), reprinted in Zunz, *Gesammelte Schriften*, 3:13. I have used parts of the translation from Wallach, *Liberty and Letters*, 66–67.

13. Leopold Zunz, *Deutsche Briefe* (Leipzig: Brockhaus, 1872).

14. Ibid., 17.

15. Ibid., 44–48.

16. Ibid., 45.

17. Ibid.

18. Ibid.

19. On the biographical information presented here, see "Kohut, Adolf," in: Salomon Wininger, *Grosse jüdische National-Biographie* (Cernauti: Orient, 1925–1936), 3:495–496.

20. Adolf Kohut, *Memoiren eines jüdischen Seminaristen: zur Würdigung des Breslauer jüdisch-theologischen Seminars Fränkelscher Stiftung* (Prag: n.p., 1870).

21. Ibid., 1, 2, et passim.

22. Adolf Kohut, *Unsere drei Dichterheroen und das Pfaffenthum: Ein Trifolium klassischer Zeugen gegen Ultramontanismus, Jesuitismus und Muckerthum* (Leipzig: Herrmann, 1872).

23. Ibid., 8.

24. Adolf Kohut, *Die Erlebnisse und Huldigungen des Herrn Cultusministers Dr. Falk während seines Aufenthalts am Rhein* (Düsseldorf: Mewes, 1875).

25. For an overview of other Jewish reactions to the *Kulturkampf*, see Toury, *politische Orientierungen*, 246–261; Tal, *Christians and Jews*, 125–139; and A. Joskowicz, "Liberal Judaism and Confessional Politics of Difference in the German *Kulturkampf*," *LBIYB* 50 (2005), 177–197.

26. "Ein neuer, allgemeiner Kampf," *AZJ* 35 (October 24, 1871), 858.

27. Ibid., 857.

28. Ibid.

29. "Ein weltgeschichtlicher Wendepunkt," *Jüdische Zeitschrift für Wissenschaft und Leben* 10 (1872), 2.

30. "Wider den Strom," *IWS* 3 (April 3, 1872), 107.

31. Ibid. The notion that it was not Protestantism but merely state interest, which had motivated the liberal and governmental initiatives for new confessional legislation, also characterized the *AZJ*'s view: "Die neuen preußischen Religionsgesetze und das Judenthum," *AZJ* 37 (February 4, 1873), 83; and "Ein politischer Brief," *AZJ* 39 (January 26, 1875), 68. For a more detailed analysis of the Jewish press, see Joskowicz, "Liberal Judaism."

32. See, for example, "Berlin, 29. Jänner," *AZJ* 37 (February 4, 1873), 87.

33. Virchow had argued that it would have been a bad investment and ultimately misleading to hire a Jew for a low-pay assistantship if he has no realistic
chance of becoming a full professor; Meilitz, "Berlin, den 12. Mai," *AZJ* 32 (May
26, 1868), 436; "Bonn, 10. Juni," *AZJ* 32 (June 23, 1868), 516–517; "Bonn, 3. August,"
AZJ 32 (June 11, 1868), 657–658; "Berlin, 12. April," *AZJ* 33 (April 27, 1869), 330–331;
and "Broschürenliteratur," *AZJ* 33 (May 25, 1869), 408–411. On Virchow's otherwise complicated relationship to Judaism—beyond his well-known opposition to
political antisemitism—see Andrew Zimmerman, "Anti-Semitism as Skill: Rudolf
Virchow's 'Schulstatistik' and the Racial Composition of Germany," *Central European History* 32, no. 4 (1999), 409–429.

34. Rudolf Virchow, *Sämtliche Werke* (Hildesheim: Olms: 2006), 33:359–375.

35. The *AZJ* gratefully cited Virchow's speech, for example, "Berlin, 20. Januar,"
AZJ 37 (January 29, 1873), 70.

36. "Der Kampf zwischen Kirche und Staat," *IWS* 3 (July 17, 1872), 228; my
italics.

37. Sometimes the liberal Jewish press even objected to the exclusion from regulations, which were criticized as coercive by the Catholic Church, like those concerning the contested state supervision of educational institutions. See, for example,
"Die Gleichstellung der Culte in Preussen," *AZJ* 43 (March 18, 1879), 179–181; and
"Staatsaufsicht," *IWS* 8 (July 18, 1877), 225–226.

38. "Bonn, 16. Februar," *AZJ* 37 (March 4, 1873), 156.

39. B. Jacobsohn, *Der Deutsch-israelitische Gemeindebund nach Ablauf des ersten
Decenniums seit seiner Begründung von 1869 bis 1879: Eine Erinnerungsschrift* (Leipzig:
Schuwardt & Co., 1879), iii. The DIGB nevertheless emphasized its nonpolitical
character in the sense of party politics.

40. On the Protestantenverein and its anti-Catholic program, see Claudia Lepp,
*Protestantisch-liberaler Aufbruch in die Moderne: der Deutsche Protestantenverein in der
Zeit der Reichsgründung und des Kulturkampfes* (Gütersloh: Kaiser, 1996). The first
circular to announce the founding of the organization notes their will to unite Jews
"in north and south"; "An die deutsch-israelitischen Religionsgemeinden" (1869),
CAHJP M1/8, 11–12.

41. "Bericht über die Versammlung von Mitgliedern deutsch-israelitischer Gemeinden die Gründung eines Gemeindebundes betreffend, abgehalten am 20. April
1871 während der Ostermesse in der Synagoge zu Leipzig," CAHJP M1/12, 24–30,
here 3.

42. Ibid, 2. The parenthetical note is in the original printed version of the
speech.

43. "Verhandlungen der Constituirenden Versammlung des Deutsch-Israelitischen
Gemeindebundes (Zweiter Gemeindetag)," CAHJP M1/8, 29–39, 10; and "Der
zweite deutsch-israelitische Gemeindetag," *AZJ* 36 (April 30, 1872), 323–330.

44. "Verhandlungen der Constituirenden Versammlung," 10.

45. "Der deutsch-israelitische Gemeindebund," *Der Israelit* 8 (May 5, 1872 [5632]), 433–434; and "Der deutsch-israelitische Gemeindebund," *Der Israelit* 8 (May 29, 1872 [5632]), 477–478.

46. Mordechai Breuer, *Modernity within Tradition: The Social History of Orthodox Jewry in Imperial Germany* (New York: Columbia University Press, 1992), 333–336.

47. Ibid., 298.

48. "Der Liberalismus und das Judenthum," *AZJ* 36 (June 4, 1872), 441–443; *AZJ* 36 (June 11, 1872), 463–466; and *AZJ* 36 (June 25, 1872), 501–504.

49. Michael B. Gross, "Kulturkampf and Unification: German Liberalism and the War against the Jesuits," *Central European History* 30, no. 4 (2001), 545–566; Michael B. Gross, *The War against Catholicism: Liberalism and the Anti-Catholic Imagination in Nineteenth-Century Germany* (Ann Arbor: University of Michigan Press, 2004) 258–280; Margaret Lavinia Anderson, *Practicing Democracy. Elections and Political Culture in Imperial Germany* (Princeton, NJ: Princeton University Press, 2000), 99; Blaschke, *Offenders or Victims,* 78–79; and Róisín Healy, *The Jesuit Specter in Imperial Germany* (Boston: Brill Academic Publishers, 2003), 68–69.

50. In two roll-call votes, four Jewish deputies in the house refused to support the bill. On June 17, Lasker, Bamberger, and Sonnemann rejected the law and Isaac Wolffson abstained; in the final reading Lasker and Bamberger voted nay, Sonnemann was absent, and Wolffson abstained again; RT, June 17, 1872, 1094–1095, and RT, June 19, 1872, 1149–1150.

51. "Die Juden und die Jesuiten," *AZJ* 26 (July 2, 1872), 523–525; and Abraham Geiger, "Die jüdischen Reichsboten bei der Jesuitenfrage," *Jüdische Zeitschrift für Wissenschaft und Leben* 10 (1872), 278–281.

52. Lasker, RT, June 19, 1872, 1123–1126; Ludwig Bamberger, "Die Motive der liberalen Opposition gegen das Jesuitengesetz," *Die Gegenwart*, June 22, 1872, 337–338; and idem, "Der Genius des Reichskanzlers und der Genius des Reichstages," *Die Gegenwart*, July 5, 1872, 1–3.

53. See, for example, Ludwig Bamberger, "Die erste Sitzungsperiode des ersten deutschen Reichstags," *Jahrbuch für Gesetzgebung, Verwaltung und Rechtspflege des deutschen Reiches* 1 (1871), 159–199.

54. On Catholic conservatives acknowledging Lasker's sometimes more conciliatory stance, see Olaf Blaschke, *Katholizismus und Antisemitismus im Deutschen Kaiserreich* (Göttingen: Vandenhoeck & Ruprecht, 1997), 47.

55. Leo Baeck Institute, New York, AR 1196 II, Wahlaufruf, Frankfurt a. M., January 4, 1874, Lasker-Comité.

56. Against the bill (without naming it) "Der Liberalismus und das Judenthum," *AZJ* 36 (June 25, 1872), 501–504; demanding stronger laws against Catholicism as the bill was drafted: "Berlin, 22. Mai," *AZJ* 36 (June 25, 1872), 452–453.

57. National liberal papers such as the *Vossische Zeitung* and the *National-Zeitung*, and even the conservative *Kreuzzeitung*, did not comment on the religious affiliation of the dissenting votes among liberals (based on the issues of June 16–25, 1872, of these newspapers).

58. Moritz Busch, *Tagebuchblätter* (Leipzig: Grunow, 1899), 366 and 367. Busch noted that he tried to pass on this suggestion to the national liberal *Weserzeitung*, which refused to publish on the matter, however, a fact Busch attributed to the Jewish dominance over the German press.

59. There were a few notable exceptions, especially some decades later. See Julius Bachem, *Erinnerungen eines alten Publizisten und Politikers* (Cologne: Bachem, 1913), 106.

60. "Die Motive der ultramontanen Presse," *AZJ* 44 (September 28, 1880), 609–612; and "Berlin, 6. Mai," *Jeschurun* 16 (May 1883), 300. See Blaschke, *Offenders or Victims*, 80, for other examples.

61. Toury, *Die politischen Orientierungen*, 247–248; Tal, *Christians and Jews*, 103–109; and Blaschke, *Offenders or Victims*, 78.

62. "Die neuen kirchlichen Gesetze für Preußen," *IWS* 4 (February 5, 1873), 41–42; and *IWS* 4 (February 12, 1873), 50–51.

63. PHdA, May 24, 1876, 1710–1711.

64. Letter of the Jüdisch-Theologisches Seminar in Breslau to Ausschuß des DIGB, March 25, 1875, in CAHJP M1/21, 25–26; and letter of Berliner Hochschule für die Wissenschaft des Judenthums to Ausschuß des DIGB, May 5, 1875 (or 1874), in CAHJP M1/21, 30–31.

65. "Die Preussisch-jüdische Gemeinde-Verfassungsfrage: Denkschrift zur Vertheidigung des einheitlichen Rechtsverbundes der jüdischen Gemeinden in Deutschland," ed. Deutsch-Israelitischer Gemeindebund (November 1873), 8. A copy is extant in GStAPK, Rep. 84a Justizministerium, no. 1207, pp. 85–100.

66. Ibid., 17.

67. Ismar Schorsch, *Jewish Reactions to German Anti-Semitism, 1870–1914* (New York: Columbia University Press, 1972), 30. This misinterpretation is reproduced by James F. Harris, "Eduard Lasker: The Jew as National German Politician," *LBIYB* 20 (1975), 164. Previous scholarship has often misread this remarkable letter. Uriel Tal falsely attributed the files of the DIGB on the *Austrittsgesetz* to those on the same law in the Prussian Ministry of Justice (formerly Bundesarchiv Koblenz P135/1207, today GStAPK, Rep. 84a Justizministerium, Nr. 1207; Tal's reference is to a microfilm reproduction of that Prussian ministry's collection in the CAHJP). He consequently mistook Kohner's letter for the DIGB's official petition rather than a behind the scenes effort to lobby for their position; Tal, *Christians and Jews*, 115n96, 116n97. The file in the Prussian ministry contains neither this letter, nor most other documents Tal claims to be there, including a memorandum of Joseph Caro to the DIGB and the expert opinion of the *Lehrercollegium der Hochschule für die Wissenschaft des Judenthums*. Rather all of these are to be found in the files of the DIGB in CAHJP M1/21, Lasker'sches Austritts-Gesetz 1874.

68. See, for example, Kohner's apology for sending out a circular letter to all communities without consulting the board; letter of Kohner to the Board, August 28, 1874, in CAHJP M1/2, 408–410. As only the draft of Gneist's letter to Gneist with the notes of various reviewers within the DIGB is extant, it is possible that the

letter was never mailed. The collected papers of Gneist do not contain a copy of the letter; see GStAPK, VI HA, Nachlass Rudolf von Gneist.

69. Gneist was also active in organizations such as the Verein zur Unterstützung hilfsbedürftiger jüdischer Studirenden; "Berlin, im März," *Der Israelit* 8, first supplement (March 20, 1872 [5632]), 270.

70. Draft letter of Moritz Kohner to Rudolf von Gneist, April 16, 1876, in CAHJP Mī/21, 47–48.

71. Ibid., 47. The first draft of the letter had used the phrase "the small Bavarian, blotting-paper-like ultramontane press."

72. Ibid.

73. Ibid., 48.

74. Ibid., 50.

75. See Otto Glagau, *Des Reiches Noth und der neue Culturkampf* (Osnabrück: Wehberg, 1879), and Glagau's periodical *Der Kulturkämpfer* (1880–1888). On demands by the Catholic *Germania* for a *Kulturkampf* against Jews, see Blaschke, *Katholizismus und Antisemitismus*, 48. On earlier accusations by Catholics, see also David Blackbourn, "Catholics, the Centre Party, and Anti-Semitism," in *Populists and Patricians: Essays in Modern German History* (Boston: Allen & Unwin, 1987), 168–187; and Uwe Mazura, *Zentrumspartei und Judenfrage, 1870/71–1933: Verfassungsstaat und Minderheitenschutz* (Mainz: Matthias-Grünewald-Verlag, 1994), 41–46.

76. See, for example, the comments of Bachem, PHdA, November 22, 1880, 256–262. On the debate, see also Mazura, *Zentrumspartei*, 73–84. On the debate and a surge in Catholic antisemitism around 1879–1881, see Blaschke, *Katholizismus und Antisemitismus*, 122–125.

77. Peter Pulzer, *Jews and the German State: The Political History of a Minority, 1848–1933* (Oxford, UK: Blackwell, 1992), 121.

78. Ibid., 96–105, on that turn.

79. This was due to a large degree to the influence of the party's leading politician, Ludwig Windthorst; see Margaret Lavinia Anderson, *Windthorst: A Political Biography* (Oxford, UK: Clarendon Press, 1981), 251–260. On the faction within the Center Party emphasizing interdenominational relations, see Margaret Lavinia Anderson, "Interdenominationalism, Clericalism, Pluralism: The Zentrumsstreit and the Dilemma of Catholicism in Wilhelmine Germany," *Central European History* 21, no. 4 (1988), 350–378.

80. See Vicki Caron, "Catholic Political Mobilization and Antisemitic Violence in Fin de Siècle France: The Case of the Union Nationale," *Journal of Modern History* 81, no. 2 (2009), 294–346; and Johannes Heil, "Antisemitismus, Kulturkampf und Konfession: die antisemitischen 'Kulturen' Frankreichs und Deutschlands im Vergleich," in *Katholischer Antisemitismus im 19. Jahrhundert: Ursachen und Traditionen im internationalen Vergleich*, ed. Olaf Blaschke and Aram Mattioli (Zurich: Orell Füssli, 2000), 195–228.

81. On the Jewish turn to republicanism, see Philip Nord, *The Republican Moment: Struggles for Democracy in Nineteenth-Century France* (Cambridge, MA: Harvard University Press, 1998), 64–89.

82. Michael Jeismann, *Das Vaterland der Feinde: Studien zum nationalen Feindbegriff und Selbstverständnis in Deutschland und Frankreich, 1792-1918* (Stuttgart: Klett-Cotta, 1992), 189.

83. Claude Digeon, *La crise allemande de la pensée française, 1870–1914* (Paris: Presses universitaires de France, 1959); and Jean-Marie Mayeur, "Une mémoire-frontière: l'Alsace," in *Les Lieux de mémoire*, ed. Pierre Nora (Paris: Gallimard, 1986), 86–90.

84. *UI* 32 (October 15, 1876), 106.

85. *AI* 33 (February 15, 1872), 121–122.

86. *AI* 35 (January 15, 1874), 37; *AI* 35 (November 1, 1874), 644–646; *AI* 36 (January 15, 1875), 35–36; and *AI* 36 (December 1, 1875), 709–710.

87. *AI* 35 (November 1, 1874), 645.

88. "Alsace-Lorraine," *AI* 35 (January 1, 1874), 11–13.

89. Ibid., 13.

90. *AI* 37 (January 1, 1876), 8.

91. *AI* 36 (January 15, 1875), 36.

92. *UI* 27 (June 15, 1872), 613–614; and *AI* 33 (May 15, 1872), 319.

93. *UI* 27 (December 15, 1871), 227–237.

94. *UI* 31 (October 1, 1875), 68–70. Bloch's strange relationship to Germany and anti-Catholicism there is also illustrated by the fact that he stated once that Alsace was lost as divine punishment for the ultramontane excesses against Jews; *UI* 27 (June 15, 1872), 616–617.

95. *UI* 27 (March 1, 1872), 391.

96. Kaplan, *Between the Devil*.

97. Till van Rahden, "Unity, Diversity, and Difference: Jews, Protestants, and Catholics in Breslau Schools during the Kulturkampf," in *Protestants, Catholics and Jews in Germany, 1800–1914*, ed. Helmut Walser Smith (Oxford, UK: Berg, 2001), 217–242.

98. Indeed the *Archives israélites* were expecting the separation of church and state already in the 1870s when such legislation was not realistic; *AI* 33 (July 15, 1872), 419; *AI* 26 (June 15, 1873), 363; and *AI* 36 (April 1, 1875), 195–196.

99. There was, however, a period in the late 1870s when many Jewish commentators in Germany perceived antisemitism as a Catholic ruse. See Joskowicz, "Liberal Judaism."

100. Michael R. Marrus, *The Politics of Assimilation: The French Jewish Community at the Time of the Dreyfus Affair* (London: Oxford University Press, 1971), 99; and Christian Wiese, "Modern Antisemitism and Jewish Responses in Germany and France, 1880–1914," in *Jewish Emancipation Reconsidered: The French and German Models*, ed. Michael Brenner, Vicki Caron, and Uri R. Kaufmann (Tübingen: Mohr Siebeck, 2003), 129. From the beginning, there were also a few other voices. Lazar

Wogue argued for example in 1881 that French Jews should not imagine they were protected from antisemitism by a cordon sanitaire made of the principles of 1789; L. Wogue, "La question juive," *UI* 36 (January 1, 1881), 227–229.

101. Edouard Adolphe Drumont, *La France juive: essai d'histoire contemporaine* (Paris: Marpon and Flammarion, 1886). On the comparison of German and French antisemitism, see also Shulamit Volkov, "Comparing Germany with the French Republic," in *Germans, Jews, and Antisemites: Trials in Emancipation* (New York: Cambridge University Press, 2006), 145–155.

102. Pierre Birnbaum, *The Jews of the Republic: A Political History of State Jews in France from Gambetta to Vichy* (Stanford, CA: Stanford University Press, 1996), 123–127.

103. Heber Marini, *Le fin mot sur la question juive* (Paris: n.p., 1886).

104. Ibid., 14.

105. Ibid., 25–26.

106. Isidore Cahen, "Deux réponses à Drumont," *AI* 47 (November 18, 1886), 361–362; *AI* 47 (November 25, 1886), 369–371; and *AI* 47 (December 2, 1886), 377–379.

107. *AI* 47 (November 25, 1886), 370.

108. Drumont had not only negative things to say about Weill; Drumont, *France Juive*, 1:466, 2:248.

109. On his life, see Joë Yehoshua Friedemann, *Alexandre Weill, écrivain contestataire et historien engagé (1811–1899)* (Strasbourg: Librairie Istra, 1980).

110. Alexandre Weill, *Feu contre feu: réponse à un ultramontain* (Paris: Bureau de la Revue indépendante, 1845).

111. Friedemann, *Weill*, 102–106; and Alexandre Weill, *Lettres fraternelles à Louis Veuillot* (Paris: Dentu, 1858).

112. Alexander Weill, *Zehn Monate Volksherrschaft vom 24. Februar bis zum 10. Dezember 1848* (Frankfurt a. M.: Hermann'sche Buchhandlung, 1857); the later French version has a more democratic preface: Alexandre Weill, *Dix mois de révolution depuis le 24 février jusqu'au 10 décembre 1848 avec un précis: Le progrès dans l'histoire* (Paris: Tous les libraires, 1869).

113. Alexandre Weill, *Moïse et le Talmud* (Paris: Amyot, 1864).

114. See James Darmesteter, *Coup d'œil sur l'histoire du people* (Paris: Librairie nouvelle, 1882); and idem, *Les prophètes d'Israël* (Paris: C. Lévy, 1892).

115. Alexandre Weill, *L'Isaïe du Faubourg Saint-Honoré* (Paris: Dentu, 1881).

116. Alexandre Weill, *La France catholique et athée (Réponse à 'La France juive')* (Paris: Dentu, 1886).

117. Ibid., 5–7, 35.

118. Ibid., 1.

119. Ibid., 7.

120. Ibid., 34. Gustave Tridon, *Du molochisme juif: études critiques et philosophiques* (Brussels: Maheu, 1884). On Tridon, see also Chapter One.

121. Review of *Lettres fraternelles à Louis Veuillot*, by Alexandre Weill, *AZJ* 22 (November 1, 1858), 613–614; and S. Cahen, review of *Lettres fraternelles à Louis Veuillot*, by Alexandre Weill, *AI* 19 (November 1858), 664.

122. Isidore Cahen, "Sur un article du journal *Le Siècle*," *AI* 25 (1864), 555–556.

123. *AI* 30 (December 15, 1869), 742. He continued to give positive reviews of his works nevertheless, such as: *AI* 43 (March 16, 1882), 83.

124. Small clusters of articles in the Jewish press equating antisemitism and clericalism did appear earlier. See, for example, B. M., "Antisémitisme et cléricalisme," *UI* 52 (November 6, 1896), 196–98; and "Intolérance," *UI* 52, (November 27, 1896), 298.

125. On Jewish reactions to the Dreyfus affair, see Philippe E. Landau, *L'opinion juive et l'affaire Dreyfus* (Paris: A. Michel, 1995); Catherine Nicault, "L'israélitisme au tournant du siècle: Remise en causes ou réaffirmation?" in *Antisémythes: l'image des Juifs entre culture et politique, 1848–1939*, ed. Marie-Anne Matard-Bonucci (Paris: Nouveau Monde, 2005), 253–264; and Pierre Birnbaum, *The Anti-Semitic Moment: A Tour of France in 1898* (New York: Hill and Wang, 2003), 315–31. These works have generally rejected the earlier claims by scholars such as Hannah Arendt that Jews were reluctant defenders of Dreyfus. For the position of some of the older scholarship, see also Marrus, *The Politics of Assimilation*, 196–242; and Jean-Denis Bredin, *The Affair: The Case of Alfred Dreyfus* (New York: Braziller, 1986), 297–299.

126. H. Prague, "Chez nos ennemis," *AI* 56 (December 26, 1895), 412; Jean-Denis Bredin, *The Affair: The Case of Alfred Dreyfus* (New York: Braziller, 1986).

127. On the decline of antisemitism before Dreyfus, see Robert F. *Byrnes, Antisemitism in Modern France: The Prologue to the Dreyfus Affair* (New Brunswick, NJ: Rutgers University Press, 1950), 320–324.

128. On the congress, see "Le congrès de Lyon," *UI* 52 (December 4, 1896), 325–330; S., "Antisémitisme," *UI* 52 (December 4, 1896), 330–32; "Le congrès de la Démocratie Chrétienne," *UI* 52 (December 11, 1896), 367–371; L. K., "Serrons les Rangs!" *UI* 52 (December 18, 1896), 402–404; B. M., "La Terreur antisémite," *UI* 52 (December 25, 1896), 429–433; and "Le congrès de Lyon," *UI* 52 (January 1, 1897), 474–476. See also: "L'Antisemitisme en Autriche," *AI* 62 (April 23, 1896), 138–139; "Polémique: un précieux aveu," *AI* 57 (June 4, 1896), 187; Zadig, "Les antisémites et les élections consistoriales," *AI* 62 (October 29, 1896), 355; and Louis Lévy, "L'antisémitisme de Saint Thomas d'Aquin," *UI* 52 (November 6, 1896), 208–211.

129. Among the exceptions is Louis Lévy, "Les fautes passées et le devoir présent," *UI* (January 21, 1898), 552–556; see, however, the same author's hesitant response to attacks from the *Osservatore Romano* in Louis Lévy, "Politique cléricale," *UI* 53 (August 12, 1898), 665–668.

130. James F. Brennan, *The Reflection of the Dreyfus Affair in the European Press, 1897–1899* (New York: P. Lang, 1998), 40–45, 71, 75, et passim.

131. Malcolm O. Partin, *Waldeck-Rousseau, Combes, and the Church: The Politics of Anticlericalism, 1899–1905* (Durham, NC: Duke University Press, 1969), 3–90.

132. See, for example, R. T., "Judaïsme et Catholicisme," *UI* 54 (June 30, 1899), 457–460; R. T., "La morale jésuitique," *UI* 55 (September 22, 1899), 5–8; L. L., "L'Œuvre des Assomptionnistes," *UI* 55 (February 2, 1900), 618–620; L. L. "La France noire," *UI* 55 (February 2, 1900), 629–632; R. T., "L'antisémitisme et le Catholicisme," *UI* 55 (February 23, 1900), 709–712; R. T., "Le Néo-Catholicisme," *UI* 55 (June 1, 1900), 325–328; L. Lévy, "Les deux catholicismes," *UI* 56 (May 17, 1901), 268–273; B. T., "L'histoire et les historiens," *UI* 55 (June 15, 1900), 389–392; B. S., "Réveillons-nous!" *UI* 55 (July 13, 1900), 522–526; and "La 'Libre parole' et l'Affaire Dreyfus," *UI* 56 (March 22, 1901), 20–23.

133. B.-M., "La loi sur le recrutement des fonctionnaires," *UI* 55 (December 8, 1899), 357–361; *UI* 55 (December 22, 1899), 421–425; *UI* 55 (March 16, 1900), 805–808; H. Prague, "M. de Cassagnac et la tolérance," *AI* 40 (November 30, 1899), 381–382; and H. Prague, "Causerie," *AI* 60 (December 14, 1899), 397–399. For a classic Dreyfusard position on the clergy, see the statements of the founder of the Ligue des droits de l'homme: Ludovic Trarieux, *Le cléricalisme et l'affaire Dreyfus* (Paris: Ligue française pour la défense des droits de l'homme et du citoyen, 1900).

134. On the debates on the laws, see Ouzuf, *L'école*, 177–184. For a critical account of the consequences of the associational laws, see Christian Sorrel, *La république contre les congrégations: histoire d'une passion française, 1899–1904* (Paris: Cerf, 2003).

135. "M. Waldeck-Rousseau et l'antisémitisme," *UI* 56 (January 25, 1901), 599; B.-M. "Le discours de M. Lasies," *UI* 56 (February 1, 1901), 613–617; and H. Prague, "Débats parlementaires," *AI* 62 (January 31, 1901), 33–35.

136. R. T., "Les résultats de l'affaire Dreyfus," *UI* 56 (August 9, 1901), 645–648.

137. Joseph Reinach, *Histoire de l'affaire Dreyfus* (Paris: Éditions de la Revue blanche/Fasquelle, 1901–1911).

138. On the Reinach family, see Pierre Birnbaum, *The Jews of the Republic: A Political History of State Jews in France from Gambetta to Vichy* (Stanford, CA: Stanford University Press, 1996), 7–19.

139. For a critique of the historiographical tradition emerging from Reinach's work, see Ruth Harris, *Dreyfus: Politics, Emotion, and the Scandal of the Century* (New York: Picador, 2010), 5–7. On the rhetoric of plot theories during the Dreyfus affair, see Richard Griffiths, *The Use of Abuse: The Polemics of the Dreyfus Affair and its Aftermath* (New York: Berg, 1991), 41–52.

140. Reinach, *Histoire de l'affaire Dreyfus*, 1:215–217.

141. "La 'Libre parole' et l'Affaire Dreyfus," *UI* 56 (March 22, 1901), 20–23; and H. Prague, "Causerie," *AI* 62 (February 28, 1901), 57–59. Reinach's work remains a source for many later accounts and their references to clerical involvement in the affair, such as Georges Sorel, *La révolution Dreyfusienne* (Paris: Rivière, 1911), 55–63. Ruth Harris emphasizes the role of anticlerical interpretations, especially involving the activities of the Assumptionist order, on the anticlerical legislation of 1901–1905; Ruth Harris, "The Assumptionists and the Dreyfus Affair," *Past and Present*, no. 194 (2007), 175–211.

142. Kaplan, *Between the Devil*, 103–106.

143. Henri Tubiana, "Les croisades au XIXᵉ siècle," *Revue socialiste* 4, no. 19 (July 1886), 634–636; Henry Tubiana, "Les Droits du Consistoire," *UI* 39 (1883–1884), 442–443 reproduces an article from *Solidarité: journal politique*. On antisemitism in the *Revue socialiste* in this period, see Byrnes, *Antisemitism*, 156–158; and Nancy Green, "Socialist Anti-Semitism, Defense of a Bourgeois Jew and Discovery of the Jewish Proletariat: Changing Attitudes of French Socialists before 1914," *International Review of Social History* 30, no. 3 (1985), 378–380.

144. Tubiana's first publication appeared under this name in 1884 and was then relaunched twice in 1885 and 1866 under the title *Gazette de l'Algérie*, each time with only several issues.

145. No. 3 has the title *Le pariah juive*, Nos. 4 and 5 *L'anticléricale juif*, and Nos. 6 and 7 *À bas les jésuites*. The only extant copies I could locate are in the Bibliothéque Nationale in Paris, where they are listed as distinct newspapers. Each broadsheet has the exact same layout and is printed by Mustapha. Tubiana did, however, change the spelling of his first name in the course of the publication. Previous scholarship has sometimes confused the paper for an antisemitic publication; Pierre Birnbaum, "French Jews and the 'Regeneration' of Algerian Jewry," in *Jews and the State: Dangerous Alliances and the Perils of Privilege*, ed. Ezra Mendelsohn (Oxford, UK: Oxford University Press, 2003), 94; see also the celebratory biography of Louis Bernard: Louis Alphonse Maugendre, *La renaissance catholique au début du XXe siècle: Louis Bernard* (Paris: Beauchesne, 1971), 6:54.

146. Tubiana, "Les croisades." Tubiana was not the only author to discover the small Algerian Proletariat as a revolutionary force and as counterexample to the claims of antisemites that Algerian Jews were rapacious small capitalists. See Louis Durieu, "Le Prolétariat juif en Algérie," *Revue Socialiste* 29, no. 173 (1899), 513–533. French socialists would only later discover the Jewish proletariat; see Green, "Socialist Anti-Semitism," 392–398.

147. Tubiana, "Les croisades," 636.

148. Patricia M. E. Lorcin, "Rome and France in Africa: Recovering Colonial Algeria's Latin Past," *French Historical Studies* 25, no. 2 (2002), 295–329.

149. Tubiana, "Les croisades," 634.

150. Tubiana had referred to Rome as a precedent for colonial policy himself around the same time. Using the historical example for a different purpose, he suggested that the French should follow Rome in giving equal citizenship rights to all inhabitants of French Algeria and thus bind them to France more effectively; Henry Tubiana, "L'assimilation aux droits civils chez les musulmans," *Gazette de Algérie*, July 11, 1884 and July 20, 1884; and "Christianisme et scepticisme," *Gazette de Algérie*, August 17, 1884.

151. On antisemitism in Algeria, see Geneviève Dermenjian, *La crise anti-juive oranaise, 1895–1905: l'antisémitisme dans l'Algérie coloniale* (Paris: L'Harmattan, 1986).

152. *Le Temps*, November 8, 1884.

153. Henry Tubiana, "L'assimilation aux droits civils chez les musulmans," *Gazette de Algérie*, July 11, 1884.

154. *L'anticlérical juif,* no. 4 [1898].

155. Tubiana also attacked the Jewish consistories with anticlerical language in this period; Henri Tubiana, *Le Peuple juif, étude sociologique* (Paris: Challamel aîné, 1898), 6, reprinted in Henry Tubiana, "3ᵉ Lettre ouverte à MM. Méline, Barthou, Milliard, ministres," *Le Paria juif,* no. 3, [1898].

156. Stephen Wilson, *Ideology and Experience: Antisemitism in France at the Time of the Dreyfus Affair* (Rutherford, NJ, and London: Fairleigh Dickinson University Press and Associated University Presses, 1982), 231; Zosa Szajkowski, "Socialists and Radicals in the Development of Antisemitism in Algeria (1884–1900)," *Jewish Social Studies* 10, no. 3 (1948), 257–280; and Dermenjian, *La crise anti-juive oranaise*, 223–229. In many respects their antisemitism was more successful than their anticlericalism; Oissila Saaïdia, "L'anticléricalisme article d'exportation? Le cas de l'Algérie avant la première guerre mondiale," *Vingtième Siècle*, no. 87 (2005), 101–112.

157. For an example of Jewish anti-Catholicism in Algeria from an author with different political commitments, see Paula Daccarett, "1890s Zionism Reconsidered: Joseph Marco Baruch," *Jewish History* 19, no. 3/4 (2005), 315–345.

158. The Archives nationales in Paris house twelve full boxes of congratulatory missives to Émile Combes (AN 73 AP 1–12). I looked through boxes 1, 9, and 10, which include among others all letters and telegrams from Algeria and the departments of Haut-Rhin (Territoire de Belfort) and Seine.

159. AN 73 AP 1/Oran: Telegram from Léon Rouach, April 12, 1903; Telegram from Kalfon, Chouraqui, Eli Amar, and Mouty, May 10, 1904; and Letter from Rouach and Elie Dahan in the name of 2,300 republican voters, January 6, 1905.

160. AN 73 AP 1/Alger: Letter from Chief Rabbi Abraham Bloch, January 4, 1905.

161. On Bloch's and the Consistory of Algiers's struggles with the consequences of the 1905 law, see "La séparation et le Judaïsme algérien," *UI* 60 (April 21, 1905), 147–149; "La séparation et l'Algérie," *UI* 60 (June 2, 1905), 339–341.

162. Kaplan, *Between the Devil*, 106–107.

163. On the origins of this story, its different versions, and the difficulties of verifying it, see Philippe E. Landau, *Les Juifs de France et la Grande Guerre: un patriotisme républicain, 1914–1941* (Paris: CNRS, 1999), 195–210.

164. Danielle Delmaire, "Antisemitisme des catholiques au vingtième siècle: de la revendication au refus," in *Catholicism, Politics and Society in Twentieth-Century France*, ed. Kay Chadwick (Liverpool, UK: Liverpool University Press, 2000), 29. On Barrès and the eventual reappearance of divisions within the *union sacré*, Gérard Cholvy and Yves-Marie Hilaire, *Histoire religieuse de la France contemporaine* (Toulouse: Privat, 1985–1988), 2:246–252.

165. "La caractéristique des élections," *AI* 59 (May 5, 1898), 137–139; B.-M., "Les élections et l'antisémitisme," *UI* 53 (May 6, 1898), 197–201; and "Après le second tour de scrutin," *UI* 53 (May 27, 1898), 293–296.

166. H. Prague, "Un spectacle consolant: Les antisémites et les élections en Allemagne," *AI* 59 (June 23, 1898), 193–194; B.-M., "Les élections allemandes et l'affaire Dreyfus," *UI* 53 (June 24, 1898), 421–425; and "Les élections allemandes," *UI* 53 (July 8, 1898), 499–500.

167. "Der Antisemitismus in Frankreich," *AZJ* 62 (April 15, 1898), 169–170.

168. "Die französischen Juden," *AZJ* 62 (June 17, 1898), 277–278; Pinchas Pfeifer, "Der Antisemitismus in Frankreich," *AZJ* 62 (September 23, 1898), 448–449.

169. Ludwig Fuld, "Der Antisemitismus in Frankreich" *Im deutschen Reich* 4 (February 1898), 69–73.

170. "Der französische Antisemitismus," *AZJ* 63 (January 1, 1899), 1–2; and "Les catholiques allemands et l'affaire Dreyfus," *AI* 59 (October 27, 1898), 347–348.

171. "Der Toleranzantrag des Centrums," *AZJ* 64 (December 7, 1900), 577–578. The Center Party submitted their bill to the Reichstag five times between 1900 and 1912, without any success. On the bill and the role of Judaism in the debate, see Mazura, *Zentrumspartei*, 146–151.

172. Mazura, *Zentrumspartei*, 114–142; Breuer, *Modernity within Tradition*, 341; and Dorothee Brantz, "Stunning Bodies: Animal Slaughter, Judaism, and the Meaning of Humanity in Imperial Germany," *Central European History* 35 (2002), 185–186.

173. Blaschke, *Katholizismus und Antisemitismus*. 144–154; and Hermann Greive, *Theologie und Ideologie Katholizismus und Judentum in Deutschland und Österreich 1918–1935* (Heidelberg: Schneider, 1969).

174. Lisa Fetheringill Zwicker, *Dueling Students: Conflict, Masculinity, and Politics in German Universities, 1890–1914* (Ann Arbor: University of Michigan Press, 2011), 187–189.

175. Toury, *politische Orientierung*, 170–177; see also the table with an overview of Jewish deputies in Hamburger, *Juden im öffentlichen Leben Deutschlands*, 252–253.

176. Marjorie Lamberti, *Jewish Activism in Imperial Germany: The Struggle for Civil Equality* (New Haven, CT: Yale University Press, 1978), ch. 4; and Toury, *politische Orientierungen*, 255.

177. Lamberti, *Jewish Activism*, 58–59; and Toury, *politische Orientierungen*, 256–257.

Conclusion

1. Ruth Klüger, *weiter leben: Eine Jugend* (Göttingen: Wallstein, 1992), 212–213.

2. On other Jewish positions on Luther, see Christian Wiese, "'Let His Memory Be Holy to Us!' Jewish Interpretations of Martin Luther from the Enlightenment to the Holocaust," *LBIYB* 54 (2009), 93–126.

3. See Tara Zahra, *The Lost Children: Reconstructing Europe's Families after World War II* (Cambridge, MA: Harvard University Press, 2011), 138–143; Joyce Block Lazarus, *In the Shadow of Vichy: The Finaly Affair* (New York: P. Lang, 2008); Catherine Poujol and Chantal Thoinet, *Les enfants cachés: l'affaire Finaly (1945–1953)* (Paris: Berg International, 2006); and Paule Berger Marx, *Les relations entre les juifs*

et les catholiques dans la France de l'après-guerre 1945–1965 (Paris: Parole et silence, 2009), 225–265.

4. See Carol Ann Rittner and John K. Roth, *Pope Pius XII and the Holocaust* (London and New York: Leicester University Press and Continuum, 2002); Frank J. Coppa, *The Papacy, the Jews, and the Holocaust* (Washington, DC: Catholic University of America Press, 2006); and Daniel Jonah Goldhagen, *A Moral Reckoning the Role of the Catholic Church in the Holocaust and Its Unfulfilled Duty of Repair* (New York: Vintage Books, 2003).

5. Joan Wallach Scott, *The Politics of the Veil* (Princeton, NJ: Princeton University Press, 2007).

6. Talal Asad, *Formations of the Secular: Christianity, Islam, Modernity* (Stanford, CA: Stanford University Press, 2003). For a similar critique of secularism, focusing on notions of secular time, see Dipesh Chakrabarty, *Provincializing Europe: Postcolonial Thought and Historical Difference* (Princeton, NJ: Princeton University Press, 2000).

7. See Asad, *Formations*, 100–124.

8. The classic expression of this critique from the standpoint of Jewish history was articulated in Salo W. Baron, "Ghetto and Emancipation," in *The Menorah Treasury: Harvest of Half a Century* (Philadelphia: Jewish Publication Society of America, 1964), 50–63.

9. Zygmunt Bauman, *Modernity and the Holocaust* (Ithaca, NY: Cornell University Press, 2000).

10. Olaf Blaschke, "Das 19. Jahrhundert: Ein Zweites Konfessionelles Zeitalter?" *Geschichte und Gesellschaft* 26 (2000), 38–75; *Konfessionen im Konflikt: Deutschland zwischen 1800 und 1970: ein zweites konfessionelles Zeitalter*, ed. Olaf Blaschke (Göttingen: Vandenhoeck & Ruprecht, 2002).

11. See Gauri Viswanathan, *Outside the Fold: Conversion, Modernity, and Belief* (Princeton, NJ: Princeton University Press, 1998).

12. James Pasto, "Islam's 'Strange Secret Sharer': Orientalism, Judaism, and the Jewish Question," *Comparative Studies in Society and History* 40, no. 3 (1998), 437–474; Gil Anidjar, *The Jew, the Arab: A History of the Enemy* (Stanford, CA: Stanford University Press, 2003); and *Orientalism and the Jews*, ed. Ivan Davidson Kalmar and Derek J. Penslar (Hanover, NH: University Press of New England, 2005). For an attempt to read together Jews and Muslims as minorities, see also the special issue *Juden und Muslime in Deutschland* of the *Tel Aviver Jahrbuch für deutsche Geschichte* 37 (2009) and Ethan Katz's forthcoming book on the history of Jews and Muslims in twentieth-century France.

13. Shmuel Feiner, *The Origins of Jewish Secularization in Eighteenth-Century Europe*, trans. Chaya Naor (Philadelphia: University of Pennsylvania Press, 2010). Feiner's work is informed in this regard by Azriel Shohet, *'Im 'hilufe tekufot: reshit ha-Haskalah be-Yahadut Germanyah* (Jerusalem: Mosad Byalik, 1960).

14. David Biale, *Not in the Heavens: The Tradition of Jewish Secular Thought* (Princeton, NJ: Princeton University Press, 2011).

15. On the notion of a *Kulturkampf* within Judaism, see also Shmuel Feiner, *The Jewish Enlightenment* (Philadelphia: University of Pennyslvania Press, 2002), part 2, "Jewish Kulturkampf"; and Moshe Pelli, *Haskalah and Beyond: The Reception of the Hebrew Enlightenment and the Emergence of Haskalah Judaism* (Lanham, MD: University Press of America, 2010), 36.

16. For the claim that Islam is replacing Catholicism, see Olivier Roy, *Secularism Confronts Islam* (New York: Columbia University Press, 2007), 2. For an argument on discontinuities, see Matti Bunzl, "Between Anti-Semitism and Islamophobia: Some Thoughts on the New Europe," *American Ethnologist* 32, no. 4 (Nov. 2005), 499–508.

Index